THE TAUBER INSTITUTE SERIES FOR
THE STUDY OF EUROPEAN JEWRY

The Tauber Institute Series is dedicated to publishing compelling and innovative approaches to the study of modern European Jewish history, thought, culture, and society. The series features scholarly works related to the Enlightenment, modern Judaism and the struggle for emancipation, the rise of nationalism and the spread of antisemitism, the Holocaust and its aftermath, as well as the contemporary Jewish experience. The series is published under the auspices of the Tauber Institute for the Study of European Jewry—established by a gift to Brandeis University from Dr. Laszlo N. Tauber—and is supported, in part, by the Tauber Foundation and the Valya and Robert Shapiro Endowment.

For the complete list of books that are available in this series, please see www.upne.com

*Ulrich Sieg
Germany's Prophet: Paul de Lagarde and the Origins of Modern Antisemitism

David G. Roskies and Naomi Diamant
Holocaust Literature: A History and Guide

*Mordechai Altshuler
Religion and Jewish Identity in the Soviet Union, 1941–1964

Robert Liberles
Jews Welcome Coffee: Tradition and Innovation in Early Modern Germany

Sharon Faye Koren
Forsaken: The Menstruant in Medieval Jewish Mysticism

Nils Roemer
German City, Jewish Memory: The Story of Worms

David Assaf
Untold Tales of the Hasidim: Crisis and Discontent in the History of Hasidism

Jehuda Reinharz and Yaacov Shavit
Glorious, Accursed Europe: An Essay on Jewish Ambivalence

Eugene M. Avrutin, Valerii Dymshits, Alexander Ivanov, Alexander Lvov, Harriet Murav, and Alla Sokolova, editors
Photographing the Jewish Nation: Pictures from S. An-sky's Ethnographic Expeditions

*A Sarnat Library Book

Germany's Prophet

Paul de Lagarde & *the Origins of* Modern Antisemitism

ULRICH SIEG

TRANSLATED BY
LINDA ANN MARIANIELLO

Brandeis University Press
Waltham, Massachusetts

BRANDEIS UNIVERSITY PRESS
An imprint of University Press of New England
www.upne.com

Manufactured in the United States of America
Designed by Eric M. Brooks
Typeset in Bulmer by Passumpsic Publishing

Originally published in German as Ulrich Sieg, *Deutschlands Prophet: Paul de Lagarde und die Ursprunge des modernen Antisemitismus*, Carl Hauser Verlag, Munchen 2007.
ISBN 978-3-446-20842-1

Library of Congress Cataloging-in-Publication Data
Sieg, Ulrich.
Germany's prophet: Paul de Lagarde and the origins of modern antisemitism / Ulrich Sieg.
pages cm.—(A Sarnat Library book) (Tauber Institute series for the study of European Jewry)
Includes bibliographical references and index.
ISBN 978-1-58465-755-2 (cloth : alkaline paper)
1. Lagarde, Paul de, 1827-1891. 2. Lagarde, Paul de, 1827–1891—Political and social views. 3. Antisemitism—Germany—History—19th century. 4. Intellectuals—Germany—Biography. 5. Nationalists—Germany—Biography. 6. Nationalism—Germany—History—19th century. 7. Nationalism—Religious aspects—History—19th century. I. Title.
DD205.L3S55 2013
305.892'4043092—dc23 2012050371

5 4 3 2 1

This publication was made possible through the generous support of Brandeis University's Bernard G. and Rhoda G. Sarnat Center for the Study of Anti-Jewishness, which aims to promote a deeper understanding of anti-Jewish prejudice, as well as Jewish and non-Jewish responses to this phenomenon, from both a historical and contemporary perspective.

The English edition was made possible by Geisteswissenschaften International—Translation Funding for Humanities and Social Sciences from Germany, a joint initiative of the Fritz Thyssen Foundation, the German Federal Foreign Office, and the German Publishers & Booksellers Association.

University Press of New England is a member of the Green Press Initiative. The paper used in this book meets their minimum requirement for recycled paper.

Whoever is stubbornly opposed to punishment will suddenly be ruined beyond all hope.

QUOTATIONS *29, 1*

Contents

Foreword

The reputation of Paul de Lagarde has undergone great transformations over the last century and a half. If known by an English readership at all, it is primarily through Fritz Stern's 1961 classic work, *The Politics of Cultural Despair: A Study in the Rise of Germanic Ideology*, wherein Lagarde appears as an early exponent of a brand of Germanic nationalism driven by a deep-seated cultural pessimism and a profound discontent with German culture, politics, and religion. The German Empire, or Kaiserreich (1871–1918), had emerged as a federal state in the wake of the military victory over France and crowned the Prussian King Wilhelm I as its emperor. Far from joining the jubilation of other German nationalists, Lagarde lamented that Germany had lost its way and the Kaiserreich amounted to a self-satisfied northern European federal state under the control of Prussia. He railed in apocalyptic terms against the entangled alliance of Judaism and liberalism. Only the spiritual national rebirth that he espoused could save Germany from its doom. Thus, he became a prophet of a specific vision of Germany and an ideal of Germanness that sought the organic integration of religion, politics, culture, and history.

His urgent calls for a redemptive rupture from the malaise of the present and a looming apocalypse required a new political ethos that combined the boldness of a revolutionary with the moral grounding and aristocratic self-certainty of a conservative. Stern accordingly looked to Lagarde and two other conservative revolutionaries, Julius Langbehn (1851–1907) and Arthur Moeller van den Bruck (1876–1925), as central figures who ultimately paved the way for the ascendancy of authoritarian and totalitarian ideology in Germany. This thesis regarding the unique ideological underpinnings of the Third Reich informed and shaped subsequent accounts by historians of German thought and scholars of modern antisemitism. Lagarde's popular *Deutsche Schriften* conveyed his ideological prophecy of a Germany reborn. In this collection of writings, he calls for the liberation of German existence from godless materialism and redemption by an organic transformation of Christianity infused with Germanness. And as Lagarde revised each successive edition of the *Deutsche Schriften*, he increased the frequency with which Jews were portrayed as parasites and bacilli infecting and depleting the German nation. Lagarde's antisemitic polemics posited extreme solutions to the religio-national struggle against Jews and Judaism. One climax of his antisemitic vitriol offered Jews in Germany the following ultimatum: become reborn completely in the German nation or be expelled.

But this is only a partial picture of Lagarde.

Ulrich Sieg presents a portrait of Paul de Lagarde (born Paul Bötticher) that goes beyond Stern's assessment by illuminating elements of his personal, scholarly, and public life. Lagarde's political celebrity may have come from his jeremiads about the decline of Germany and the danger of Jews and Judaism, but Lagarde's reputation as an influential and pioneering scholar of the Septuagint (LXX, the main Greek translation of the Hebrew Bible/Old Testament) who made long-lasting contributions to the field of biblical studies is an integral if perplexing part of the story. Lagarde appears as a much more complicated figure than would appear at first glance. He often sought out and corresponded with prominent public and political figures of his day and, in turn, found himself sought out by them. Lagarde, who never ran for political office, did offer his qualified support and sympathy for various *völkish* antisemitic parties, but he consistently rejected currents of Aryan Christianity and antisemitic worldviews drawn from racial science. While Stern along with some of Lagarde's notable contemporaries deemed his assault upon normative Christian doctrines and institutions in Germany as signaling Lagarde as a pagan who had broken with Christianity, a number of others, including several clerical figures, accepted his self-perception as a pious Christian servant.

One of the most striking elements of Lagarde's biography relates to his biblical scholarship. The man who authored politically charged pieces collected together in the *Deutsche Schriften* also became recognized as an accomplished scholar of the ancient Near East who partook in a second Renaissance of Oriental studies in the German Empire in the last third of the nineteenth century. While Lagarde served as a professor of Oriental studies at the University of Göttingen, his contributions to biblical scholarship made him a leading scholar of the Septuagint. Indeed, his investigations into ancient pre-Christian sources and extant witnesses of the Septuagint have only grown in significance since the 1947 discovery of the Dead Sea Scrolls.

Lagarde argued that there was a single source of the Septuagint, which was edited and disseminated in the second century. The discovery of the Dead Sea Scrolls and other manuscripts during the last several decades seems to have only extended the plausibility of Lagarde's theory of an urtext, a unitary archetype, as the source of the Masoretic text, the redacted standard Jewish vocalized Bible. It should be noted that his convictions regarding the reliability and spiritual superiority of the Septuagint over the Jewish Masoretic version of the Hebrew Bible dovetailed perfectly with his theological antisemitism. He never managed to complete his life's work, a critical edition of the Septuagint and its sources. He did, however, produce a plethora of other scholarly materials. He searched for, studied, and published critical editions of a wide range of manuscripts. He published recensions of Talmudic materials such as Aramaic translations of the Prophets and Chronicles, the Gospels in Arabic, and Apocrypha in Syriac. He assembled and interrogated Latin, Greek, Persian, Egyptian, Coptic, Syriac, and Armenian texts, translations, and recensions as well. While biblical scholars still invoke and rely on his scholarly oeuvre, most do not offer analyses or assess the relevance of his disturbing nationalist and antisemitic persona, even though for Lagarde they were closely related.

Lagarde's dual legacy recalls that of his eighteenth-century predecessor at the University of Göttingen, Johann David Michaelis (1717–1791). In biblical studies, Michaelis has largely been seen as a crucial figure who advanced historical and linguistically informed approaches to the field and therefore became a pioneer of the yet to be realized field of Orientalism. Modern European historians, however, have focused on his political diatribes against Jewish emancipation in enlightened Europe. In the long shadow of Edward Said's *Orientalism*, perceptions have begun to change. Rather than seeing scholarship on the ancient and Near East as an autonomous sphere of production, scholars such as Jonathan Hess, Suzanne Marchand, Susannah Heschel, Amnon Raz-Krakotzkin, Christian Wiese, Derek Penslar, and Ivan Kalmar have begun to trace the intricate interweaving of empire, nation, race, religion, and science in scholarly and political depictions of Jews and Judaism.

This biography provides the reader a palpable sense of Lagarde's complex character (public and private, scholarly and political) by drawing on a wealth of available materials such as published works, personal correspondence, diaries and poetry, and institutional history, while also registering the significance of his ambitions, triumphs, and failures. Ulrich Sieg follows and assesses Lagarde's legacy and influence upon subsequent German *völkish* antisemites such as Julius Langbehn and the notorious Alfred Rosenberg (1893–1946). Sieg even explores the ways in which Hitler may have read and interpreted Lagarde by looking at marginalia contained in Hitler's personal copies of Lagarde's writings.

A number of questions then arise for a present-day encounter with Lagarde. How did Lagarde's personal beliefs and scholarly convictions intersect? How did his scholarship into early and pre-Christian textual variants of the Septuagint coincide with his theological commitment to strip what he saw as the perverse influence of St. Paul—whom he understood as a Pharisee who so decisively Judaized Jesus and his legacy—from the Old and New Testaments?

How did Lagarde's status as an expert on Jewish texts lead him into public disputes regarding the authority of the Talmud and nature of normative Judaism in the present? These are just some of the questions Sieg addresses. As for Lagarde's character, Sieg offers a rich and vibrant picture of a troubled and flawed scholar over the various stages of his life and career—from his traumatic childhood to his struggles as a young teacher and schoolmaster desperate to win political and academic allies so as to be offered a university professorship to his endless lack of confidence and concomitant egomania. He had heated controversies and a fair degree of success in his career, but his monumental Septuagint project (Göttingen LXX) remained unfinished. Like many academics, Lagarde was sensitive to criticism but obsessive about recognition.

Sieg takes his readers into a world wherein a scholar relied on all sorts of political and personal influence in order to acquire rare, ancient manuscripts from around the world, and study them in the privacy of his home. A fire in 1880 at the wood home of Europe's leading ancient historian of Rome, Theodor Mommsen, changed these practices. Lagarde's contempt for the practices, standards, and outcomes of his contemporary academics is juxtaposed against his own practices, standards, failures, and successes in the realm of scholarship. Lagarde's relationships with colleagues, students, foes, and allies are explored in detail. While Lagarde could be dismissive and cantankerous when it came to the work of competitors and rivals, he was generally thin-skinned and vindictive when his own work came under the scrutiny of others. His long-lasting disputes with Jewish Orientalists who took part in the Wissenschaft des Judentums (Scientific Study of Judaism) did not remain a purely scholarly affair. In addition to his public attacks on Jews and Jewish scholarship, he eventually played a key role in one of the more notable antisemitism trials of the late nineteenth century, the so-called Talmud Trial in Marburg in 1888. The state prosecutor for Hessen charged Ferdinand Fenner, a schoolteacher and publicist of antisemitica, with defamation of a state-protected religion. Lagarde eagerly participated as an expert witness on behalf of the defendant. The prosecution featured a written statement by Hermann Cohen, the Jewish founder and leader of the Marburg school of neo-Kantian philosophy at the University of Marburg. The trial became famous not only because of the celebrity academics involved but also because antisemitic political agitation had become an increasing political force in the region and the mechanism of the trial would serve the public fascination with antisemitic claims about Jews and Judaism. As was typical with similar cases, the alleged slanderer could use the trial as a venue to convey and legitimate his antisemitic worldview. And the court asked Lagarde and Cohen to answer two questions related to Fenner's publicist activities: were Jews beholden to the Talmud, and did the Talmud sanction dishonest behavior with non-Jews? Journalists packed the Marburg courtroom, and several regional and national newspapers printed accounts and analyses of Lagarde's and Cohen's respective answers to these questions, eager to satisfy the public's appetite for the drama of a political trial. This remarkable episode challenges present-day readers to reflect upon how claims to scientific expertise inflect legal and public opinion about some of the most contested and combustible issues of the day.

Even though Lagarde rejected the purely racial antisemitism of his day, notions of race nevertheless constantly seep into his articulations of nation and religion: conjoining terms of blood and national community such as *blutsmässige Volksverbundenheit*. Sieg's study of Lagarde challenges the reader to explore the myriad aspects of Lagarde's life and career in his day, and assess his significance and his difficult legacy for our own times.

EUGENE R. SHEPPARD
BRANDEIS UNIVERSITY

Author's Acknowledgments

Biographies do not leave their authors unaffected. For many, they trigger turbulent processes of transference that can even extend to the level of dreams. But I had to do it more through dissociation. Not infrequently, I was plagued by the question of whether a study of the "misanthrope" Paul de Lagarde was really a mistake. But the figure of Lagarde, his unbelievable hatred and fervent enthusiasm for science, continued to enthrall me. Today I am pleased to have completed a book about this broken human being, whose influence turned out to be so profound. And I hope that I will not be seen in a different light for having done so.

Many people have supported me. The Deutsche Forschungsgemeinschaft (German Research Foundation) has once again proven itself as a pillar of fundamental work in the liberal arts. The Gerda Henkel Foundation made an extension of the project possible, thereby providing crucial, uninterrupted time for writing. At the invitation of Clemens Wischermann, I spent two months at the Norm und Symbol Special Research Center at the University of Konstanz. During my time at Lake Constance, I composed the chapter "A House Like a Fortress," whose somber mood was in marked contrast to the beauty of the landscape and the hospitality of its residents.

My perennial connection to theological research introduced me to new perspectives. Friedrich Wilhelm Graf helped with expert opinions and contacts, and advocated sober analytical detachment. In Marburg, Dietrich Korsch was an equally thoughtful and warmhearted partner in conversation. When I confronted the students in my courses with certain antisemitic idiosyncrasies, they not only mustered the necessary patience but also expressed genuine interest. Their fresh ideas and curious inquiries became an important source of inspiration.

Technical support from the Göttingen State and University Library went far beyond the call of duty. The library's head, Helmut Rohlfing, solved organizational problems. Bärbel Mund clarified difficult provenance issues, and I could always rely on the skills of Wiard Hinrichs in the case of practically unreadable notes or letters. Long walks with Carola Dietze, who was working on her groundbreaking study of Helmuth Plessner, will always remain pleasant memories. Sometimes I envied her for having a much more sympathetic "hero." But the two of us also found that we had a surprising amount in common and, despite very different life experiences, each of us had become an "established outsider" in his or her own way.

It became clear to me one day that I had to actually write the book which had only been a dream until then. Oxford's Wadham College provided the necessary seclusion to review the collected materials. Despite having many obligations of his own, Jörn Leonhard was an exemplary host. And our ironic conversations in the Senior Common Room made the abysmal nature of my subject clear to me. Thanks to the efforts of Kinichi Ogura and Takayuki Shibata, I was even able to study source materials about Lagarde and his impact in faraway Japan.

Exchanges with such comprehensively educated scholars as Reinhard Brandt, Peter Krüger, Fritz Osterwalder, Peter Pulzer, and Reinhard Rürup provided me with valuable suggestions. In an era of rapid paradigm shifts and self-assertive fashionable "design theory," these exchanges helped sharpen my awareness of just how endangered spiritual traditions are. Among the scholars of my generation, I am much indebted to Heike Behlmer, Michaela Haibl, Thomas Hertfelder, Andrea Hopp, Martin Liepach, Thomas Meyer, Helmut Walser Smith, and Till van Rahden. They asked relevant and leading questions, suggested instructive literature, and acquainted me with rare sources. Above all, they encouraged me to trust my own discoveries and to clearly highlight departures from established images of Lagarde.

The collaboration with Martha Bunk and Tobias Heyl of Hanser Verlag was simply a joy. He and Philip Blom made certain early on that, no matter the research pressures, I never lost sight of creating a "readable book." Jörg Hackeschmidt, with whom I carried on inspiring discussions, extended his hospitality to me in Berlin. Michael Dreyer viewed my very German subject from the far shores of America and helped me better understand its peculiarities. Ewald Grothe diligently studied the entire manuscript and once again proved to be an unerring critic, as well as a close friend. Anne Nagel got an earful of my ideas in their nascent state. She encouraged me and gave wise advice. Without her human warmth, life would be much the poorer. My friendship with Astrid Milenz is enormously enriching and especially fortunate indeed. It is to her that I would like to dedicate this book.

ULRICH SIEG

MARBURG, NOVEMBER 2006

Translator's Comments

The process of translating this remarkable biography of Paul de Lagarde has been a distinct honor and challenge. Ulrich Sieg is intimately familiar with nineteenth- and twentieth-century German history, and his voluminous knowledge of source materials in such diverse fields as philosophy, the history of ideas, and theology has earned my sincere respect. He has also conducted extensive research into the published and unpublished writings of Paul de Lagarde, which provide detailed insight into this complex man and the time in which he lived. Not only does this help those of us living today to understand the roots of modern antisemitism; it also connects the dots between the major trends in nineteenth-century thought and Lagarde's influence on twentieth-century minds. As Professor Sieg so aptly points out, Lagarde's ideas met with widespread acceptance during very different periods. But they were ultimately used as propaganda tools in the National Socialist era.

With the downfall of the Third Reich, Lagarde consequently disappeared from the historical radar screen for decades. In translating this work, we have made every effort to preserve the subtleties of the original German. Our goal has always been to make the work an interesting read that deepens an overall understanding of those trends in German history that led up to the Second World War. We have chosen to leave certain words in the original German, either because they are commonly understood (e.g., Reich or Mensch) or because they do not easily translate into English. When a German term appears in the text for the first time, we include the English translation in parentheses. It appears thereafter in italics, unless the term can be understood as a proper noun, in which case it is set roman. An example of such a word would be Reichsgründung, which describes the period of the founding of the German Reich that began in 1871.

This translation could not have happened without the wonderful collaboration with the Tauber Institute for the Study of European Jewry at Brandeis University. I would especially like to thank Sylvia Fuks Fried and Eugene Sheppard for their help and support. Warm thanks are also due to Lys Ann Weiss, managing editor of the University Press of New England, for her excellent assistance with the endnotes and other publishing-related matters.

The author, Ulrich Sieg, was available throughout to provide explanations, feedback, and encouragement. He was particularly helpful with the many brief quotes that add color and complexity to the text but that also present a creative challenge for the translator.

Finally, I would like to thank my fellow German translators who, as members of the German List Division of the American Translators Association, were generous with their time and insights. Although I was aware of it already, I was nevertheless moved by the enormous talent and breadth of knowledge that are represented in our association. Special thanks are due to Thomas Huber, William McJunkin, Sibylle Frnka, Nina Gettler, Sigrid Coats, and Lotte Schmitz.

For my own part, I would be remiss not to thank my alma mater, Yale University, for the wonderful liberal arts education that has enabled me to remain curious and open to lifelong learning.

LINDA ANN MARIANIELLO
SANTA FE, NEW MEXICO
WWW.ALLA-BREVE.US

Germany's Prophet

1

A Man of Contradictions

On a bitterly cold Christmas Day, a considerable number of academics gathered at the Central Cemetery in Göttingen. They came together to pay their last respects to a highly controversial man. The man in question was Orientalist and cultural critic Paul de Lagarde. Lagarde had nursed a broken relationship to Christianity and pilloried the double standards of the church in his writings. So it was not without an internal struggle that he had refused pastoral support and charged the university with the task of organizing a dignified burial on short notice. Prorector Ulrich von Wilamowitz-Moellendorf was obliged to swiftly prepare an oration, as Lagarde had told no one other than his wife about the seriousness of his illness and the pending cancer operation. Only three days later, he died in the Mariahilf Hospital in Göttingen. The date was December 22, 1891. Surely most people would have made do with the customary formulas for interment. For Wilamowitz, the proud authority on Classical Greece, it was certainly out of the question for him to portray Lagarde in anything but a worthy fashion. And so he delivered a notable address that was mentioned in the national press and was apparently remembered by those in attendance for a long time thereafter.[1]

Wilamowitz, the son-in-law of Theodor Mommsen, shared with Lagarde the positivist creed of self-sacrificial attention to detail and the conviction that scholarly argument was indispensable to the advancement of knowledge. He showed particular respect for the seriousness with which Lagarde had faced the ethical dimension of life. It was hardly coincidental that Wilamowitz began his address with remarks about Lagarde's valiant end. Having only recently returned from a trip to various libraries in Italy, the Orientalist had not burdened a single colleague with concerns about his health. Rather, he sat at his writing desk until shortly before the operation, poring over philological problems.[2] But with all due respect for the scholarly ethos of the deceased, Wilamowitz was not one to simply cover up conflicts. He let it show through in his eulogy that Lagarde had pursued overly ambitious scholarly projects that could not be realized. At the same time, he read the riot act to his Göttingen colleagues, whom the strangely solitary Lagarde had barely noticed and occasionally derided. With solemn diction that was also entirely on the mark, Wilamowitz gave voice to Lagarde's linguistic skills: "There is arguably no one here who can spell in all the languages in which his texts were printed."

Lagarde's colossal knowledge should not be seen as an end in itself, as it served a larger purpose. His intention to pioneer a critical edition of the Old Testament had demanded both courage and an unrelenting willingness to work, and could hardly be surpassed in terms of difficulty. Wilamowitz, who ranked among the most outstanding scholars of his generation, was usually very sparing in his praise and did not leave the slightest doubt as to the inherent worth of Lagarde's undertaking: "I have a broad enough view of things to be able to say that there is no more difficult and, therefore, no finer edition of textual criticism, bar none. Anyone who attacked it fifty years ago must have told himself he was staking his life on it. He had a certain boldness that he never lost, not even after he had long since realized that he wouldn't see the Promised Land from the mountaintop." By means of this biblical imagery, Wilamowitz had moved his address into the field to which Lagarde owed his prominence.

Although the man of letters from Göttingen possessed vast knowledge of the Coptic and Syrian languages and had written a host of specialized scholarly works, he was known to the broader public as a fierce critic of his time. Lagarde had thus cultivated a prophetic air that fit well with the dark tone of his culturally pessimistic remarks. Wilamowitz, who tended to be gravely earnest himself, portrayed his colleague as a "Crier in the Wilderness," whose "prophetic nature" had given him the right to preach.[3] He boldly reminded his listeners of "Heraclitus and Parmenides, Augustine and Giordano Bruno, Jean-Jacques Rousseau and Thomas Carlyle," who were renowned for moving their contemporaries to the very core. After all, Wilamowitz added soberly, none of these men were entirely without personal weaknesses. As to what this meant in Lagarde's case, the eulogy left the question open. Wilamowitz ended with the comment that Lagarde had always thought of the Gospel as "Good News." The Göttingen Old Testament scholar Rudolf Smend recited the Reformed Church prayers and made certain that Lagarde's repudiation of church beliefs hardly entered the minds of those present. Even the grave site suggested that a devout life cycle had been completed. The simple stone cross still bears the epitaph that the ultraconservative theologian Ernst Wilhelm Hengstenberg once wrote in his own family album: *Via crucis est via salutis*. ("The way of the cross is the way of salvation.")[4]

With reference to the words that Shakespeare's Mark Antony spoke at the bier of Julius Caesar, Wilamowitz gave expression to the hope that Lagarde's good deeds would outlive him. Presumably, as was so often the case with funeral sermons, "Thy wish was father to the thought" (Shakespeare, *Henry IV*). The reality would soon look quite different. Immediately following the burial, the fight over Lagarde's spiritual legacy began. Even the journalistic rendition of Wilamowitz's eulogy may have been taken by many as too complimentary and was not free of polemical undertones. Lagarde had many enemies among academicians; he would not accept any other viewpoint than his own and had entangled himself in many a scholarly feud. A classic example of double entendre was the obituary by the successor to his post, Julius Wellhausen.[5] Admittedly, he emphasized Lagarde's scholarly ambition, which spanned religion and ancient languages in equal measure. But Wellhausen left no doubt that Lagarde had approached the solution to the most complex problems with an antiquated worldview and narrow methodological awareness: "Religiously speaking, he labored under a belief in the orthodoxy of Friedrich Wilhelm IV, an ecclesiastical version of Romanticism. Academically, he was ruled by the usual comparative method of the time, a rather untamed means of comparing." From on high, he commented on Lagarde's enthusiasm for learning, which made difficult languages like Persian and Coptic accessible to him during his studies without the help of adequate grammars, thereby impressing even celebrated scholars like Friedrich Rückert. "Apart from that, he can be described as self-taught." Wellhausen likewise commented unequivocally on Lagarde's publishing practice of presenting even marginal research results to the public. From Wellhausen's perspective, the ambivalent verdict of the academic world was entirely understandable, because Lagarde had never managed a comprehensive account of his results. Surely this outstanding Old Testament authority summed up the weaknesses in Lagarde's oeuvre. Lagarde's contentiousness was considered so notorious that it actually took up considerable space in an 1897 article that appeared in Meyer's Conversation Lexicon.[6] Nevertheless, a person seldom goes wrong in suspecting that not only purely scholarly reasons lie behind learned disputes but also ideological conflicts and personal animosities.

Lagarde had voiced opposition to Wellhausen's promotion many times. He simply didn't like the talented scholar, who had created a sensation with his *Geschichte Israels* (*History of Israel*), only to switch from theology to Oriental studies on grounds of conscience. In addition, Lagarde's rigid positivism made him skeptical of Wellhausen's intellectual delight in experimentation. In the fall of 1881, Lagarde told a colleague in Königsberg: "He [Wellhausen] opines very evasively and astutely that understanding and astuteness, which he sometimes passes off as fantasy and hatred, can replace pedantic source study."[7] On July 9, 1887, Lagarde was even more explicit with ministerial advisor Friedrich Althoff, who was the deciding authority in matters of appointment in the Prussian Ministry of Education and Cultural Affairs. About Wilamowitz's "bosom buddy," whose appointment in Göttingen was being deliberated, he said very caustically: he "takes false credit," is "badly behaved," and would "never again darken" the doorstep of Lagarde's home. The main reason for this harsh judgment was political in nature. Wellhausen was a left-liberal sympathizer, and Lagarde denigrated him to Althoff on May 18, 1888, as tainted by "Jewish liberalism." Moreover, he was of the opinion that a bloc of left-liberals had arranged for Wellhausen's "achievements [. . .] to be grossly overestimated in the most colossal manner." Wilamowitz, who since his Göttingen appointment in 1883 had endeavored to be on good terms with the unsociable Lagarde, appears to have known very little about his denigration of Wellhausen. But the vehemence of Lagarde's antisemitism must have been absolutely clear to Wilamowitz, because the embittered scholar had given free reign to his resentment during the final years of his life.

The opinion leaders of political antisemitism reacted promptly to Lagarde's death. The opportunity had finally presented itself for their movement to take full, unrestricted advantage of a recognized academician. The subversive agitator Theodor Fritsch styled Lagarde as the mastermind of the people's antisemitism. He placed special emphasis on the fact that the Orientalist stood vividly before the eyes of those who read his anti-Jewish articles. With a sense of self-promotion, Fritsch made scornful remarks about the alleged publication practices of contemporary journalism: "The illustrated journals mainly serve the Jews and feature the likeness of every Jewish chess talent, piano virtuoso and magician, yet they have no space for a great German thinker."[8] Fritsch, who approached Lagarde with some reserve during his lifetime, lived both for and through politics, and had no scruples when it came to choosing his means. Lagarde, who felt that his own appearance was unbecoming, expressly forbade the publication of his portrait and looked at "political mass marketing" with contempt (Hans Rosenberg).[9] But the mere fact that his name could be used in antisemitic circles for propaganda purposes reveals the nature of his reputation. Even the *Bayreuther Blätter*, whose readership extended far beyond orthodox Wagnerians, did not want to be on the sidelines; Ludwig Schemann was the person responsible for drawing up a grandiose obituary for that publication. As the founder of the Gobineau Society, he was among the leading architects of antisemitism in the Wilhelmine era.[10] The memory of Paul de Lagarde would soon take on a remarkably hagiographic quality. Thus, all three biographies written by his contemporaries would come from his private milieu and would strive to lend the misanthropic scholar a friendly, cosmopolitan air.

Anna de Lagarde's recollections are the most important source for a biography of Lagarde: they convey personal impressions and occasionally cite documents that have been lost over the years. As with Marianne Weber, the wife of Max, Anna de Lagarde lived entirely for her husband. Following his death, she considered it her distinct honor to keep his memory alive.[11] Nevertheless, her will to power should not be underestimated. In her careful preparation of his personal effects, she destroyed documents that told of painful private matters. Her relationship with her husband was clothed in admiration and awe, so the biography tends to ignore or whitewash unpleasant facts. Nonetheless, it would be erroneous to entirely dismiss Anna de Lagarde's recollections as unreliable, for they provide multifaceted insight into the private life of a secretive scholar about whose feelings and convictions we are anything but certain. Due to their affective proximity to contemporary values, they also have worth as independent source material.

The second biography is by Ludwig Schemann. The Göttingen librarian idolized Paul de Lagarde, but was reserved toward the academic world. He earned his professional reputation as a journalist in the service of Bayreuth circles whose antisemitic orientation intensified around 1900. With regard to content, he closely followed Anna de Lagarde, who presented her husband as the advocate of a self-contained, heroic attitude toward life. Moreover, his inspiringly formulated biography illustrated the extent to which antisemitism strove for bourgeois acceptance and had already gained it in part. For Schemann, the rejection of parliamentary or humanistic values was nevertheless out of the question. What may have been significant to his worldview was the catastrophe of World War I, which had induced him to conclude that Germany had been destroyed by an "addiction to the opiate of democracy."[12]

Lagarde's student Alfred Rahlfs maintained considerably greater distance from the prevailing circumstances and his professor's personality. Rahlfs continued with the Septuagint undertaking with which Lagarde had hoped to raise the textual foundation of the Old Testament to a new level. A benevolent eloquence indeed marks the 1927 study that was drawn up for Lagarde's hundredth birthday, but it also contains a large number of doubtful remarks about his fiery intellectual temperament. From personal experience, Rahlfs knew about a fragment that his teacher had left behind in the Septuagint research: "Despite great love for the cause and despite his enormous capacity for work," as he trenchantly expresses it, "Lagarde had [. . .] not managed to even partially finalize any work."[13] At the same time, Rahlfs was not blind to Lagarde's human weaknesses and, from his point of view, Lagarde was incapable of "distinguishing between the practical and the personal." The Göttingen biblical researcher nevertheless exhibited great loyalty to Lagarde, to whom he owed his place in life. Characteristically, Rahlfs barely approached the dark abyss of Lagarde's political activity. All three biographers defended Lagarde against accusations that he was autocratic, lending him an aura of altruistic veracity and bourgeois respectability. On the other hand, they did not capture any of the brisance of his worldview or the wide resonance it found.

Lagarde attained a high degree of prominence through his *Deutsche Schriften*, a collection of essays that first appeared in 1878 and combined political texts of varied origin. With a prophetic air, they invoked a "national religion" as the answer to the contemporary crisis of meaning. Lagarde gave voice to widespread discontent with the modern age; he turned against industrialization, urbanization, and bureaucratization, and called for strict separation of church and state. At the same time, he fought against liberalism, which he blamed for the excesses of capitalism and the lack of faith among his contemporaries. Lagarde played a special role in the history of nationalism. In colorful terms, he expressed the need for a comprehensive worldview, a need shared by many of his contemporaries. He opposed all forms of pluralism with inexorable resolve. At the same time, he favored the fusion of enemy stereotypes that would become a distinguishing feature of modern nationalism. Though considerably shortened and styled according to popular taste, his writings were rather widely disseminated.[14] Moreover, Lagarde cast his spell on aspiring authors. At the beginning of the twentieth century, a whole range of figures like Martin Buber, Maximilian Harden, and Friedrich Paulsen studied him intensively. Christian Morgenstern even wanted the words "Read Lagarde!" to be placed on his tombstone. During the First World War, Lagarde was celebrated as the "herald of German character" whose worldview was ideally suited to putting the "ideas of 1789" in their place. In the period of the Weimar Republic, he became a fixed point of reference for nationalistic groups that found his aggrandizement of a Greater German Reich attractive. Lagarde's rejection of racism as "materialistic" limited his usefulness to the Third Reich. Nevertheless, he was an important forerunner of the National Socialist movement, and Alfred Rosenberg's office went to considerable lengths to propagate his ideas about "German religion." Finally, it can be no mere footnote to National Socialist history that, after the "Machtergrifung" (Seizure of power), Adolf Hitler studied Lagarde's *Deutsche Schriften* extensively. And then, in 1945, the examination of Lagarde was almost entirely abandoned.

Although the scholarly and historical significance of Lagarde's ideas cannot be contested, he rates as one of the least examined and lesser-known figures in German history. While handbooks and complete overviews readily mention him, they seldom contain in-depth remarks. Significantly, there are no newer studies that meet scholarly expectations. An important reason for this may well be the canonical rank of Fritz Stern's monograph *The Politics of Cultural Despair: A Study in the Rise of Germanic Ideology*, which decisively shaped the image of Lagarde in the early 1960s. Along with Julius Langbehn and Arthur Moeller van den Bruck, the Göttingen Orientalist was elevated to a mastermind of radical conservatism, without whose fateful rejection of the modern age the catastrophe of National Socialism would be incomprehensible. Many historians adopted Stern's assessment and portrayed Lagarde as an embittered scholar, passionate antisemite, and ardent nationalist. This was in no way erroneous, yet this appraisal of Lagarde, equal parts simplistic and pejorative, rapidly dampened the hermeneutic ambitions of interpreters. The once greatly admired oeuvre of this Göttingen scholar would serve only as a quarry for antisemitic and emphatically nationalistic quotations. Curiously enough, research followed Lagarde's self-styling. But whereas he always emphasized the hermetic uniformity of his worldview, he was actually responding sensitively to the changing times. The fact that Lagarde was a masterful recycler of certain texts is hardly coincidental. This applies even more so to his *Deutsche Schriften*. Thus, a number of articles were taken as a symptomatic reaction to the problems of the Bismarck era and date back to the repressive atmosphere of the 1850s.

Stern's work certainly has great merit. When it appeared in 1961, a critical view of the past was of great concern. Brilliantly written, it looks at the shadow side of German history and makes clear just how radically the contemporary critique of uprooted intellectuals could change into jet-black cultural pessimism. Admittedly, one opens the door to epistemological difficulties by conceptualizing the German Empire and the Weimar Republic as the prologue to National Socialism. Thus, it is apparent that the singularity of national developments cannot be precisely understood without an appropriate comparative perspective. American historian Helmut Walser Smith only recently pointed out that traditional historical scholarship "got stuck in a quagmire of nationalistic teleologies" and "life as it really was remained uninvestigated."[15] This probably holds true to an exceptional degree for the history of ideas, a fact that was hardly noticed for decades by Germany's socio-historically dominated faculties. Especially in the nineteenth century, scholarly ideas and intellectual trends almost effortlessly exceeded state limits. Should one therefore mistake the traditional rhetoric they are clothed in for their objective content, the path to understanding will be blocked. Even Lagarde, depicted mostly as a loner within the history of ideas, kept up an extensive correspondence that linked him with leading intellectuals and countless scholars throughout Europe. So it is revealing to see how Lagarde's concept of "national religion" differs from the thoughts of Ernest Renan, who concurrently propagated a religiously tinged national understanding in France. Lagarde's admiration turned to Great

Britain and Thomas Carlyle, whose heroicized writing of history he regarded as the paragon of defiant resistance to modernity. In his critique of historicism and his rejection of the church-state entity, Lagarde again displayed views similar to pundits of note like Jacob Burckhardt and Friedrich Nietzsche.[16]

Lagarde already exercised considerable influence during his lifetime, as his Göttingen estate impressively shows. It contains letters that precisely state how Lagarde meant for his *Deutsche Schriften* to be construed. Until now, this evidence of the careful guidance Lagarde provided to his readers has been either underestimated or ignored. This also holds true for the analysis by Fritz Stern, who adopted Lagarde's self-styling as an ostracized outsider and only allowed his effective history to begin posthumously. Stern's opinion has remained decisive in the research, such that Lagarde is primarily considered a figurehead of the nationalist movement. Lagardism cast a veil over Lagarde, so to speak. In this way, the late Romantic thinker became a Wilhelmine era figure.[17] In fact, the as yet unclassified portion of his estate most notably documents the scholar's contemporary resonance. Thus, a collection of papers and reviews attests to the interest in his writings. Myriad letters show just how closely the pundit tracked the response to his political writings and tried to maneuver it whenever possible. His band of followers was admittedly not that large, but it was carefully cultivated and could list many respectable persons among its members.

The question that generally confronts us is whether the traditional organization of the German Empire in the period before and after Bismarck's chancellorship can be considered absolute. At any rate, this periodization is not fair to the intergenerational character of the religious and cultural problems that were caused by the swift changeover from an agrarian society to a modern industrial one. The example of Lagarde, in particular, shows the extent to which fin-de-siècle problems are traceable to ideological circumstances and developments during the Gründerzeit, the period of rapid industrial expansion from 1871 onward. At the same time, it makes clear just how far-reaching the consequences of the "dechurchification" and de-Christianization processes were. Attention thereby turned to the burden of modernization, and compensatory efforts to deal with it engendered a powerful thirst for meaning. So it was hardly coincidental that, in order to meet with the approval of a broad spectrum of people, nationalism was dressed up as a religious venture. Promulgators of nationalism linked themselves to the familiar hope of salvation, thereby reaching precisely those persons who were overwhelmed by the rapid social changes in the latter half of the nineteenth century. Lagarde ranks among those "false prophets" whose importance should not be marginalized. Such outsiders appeal to the majority. Like seismographs, they proclaim a crisis in society.

Lagarde's concept of a national religion was of central importance to the cultural critique of the Bismarck chancellorship. On the one hand, it involved legitimizing nationalism as the final arbiter of meaning. On the other hand, Lagarde's cultural philosophy represented a spiritually motivated answer to the changes of the modern age. National religion can only be grasped by taking into account the tension among theology, culture, and politics. Normative criteria help very little in analyzing his neo-Romantic "reenchantment" of the world, which ensued primarily via aesthetic categories.[18] Most important for Lagarde's style was his purposeful blurring of the differences between the written and spoken word. He repeatedly drew upon pastoral stylistic elements that thereby lent his nationalistic worldview religious consecration. Combined with the biblical derivation of his anti-Jewish decrees, this accounted for his significance within the antisemitic movement.

Israeli historian Moshe Zimmermann noted twenty years ago that the history of antisemitism was written mostly without the participation of antisemites, and not much has changed in the meantime. Another salient methodical finding also comes into play: as drastic as the antisemitic source language is, parts of the scholarly literature are every bit as top-heavy and overtheorized. It is not coincidental that Oxford scholar Peter Pulzer's work *The Rise of Political Anti-Semitism* has occupied a key position for decades; it appropriately interlinks theoretical reflection and keenly detailed descriptions.[19] Following the National Socialist dictatorship's decivilization, most historians shuddered at the precise representation and inherent logic of the antisemitic thought world. Perhaps this applied even more to motives that allowed individuals to become antisemites. Instead of psychologically empathetic interpretations, some favored normative declarations that paraded antisemitism as the "sentiment of the riffraff" (Theodor Mommsen). The reduction of hermeneutic claims certainly resulted in our knowing decidedly little about the personal motives and characteristics of antisemitism. The only way for this to change even slightly is for the historical principle of charity, which demands empathetic reading through a temporary suspension of suspicion, to be applied to the topic of antisemitism.

To write the biography of an antisemite is no easy task. It means the emotional examination of antipathies that feel very foreign and strangely, urgently present at the same time. Furthermore, to attempt a "thick description" (Clifford Geertz) demands convincing evidence. Lagarde's estate fortunately contains many documents in which the Orientalist expressed his views with typical, ruthless candor. Since Anna de Lagarde shared her husband's hatred of Jews, she appears to have refrained from broaching the topic. In any case, the leading representatives of contemporary antisemitism, from Theodor Fritsch to Julius Langbehn to August Rohling and Richard Wagner, were all prominently represented. Even Jewish responses to antisemitism come into sharp relief, because the eminent academic was in contact with many representative scholars of Judaism.

To define Lagarde in terms of his antisemitism certainly does not go far enough, as his reach extended well beyond antisemitic circles. Irrespective of his sharp criticism of ecclesiastical faith, he also had many followers in the field of academic theology. Outside the walls of the university, he was considered the virtual embodiment of true religious feeling. A sharp critic of education, he spoke to the hearts of many who rejected the Prussian school system and its authoritarian traits. The fact that, at the turn of the twentieth century, Lagarde was thought of more as a grandiloquent cultural pessimist than an antisemite also deserves mention. Before Nietzsche became the focal point of bourgeois reform efforts around 1910, Lagarde possessed an authority in ideological matters that is difficult to grasp from today's perspective. His supporters fancied him the "Prophet of Germanness" whose earnest convictions could lead them out of the contemporary cultural crisis. At the 1914 Leipzig International Book and Graphics Exhibition, Diederichs Verlag even built a "Lagarde Chapel" that was intended to underscore the quasi-religious character of his message.[20] Finally, we should not forget that the danger of antisemitism owed in large part to its ideological smoothness. This very thing speaks in favor of involvement with a thinker like Lagarde, whose shimmering, multicolored works were taken up by divergent ideologies.

Paul de Lagarde was a man of contradictions. As a hardworking philologist known for his skeptical positions, he abandoned himself repeatedly to bold speculation that cast his scholarly oeuvre in a doubtful light. He composed delicate poems, as well as hateful treatises, and did not seem to notice that he abruptly changed the diction within one and the same text. Surely he placed great value on tact and keeping one's distance, and his praise for the social ideal of the English "gentleman" was stylishly worded. But he dealt with internal academic and administrative matters with a directness, at best, that earned him a multitude of enemies and the interest of the judiciary. As richly documented as Lagarde's personal restraint is, there can be no doubt that he purposefully aimed at political efficacy. In his polemical treatises, pedantically implemented reform programs alternate with bold visions whose realization lies in the distant future. On the surface, Lagarde's unhappy, characteristically workaholic, disappointed, and bitter life displays no fascinating traits. Nonetheless, he cast his spell as a "prophet of doom" in every shade under the sun.

All of this raises the question: what was Lagarde really about? This book seeks an answer. It challenges the assumptions of today's teleologists and focuses on synchronous elements of the past so as to gain a better understanding of a difficult human being. Nevertheless, the shadowy lines of German history are open to debate. How can it be otherwise for an intellectual who was still influenced by the fateful mind-set of late German Romanticism and wanted to establish radical conservatism in the spirit of the Middle Ages? In addition, Lagarde's idiosyncratic appeal extends deeply into the world of National Socialism and calls for diachronic perspectives. There will always be risk involved in approaching a thorough characterization of a psychologically disabled person and his ideological obsessions with German history. In the end, only the reader can decide whether the outcome is a successful one.

2

Dismal Childhood

In each of the various German states, the end of the Napoleonic era was accompanied by multifaceted expectations.[1] Economically, people were focused on overcoming trade barriers. On the political front, they hoped for the adoption of prospective constitutions that would create centralized states. But the climate of reform did not last long. The German Confederation superseded longed-for German unity. Austrian chancellor Clemens von Metternich realized his main restorative goals with the issuance of the Carlsbad Decrees on September 20, 1819. Newspapers and magazines were subject to censorship and nationally minded student associations were forbidden. The autonomy of the universities was now a thing of the past. "Demagogues," that is, those who undauntedly proclaimed the people's right to freedom, were tracked down and incarcerated. Of course, Metternich's attempt to stop the passage of time, while considerably successful, was also illusory. The Holy Alliance was supposed to preserve peace in Europe. But in the long run it was unable to prevent conflicts of interest between Russia and Austria. Regardless of censorship policies, nationalistic and liberal ideas still took root in people's minds. And social change went forward no matter how many restrictive laws were enacted. Years of peace saw an increase in the wealth of the bourgeoisie, engendering feelings of self-importance and encouraging political participation. But there were definite limits to economic change within the German Confederation. While smoking factory chimneys and fast spinning machines announced the start of the Industrial Revolution in England, premodern slowness was mostly still the rule in Germany. Far more than the reform-oriented bourgeoisie could have wished for, complacent petty princes and obscure tariff regulations shaped the territorially splintered country.

The Berlin of Friedrich Wilhelm III, into which Paul de Lagarde was born on November 2, 1827, reflected the contradictions of the epoch. On the one hand, rural flight and improved medical care led to rapid population growth. Between 1800 and 1850, population figures climbed from one to four hundred thousand. On the other hand, industrialization was still in the early stages and did not offer enough jobs for the many who came along. In addition to large manufacturers, small enterprises and retailers shaped the face of a city that knew many forms of social inequality. But this was not the picture that Lagarde painted in recalling the Berlin of his youth. Instead, he presented an absolutely cordial, paternalistically idyllic city that could still offer people a *Heimat*, or homeland, understood by Lagarde in a romantic nationalist register to embrace one's organic rootedness in a place through birth, upbringing, culture, language, and topography, and ultimately, destiny.[2]

His pastel-colored depiction of Biedermeier Berlin not only marginalizes the inner tensions and transformational tendencies of the epoch; it is also unsuited to a realistic understanding of the Prussian bureaucratic state, whose shadow side Lagarde knew only too well. This even holds true for the university, which was world famous in the late nineteenth century. After Wilhelm von Humboldt left office in protest against the Carlsbad Decrees, very little could be felt of the impulse toward reform that characterized the founding period: there were admittedly still outstanding scholars teaching at the University of Berlin, but very few took an active role in political life. Most professors valued their prestigious social positions and, whenever possible, avoided sounding critical of the state. The philosopher Hegel even went so far as to behold what was then the apogee of human progress within the Prussian state.[3]

As with many German academics, Paul Bötticher—for that was Paul de Lagarde's original name—came from an old and noble pastoral family. His father, Wilhelm Bötticher, was an ambitious, self-confident man.[4] The elder Bötticher studied theology and came into conflict with the authorities early on when he protested the dismissal of Berlin theologian Wilhelm Martin Leberecht de Wette. De Wette's offense had been a letter of condolence to the mother of Karl Ludwig Sand. Sand had murdered the poet August von Kotzebue in 1819 on suspicion of being a Russian agent, and was later executed in an atmosphere of great public interest. But Wilhelm Bötticher would soon decide in favor of a more orderly lifestyle. In 1824, he accepted a teaching position at the Friedrich Wilhelms Gymnasium in Berlin. Shortly thereafter, he married Luise Klebe, the daughter of a prominent commissioner of economics, and established a household of his own. Wilhelm Bötticher was a dutiful pedagogue and an outstanding authority on the Old Testament. The famous theologian Friedrich Schleiermacher was among his friends and a regular visitor to his home. The title of "grammar school professor" revealed the universal esteem in which Wilhelm Bötticher was held. When his wife became pregnant in 1827, their familial happiness seemed complete.

A tragedy marked the beginning of Paul Bötticher's life. His mother, who was then barely nineteen years of age, passed away only twelve days after he was born. His father apparently never recovered from this cruel blow of fate. The formerly open-minded theologian had been among Schleiermacher's young devotees, yet he now became an obdurate Pietist who placed dogmatic interpretation of the Holy Scriptures above all else. He treated his son with hostile severity and subliminally blamed him for his wife's death. A taciturn, genuinely depressing atmosphere blanketed the family. A serious attitude toward life was conveyed to the child as a matter of course. There were no toys, and laughter was not permitted.

Paul Bötticher suffered as a result of his father's coldness. In retrospect, he described his early childhood years as "abysmally sad."[5] Wilhelm Bötticher prompted his son to intensively study the Bible, but denied him any information about his mother. The father-son relationship showed signs of conflict early on.

As coldhearted as he was demanding, the father was stingy with his praise yet openly showed his displeasure with his son's behavior. Even the boy's artistic talent was treated dismissively. So Paul Bötticher could only play piano during his father's absence in the evenings, which were actually intended as "family devotion" time. Along with grim defiance, the lonely, isolated boy developed an early desire for fatherly approval. Just how despairing Paul Bötticher's early years were can be intuited from a later remark that "if a child, like a tree, grows crooked from the cradle, it will never straighten and never be a joy to man." He tellingly opted for the image of Immanuel Kant, who endured a rigidly pietistic upbringing himself.[6]

His father married again in 1831 and, after his two brothers were born, Paul Bötticher felt relegated to the margins of the family. From an early age, he sought refuge in a fantasy world. He abandoned himself to daydreams about his mother and regarded not having known her as the greatest sorrow of his life. It seems that his only close relationship was to the youngest member of the family, his sister Anna, who was born in 1835 but died at the tender age of three. Even so, his mother's two aunts, Eleonore Klebe and Ernestine de Lagarde, looked after the shy child whose body language revealed deep insecurity. With them, Paul Bötticher found the support that his father denied him and love that didn't ask for anything in return. Ernestine de Lagarde, who came from the Huguenot branch of the family, would later adopt him and become his greatest supporter. But there can be no doubt whatsoever that his childhood years were joyless. For his entire life, he wrote poems that he hoped would help him overcome early wounds and feelings of loneliness. As early as 1850, Paul Bötticher circulated a book of poetry among his friends in which he recorded childhood impressions in elegiac language. The dreamy verses express just how great his need was for a "healing world":

The clouds come down on the horizon so light:
the day dies softly, smothered by the glowing kiss of night.

Where linger the white sails that set from here this day?
Who knows if ever they'll return to this still estuary?

And you would like to dwell nearby, to that which you like best,
bring it to you here from afar, the dreams when ere you wish.[7]

His deceased mother was the antithesis, as it were, of the hated father, in the face of whose drastic child-raising methods the boy was helpless. But the boy also showed early signs of rebellion. Thus, he protested the uplifting get-togethers in his parents' home that he considered the paragon of hypocrisy. Nevertheless, Paul Bötticher exhibited many of his father's violent and impatient character traits. He shared his father's interest in the biblical world and its rigorous understanding of truth, which interpreted every form of compromise as a weakness. Wilhelm Bötticher drafted numerous scripts that, despite their show of erudition, primarily targeted the moral betterment of mankind. Tacitus stood at the center of his oeuvre, although he was not primarily of interest to Bötticher as a historian of the Roman Empire. Rather, the pietistic Latin teacher made every effort to prove Tacitus' Christian roots. The title of his main, two-volume work, which appeared in Berlin in 1840, leaves nothing to be desired regarding bluntness and, for this reason, has been reproduced here in its entirety: *Prophetic Voices from Rome or the Christian in Tacitus and the Typically Prophetic Character of His Works regarding Rome's Relationship to Germany: A Paper on the Philosophy of History and the Deeper Appreciation of This Roman Historian.* The treatises of Wilhelm Bötticher, who suffered from deafness in old age, became more sectarian as the years passed. In his self-published, self-financed leaflets, he castigated his contemporaries for their superficial belief and lack of faith. A harsh anti-Judaism appeared in these leaflets as well. The March Revolution of 1848 thus led to the polemical treatises *Herrschaft der Juden* (*The Domination of the Jews*) and *Die Zukunft Israels und der Christenheit* (*The Future of Israel and Christianity*). His final leaflets of 1850 examined *Unsere jetzigen Zustände im Spiegel des göttlichen Wortes* (*Our Present Circumstances as Reflected in God's Word*) and came to damning conclusions about the present.

Wilhelm Bötticher found humanizing stability in parish life, which also made a significant impression on his son. In his first years, Paul got to know Schleiermacher and played at his feet. Six-year-old Paul was instructed to copy the account of Schleiermacher's death several times for the Pietist community. The dutiful lad performed the task with great care that won him accolades. Although he would later have differences with Schleiermacher, there can be no doubt that the theologian made an impression on him. His idealized concept of religious community, in particular, came from Schleiermacher, who had categorically rejected theological rationalism and fought for the right to personal feelings and imagination.[8] At the same time, Paul Bötticher met Romantic poets like Adelbert von Chamisso and Prussian reformers like the elderly Hermann von Boyen. Surely these were stimulating interludes, but their impact quickly faded into the background of a daily routine defined by austerity and lovelessness. The rather vulnerable boy retreated into the world of books from an early age. He read everything he could get his hands on, and was especially attracted to fairy tales and sagas. His loneliness was furthered in the process, but his achievements in school were not harmed a bit by his literary meanderings. The transfer to his father's grammar school also seems to have merely aroused his ambitions.

Paul Bötticher was an intellectually curious person by nature and was not fazed by difficult works; he slogged through Barthold Niebuhr's *Römische Geschichte* (*History of Rome*) and studied his views on source criticism. He was perhaps even more enamored of exploring medieval poetry through the editions of Karl Lachmann, whom he valued as an editor of Gotthold Lessing's correspondence. Paul Bötticher also admired Lessing for his sober diction and incorruptible love of truth, whereas he showed very little interest in Goethe and Schiller. Jacob Grimm's *Deutsche Mythologie* (*German Mythology*), which appeared in 1835, may well have been the most important work that he encountered during his school days. It offered philological access to the country's past, including romantic glorification of its ancestors. Paul's penchant for reading was not always in harmony with the principal values of the Friedrich Wilhelms Gymnasium, where Friedrich Ranke (brother of the famous historian) ran a tight ship. Several years beforehand, Otto von Bismarck had spent an unhappy time there at the behest of his parents, who coerced him into a proper education. In contrast to the educationally assiduous Paul Bötticher, Bismarck regarded the classicists as nothing more than a source of quotes: his reading "neither shaped his character nor his mind."[9] However, the quixotic enthusiasm of the young Bötticher turned out to be somewhat of a problem.

As his father once had, Paul Bötticher ran into trouble with the authorities. In retrospect, he sought to make the altercation appear minor. He and a group of fellow students organized a musical event to raise money for the building of the Cologne Cathedral. Even though the national building project was welcomed by the Prussian king, the authorities opposed the event. Berlin's chief of police approached the headmaster in a most personal way, stating that it was "not fitting" for the students of a "Protestant Gymnasium" to support the building of a "Catholic church." This statement may not have reflected the whole story, of course, since the patriotism of Friedrich Wilhelm IV also had a superficial side. Despite his bold support of the Cologne Cathedral, the monarch knew full well the explosive power of nationalist thought and regarded its dissemination in the Prussian schools with skepticism.[10]

Paul Bötticher protected himself from rebuke and criticism with a studiousness that was rare, even in the inquisitive nineteenth century. Along with Latin, taught to him by his father, he acquired knowledge of ancient Greek and extensive skills in the Hebrew language. Since he showed early enthusiasm for biblical studies and wanted to access the original sources, he also studied Arabic and Syriac. He even devoted himself to English and Spanish, modern languages that played no role in the schools of that time. Father Wilhelm met his son's studiousness with dismissive coldness: he took the prizes that his talented son received for his language skills and gave them to the needy. It never even occurred to Wilhelm Bötticher to order the grammar books and lexica that his son needed. This behavior seems to have merely increased Paul Bötticher's resolve. He wrote down myriad words and grammatical explanations in narrowly spaced, lined notebooks in his minute yet accurate script. As cumbersome as this task was, it made personal access to foreign languages easier and strengthened his confidence in his own abilities. By organizing the materials in this way, the diligent autodidact aided his keen memory. In 1844, at the age of sixteen, Paul Bötticher completed his *Abitur*, grammar school examinations required for entrance into higher education. His certificate reveals just how much confidence people had in him.[11]

Bötticher's "exemplary conduct" and "persistent industriousness" were praised as having prompted him to autonomous scholarly work. His "German compositions" were acknowledged to be "decisively mature." In Hebrew, he showed not only secure mastery of the grammar but a sense of contextual nuance as well. Particularly highlighted was his knowledge of "Hebraic antiquity," which, in addition to his pursuit of Syriac and Arabic, pointed to his systematic study of Oriental languages. Furthermore, Paul Bötticher didn't exactly hide his light under a bushel "and often [made] rather joyful reference in his written work" to practically unknown "Semitic dialects." Finally, on the subject of religion, his examiners extolled his familiarity with the Holy Scriptures and with "doctrine and ethics." The board of examiners exempted the outstanding student from oral exams. The board confidently expressed the hope that he would "always continue to strive with the same zeal and aspire to great success."

Just a few weeks later, Paul Bötticher began to study theology and Oriental languages at the University of Berlin.[12] It was the year of Friedrich Nietzsche's birth and, at Prussia's most important university, Aristotle researcher Adolf Trendelenburg set the tone. Following Schleiermacher's death, the highly conservative Ernst Wilhelm Hengstenberg was the leading figure on the Theology Faculty. The founder of the *Evangelische Kirchenzeitung* (*Journal of the Evangelical Lutheran Church*) had made a name for himself as a defender of God's mercifulness and an outstanding expert on the Old Testament. Since he was a friend of Wilhelm Bötticher, it went without saying that he would take Bötticher's son under his wing. Paul Bötticher's relationship with Hengstenberg was ambivalent. While he admired the outstanding biblical scholar, who approved his choice of a research area, the powerful senior professor was also hard for the easily intimidated young man to take. In the end, the positive aspects of Hengstenberg's charisma seem to have won out. Paul Bötticher listened almost exclusively to him, in any case, and barely noticed the other two theology professors, August Neander and August Twesten. On the other hand, he devoted himself to languages, studying Chinese and Tartar literature with the Orientalist Julius Petermann and attaining vast knowledge of Coptic under Egyptologist Moritz Gotthilf Schwartze.

The most influential person in Paul Bötticher's life was the poet and Persia scholar Friedrich Rückert. Rückert had already made his mark as a young man with his anti-Napoleonic *Geharnischte Sonette* (*Sonnets in Arms/Harsh Words*). Called to Berlin in 1841 by Friedrich Wilhelm IV, Rückert was an unsurpassed translator of Oriental literature, as well as a worldly and exceptional person. Bötticher prepared a Persian greeting for a visit to his home that made the favorable impression he had hoped for. An animated friendship soon developed, one that went far beyond the framework of academic pursuits. The warmhearted Rückert became a kind of ersatz father figure with whom Bötticher could share his concerns. When Bötticher wanted to learn difficult languages like Finnish on a whim, Rückert expressly urged the budding scholar not to overextend himself. Bötticher also met three young Orientalists, Richard Gosche, Friedrich Dieterici, and Friedrich Max Müller, at Rückert's lectures on Persia. All three would later become influential in the field.[13]

Paul Bötticher proved very energetic in his studies. Both in Oriental languages and in theology, he made every effort to obtain a broad-based education. But since he was not called to the ministry, he drew the line at applied theology. He went to the University of Halle in 1847 in order to expand his knowledge and mainly grappled with linguistic problems there. Notably, he wished to establish his own area of specialization early on. So he toyed with the idea of training missionaries to the Jews and corresponded with the Rostock theologian Franz Delitzsch about it. As proof of his serious intent, Paul Bötticher sent him a Hebrew poem that was favorably received by the Rostock professor. On October 4, 1847, Delitzsch let the young scholar know in a self-assured tone of bold conviction, "How beautiful it would be if a Christian went so far as to make the message of the cross more accessible to the Jewish people in their native language." In the smooth talk of someone experienced in manipulating people, he added, "Yes, I can assure you without flattery that the entire manner and style in which the Hebrew poem was written have convinced me that you have found your calling."[14]

But Delitzsch's attempt to win Bötticher to the cause of missions to the Jews ultimately failed, because pure scholarship held a far greater attraction for him than any mundane occupation. Though barely twenty years old, he published his first paper that same year. Titled "Horae aramaicae" (Aramaic Hours), it furnished a directory of Armenian, Indian, and Persian words that had been translated into Aramaic.[15] As regards content, the unsystematic execution gave many indications of the work of a beginner. But it presented Bötticher's extensive linguistic knowledge to the public and attested to his feeling for open research questions. Thus, the young scholar stressed the usefulness of the Septuagint and regretted "that no one was attending to it." When he made this statement, Paul Bötticher could not yet have known that he would wrestle with the Greek translation of the Old Testament for his entire life. But the serious diction already indicates how convinced he was of the importance of this topic.

The doctoral process at the University of Berlin proceeded as expected without a hitch. Typical of his overly wary nature, Bötticher had inquired submissively beforehand in Kiel as to whether he could receive a doctorate there. This would also have presented no problems: Justus Olshausen, the responsible Orientalist, benevolently informed him on October 25, 1848, that "I look forward in advance to making your acquaintance on the scholarly plane. May a personal meeting ensue in the near future!" But the up-and-coming scholar finally decided in favor of a doctorate from the renowned Friedrich-Wilhelms-Universität (as the University of Berlin was renamed in the early nineteenth century). On May 19, 1849, he submitted his thesis on Arabic color theory. As was the practice at that time, his dissertation was written in Latin and pertained to the clarification of a special scholarly problem.[16] To his petition, Paul Bötticher attached his own study *Rudimenta mythologiae semiticae. Supplementa lexici aramaici* (*Rudiments of Semitic Mythology: Supplements to Aramaic Lexica*), which had just come out in Berlin the previous year. The assessment of the Orientalist Julius Petermann was a mixture of accolades and skepticism.

He pointed out how precarious it was to apply "the views of later authors to [. . .] earlier times," as Paul Bötticher had done in his Semitic mythology. "Greater importance was" consequently "attributed to individual gods than was originally given to them by the populace." However, Petermann judged the questionable methodology less meaningful than the absolutely remarkable language skills of the applicant, his "studiousness," and his aptitude for making associations. As was usual for problem-free doctoral processes, linguist Franz Bopp fell into line with the vote of the head examiner. Bötticher also successfully passed the oral portion of the doctoral examination on June 14, 1849. After questioning him about Spinoza and Kant, only the strict Trendelenburg offered the criticism that "a more incisive understanding could have been wished for." The unanimously conferred rating was *multa cum laude*, which corresponds to today's highest academic distinction, summa cum laude.

Although Paul Bötticher had single-mindedly and successfully completed his studies, this did not lead to emancipation from his parental home. Revealingly, the main conflict in the 1848–1849 revolution was of a purely private nature to him. He was angry that his father presented him at public events as the chief witness for his own political convictions.[17] There was not the slightest disagreement as to content, however. Out of loyalty to the Prussian crown, Paul Bötticher placed a black-and-white cockade on his hat and loathed democracy as "mob rule." He interpreted the suppression of the revolution as the victory of morality over subversive power. But the true test of his dreamy royalism was imminent. In November 1849, he was forced to admit that the conservative establishment had fabricated evidence in order to charge left-liberal [reformer] Benedict Waldeck in court. To Bötticher, behavior that was intended to show the Prussian *Landtagsabgeordneter* (member of the legislative assembly) at the center of revolutionary activities was unlawful beyond doubt. So as to publicly express his rejection of the conservatives, he cut the black-and-white cockade off his hat in a rage. He simultaneously broke off relations with Hengstenberg, one of Waldeck's strongest opponents, who presented himself apologetically for party discipline after the affair was exposed. Bötticher considered himself politically homeless from then on and was firmly convinced that "radical conservatism" would only be realized in the distant future.

The year 1850 brought great changes for Paul Bötticher. On April 6, 1850, his father died at the age of fifty-three following a short but severe illness. His son felt no sorrow whatever, bespeaking the broken relationships in the Bötticher home. Thanks to the energetic intercession of Hengstenberg, Paul had received a secular scholarship from the City of Berlin in November 1849. Perhaps he now thought that he could spend it as he saw fit. The Orientalist aspired to an academic career and switched to the University of Halle, where he hoped to earn his teaching certificate. And it was in Halle that he met an officer's daughter, his future wife, Anna Berger. Many years later, she still recalled what a vulnerable impression the young scholar had made on her: "One saw vestiges of his having just survived a long period of suffering in his parental home and, at the same time, a sigh of relief after shedding a heavy burden that he had carried for a long time. He was indescribably unpretentious, abundantly complaisant all around, and thankful for every kindness."[18] As early as July 7, 1850, these two shy people became engaged and were happy to have found one another.

Shortly thereafter, Paul Bötticher set off on a long trip that led him to the symbols of national unity in the Rhineland and, later on, to Switzerland. He was not accompanied by his future wife but rather by his great-aunt, Ernestine de Lagarde, who also financed the trip. In Bonn, he met Ernst Moritz Arndt. The poet had, indeed, long since passed the zenith of his creative power, but he still impressed the young scholar with his nationalist views. In a letter to his bride, Paul Bötticher effusively expressed his excitement over the Cologne Cathedral he had glamorized as a schoolboy: "My God, my God, what a structure! [. . .] May God allow me to *see* it when it's completed, and a unified Germany as well."[19]

But it would not be long before his mood changed. He no longer had anything good to say about Catholicism, which he had regarded as the expression of true religiosity until now. The choral music seemed to him as if it "blared," and the idea of the Papacy was simply indefensible. He was downright ferocious in his expression of the future of Catholicism: "I hope that the course of history will make the Catholic Church ever more into a deserted ruin."[20] Bötticher's letters from 1850 not only show unbridled euphoria and wrathful hauteur; they also express great faith in Anna Berger's family. A letter of August 11 to his parents-in-law makes clear just how deeply the political conflicts in the Waldeck trial had affected his religious identity: "I often feared that the battles I fought to free myself from Pietism might do more than they have to help me enter into the warmth of piety." He continued in very personal terms: "This, my Christian Pagan religion, is now my only sanctuary and calms me like a mother's eyes calm her child when they behold it, like a mother's arm that carries it." But the young scholar could not abandon himself to these kinds of early primal feelings very often. Because he wanted to support his claim to a professorship in good time, he already planned to qualify for a teaching position the following spring in Halle. His most important advocate was Friedrich Rückert.

The experienced scholar Rückert knew the procedure for the main academic rite of passage.[21] In no way was he permitted to make the faculty in Halle feel as if he were getting mixed up in their affairs. Thus, he formulated his letter of February 2, 1851, conservatively but left no doubt as to "the worthiness and qualifications of the applicant," whom he called his "young friend." He made provisions for possible criticism by remarking that no one "can pursue the study" of all "Oriental languages and scholarship [. . .] with equal mastery." In any case, Paul Bötticher's skills were sufficient for the lecture position in question. A review that the Göttingen Orientalist Heinrich Ewald had written for the 1848 *Jahrbüchern der biblischen Wissenschaft* (*Yearbook of Biblical Scholarship*) was added to the application. The critique pertained to Bötticher's *Rudimenta mythologiae semiticae*, which Ewald regarded as a particularly enterprising work. Moreover, as he was rather brusque in his dealings, Ewald was not the kind of man to emphatically praise the achievements of a young scholar. He criticized Bötticher's historical knowledge as insufficient for an in-depth representation of the Old Testament. On the other side of the equation, however, he acknowledged Bötticher's solid language skills, which he felt would be best applied to the field of Oriental studies. The March 5, 1851, assessment of local expert Emil Rödiger also turned out to be positive, whereupon the habilitation paperwork was passed around among the faculty. A work dedicated to Friedrich Rückert, briefly titled *Arica*, dealt with sound shifts in Indo-Germanic languages. No critical objections were raised. The probationary lecture on "Das Verhältnis der indogermanischen Sprachen zu den semitischen" (The Relationship between Indo-Germanic and Semitic Languages) that took place on March 19 was also well received. Attendees applauded Bötticher's prolific language skills, in particular, and the "independent judgment" of the candidate.

On May 20, Paul Bötticher defended his thesis concerning the philosophical basis of theology and the Aryan origins of Armenian. Now nothing remained to prevent him from beginning his teaching career. As usual, a certain amount of time passed before he presented his lecture debut to the students in Halle on November 1. As the title suggested, the lecture dealt with the twelfth-century Jewish poet and religious philosopher Yehuda Halevi. With respect to content, however, Bötticher offered an extensive cultural history of Judaism.

The new university lecturer proudly pointed out that, as an Orientalist, he did not need *Captatio benevolentiae* (to garner goodwill), because the importance of his research area was irrefutable. He placed himself within the tradition of Goethe, whose positive image of the Orient had also impressed Rückert. But the period of Romantic yearning in academia had passed, and the most precise study of Jewish historical sources was the order of the day. Bötticher emphasized that special, wide-ranging skills were important if a person wished to do justice to a complex subject like Judaism. He underscored the fact that the synagogue, which "had given the Jews the power to oppose their numerous enemies," had been invented in Babylonia.[22] And it seemed undeniable to him that the Arabian challenge had decisively inspired a rise in Jewish culture. Bötticher established a similarly fundamental connection with respect to Sephardi culture in Spain. Poetry could only flower there after Jewish life was firmly rooted, because an inextricable link existed between the art of versification and love of one's country. Subtle, sophisticated Jewish poetry certainly need not fear comparison with that of other cultures. By means of example, Bötticher quoted from his own translations of Sephardi verse, which expressed his high regard for Andalusian Jewish culture and lent his lecture debut a solemn character. But his appraisal of Judaism remained ambivalent, as a closer look at his provisional lecture shows.

In his provisional lecture, which was part of the certification process of the habilitation, Bötticher made decisive statements about the relationship between Indo-Germanic and Semitic languages. He acknowledged Wilhelm von Humboldt's idea that the essential character of a language was manifested in popular speech. He clearly emphasized the differences between the two linguistic communities that can be traced back to Noah's sons, Shem and Japheth. Semites "lacked the ability to see the totality," which led to the realization that they had never once developed a philosophical system.[23] A Semite's individualistic awareness was so pronounced that even the cosmos was perceived as scattered. By contrast, the Japhetic worldview aimed for holistic coherence, which proved beyond a doubt the missing kinship with the Semites. These were bold generalizations that, furthermore, tended to disavow the philosophical dignity of Semitic perception. The inscrutability of these value judgments may not have occurred to most of those listening, but they were part of a philosophical tradition that was generally accepted. Since the days of Johannes Fichte, it had become customary to criticize Jewish thought as being far too particularistic.[24] However, Bötticher's passion for Sephardi Jews was conspicuous, and it was no accident that it met with reservations.

On December 19, 1851, Bötticher's friend Max Karow informed him that he "definitely did not share his fascination with the Spanish-Jewish poets." These sorts of judgments may have made little impression on the young university lecturer. In any event, he did not choose his academic contacts according to their religious affiliations. So he sent a letter to the Jewish linguist Heymann Steinthal, who was then studying in Paris. The eminent popular psychologist, who also possessed outstanding linguistic abilities, understandably refused to comment in detail on Bötticher's research in May 1852. He was so busy with

Chinese culture at present that he was unable to get involved in the Near Eastern world.

Along with expanding his network of academic contacts, Paul Bötticher tried to build a student following in Halle. Like many fledgling university lecturers, he didn't have an easy time of it. His Oriental research areas required considerable knowledge and were accessible to only a few students. Moreover, tenured professors claimed the theological survey lectures for themselves, as they yielded the most student funding. But the Berlin scholarship protected Bötticher from financial worries for the time being. During the winter semester, he lectured on his own research interests, such as Egyptian hieroglyphics, which did not draw many students. Friedrich Rückert offered him the most personal support. In him, the young scholar had found a warmhearted mentor.

Rückert enjoyed the support of the Prussian king, yet was an outsider at the University of Berlin. The fact that he only lectured in wintertime and spent every summer in his Franconian homeland surely contributed further to his isolation. Rückert knew the pitfalls of academic life from personal experience. Time and again, he warned the impatient university lecturer against raising his hopes too high. In his courses, he had observed Bötticher's rapid progress in Persian and Arabic.[25] Rückert could imagine what Bötticher, who had invested a great deal of energy in his career, thought of less industrious scholars. In addition, a stagnant curriculum vitae posed personal problems for academics. In the bourgeois nineteenth century, professional advancement and private happiness were closely connected, and marriage to Anna Berger was unthinkable without a permanent position. Of course, Rückert was not among the power-conscious scholars who had a decisive say in the filling of professorships. With a touch of irony, he told Bötticher in July 1850—which is to say, long before his postdoctoral qualification for a teaching position—about his lack of influence in appointment matters. He could only construe it as a "joke" or a "fit of one-sided ideality" that an unworldly scholar such as he should procure "a real post [. . .] by virtue of a few sheets of stationery."[26]

Rückert's importance to the young scholar was mainly of a personal nature. He had a moderating influence on Bötticher's obsession with work, yet also gave him the feeling that he was working on truly important things. The professor even learned Coptic, because his student convinced him of its beauty and value for religious history. In the summertime, he gladly invited him to his estate, Neuses bei Coburg, where the nervous junior scholar could relax. Rückert actually read Bötticher's poems and, with a sound feeling for the language, recognized what was missing. In April 1852, he phrased his critique sensitively so as not to hurt the highly motivated poet. As he put it, "Your verses are lovely, ingenious and deep, only too much so." In one respect, however, Rückert's influence was questionable. He encouraged the university lecturer's hostility toward theory, which soon took on harsh characteristics. In contrast to the moderate Rückert, Bötticher was not given to acknowledging the validity of other viewpoints. Even when he rebelled against prevailing opinions or polemicized against the drill for learning foreign languages, for example, he left no room for contradiction. In his rejection of methodological constraints, he was a child of the principled nineteenth century.

A second key figure for the ambitious linguistic researcher was Jacob Grimm, who lastingly validated his worldview. This was particularly true of Bötticher's esteem for the ancestors and his belief in the future of the German nation. Both scholars shared Johann Herder's conviction that the people were the true guardians of culture. Bötticher had special respect for Grimm's strength of character. During the protest of the Göttinger Sieben (Göttingen Seven), Grimm had counted on his dismissal for his commitment to the Hanover constitution. Like his courageous comrades-in-arms, he was convinced that faculty members had to stand by their constitutional oath if they did not want to lose the respect of their students. Liberal public sympathy was on the side of the Göttingen Seven, but many found their political move too radical. For Bötticher, it was clear which side he stood on.[27] He admittedly rejected the liberal value system, but this did not mean that he held self-aggrandizing potentates like Ernst August von Hannover in high regard. The king's contempt for the teaching profession was downright proverbial: as he put it to Alexander von Humboldt, "Professors, whores and ballet dancers can always be had for money." So Bötticher was especially happy when Friedrich Wilhelm IV gave the Brothers Grimm an honorable reception in Prussia.

Jacob Grimm and Paul Bötticher were also alike in their unqualified dedication to scholarship. A philological precision was inherent to both researchers, and could sap the energy of both. But unlike Bötticher, Grimm possessed a feeling for the limits of his working capacity. In any case, the shy Bötticher never got to know the famous Germanist well. He was much too timid to steal time from a national hero like Grimm. As a consequence, his letters to Jacob Grimm were formal and not particularly expressive.[28] This does not mean, however, that his brief acquaintance with Grimm meant little to him—on the contrary. The title of his principal work, *Deutsche Schriften*, was in itself reminiscent of Grimm's *Deutsche Mythologie*. And by adopting linguistic idiosyncrasies like the systematic use of lowercase, he tried to underscore this connection. Bötticher placed less value on his contact with Heinrich Ewald. However, the Göttingen Orientalist provided him with considerable help at the start of his career.

Heinrich Ewald, who like Jacob Grimm had defied the Hanoverian king in 1837, belonged to the political figureheads of the Vormärz (lit. pre-March era, the period leading up to the failed German revolution of 1848–1849). His scholarly oeuvre, however, did not receive the same early recognition. The Old Testament scholar developed a rigid attitude toward his research topic and turned his back on differing opinions. The fact that other scholars posed questions that he believed he had already answered left him speechless. His writings displayed a self-aggrandizing style that blurred the lines between his own worldview and genuine, scholarly statements. There was admittedly something in his maxim that great importance attached to the philological details of biblical exegesis. But his pathos increasingly marred his capacity for self-criticism.[29] Paul Bötticher approached the irascible scholar with caution, but not without skill. In a letter of September 18, 1847, he thanked Ewald "for pointing the way to the sanctity of the Old Testament." In addition, he rather proudly highlighted his own efforts in the field of Oriental languages and "Rückert's leadership" in the interpretation of "difficult Arabian and Persian poets."[30] Ewald turned out to be well disposed and soon endeavored to help the young scholar. For example, he bought an Arabic-Hebrew manuscript from Bötticher so that the latter could finance the printing of his dissertation. He magnanimously gave Bötticher the option of buying it back from him anytime for the same price. And his review of the *Rudimenta mythologiae semiticae* came at just the right time for Bötticher's habilitation process in Halle.

Although Paul Bötticher was convinced that people were seeking to impede his progress, he actually enjoyed considerable support. Thus, he was able to express his thanks to the Prussian minister of culture on January 1, 1851, for having been released from "military service" [. . .] by the king, "upon the recommendation of my teacher and friend, Friedrich Rückert" and "through the intervention of Mr. Alexander von Humboldt" [. . .] "so that I may be at leisure to pursue my studies without interruption."[31] But, as with many other things, Bötticher could not rejoice at this perquisite for long. In a letter to the Ministry of Culture, he requested immediate permission to take manuscripts home from the library that, according to the rules and regulations, were only permitted to "important scholars." Furthermore, he asked for financial assistance with two papers in the field of Oriental languages. He explained that, without the "publication of more extensive works," it would be impossible for a "defenseless young scholar" to "commend himself" to the ministry "for advancement." Considering that the young scholar did not yet have his *venia legendi* (permission to lecture), these requests were rather presumptuous of him.

Only after successfully completing the habilitation process was Paul Bötticher really convinced of his ability to become a professor. A good example of his newly acquired self-confidence is the introduction to his *Vorlesungen über Religionsgeschichte Vorderasiens* (*Lectures on the Religious History of the Near East*), which was delivered on February 26, 1851.[32] In it, he advocated an organological view, according to which religion had "precisely the same meaning for a person's spirit" as "blood did for the life of the body." Apodictically, he designated the "immanence of God in man" as "the sine qua non of religion, *of all* religions." As a result, "even so-called heathen religions" had to be granted a certain degree of "relative truth." From this perspective, studies in comparative religion were accorded theological justification. His dissociation from Romanticism, which lacked "all humility, all respect for facts," is of similar, fundamental importance. His strictly positivistic scholarly understanding is apparent here and, in fact, at the service of nationalistic values, although this single instance may not be reflective of his authoritative worldview.[33] Behind it lay the philosophical conviction that only an accurate evaluation of scholarly facts could reveal signs of God in the course of history. Bötticher's avowal of God's immanence was in no way unusual during the heyday of historicism. It took on rather individual traits when he dismissed other scholarly positions as "carnival tricks." Certainly such a harsh position would not help him obtain the needed financial support for a successful academic career.

The secular scholarship that enabled Bötticher's habilitation in Halle had a condition attached to it.[34] Within two years, the person being sponsored by Berlin had to earn his Licentiate (Latin: permission to teach). In order to reinforce this requirement, the final quarterly installment of the scholarship was only paid out after the title of Doctor of Theology was granted. But Bötticher, who wanted to concentrate entirely on his research, did not accept this condition. As a result, he turned to the theological faculty in Erlangen to obtain an honorary Licentiate. Aided by campaigning on his behalf by Franz Delitzsch, the bold undertaking succeeded. On August 1, 1851, Bötticher received the sought-after diploma, which he promptly presented in the Prussian capital. However, the magistrate refused to accept Bötticher's dubious course of action and insisted on his taking the Berlin examination. The penniless university lecturer turned to Hengstenberg in his hour of need. In his letter of April 25, 1852, he used every argument in the book, including his medical attestation, according to which he was forbidden to use his eyes for serious work. In addition, he claimed that the theologians in Erlangen would surely be offended if their examination was not recognized in Berlin. Finally, he pointed out that he had used the exam preparation time more sensibly for his own publications. Bötticher had expressed his concerns so directly that they bordered on defiance.

Even so, he knew full well that he was skating on thin ice. So he asked Hengstenberg "to consider this letter and everything in it as written only to you, and to destroy it."[35] Hengstenberg, who regardless of his political differences with Bötticher was well disposed toward him, answered immediately and unequivocally. That same day, he let Bötticher know that granting his request was out of the question, because the "decision" about the scholarship was "approved by the King" himself and could "not be contravened" by the Berlin theological faculty. Hence, he could offer "no other advice" than to take the compulsory exam. Bötticher showed himself to be inflexible, however, and did without the final scholarship installment.

The young man tended to regard nothing other than his own standards as binding. Even during his first reviews, he wielded a sharp knife and had no regard for authority. Thus, he made remarks about two Old Testament experts that were as trenchant as they were disparaging: "Mr. Umbreit is a genius at dilettantism, while Mr. Hitzig works as a dilettante in the field of geniuses."[36] Concerning the powerful Hengstenberg, with whom he enjoyed a relationship of trust, he held that Hengstenberg only adopted a position "of comprehension and understanding" and was effectively "free and devoid of all poetry." Even in a nineteenth-century academic culture that was fond of arguing, such explicit value judgments did not represent the best career strategy, so Paul Bötticher soon found himself an object of fierce attacks. Rückert's successor in Erlangen, Friedrich Spiegel, published a review of Bötticher's habilitation paper, *Arica*, in 1851 that criticized his unsystematic approach. Shortly thereafter, he subjected Bötticher's most recent work, *Wurzelforschungen* (*Researching the Roots*), which was devoted to the idiosyncrasies of the Egyptian, Indo-Germanic, and Semitic family trees, to detailed criticism. The critique basically targeted the fact that the ambitious university lecturer did not reveal the principles of his linguistic comparison. Bötticher belonged to that scholarly group which could dish it out but couldn't take it. He blew off steam in a reply that did not observe the proper form and offered personal justification. Thus, he pointed out that pecuniary problems had compelled him to sell important books and that he was self-taught in most fields. Furthermore, he harshly criticized Spiegel for not having read "the books he reported on," describing his reviews as "denunciations." Spiegel didn't mince words in his counterreply and averred with the renown of a full professor that "men in this field of endeavor" have long since formed an opinion of Bötticher's publications. This statement touched off an unpleasant altercation, one that could not have interested Bötticher in the least, which dragged on for quite some time.[37]

Paul Bötticher acted with no safety net and no place to hide. He didn't have a powerful advocate in the fraternity, and he lacked the financial means to wait long for a professorship. He had neither the patience nor the basic social skills to carefully sound out the situation. Bötticher's anxiety expressed itself in an unsolicited application to the University of Jena that had no prospect of success. The letter of response from university trustee Moritz Seebeck, dated June 3, 1852, made every effort to avoid offense. In a conciliatory but also markedly vague manner, the official spoke of better days and promised that he "would not forget your interest in Jena as made known to me."

At this point, however, Bötticher already had another possibility in mind. It was his sense of mission that, at least in terms of written communication, allowed him to overcome great social barriers. In April 1852, he had been in written contact with Christian Carl Josias von Bunsen, the Prussian minister to London. Baron von Bunsen had made a name for himself as a church historian, and assumed that he could exploit the indigent university lecturer for his own scholarly purposes. He promptly turned to the Prussian king to ask a favor: he would like the king to approve a two-year research grant for Bötticher. Bunsen's interest pertained to Bötticher's expertise in Coptic and Syriac, and Bunsen expected him to work on the textual basis of the New Testament.[38] For Bötticher, this option presented a way out of his financial misery. In addition, there was the attractive prospect of reading source texts in the British Museum, which had only recently acquired valuable Syrian manuscripts.

3

With Scholarship into the World

At the end of September 1852, Paul Bötticher set out for London. He was filled with pride and self-confidence, because several famous men had interceded with the king on his behalf regarding his research residency. His advocates included the widely traveled naturalist Alexander von Humboldt, conservative publicist Ludwig von Gerlach, and statesman Joseph Maria von Radowitz. Whether political motives played a role in the support Bötticher received cannot be ascertained with certainty; what is undeniable is that his supporters were predominantly in the archconservative camp. On September 27, Friedrich Rückert sent him on his way with a final farewell. He affectionately advised his difficult student: "Now go with God and imbibe the sources fully. But don't overload the carriage." Rückert presumably sensed that his words would fall on deaf ears for, in the presence of rare manuscripts, Bötticher's passion for work knew no bounds. Nevertheless, he must have appreciated Rückert's expression of concern.

On his way to England, Bötticher first stopped in Göttingen, where a large philology conference was taking place. The unsociable researcher apparently found personal contact with other scholars stressful. Just as he could not understand that scholarship was a form of social exchange, he could not grasp the necessity of personal contacts for career development. Bötticher instead compensated for his insecurity by passing drastic judgments on his fellow philologists. On October 5, he wrote to his fiancée from Koblenz: "For me, the most repulsive thing about the conference was the stench of the fraternity that assaulted me everywhere. By the sweat of its brow, the intellectual proletariat finishes its articles, as is required of it, yet knows nothing of the scholarship which sets it free and makes it blessed."[1]

Bötticher was actually on familiar ground with his harsh rejection of the academic establishment because, since the dawn of Romanticism, the idea of heroic seclusion had been a primary component of academic self-styling. But his derisive speech was also an expression of inner tensions and exclusive haughtiness. Even so, Bötticher's rejection of the "fraternity" should not be overrated. On October 1, he had told Anna Berger that the conference was "brilliant," and the tone of his report on his Göttingen experiences was rather favorable. He opined that he found Theodor Benfey, the Sanskrit researcher who had dubbed Bötticher the "Black Hussar among young Orientalists," downright charming. This evidence presumably documented one of the mood swings that were characteristic of Bötticher from early on and, when he reached the point of exhaustion, led him to make tactless and, indeed, brutal statements.[2] Furthermore, in the fall of 1852, he was steeped in the importance of his own assignment. Lastly, the Prussian king had personally chosen him to examine the newly acquired Syrian documents in the British Museum.

When Paul Bötticher arrived in London, it was Europe's largest city. More than two million people lived there by the middle of the nineteenth century. Since the Great Exhibition of 1851, the city's symbol had been the Crystal Palace, an enormous building of glass and iron that demonstrated the technical possibilities of modern architecture. Steam power and mechanical production had reached London, launching an abundance of new opportunities for work. Industry and trade flourished. The London Stock Exchange was the most important in the world. Untold numbers of people flocked to the center of the British Empire, where seemingly undreamed-of possibilities were on offer. Of course, the shadow side of industrialization was highly visible. The majority of workers lived in slums, and their life expectancy was correspondingly short. The gap between rich and poor spawned a fierce critique of contemporary issues that demanded rapid changes in social conditions. Yet very few people could resist the fascination of the metropolis. Even a grim cultural pessimist like the Scottish writer Thomas Carlyle characterized London as the "heart of the universe, which incessantly ejects and sucks in a tide of human troubles with a power that nearly robs the senses."[3]

Paul Bötticher was open to several of the city's attractions. Thus, he delighted in going to the theater. He enjoyed mingling with members of the upper classes who visited the Bunsen home and, insofar as his crowded schedule permitted, was not disinclined to accept private invitations. But Bötticher was not a truly attentive observer of his surroundings. Rather, he often abandoned himself to fantasies in which the Moloch (the Thorny Devil), London, was contrasted with a purely natural world. His idyllic description of a Scottish street musician is symptomatic of such fantasies. A man played the bagpipes while his sister, "a charming creature about fourteen years of age," danced to the music. The "ancient Celtic ways" appealed to him, but he attached dark thoughts to the scene: "Where will this pretty, wretched child end up," he asked his in-laws on November 1, 1852, "other than in the humiliation which devours thousands each year in London?"[4]

Even though many German émigrés were forced into exile in England after the failed March Revolution and shared his dim view of the present, Bötticher made no effort to contact members of these circles. He might have had a great deal in common with the sartorial apprentice Wilhelm Weitling, in particular. Weitling used religious diction to attack contemporary politics and believed the kingdom of God on earth was imminent. At the beginning of the 1850s, Karl Marx also worked in the reading room of the British Museum. Like Bötticher, he was convinced that modern society was characterized by profound disaffection. Both saw a crisis syndrome in the quickly progressing division of labor. But, in contrast to Marx, Bötticher did not search for the causes of alienation in the economic sphere. Instead, his observations induced him to consider the speculative, cultural, and philosophical aspects.

Bötticher even diagnosed the same problem in England that would cause him to doubt the future of German society. On December 17, 1852, he wrote to Anna Berger's younger sister Mathilde, with whom he had also built a relationship of trust, that modernity's lack of faith would surely lead to moral collapse. He compared the current state of religious life with the "great despair of the ancient heathen world [. . .] out of which Christianity emerged." So as to hold a mirror up to his own time, he planned to write a comprehensive history of the Late Classical period. But, as with so many of his ideas, his audacious plan would go unrealized. An important reason for his failure to complete such projects lay in his fragile self-esteem. Thus, he candidly advised Mathilde Berger in the same letter: "More often than not, I lack faith in myself to such an extent that I try to hide the deficiency from myself with all sorts of boasting." However, there can be no doubt as to his desire for political action. Bötticher considered existing institutions antiquated and therefore advocated "systematized anarchy," which would provide individuals with an opportunity for self-development.[5] But it would be erroneous to imagine that an elaborate political theory stood behind his affirmation of anarchy.

Bötticher's letters contain many avowals of religious freedom that are reminiscent of his pietistic roots. This is especially true of his idea for spiritual renewal, which contains the radical renunciation of all contemporary half measures. To his fiancée, he expressly identified "rebirth" (*Wiedergeburt*) as "the great Word of Christianity" (*das grosse Wort des Christentums*).[6] He planned to start a new life with her in the mountains and forever turn his back on the rotten world of big metropolises.[7] Surrounded by a goodly swarm of children, he wanted to lead the life of a hill farmer. Surely this was an unrealistic idea that even he may not have taken too seriously. Nonetheless, it discloses much about the Christian roots of his radical critique of contemporary life, which could escalate into across-the-board condemnation and sinister prophecies. So it was that he wrote to Anna Berger in draconian language: "Everything is false, and I fear that European civilization must be destroyed, root and branch." Bötticher's drastically formulated rejection of the present makes plain the religious orientation of his worldview. At the same time, his letters illustrate how closely his spiritual equilibrium was linked to contact with his *Heimat*. However much his correspondence needs to be interpreted, it represents only one facet of his London experience. His daily life was dominated by scholarly pursuits and numerous obligations to Bunsen.

Bötticher's stay in London was mainly characterized by arduous research in the British Museum. Since he also had duties to fulfill in his role as attaché to the Prussian minister, his time for excursions or cultural events was quite limited. In any case, it is hard to imagine the industrious Orientalist as a loafer. Over the years, he would be constantly pressed to use his working time in foreign libraries as effectively as possible. An almost feverish euphoria seems to have periodically gripped him in the metropolis. Thus, he wrote these pithy lines to Germany: "Live fast and die fast is my motto. My duty is to take care that everything goes well, both during and after."[8] In the long run, Bötticher's respect for English institutions was of greater importance than his commitment to an impetuous life. As did many continental Europeans, he regarded these institutions as a bulwark against the democratic Zeitgeist. After all, the March Revolution had not taken place on the island, where respect for the law and a capable aristocracy had apparently guaranteed social stability. Basic regulatory measures played a subordinate role in this prettified picture of England. But the probable reality was that London remained peaceful in the spring of 1848 because of the deployment of 150,000 civil-service policemen, rather than any broad social consensus.[9]

Bötticher studied the manners of the English upper class in detail at the Bunsen residence. His outstanding command of the English language, which very few of his countrymen could claim at such a level, worked to his advantage in his political undertakings on the minister's behalf. The world of refined people fascinated Bötticher. So he proudly confided to his future father-in-law: "I am so posh that even the least in my social set is still a baron." He let his fiancée know that "among genteel people, one learns how to best leave feelings and thoughts unexpressed."[10] Bötticher, the traveler, admired English manners as the epitome of civility and professed the gentlemanly ideal. He was such an Anglophile that he went so far as to read the *National Zeitung* of London for his entire life, although he had virtually nothing in common with its liberal political bias; he found the paper exemplary in its embodiment of his own, characteristically British idea of civilized behavior. Bötticher's adulation of the English gentleman was ambiguous, of course. While he himself often adopted a ruthless tone, he expected polished manners from his peers. It seems to have escaped him that a certain nonchalance in the face of human weakness was also part of good manners. And the obstinacy with which he nursed personal enmities did not fit at all well with the equanimity he so admired in the English way of life. Yet in order to understand his vehement rejection of German provinciality, we must surely bear in mind how deeply the erudition of the English gentleman impressed him as a young man.[11]

Bötticher assiduously carried out his duties as Bunsen's private secretary. In the end, he remained nothing more than an onlooker in the world of diplomacy, and his initial admiration for Bunsen grew into its dark opposite. He had the impression that his host was taking advantage of him. In a moment of personal disappointment, he wrote to his bride in a fierce and complacent manner: "He [Bunsen] knows that I see through him and has shown me such weaknesses that he would hate me, were he capable of anything that pertains to a man, a real man, that is."[12] In reading such statements, it is surely important to consider that Bötticher had to exercise the utmost restraint in everyday life, and his tough stance on paper was his way of compensating for it in the extreme. The fact that Bunsen had not been entirely aboveboard with his guest must also be considered. As it happened, the English researcher Lord William Cureton was monopolizing the manuscripts that Bötticher wanted to study. Bötticher initially cherished the hope that Cureton would be prepared to collaborate, but this soon turned out to be a chimera. So Bötticher had to look for another field of research, and the urbane Bunsen used the opportunity to steer him onto his own scholarly terrain. He suggested an edition of "the oldest ecclesiastical laws," for which a detailed knowledge of Syriac was essential. Bötticher had actually planned on writing a comprehensive edition of New Testament sources, and canonical problems were the last thing he wanted to work on. But what else could he do, other than resign himself to the new task.

In January 1853, Bötticher set off for Paris to study Syriac manuscripts that were supposed to give insight into the oldest canons. The trendiness and vitality of the French metropolis escaped him, however. Informed by his rigid ideas about cleanliness, he found the dirty city more distressing than exciting. Bötticher lived in seclusion and, in order to go easy on his wallet, subsisted on "cauliflower and white beans."[13] As his correspondence with Anna Berger shows, the loneliness of the outland caused his identification with his own roots to intensify. After having spoken with an Italian priest, he wrote to his fiancée in January 1853: "Thank God that I am a German and a Protestant." As in London, Bötticher had no contact whatever with the émigré community in Paris. He could have gotten to know many interesting people while he was there. Around one hundred thousand Germans lived on the Seine, making

Paris the "sixth largest German city at that time."[14] But Bötticher was only interested in his work on Syriac canonical sources. All the same, he struck up a friendship with one of the most important scholars of his day, the Orientalist Ernest Renan, who was the librarian at the Bibliothèque Impériale. Renan provided the German researcher with valuable manuscripts. Bötticher and Renan had a lot in common: both had lost their faith in the church and hoped that scholarship could provide a solid foundation for religion. They were both skeptical about the Old Testament, because they considered the conditions under which it had been handed down to be highly unreliable. Familiar with the left-leaning, Hegelian Tübingen School, Renan argued for the consistent application of textual criticism to the Old Testament and the departure from favored legends like Moses' authorship of the Pentateuch.[15] To Bötticher, who had always tended toward puristic positions in matters of textual criticism, this was grist for the mill. The two scholars' essentialistic views on Judaism may have been even more significant to their mutual understanding. For both, semitophilic noises would soon taper off, and anti-Jewish themes increasingly took on greater importance.

At the Bibliothèque Impériale, Paul Bötticher experienced a scholarly appreciation to which he had been unaccustomed in Germany. This was mainly because he was able to develop his own strengths—broad knowledge of languages and philologically precise work with original manuscripts—to the best of his ability there. Bötticher's Parisian findings gave important impetus to Syriac philology. They underscored how valuable Syriac was for New Testament study and for patristics, because an abundance of important Greek texts had been preserved in the translations of Syriac Christians. Bötticher attributed special importance to the *Didascalia Apostolorum*, the oldest comprehensive treatise in the area of canon law. He euphorically told his fiancée that he had "made a discovery of the greatest importance," one that surpassed all his previous accomplishments.[16] And, in fact, the Syriac *Didascalia* helped shed greater light on the roots of apostolic canon law. Upon his return to London, Bötticher convinced Bunsen of the worth of his discovery. He spent his last seven months in London researching an edition of the *Didascalia Apostolorum Syriac*, to which he attached high hopes of publication. Immediately prior to his departure in September 1853, he managed to finish work on the manuscript. But it took until the following year for him to raise the money to print the study, which he self-published in a limited edition of one hundred copies.[17]

Because he hoped to use his research results to further his career, he also returned from London earlier than expected. Like so many academics who received generous scholarship support, he underestimated the difficulty of finding a permanent position within the extremely factional German university system. Immediately upon his return in October 1853, he informed Heinrich von Mühler, the Prussian minister of culture, of his desire to resume his lecturing activities in Halle during the winter semester. Furthermore, he forwarded his *Ausgabe der Apostolischen Constitutionen* (*Edition of the Apostolic Constitutions*) to Mühler and asked him "to pass it on to a specialist in church history and canon law for evaluation," since Orientalists wouldn't know what to do with it.[18] And if this request already sounded presumptuous, then the minister of culture must have rubbed his eyes in disbelief at the adjoining judgment. Bötticher deemed it appropriate "to confer a special *Professur* (professorship) on him" because no one could doubt his "studiousness." He expressly pointed to the importance of the documentation that he "had produced in England and France at the expense of the state." In an idiosyncratic undertone, he concluded with a warning: "If I were not to have a fixed salary to keep me from want, I would dissipate my energies by working to subsist and use them up prematurely." Given that Bötticher had received a very impressive grant at the behest of the king and completed his research only thirteen months later, this was downright impertinent. But the potential threat from a humanities scholar was extremely limited. Without taking time to respond, the ministry passed Bötticher's request on to the Philosophy Faculty in Halle.

The Halle faculty had no tolerance for the university lecturer's behavior.[19] On December 21, 1853, the classical philologist Gottfried Bernhardy delivered his assessment. It found fault with the marginality of Bötticher's research topics, which would not permit the awarding of a *Professur*. In addition, Bernhardy let it be known that the edition of the London sources was to be expected and the applicant was only at the beginning of a long road: "But as soon as he [Paul Bötticher] fulfills the promise contained in the account of his travels, and thoroughly edits and publishes a substantial number of the Oriental literary treasures he has collected, then his knowledge and talent would be more clearly recognizable." And with that, judgment was passed on the application. That same day, the Philosophy Faculty told university trustee Ludwig Pernice that it was not interested in a special *Professur* for Bötticher. They justified the ruling by stating: "His written work is still fragmentary and leaves much to be desired in terms of thoroughness, to say nothing of diligence. But his academic activity is still in the early stages." In Berlin, Culture Ministry officials waited until February 1, 1854, to inform Bötticher of the results of the evaluation. They dryly summed up that the young applicant was simply not yet ready for a professorship.

The news must have been shattering for the ambitious university lecturer. Bötticher had not only overestimated the worth of his research grant but his standing in Halle as well. Since no member of the Philosophy Faculty was prepared to speak on his behalf, he knew what his future prospects were there. On top of that, he had continuing problems with the critics, who had not been idle during his trip to England.

Friedrich Spiegel, the Erlanger scholar of Persia, had resumed his critique of Bötticher's early work, and Bötticher's response was nasty. More important than this ongoing dispute was the fact that Bötticher's Coptic edition of the history of the Apostles had incurred the displeasure of Göttingen Egyptologist Heinrich Brugsch. In 1853, Brugsch published a detailed critique in the prestigious *Zeitschrift der Deutschen Morgenländischen Gesellschaft* (*Journal of the German Orientalist Society*) that was unsurpassed in its harshness. He held nothing back in attempting to prove that Bötticher's knowledge of Coptic was superficial and his methodology insufficient. Modern scholarship since disputes this view, but the damning judgment of the senior professor did nothing to enhance Bötticher's reputation at the time. Notably, Bötticher sold his early work on the Coptic language for wastepaper, as no one was interested in it any longer.[20] In just a few months' time, his prospects for a professorship had dramatically worsened.

Given his financial situation, Paul Bötticher was faced with an important decision. Should he continue to hope for a university appointment or instead aspire to a secure teaching position, although it was not highly paid? The second option was favorable, particularly as the decision to teach school did not, in principle, foreclose the possibility of an academic career, and he could finally marry Anna Berger. In fact, many a nineteenth-century scholar spent a number of years as a grammar school teacher in order to tide themselves over while waiting for a professorship. Bötticher opted for security, but not without gnashing his teeth. The approval of his great-aunt, Ernestine de Lagarde, was very important to him. The couple had arranged for the elderly woman to move in with them after the wedding. Moreover, he had decided to change his name to de Lagarde. His final motive for doing so cannot be ascertained with certainty. Throughout his life, he emphatically stated that he wanted to prevent the Huguenot family name from dying out. But surely his hatred for his deceased father must have also played an important role. Paul Bötticher wanted to publicly document the break with his family of origin and his former life. Finally, the prospective inheritance must have been of importance to the young Orientalist, who clung to scholarship with every fiber of his being. As it turned out, the name change was a protracted affair. So the marriage took place on March 27, 1854, under the name of Bötticher in the presence of a small circle of family members.

Paul Böttticher's future wife would have preferred to adhere to bourgeois conventions, but Bötticher considered the adoption an "absolute necessity." On August 7, 1853, he wrote to Anna Berger in unmistakable terms: "I want to be rid of everything from my old life!"[21] Immediately upon his return from London, he wanted to visit his father's grave site and was not entirely displeased to learn that it no longer existed. In his family history, he spoke of the grave with laconic brutality: "They dug him up, and someone else is rotting in it."[22] Paul de Lagarde also tended to deal with his early work by means of *damnatio memoriae*. He regarded all his writings published before the adoption on October 9, 1854, as sins of youth to be stricken from his publications record. His numerous treatises on politics and cultural philosophy soon appeared under the name de Lagarde. However, he attached no importance to the apparently aristocratic title. He sometimes thought, in fact, that exalted family "claims of nobility" were "unfounded."[23] Thus, it became customary to simply call the author, who placed great value on his appeal to ordinary people, "Lagarde." And so it shall remain in this biography.

Toward the end of his London stay, Lagarde wondered whether he should join the conservative party in Prussia. His political stance was ostensibly beyond debate. During the March Revolution, he stood on the side of the king and the existing order, and considered them worth defending despite all injustice. He spelled out his self-image in a letter to Heinrich Ewald on July 5, 1849, in which he called himself "an aristocratically disposed young man by virtue of birth and conviction."[24] His sojourn in England had strengthened his belief in the value of stable institutions. Nevertheless, Lagarde did not believe that true conservatism had a future in Germany.

He put his views down on paper in late summer 1853. In an essay simply titled "Konservativ?" he positioned himself politically for the first time. Since Lagarde's tone so directly relates to the topic, the quotations that follow from the original are rather extensive. Significantly, his political commentaries are almost never a matter of discursively constructed text. What we are dealing with is more of an imploring rhetoric whose effectiveness depends on speaking directly to the reader, on the suggestive power of imagery, the use of repetition, and other persuasive measures.[25]

Lagarde emphasized his position as an outsider in a forceful and self-styling fashion that issued from an intellectual honesty that did not allow for personal considerations. Apparently sure of himself, yet also vague as regards content, he said, "The direction of my life is certain and will not change" (p. 5). This statement is linked to his political self-assessment as a "radical conservative," which sheds light on Lagarde's ideological rigidity, as well as his impatient temperament: "My conservatism is too great to be anything but radical and has no hope of ever gaining influence, as I would have to conform in the political arena for too long. I'm afraid I would collapse from exhaustion before my turn to exert influence would come" (pp. 5ff.). In any case, Lagarde's definition of conservative was extremely willful and reflected the political situation after the failed revolution of 1848–1849. He used the term *conservative* to describe any Prussian citizen who made an effort "to preserve the characteristic efficiency of Prussian life" (p. 6). Even though its eye was on the future, his conservatism actually concerned a worldview whose values were rooted in the past. From the perspective of Lagarde's "radical conservatism," which appealed to malcontents of every stripe, the present must have seemed fundamentally deficient.[26]

The "German question" stood behind this train of thought and, in Lagarde's opinion, had no hope of a peaceful resolution. He saw Prussia as "a product of necessity" (p. 6) that could only justify its existence as a state by assuming a leading role in German unification. Lagarde used a metaphor to describe the political situation that would become part of the classic twentieth-century arsenal of leftist revolutionary justifications: "Consequently, the State of Prussia will be conservative if and when it fights tooth and nail to achieve the goal it espoused when it came into being: to cultivate the German way of life, to preserve whatever can still be preserved in Germany. This is no peaceful assignment, and whoever wishes to eat eggs should not balk at breaking eggshells" (p. 7). At this point, we see that Lagarde's worldview was not about genuine conservatism but rather a form of utopian thought that projected his own wishful thinking and values into the future. Lagarde's political ideal was tied to Jacob Grimm's conservative thinking and appears strangely unreal in the process. He advocated a German empire in which dukes would occupy a decisive intermediary position between the populace and the ruling class. But since hardly any persons were suited for such a task, this would mean the creation of a new aristocracy. Lagarde had in mind a social institution that, like the English gentry, could take on important societal responsibilities. By audaciously removing the newly functioning elite from power politics and all other social realities, he saw a magic bullet in the aristocracy's emergence that would reform German affairs.

Lagarde's language was so radical as to render impossible his attempts to realize his political ideals in the near future: "My conservatism in the field of politics is so reactionary that it harks back to the days of the Salian Franks and the Anglo-Saxon monarchs, and it would be best to strike off anything that has happened between then and now" (p. 9). Such sentiments were very close to those of the established historian Georg Waitz, who cultivated the Romantic return to the "good old days" of the Middle Ages. With this mode of thought, whose linguistic radicality prefigures Nietzsche's reassessment of pre-Socratic philosophy twenty years later, he simultaneously managed to turn against the "ideas of 1789." Instead of equality for all citizens, he advocated rule by noble families and fashioned the aristocracy into the genuine Teutonic life form. Lagarde's position regarding the contemporary educational debate also contained a revaluation of *Volksgedanke* (concept of the German nation). Real public education would only be possible in an aristocratically governed state, whereas the existing, bloated educational system was inherently worthless. Lagarde had particularly harsh words for conventional rote learning: "To rattle off the German emperors, Prussian kings, and the elements of modern chemistry one by one is of no use, because even a parrot would be perfectly capable of learning in this way" (pp. 11ff.). On the other side of the coin, he glorified the world of the Middle Ages, "when all learning took place under the tutelage of masters" (p. 12) and still embraced the entire person.

Lagarde forcefully criticized the existing arbitrariness in religious matters as an expression of inherent weakness in the character of organized religion. His arguments fired shots at Protestantism, which had become an unholy multiplicity of splinter groups and schools of thought. He spoke rather contemptuously of his contemporaries' earnest beliefs: "As far as the church is concerned, I have a highly personal opinion about more than one of its variants. [. . .] [W]ho can claim that an honorable person, someone who knows himself, would or should get involved with these—if I exempt Catholicism, which is at least a noble and powerful authority—idiosyncrasies of spiritually and mentally lazy individuals?" (pp. 12ff.). Lagarde judged the political orientation of Protestantism completely unacceptable. Not only was this orientation in conflict with the transcendental nature of all religions, it was also demonstrably corruptible in the extreme: "Protestant clerics of all stripes are nothing other than theologically dyed projections of political ambitions, maggots that take on the color of whatever fruit they are eating" (p. 13). He portrayed the dreariness of Protestant everyday life through striking examples that showed how pastors had lost their living faith in God. Such descriptions also intimate Nietzsche, who explained the unbelief in parsonages by the fact that pastors' children had frequently observed their fathers praying.

Lagarde's harsh words suggest personal disappointment and loneliness. The young scholar could not rediscover his Romantic ideals in the present and sharply condemned academic theology. He saw an important reason for its failure in the overestimation of the Apostle Paul, whose Jewish roots had been wrongfully pushed into the background: "[W]hat Paul taught was not the Gospels, but rather the reflection of a reflection of the Gospels in an energetic and noble, but undeniably out-and-out Jewish, spirit" (p. 14). Current theology opines that Lagarde was barking up the wrong tree, because the textual basis of the Bible remains entirely uncertain—but Lord Cureton prevented him from tackling that problem. In connection with his academic studies, Lagarde remembered that the Prophet Jeremiah had once announced the conquest of Jerusalem and the destruction of the Temple. With a grand gesture, Lagarde wrote: "I can preserve nothing here. Jeremiah said, 'Plough new fields and do not sow beneath the thorn bushes'" (p. 14). Of course, the pretentious diction reflected not only the extent of Lagarde's idealism; it also showed how exceptionally out of touch with reality he was.

Lagarde candidly reported that his friend Ernest Renan did not consider his position politically viable. However, this particular concern did not prompt him to look inward. With tearful sentimentality, he chose to refer instead to the unfortunate situation in German affairs that denied him promising political involvement. It was therefore no coincidence that Lagarde allowed two decades to pass before printing the address on conservatism. But we should not overestimate the originality of his thoughts. In the Nachmärz period (post–March 1848), a broad discussion of the political and social functions of the aristocracy took place, and Lagarde's Anglophile conservatism fit right in.[27] The distinctive feature of his position was not that he professed faith in throne and altar but that he called for a new aristocracy. Despite his adulation of the Middle Ages, Lagarde built upon principles of meritocracy that were well suited to his own highly competitive bourgeois era. His idea that a new aristocracy could be the result of purposeful negotiation would also prove influential.[28] This was even more true of his apocalyptic visions, which stirred the fears of his contemporaries and simultaneously promised a way out of the crisis.

In November 1853, Lagarde gave a lecture with the programmatic title "Ueber die gegenwärtigen Aufgaben der deutschen Politik" (On the Current Responsibilities of German Politics). As with his first essay, more than twenty years would go by before he decided to print it. The timing was good, because radical voices found a sympathetic ear during the political aftershocks that followed the stock market crash of 1873.[29] What at first glance may seem like an astounding reception to a text aimed at relevance within an entirely different temporal and political framework gains a broader clarity upon closer examination. In point of fact, Lagarde had dressed his basic convictions regarding the critique of contemporary culture in the garb of day-to-day political arguments. These beliefs actually came from the world of political Romanticism and were infused with the disappointed atmosphere of the 1850s. But their vaguely radical content allowed people of other time periods to also relate to them.

Lagarde's starting point was a question: who would bring about German unity? It undoubtedly looked to him as if the princes bore the responsibility, because they had to answer for the malaise of the small German states that their egotism had caused. In particular, they had almost always placed their own interests above those of the nation. This was a strongly normative view of German history that, moreover, projected nineteenth-century values onto the past. Naturally, Lagarde's reasoning was not especially aimed at the settlement of failed historical developments. He was mainly concerned with delegitimizing the present, which he regarded as morally corrupt and politically dead in the water. In light of his Romantic ideals, he considered the prevailing historical awareness to be grossly overrated. Great moments in history were few and far between, even if politicians would like people to think otherwise: "Throughout world history," as Lagarde pointedly expressed it, "electricity has come down solely from on high: molehills are safe from all kinds of lightning" (p. 20).

In the 1850s, German unity took a backseat to problems of domestic policy consolidation and the balance of power in foreign affairs. But unification now acquired new importance in the sphere of established culture, and Lagarde aimed for a solution that would remain in effect for a long time. In that spirit, he said, "The so-called German question can really only be answered in such a way as to make the solution valid not merely today, but tomorrow as well. I won't deny having thought about the future for some time" (p. 21). A decidedly voluntaristic understanding of nationhood dwelled in the back of his mind. All institutions had only one task: to facilitate the emergence of a true national consciousness. Accordingly, Lagarde's central question was: "How will a polity be established that will enable Germans to become a nation?" (p. 21). This question is reminiscent of Herder's ideas, according to which a nation is primarily entitled to play a cultural role in the life of the people. But allusions to the existing political situation show that Lagarde, like Fichte before him, was concerned with direct political action.

Lagarde exhibited a patronizing attitude toward the masses, even as he crafted a message that invoked an idealized picture of them. The masses knew just as little about the life of the state as they did about "the deepest political principles, which are purely ethical" (p. 22). So long as the aristocracy did not understand this, any mass reform was simply inconceivable. Regional and religious turmoil represented an additional burden for the German nation. Lagarde considered the split between Catholics and Protestants particularly fateful, because every nation that hoped to find itself needed a common goal whose core was necessarily of a religious nature. But he left us in the dark as to what the work that "the entire nation will take on" consisted of from a religious perspective. Only his affirmation of religion is emphatically clear, and he understood this to include a "sense of reality—the true, eternal reality, of course" (p. 23).

Instead of explaining the metaphysical ability of mankind, Lagarde indulged in a summary of antisemitic topoi. It was in no way coincidental that Jews of every era had met with the rejection of their fellow human beings. He roundly opposed the widespread assumption that outer circumstances were responsible for Jewish character and stated categorically: "Jews have not been corrupted by history; it's simply in their nature" (p. 24). The survival of the Jewish people had brought about a sterile culture, and he was at most prepared to acknowledge Spinoza as the product thereof: "For Maimonides and his ilk were thieves who had held Arabic Artistotelianism and dogmatism above the scriptures of their own nation. Moses Mendelssohn had worked in the pale luminosity of the German Enlightenment. The Jews took until the year 1,000 of our calendar [. . .] to adopt monogamy, the actual basis of every civilization, from the Germans" (p. 24). Lagarde even excoriated Jewish monotheism. No religio-historic gemstone was involved here; rather, it was a matter of a common phenomenon to which Jewish arrogance alone owed its unique character.

Lagarde steered clear of any type of racially motivated enmity toward Jews. In his text, he instead professed a voluntaristic and cultural definition of the nation that would be frequently cited later on: "Deutschtum (Germanness) lies not in the blood, but in the heart" (p. 26). But his remarks made it seem less likely that Jews were, on the whole, capable of leading truthful lives. In fact, he ascribed to them a *Rassenhochmuth* (racial arrogance) (pp. 25, 37) that did not allow for a flourishing communal life.

As disparaging as Lagarde's assessment of Judaism was, his remarks about contemporary Protestantism were almost more cutting with regard to intellectual fidelity and religious substance: "We can take the Jews, but not give in to them. For every religion, even fetishism, is better than the mishmash of stale, cowardly sentimentality and stagnant, putrid remains of Christendom that we call Protestantism today" (p. 26). Lagarde did not give a more detailed critique at this point. He was already convinced at an early age that Protestantism lacked ideological substance. The historical situation from which it had emerged in the sixteenth century had long since disappeared, and Luther's critique of the Papacy simply did not suffice as the basis for an independent religion.

Politically, Lagarde had high hopes for colonization, which he legitimized by means of his theory of young nations. Their role was to shape the world according to their ideas. A country need not be young in years, but could experience a spiritual rebirth, as had the German nation. It was beyond question, however, that Hungary was a "used up" country and, therefore, presented enterprising settlers from southeastern Germany with a destination. The very fact that the German people had a genuine purpose to fulfill would promote national unity. At the same time, Lagarde nurtured scholarly ideas that were already hopelessly obsolete in the 1850s. Thus, he stated apodictically: "Only tillage, livestock, breeding, and trade can make Germany wealthy—not industry" (p. 30). Behind such fantasies stood Lagarde's radically idealistic position that the real wealth of a nation lay in its inner unity. To this end, it was necessary above all—and Lagarde went that far—to adopt the perspective of the aging Faust. With great flair and little chance of realization, he called for the East and West Friesian Islands to be connected by dams so as to wrest new land from the sea.

In addition, Lagarde made the case for the creation of a new aristocracy. But, as compared with his first political treatise, the question now was less one of social order and more one of combating the camarilla: here, Lagarde's blistering anger was directed at the fraudulent advisors to Friedrich Wilhelm IV, who were decisively responsible for Germany's stagnation. The natural life of a "farmer, forester, seaman" received high praise as compared with that of a "city dweller" (p. 32), who could barely sense life's actual responsibilities. Lagarde often accused politics of disorientation and indolence, which is why it deserved urgent pedagogical reproof: "Anyone can destroy, but to explain how to create something anew is another matter. Re-creation is what it's really all about. To come here as an educator would make life worth living" (p. 32). On the political horizon, Lagarde saw a great war coming between England and France on one side and Russia on the other. Germany should remain neutral for as long as possible so as to reap the highest reward for its wartime participation. But this role lay in the distant future. Germany's most pressing task was the colonization of Austria. Right here was an opportunity for those superfluous German aristocrats who would otherwise be a heavy burden for societal development. In the long run, the goal would have to be a united "Central Europe" under German leadership (p. 34).

There would, however, be no place for Jews in the future German Empire. Lagarde called for their resettlement from the lands of the Vistula and Danube Rivers to Palestine, where they were to find a new home. Coercive measures were unavoidable for the welfare of the Fatherland, because "we Germans are made of material that is much too soft to be able to withstand the Jews, who have been hardened by Talmudic breeding." (p. 36) The recognition of cultural differences was entirely foreign to Lagarde's nationalistic thinking, so he knew of only two alternatives for the Jews: complete assimilation or emigration. Since he regarded the mission of his own religion as immoral, he appeared to be offering the Jews a choice. Upon closer examination, his striking formulation, "totally in with them, or totally out," (p. 37) expressed his rejection of all forms of collective Jewish identity. In his homogenously conceived German nation, Jews were only welcome as individuals if they decided to fully merge with the majority German population.

The text concludes with remarks about the religio-political mission of the German nation. As implied before, soulful Prussia was to expand into Austria, a country that lacked any idea of how to keep a nation together. But the most important future mission was of a radically metaphysical nature. It concerned a shift in the human mode of thinking that could only be characterized as "inner revolution" (p. 38). Its purpose was to prepare human beings for a truly religious experience that was necessarily cataclysmic. Lagarde was completely convinced of the value of this cause: "There is no such thing as normal development on the mental plane. That's exactly why it is a law of nature, because nature cannot inherit the realm of the mind. If you wish to properly understand the world, then it is entirely correct that only a miracle will transport you to wonderland. Jesus called this miracle 'new birth'" (p. 38). The world of political reality, on the other hand, lacked meaning in the long run, and definitive proposals for improving it would surely not solve the matter.

It is apparent that Lagarde's political ideas were as meager in their inner consistency as they were unrealistic. The only thing that interested him was the welfare of the German nation, whereas he ignored the concerns of minorities and other nations. In addition, these other entities served as a "projection screen" for a large number of resentments that reflected a sense of deep personal dissatisfaction. Lagarde's erratic, often contradictory remarks were mainly held together by rhetorical elements. He used them to illustrate the alleged lack of faith and depravity of his own time that would, in fact, justify the adoption of drastic reform measures. Lagarde also put forward elegiac images and bold futuristic visions that accorded with the desire for a reenchantment of the world. Once revolutionary dreams had vanished, a mood of depression prevailed in Germany. For the time being, the old powers were in the saddle again, and the solution to the national issue lay far in the future. In the sphere of the mind, there was a tendency "to make people feel small."[30] The universities were dominated by narrow positivism and the appraisal of scholarship according to its immediate usefulness. Although Lagarde's Oriental studies practice, which included a host of barely annotated text editions, was of an entirely positivistic nature, when it came to his sense of national identity, references to Romanticism prevailed. His prophecies of doom expressed the longing for an ideal world, a world that presumably existed in the distant past. And his idealized image of a latter-day Middle Ages bore the signs of a reactionary alternative to modernity.

If we compare Lagarde's treatises with a book by another author that created a furor when it first came out, it becomes exceptionally clear just how far removed from reality Lagarde's views were. In 1853, the publicist Ludwig August von Rochau released his *Grundsätze der Realpolitik* (*Principles of Realpolitik*) in Vienna. By means of these principles, Rochau had hoped to tackle the German question. Like Lagarde, he aimed for a unified Germany, but unlike Lagarde, he tried to suitably acknowledge real political power. The affirmation of power stood at the center of his considerations: "To rule means to exercise power," he stated categorically, "and only someone who has power can exercise it. This direct connection between power and sovereignty is the basic truth of all politics and the key to all of history."[31] Rochau's positive attitude toward power accommodated a widespread need because, since the revolution of 1848–1849, many people regarded political idealism as antiquated. In lieu of it, they affirmed a real balance of power that seemed to call for German unification under Prussian leadership.

Even if Lagarde judged power as an inevitable part of history, Rochau's perspective was deeply suspect in his view. To Lagarde, the principal matters involved the ethical disposition of the political players and the religious substance of the German nation. Like Thomas Carlyle, he campaigned vehemently against the heresy of his time. But he did so as a culturally skeptical moralist and not as a power politician. Moreover, Lagarde saw himself primarily as a theologian. As interested as he was in military issues, he was mainly concerned with a transpolitical goal: the redemption and salvation of the German soul. And his missionary agenda of spreading the national religion throughout Central Europe was closely linked to that goal. Lagarde, like many of his contemporaries, looked at Hegelian progressive thinking with utter contempt. It no longer seemed plausible to closely connect reason and reality. And, after the triumph of reactionary forces in Central Europe, Hegel's optimistic philosophy of history appeared every bit as whitewashed as antiquated. What's more, it would not have crossed the mind of a conservative individualist like Lagarde to see the state as a guarantor of morality.

In his conviction of the emptiness of world history, Lagarde rubbed shoulders with Kierkegaard, who deemed the March Revolution completely trivial.[32] Another point of agreement was even more significant: as different as they were, both intellectuals shared the idea that de-Christianization had led to an inner emptiness of exceptional historico-cultural importance. Furthermore, both of these elitist mavericks were extremely skeptical of their fellow men. Kierkegaard confided a bitter assessment to his diary that, right down to the diction, channels Lagarde: "People are most afraid of total bankruptcy at the moment which, it would seem, all of Europe is headed for, and they forget about the far more dangerous, apparently unavoidable spiritual insolvency that is right outside the door."[33] In contrast to Lagarde, who met everything with a serious attitude, Kierkegaard was capable of ironic turns of phrase and subtle changes of perspective. This allowed him to playfully enhance his ideas, something that was entirely foreign to Lagarde.

Lagarde had proudly written to his father-in-law from London: "Both politically and religiously, my views are becoming more and more of a complete whole."[34] His hatred of the Jews played a central role in his increasingly unified worldview. But it is exceptionally difficult to clarify when and for what reasons his originally rather positive perception of Jews reversed itself. Unfortunately, philosemitism is one of the most poorly researched areas within the modern history of ideas. There can be little doubt, however, concerning the ambivalence it engendered. That Jews regarded Christian aggrandizement of Judaism with concern and skepticism, as well as pride, was by no means coincidental. Jews had repeatedly learned that, particularly in the case of effusive souls, a positive opinion of Judaism could swiftly turn into a negative one. Moreover, Lagarde's earlier attempt to define the unity of the Jewish character partook of the same ambiguity that German idealism showed toward Judaism.[35] At the same time, his rejection of Protestantism was striking. Lagarde not only accused it of inherent emptiness and religious inconsistency; he also blamed Protestantism for Germans' inability to find their way to a national religion, without which a powerful nation was inconceivable. On the other hand, he attested to the inherent consistency and historical significance of rabbinical Judaism, because it had made survival possible in a hostile world by means of strict upbringing and rigorous schooling.

But the inner unity of Lagarde's worldview should not be overemphasized. Extreme mood swings were the order of the day with him, and they influenced his political judgment. His anger toward superficial contemporary life extended to national minorities, social strata, and religious beliefs. When he was in a dark mood, his disparaging opinions could touch on practically every group and every topic. Despite his Anglophilia, he put it this way to his future wife: "In England, the foreignness is saddest of all. So little spirit, so many rules."[36] In any case, it is not enough to trace Lagarde's cultural pessimism to his disenchantment with his academic career and to leave it at that. The first signs of his radical rejection of contemporary life were present early on. They were rooted in his joyless childhood, for which he tried to compensate with romantic ideals.

His understanding of spiritual rebirth as a means of overcoming the "world" was shaped by Pietism and corresponded to the ideas embraced by the movement. Of course, we should not push aside the fact that grammar school teaching was a bitter pill for the highly talented scholar to swallow. In the spring of 1854, he entered his probationary year as a teacher, a profession that he was scarcely prepared for and had never aspired to.

4 A Double Life

The start of Lagarde's professional career was a difficult one. In fact, it appears as though his entry into grammar school teaching precipitated a real life crisis. At any rate, he still recalled more than twenty years later how depressed he had been in 1854. So terribly ashamed at the failure of his academic ambitions, he even refrained from inviting Friedrich Rückert to his wedding. The number of family deaths had also increased during the troublesome probationary period at the Friedrich Werdersches Gymnasium. Within a short time, his grandparents and one uncle passed away.[1] As was so often the case for him when personal problems arose, Lagarde concentrated entirely on his work. His efforts paid off when a Berlin school hired him at the end of his probationary year. Unfortunately, it was only the Luisenstädtische Realschule, where his knowledge of ancient languages was not of much importance. But he succeeded in transferring to the Köllnische Realgymnasium just half a year later. As of spring 1858, he was teaching at the prestigious Friedrich Werdersches Gymnasium, site of his probationary training, where his father had once completed his *Abitur*.

By dint of his amazing scholarly prowess, Lagarde was an outsider among his colleagues. And his teaching load reflected the breadth of his extraordinary curriculum vitae. With the exception of the natural sciences, Lagarde simply had to teach in all subject areas. This was essentially of little benefit to his pupils, because many disciplines were much too far removed from his educational background and intellectual preferences. Physical education must have been a real hardship for the constitutionally tense and very nearsighted scholar. Added to that was the unusually heavy workload for a newly married man. Lagarde taught for up to forty-five hours per week. In order to increase his salary, he also took on a great deal of private tutoring.[2] And he had to publish continuously so that the academic world would not forget him.

Lagarde repeatedly complained about his situation. On April 12, 1855, he described himself to his cousin Eduard Böhmer as "a sixty-year-old man" who longed for peace and quiet. On June 17, 1855, he let Böhmer know about his state of health in rather matter-of-fact terms: "The entire machine will have to be greased again if it's supposed to be in working order!" A full year later, Lagarde remarked to Heinrich Ewald, one of his most reliable contacts in the academic world, that his eyesight was so poor that he "had not been able to recognize the students in the back rows for quite some time."[3] His remarks were presumably not calculated to arouse any sort of sympathy, because nineteenth-century respect for discipline and hard work did not lend itself to lamentations of this sort. Lagarde must have felt that his situation was unbearable during recurring periods of exhaustion. A letter to Rückert attests to just how greatly feelings of depression could envelop the extremely nervous scholar. In it, he said that he "had been rendered dead tired by life."[4] But we should not approach Lagarde's descriptions of himself without a pinch of skepticism regarding the accuracy of the source—Lagarde himself. As much as he suffered under the double burden of teaching and scholarship, it was also quite common for academics to depict themselves as devoted workers in the vineyard of the Lord. And Lagarde showed considerable authority in deploying literary conventions early on.

In any case, Lagarde soon became accustomed to his new assignments and took pleasure in the upsides of the teaching profession. He could work independently and emphasize content within the framework of standards. As early as New Year's Day 1856, he underscored to his parents-in-law "the many good aspects" of the latest developments, chief among them the financial security that permitted him to provide a solid basis for his wife's pension.[5]

Lagarde also commanded his students' respect. Character building was just as important to Lagarde as his students' academic achievement. He did not merely want to impart knowledge, but urged his students to be patriotic. He also tried to disregard their ancestry to the greatest possible extent. Even members of the nobility were not exempt from harsh rebukes, while his antisemitism did not in any way prevent him from encouraging Jewish students. Two of them, Isidor Baumann and Oskar Blumenthal, kept in touch with Lagarde for a fairly long time after completing their *Abitur*.[6] This does not mean, however, that Lagarde moved away from his antisemitic views during his time as a schoolteacher. As has been true of prejudice from time immemorial, he instead expressed his attitude through patronizing behavior. For example, having just conversed amicably with Michael Sachs, a respected scholar and the rabbi of Berlin's Jewish community, he wrote to his wife from Franzensbad in July 1857 that treating him honorably was important "because the Jews here are so numerous and loathsome." This was consistent with Lagarde's views on Jewish supremacy in Germany. On December 31, 1863, he wrote indignantly to his in-laws that one could "no longer officially mention Easter" at city council meetings. A person had to speak of "Passover" instead, or he would find himself in a bad position with respect to his own request.[7] However we may assess the importance of Jewishness to urban liberalism, this was a judgment in which hatred already dominated Lagarde's sense of reality. On July 8, 1864, Lagarde told his wife about a daydream that bore totally obsessive features. In it, he was sitting in a railway compartment with a group of Jews who were "sent back to their Oriental *Heimat* at his command." Concerning this antisemitic opinion, he commented disparagingly that "I just couldn't get rid of those people."

The shy scholar was happy that he didn't have to communicate at eye level in the course of everyday teaching. And it was precisely this fact that seems to have opened the way for him to an almost personal conversational tone. One student even praised Lagarde, saying upon reflection that he had learned "free thinking" from him. Over time, Lagarde developed a certain pride in his abilities as a teacher, a pride that was also reflected in his worldview. The discussion of educational issues takes up a great deal of space in his writings. Concrete examples from school are not infrequent, and Lagarde willingly lets on that he is speaking from personal experience. At the same time, his penchant for moralistic statements and his sentimental (appellative) language may have been strengthened by the teaching profession.[8] While Lagarde observed iron discipline in his own academic work, he categorically rejected the authoritarian elements of the Prussian school system. In a letter to the Orientalist August Dillmann, dated December 5, 1859, he compared teaching to an "ox treadmill, since no child learns anything, but is simply supposed to be trained." There was no doubt in Lagarde's mind that, if he wanted to be successful as a teacher, he had to incline himself toward the actual abilities of his students and not toward abstract principles.

In his dealings with public authorities, Lagarde displayed considerable opposition. So it was that, on January 9, 1864, he complained to the Berlin school board (*Provinzialschulkollegium*) that a colleague had tactlessly requisitioned school fees. Lagarde's idealistic standpoint was that "students [should] be reminded as little as possible [. . .] that they are being taught for money." With acute irony toward low teacher salaries, he added: "With our splendid wage rates, we dare not be concerned that, based on our outward appearance and behavior, [the students] would ever get the idea that we are paid at all." His remark was a deliberate exaggeration, as grammar school teachers already earned a solid income by the mid-nineteenth century. This was mainly due to the elite nature of Gymnasium education (*Gymnasialbildung*). Of the 29,500 teachers in Prussia in 1843, no more than one thousand taught at the grammar school level.[9] But Lagarde's complaint pointed to the marked gap between truly successful academics, such as professors or judges, and teachers. Teachers had to go to great lengths just to afford the bourgeois lifestyle. Even if they taught Gymnasia, they still needed a handsome dowry or inheritance in order to finance the obligatory housemaid. Since teachers also were accused of having received a "superficial education," it is hardly surprising that an ambitious scholar like Lagarde would occasionally express discontent over existing circumstances. What is astounding is the extent to which he identified with the teaching profession. He probably sensed that the students accepted him.

Lagarde, the teacher, also did not refrain from stating his opinions. Among other things, he was firmly convinced that one should not overburden the students with knowledge, but encourage them to form their own opinions. He simultaneously harbored doubts that very much could be achieved through strict disciplinary measures, relying instead on personal discussion and on class field trips, which were still a rarity in those days. The degree to which Lagarde sought to establish a relationship of trust with his students was unusual, and he even divulged little secrets from time to time. He enjoyed a great deal of trust in return and, even though it was a school holiday, his birthday on All Souls' Day was a very popular occasion. His students even occasionally visited him at home, also a very rare practice back then. In order to arrange a surprise party for him, they joined forces with Lagarde's housemaid, who took care of the essentials.[10] Some of them kept in touch with their former teacher throughout their lives. While this was surely a sign of social prestige, as Lagarde later became a renowned professor, Lagarde's relationships with his students had definite value in and of themselves. This can be deduced from the time repeatedly taken by the harried scholar to cultivate friendships with people from his teaching days.

Lagarde's relationships with his colleagues were not close, but they were at least free of animosity. He participated in the social niceties following large school conferences and occasionally went along to the pub. But he usually focused his attention on his own scholarly oeuvre. Scholarly correspondence seems to have been more important to Lagarde's desire for intellectual exchange than were his colleagues at school. One colleague, Georg Büchmann, published an anthology of quotations in 1864 that would become *the* best seller of the educated middle class. By 1900, at least one hundred thousand copies of Büchmann's *Geflügelten Worten* (*Familiar Quotations*) had been sold.[11] Even today, his compilation helps the reader brush up on and present literary knowledge that, in reality, very few people have at their disposal. Lagarde never commented expressly on his successful colleague. Given his earnest disposition toward life, however, he more than likely held this type of mass-market-oriented publication in contempt.

Despite the considerable workload at school, there can be no question that Lagarde put at least as much energy into his scholarly oeuvre. In doing so, he firmly believed that few scholars had comparable linguistic knowledge at their disposal, knowledge that would shed light on the problems of early Church history. He made a start with unadorned yet solid editions in which he publicly presented his London findings. Lagarde had transcribed approximately one thousand quartos in the British Museum, most of them in Syriac. With tenacity and diligence, he published one book after another, several of which were reissued in the twentieth century. In view of the limited amount of financial assistance involved, Lagarde did not feel obligated to a large academic apparatus, which also accounts for the relative strengths and weaknesses of his editions. On the one hand, they did not feign knowledge that could not be rightly obtained, given the state of knowledge at that time. On the other hand, he often left his readers clueless, because they couldn't understand many of Lagarde's conclusions.[12] The accuracy of his editions was, however, generally recognized; he carefully revised them twice on the basis of the originals. He published, in total, no fewer than sixteen books during the twelve years that he taught grammar school in Berlin.

His wife's support played a decisive role in Lagarde's productivity. She participated in his scholarly duties and undertook smaller editing tasks. In addition, she helped her husband in all matters of everyday life and bolstered his fragile sense of self-worth. The inheritance from his adoptive mother, who passed away in 1857, made his very costly editions possible in the long run. At the same time, he was able to dispense with the burdensome tutoring assignments. Just how central scholarship was to Lagarde's sense of self can be seen in his setting off, immediately upon receiving his inheritance, on a rather lengthy research trip to London. In no way should we underestimate the importance of legacies to the intellectual life of the nineteenth century. Many adjunct professors waited more than a decade for a professorship. Lacking stable, job-related income, they depended on the financial support of their families. The same is true of the great mavericks in the history of ideas. In order to ignite his passion for writing, Kierkegaard required constant access to luxury items like choice pastries and excellent wines. He did not have an eye to mass audience appeal, yet published ceaselessly until his inheritance was almost completely used up. Only an early death saved him from financial ruin. Schopenhauer was luckier: he knew how to economize, and the light of fame shone on him in his old age. Although not widely known, it is by no means insignificant that Nietzsche lived on his inheritance from a distant uncle. His many years of unsettled wandering could not have been financed solely by his small pension from the University of Basel.[13] Financially speaking, these existential philosophers owed a "debt" of gratitude to their family backgrounds.

Lagarde's situation was probably most comparable to Kierkegaard's. Like the Danish philosopher, the Orientalist laid out large sums to print his writings, hoping for a broad response. While, if nothing else, Kierkegaard's editions served as a personal indulgence, Lagarde was downright miserly. Lagarde's correspondence is filled with disputes over finances. Anger over the "malice" of the scholarly readership that did not purchase his writings would accompany him all his life. By using his own funds, Lagarde felt justified in his censure of the academic public and was capable of formulating his rebukes in the harshest terms. In his March 16, 1864, letter to Dillmann, he called his potential readers "indigent and intellectually depraved." Lagarde identified strongly with what he produced academically and, as a consequence, he would experience euphoric swells of self-worth from time to time. But the fact that he hoped for respectable earnings as an author also showed the considerable degree to which he was divorced from reality. The majority of his books were unadorned, relatively expensive, and geared toward a highly specialized audience. In addition, his self-publishing lacked the support of the book trade. Finally, numerous scholarly feuds meant that his works were hardly ever recommended within his field and almost no one bought them.

Nevertheless, Lagarde's desire to make a name for himself on a grand scale was discernible early on. He was comfortable using just about any means to achieve his purpose. With great energy, he appealed to the Ministry of Culture to acquire his writings for school libraries and was occasionally successful. His basic aim seems to have been to immortalize his life, as was once true of Kierkegaard. One of Lagarde's poems, cryptically titled "To M.v.B.," exemplifies this. It highlights the importance of fame to human existence and ends with the verses:

> If in the future you do not to it aspire,
> You'll be forgotten for all time.[14]

Kierkegaard's notes express this same point in a similarly firm manner: "Just as writing in the sand or the sea leaves no trace, so it is with all that exists and does not become spirit: a vanishing, something traceless."[15] As different as Lagarde and Kierkegaard were in terms of intellectual temperament, as we have already seen, many similarities spring to mind from a biographical perspective. For example, the separation from their fathers through death played an important role in both men's lives, and the fear that other authors would deny them posthumous fame was among their constant concerns.

In Lagarde's case, fear of plagiarism took on pathological features at an early stage. He accused many of his colleagues of intellectual theft and had researchers with whom he was on friendly terms investigated. Naturally, Lagarde was not a member of any influential scholarly network. Without the necessary protections, there was always a danger of being unduly taken advantage of or even directly exploited. Thus, in return for the vague prospect of a Berlin professorship, Baron Bunsen hoped to enlist Lagarde in the hopeless task of creating a trilingual edition of the Bible. On February 3, 1859, the Bonn theologian Albrecht Ritschl forcefully dissuaded Lagarde from accepting the proposal: Bunsen had "neither the goodwill nor the power [. . .] to practice effective patronage. You should not be deceived by him, nor support him in his vain and devious pretentions to scholarly fame." The advice of his friend and fellow scholar, whom Lagarde often visited in Berlin, fell on fertile ground. Despite how deeply he longed for academic influence, the grammar school teacher was unwavering with regard to Bunsen's offer. He went so far as to explain to the ministry "that Bunsen's planned work was infeasible and, even if it were to be carried out, useless."[16] Lagarde's directness was hardly suitable to his professional ambitions. In order to get a professorship, he needed ministerial backing and at least one powerful advocate in the field of Oriental studies.

Lagarde lacked the necessary skills of self-reflection to recognize just how greatly his aggressive nature and rejection of scholarly conventions contributed to his isolation. In any case, his conflicts with the academic establishment facilitated his friendship with Ewald, an eccentric who had attained great prominence in the wake of the Göttingen Seven protest of 1837. The Semitist had basked in glory ever since he had been called back to Georg August University in 1848. At the same time, he cultivated his outsider position within the academic establishment. Like Lagarde, he was an outstanding connoisseur of Oriental languages and a tireless worker who placed great value on his own impartial judgment. In terms of content, Ewald aspired to a theological reading of the Old Testament that balked at false theologies and simultaneously displayed multifaceted, antisemitic reservations. After Rückert's retreat into private life, Ewald was Lagarde's only stable contact in the world of academe. Lagarde valued Ewald as tailor-made for his advancement. This explains why Lagarde handled him with great diplomatic skill. In his letters to the quick-tempered Ewald, he emphasized his own role as an outsider whenever possible, offering help in small ways, but made few promises. On January 27, 1855, Lagarde alleged to Ewald that, despite a good teaching record, some had "happily lied to keep him away [. . .] from the university." In light of events in Halle, this statement was very far from the truth. But Lagarde was able to count on Ewald's well-meaning acceptance, because Ewald was deeply convinced that mediocre professors were envious of talented outsiders. Lagarde let the Orientalist from Göttingen know that he would like him to review his anonymously published

Didascalia in such a way as to keep his identity secret. Ewald agreed to this unusual request, but the results were disastrous for Lagarde. On the one hand, the way in which the review appeared fostered skeptical reactions. On the other hand, the secretive format prevented Lagarde from acknowledging his significant Parisian findings. Only at the beginning of the twentieth century did Lagarde's edition of Syriac Church law gain acceptance, at which time it was translated into no fewer than four languages.[17] The combination of two eccentric personalities like Ewald and Lagarde was not an especially ideal prerequisite for winning scholarly esteem. As compared with other scholarly correspondence, personal news played a minor role in their letters to each other. They instead focused on questions related to scholarly matters or bemoaned Germany's cultural decline.

Lagarde emphatically underscored his scholarly and religious ideals, and was unsparing in his critique of the current state of affairs. Following his transfer to the Köllnisches Gymnasium, he told Ewald how much he despised Hengstenberg's *Christology of the Old Testament.* Reactionary "Throne and Altar theology" was entirely unsuitable for young people. He closed his striking letter with these words: "Without Pentecost from above and a conflagration here below, things will not improve."[18] When it came to Prussian economic policy, Lagarde also had nothing good to say, but he expressed the hope that, with Ewald's help, he would be able to stand his ground. Admittedly, not that many options were open to the ambitious scholar. And so it was that, on May 27, 1859, he remarked in an equally depressed and categorical manner that "in Prussia, a person cannot get ahead without European renown or lots of obsequiousness." However much sympathy Ewald may have wished to show Lagarde, the latter's profile for job applications was no doubt weak. In particular, he lacked sufficient university teaching experience. Beyond that, of course, the number of scholars who could evaluate Lagarde's oeuvre was very small indeed. On November 11, 1859, the disappointed scholar got carried away and phrased it as follows: "What I write may as well be written on water, if people won't read it. No one on God's green earth even bothers with it."[19] But this kind of impassioned tone was exceptional. As a rule, Lagarde simply presented his latest findings and hoped to receive Ewald's accolades. Nevertheless, such strong dependence on Ewald must have awakened ambivalent feelings in someone as proud as Lagarde, a man who had hardly any emotional outlets. To perhaps an even greater extent, the same principle applied to his attitude toward a second advocate, the historian of antiquity Theodor Mommsen.

Lagarde had almost nothing in common with Mommsen, whose rise to fame had been meteoric. He had practically no interest in Roman antiquity and denounced Mommsen's left-wing liberalism as inherently empty, as well as disastrous for the German people. Mommsen's ironic intellectual temperament and agnosticism were foreign to Lagarde. However, in light of Mommsen's powerful position and his say regarding many openings in Prussia, he could not be ignored. All backing was admittedly hard won. Lagarde did research for Mommsen in Paris and London, and promptly provided information about the results. On March 19, 1864, when Lagarde felt that he had once again been neglected by the Prussian Ministry of Culture, he wrote to Mommsen: "Help me get away from here!"[20] Lagarde could not expect a positive reaction to this type of spontaneous request, and there is no record of any response. But his letters to Mommsen basically show that, irrespective of any and all pompous criticism of contemporary issues, he knew that he had to bow to certain realities. If a person wanted to get ahead in Prussia, then patronage was not only indispensable at the university but at the secondary school level as well.

On February 8, 1864, Lagarde rather skillfully let Mommsen know that he was seriously thinking of applying for a grammar school position in Oldenburg. He styled himself a "recluse" without any connections, who had to "do his own self-promotion." Lagarde invoked an idealistic rationale for his change of location. He needed "efficiency in the office and scholarly work in the classroom," both of which were on the decline in Berlin. Of course, the shrewdest bowing and scraping were no guarantee of success and, shortly thereafter, his hopes for a move to Oldenburg turned out to be an illusion. In the summer of 1864, when he was passed over in the restructuring of the Berlin grammar schools, Lagarde's dissatisfaction with teaching increased. Many a young colleague now drew a larger salary. In addition, he was given hardly any teaching for the more advanced students. This was particularly vexing because, on May 29, he had asked the municipal authorities in Berlin for permission to limit his teaching to four subjects: Hebrew, Greek, Latin, and religion. Otherwise, there would be a real danger of "entirely losing sight of the focus of my intellectual life."

On October 25, Lagarde used antisemitic diction to inform Mommsen of his resentment concerning the Senate's lack of due regard: "Now I know where I stand. With witless, abstract justice that would be a credit to any Talmudist, they have worked the budget over and over." Naturally, the confidential tone does not necessarily mean that Mommsen shared Lagarde's resentment. But, in the meantime, the confident, left-wing liberal almost surely harbored his own private antisemitic reservations. His letter of October 22, 1857, to the music historian Otto Jahn is exemplary. In it, Mommsen comments on his Berlin appointment in the following terms: "You may know that I don't go to the great Babel without fear and trembling: Jews, privy councilors, and relatives are not exactly the fundamental constituents of a desirable society."[21] Admittedly, a crucial difference should be considered. Unlike Lagarde, Mommsen's orientation was strictly antireligious, and he considered every religion a relic of the Middle Ages that was incompatible with a scholarly worldview. Mommsen's atheism bore explicitly affective traits. Ever since he was a young man, he preferred to be called Jens, because he loathed his Christian forename, Theodor. Mommsen's anti-Catholic and anti-Protestant statements are correspondingly numerous. Within the logic of this worldview, of course, observant Jews would have appeared reactionary to him. In any case, Lagarde's antisemitic statement didn't do him any harm. Mommsen's intervention with the city school board yielded a salary increase of fifty talers, as well as the prospect of "a better position at one of the new schools," as he promptly reported to his mentor. However, it was entirely unclear how Lagarde was supposed to realize his lifelong dream of producing a critical edition of the Septuagint. The pressures of teaching school really didn't allow him enough time for such an enormous undertaking. Moreover, not only was Lagarde a passionate teacher; his marked disposition as a contrarian also brought him into repeated conflict with the senior administrators.

Lagarde's petition of January 14, 1864, which he planned to dispatch to the city council meeting, caused the biggest stir of all.[22] Since teachers were forbidden to pursue their goals collectively, he handled the matter on his own. This approach was also in keeping with his political temperament, of course, which tended more toward ideological fanfare than careful compromise. He voiced his conviction in drastic terms that the Friedrich Werdersches Gymnasium had seen better days. He complained that the barely ventilated classrooms were heated by "enormous ovens," and the sanitary facilities were simply a health hazard. It was entirely unacceptable to collect the fecal matter of 576 students and many visitors, to store it, only to "deal with it" later on. On top of that, there was the problem of massive overcrowding. The lower classes comprised more than fifty students on average and, in light of classroom size, proper instruction was also barely feasible in the upper classes. Lagarde called for urgent measures, including the hiring of at least three teachers and appropriate building alterations. After considering the appropriateness of the text, however, he finally refrained from sending it to the city council meeting. But he circulated a printed version among influential members of the Berlin bourgeoisie, and his approach resonated with some. On January 24, a medical officer for public health, one Dr. Ludwig Ruge, informed Lagarde that he "would again take up the petition that you withdrew, along with like-minded persons." In any case, the issue was clear in terms of content: "We cannot sanction the idea of teachers and students forfeiting their health in damp, unhealthy classrooms." For this reason, the authorities had to provide "the necessary funds to renovate the Evangelical grammar school." Things took their course, and it became apparent that Lagarde had adopted the right tone. He was able to inform Mommsen that the municipal authorities had ordered the closing of the premises in question. Lagarde was certainly not someone who could constantly rejoice at improvements in everyday life. Rather, the longer he thought about it, the more inclined he was to believe that the power of public opinion did not allow for any kind of serious political reform.

Meanwhile, Lagarde's rejection of the Conservative Party had become irreversible. He was firmly convinced of his own radicality and wanted nothing to do with the business of everyday politics, whose protagonists he despised. With that in mind, he wrote to Eduard Böhmer on June 17, 1855: "I am more reactionary than any reactionary, and can have nothing in common with the liars, slanderers of and traitors to the crusading bearers of the Cross." The hatred of big cities that had already infiltrated Lagarde in London and Paris now also galled him in Berlin. He could no longer recognize the city of his youth in the rapidly expanding metropolis. The hectic pace of the new era especially disturbed him, and he therefore told the theologian Adolf Hilgenfeld that Berlin was "a vast and beastly city."[23] As with many dissatisfied persons, Lagarde linked his assessment of his own status to his appraisal of the overall political situation. According to his own experience, it appeared certain to him that a highly principled man could not succeed in Prussia. Unlike many of his contemporaries, he did not pin the slightest hope on Bismarck, whom he took to be pitiless and brutal. He regarded it as an accepted fact that Prussia's increasing military power was detrimental to the German nation. On April 20, 1863, he trenchantly told Dillmann he was convinced that the policies of Bismarck and Kaiser Wilhelm I were disastrous. With polemical virulence, he added, "If only the democratic apes wouldn't help them so much, but would build in the German tradition, seeing as Prussia is tearing it down." Revealingly, Lagarde's writings hold no indication that he had once attended the same school as Bismarck, although he knew full well that this was true. Lagarde could complain so eloquently about the silence of his political opponents, yet he generally used information advisedly, especially if it touched on the private domain. This owed not least to his conviction that the adroitness of debates should not suffer from personal considerations.

The authoritarian bias of the Prussian state was downright inescapable as far as Lagarde was concerned. As early as 1856, he had disrespectfully called Prussia a "patriarchal police state." Eight years later, he told the privy councilor from

Jena, Carl Hase: "The state of affairs in Prussia gets more unbearable from year to year. I believe it is inherent and thus consider it ineradicable, that is unless one were able to eradicate the entire state."[24] Only now and again do we hear a different tone from Lagarde, as on the occasion of the Schiller celebrations, when he gave the official speech at the Friedrich Werdersches Gymnasium. His patriotic address of November 10, 1859, underscored Schiller's national ethos and, in the tradition of Weimar Classicism, co-opted Shakespeare on behalf of German culture. Lagarde tellingly chose an authoritarian reading of Kant, who had once deeply shaped Schiller's moral philosophy. With military curtness, he said, "We are *certain* of nothing, other than the awareness of duty." Of course, the address did not echo Lagarde's real viewpoint. On December 15, 1859, he told his father-in-law that he wished he "were allowed to view the cultural period that began" with Goethe and Schiller "as finished." He extended his severe critique of Weimar humanism by stating: "As a cultural principle, 'Art' is not much help. I find it necessary to thoroughly dispose of all that literary mumbo jumbo."[25] As a rule, however, Lagarde was at great pains to avoid openly identifying with the developments of his day or even with the Prussian state.

In the summer of 1859, Lagarde wrote a paper on the decline of religious life. The original text has not survived, but important thoughts from it flowed into his essay "Über das Verhältnis des deutschen Staates zu Theologie, Kirche und Religion" ("On the Relationship of the German State to Theology, Church, and Religion"). It bears the strange subtitle "Ein Versuch Nicht-Theologen zu orientieren" ("An Essay Addressed to Nontheologians"). But a read-through quickly reveals that, to Lagarde, political and theological commentary carried equal weight. His main goal consisted of taking away the legitimacy of Protestantism as a scientifically justifiable and, from a religious standpoint, seminal philosophy.[26]

In solemn language, Lagarde emphasized the presuppositionless character of scholarly findings: "Everyone who is acquainted with science knows that its purpose is self-contained; it, therefore, seeks its own method and does not embrace any heavenly power or earthly regulations, laws, goals. Science wants to know, nothing other than to know and, in fact, only so as to know" (p. 40). Since all knowledge is essentially positivistic in nature, the rules of verifiable scientific advancement must also be applied to theology, were it to assert the overall validity of its statements. In this context, Lagarde's strictly antipluralistic understanding of knowledge is critical. For him, the perspective and subjectivity of human knowledge had no scholarly value whatsoever. In Lagarde's opinion, theology should note that there was only *one* religious denomination. There was consequently no tolerance in matters of faith, and the peaceful coexistence of united Lutheran and Catholic theologians could only be regarded as a farce. Lagarde used the example of astronomy, in which Copernicus's thinking had replaced the Ptolemaic worldview once and for all. In matters of scientific history, Lagarde, ever the cultural pessimist, was a devotee of rigid progressive thinking.[27] He outlined a grave consequence for contemporary theologians that was based on his ideal of presuppositionless research. Since they were already committed in advance to a religious creed, they were not entitled to "see themselves as servants of science" (p. 42).

Lagarde was convinced that Protestantism should merely be understood as a historical event, the fruit of the sixteenth century. In spite of all the ideological dramatization, in essence it was only a reform movement, i.e., a gradual modification of Catholicism. The "scholastic-Catholic structure" (p. 48) itself had not hindered any reformer. Luther's attitude was symptomatic of the narrow scope and nonradicality of his critique. As a pastor, his indignation pertained chiefly to the sale of indulgences. In other words, his protest was not directed against the Catholic Church as a whole but only against particular abuses. Protestantism had long been unnecessary in contemporary religious life. One could recognize its intellectual honesty by how it dealt with the New Testament. An examination of the New Testament using modern philological methods would reveal something other than what Protestantism claimed. Neither christening nor Sunday nor the doctrine of the Trinity could be proven by the gospels. Rather, they testified exclusively to the transformative impact Jesus had on the community. Even in its heyday, Protestantism had not lastingly shaped the religiosity of the German people, and the officially recognized lifestyle of its orthodoxy was a "galvanized death" (p. 51). When modern religious education placed men like "Lessing, Goethe, Herder, Kant, Winckelmann" in close proximity to Protestantism, this was a white lie (p. 51). In actuality, these figures never had anything to do with the church of their day. This was an oversimplification, of course. While Lagarde denied Protestantism its historic sources, he also delegitimized its contemporary manifestations. As a cultural critic who delighted in placing special emphasis on the clear, unemotional objectivity of his statements, he knew full well that history in the period of historicism was not only a universally accepted benchmark but a weapon as well. His assessment of the historical meaning of Protestantism is, therefore, also ideologically charged.

Lagarde emphatically stressed that nothing vital had ever come from Protestantism. Rather, it had led to the fossilization of Catholicism. The founding and upswing of the Jesuit order should ultimately be seen as a reaction to the Reformation. In the new Catholicism, Lagarde saw the enemy of nations. The Jesuits and their rigid universalism were born enemies of every organic ideology. Their rejection of nationality would lead to materialism, which would ultimately destroy all commonweal. But the new Catholicism was also ideologically insubstantial. The fact that Rome had to deny "every word that God had ever spoken throughout history" (p. 53) made this abundantly clear. It was, therefore, only appropriate to regard the new Catholic Church as a "born foe of every state" (p. 57).

Lagarde brushed aside questions posed by left-wing Hegelianism about the historical Jesus. The meaning of historical events did not consist of "becoming knowledgeable" but of providing "the nation in which they came about with the basis for a new existence" (p. 60). He mixed a large dose of enmity toward Jews into his theologically overarching nationalism. Thus, the preference of contemporary Judaism for meaningless, apparently universalist views proved it was in "need of a coherent worldview" (p. 62). Liberals, on the other hand, had no religious core and would soon be scattered to the four winds. But Christianity's concept of religion was also false. Religion was primarily "a personal relationship of pious persons to God" (p. 65) rather than a form of theological reflection. Lagarde generally disputed the importance of historical knowledge to religious life. Thus, David Friedrich Strauss's work on *The Life of Jesus* was certainly mistaken. The real problem lay not in its findings but in the value that Orthodox Christianity had placed on "historical facts" from time immemorial, while not even noticing its own "fetishism" (p. 65). No bridge led from history to religion and, as a result, Lagarde stated categorically that, "To steep oneself in what has been is not religion, but sentimentality" (p. 67). According to his beliefs, which held that science was not capable of making sense out of human existence, the excess of historical knowledge threatened to sidetrack human beings from the essentials and to smother their religious feeling.

As Lagarde saw it, the ceaseless search for God was the most lofty and important life's work. It was precisely the hidden God who possessed that decisive, instructional quality: "He asks us to look for the pearls in the rubble instead of letting them glide into our hands. He forgives, yet always remembers that atonement was necessary. Thus, he is diligent and meek, and diligence and meekness are better than laziness and pride" (p. 68). Whereas Lagarde glorified the personal search for God, he disparaged the religious communities of his time as sects. For the sole reason that they were not in a position to represent the entire *Volk*, they had no right to state support. Moreover, one was not permitted to harbor any illusions about the vitality of Protestantism. For Lagarde, it could not measure up to the dynamism of the de-Christianization process, and the scholarly education of clerics alone would soon prove fateful. At any rate, an impetus for the religious life was not to be found in theology, which was basically a historical discipline: "In that it provides a history of religion, it provides knowledge of religion" (p. 74). And yet he also was aware of the limited effect scientific criticism had upon thoughts and deeds. Feelings and convictions determine actions. "The core of a human being," as Lagarde apodictically put it, "is not the mind, but the will. He who will not see, does not see, not even if all the professors in the world hounded him with proof" (p. 75). Despite these skeptical thoughts regarding science, Lagarde longed to participate in academia. Owing to his numerous publications, academics began to pay attention to him in their circles.

It is not possible to identify the precise moment at which Lagarde became employable as a professor. Toward the end of the 1850s, his name arose in matters of appointment, although it was not exactly at the center of the discussion. An opening for a professor of Orientalism in Halle, where Lagarde had once delivered his first lectures, illustrates this point. Lagarde was not yet under serious consideration for Emil Rödiger's chair. Rödiger had moved on to the center of Prussian academic life in Berlin, and the eminent Bonn Orientalist Johannes Gildemeister, who had made a name for himself as a confirmed liberal, had been placed atop the list. Gildemeister attained early fame when he and historian Heinrich von Sybel exposed the "Holy Skirt of Trier" (*Heiligen Rock*) as a fake and ridiculed it as Catholic trickery (*Bauernfängerei*). His conversance in the Old Testament, as well as his "outstanding knowledge of Semitic languages and Sanskrit," spoke in his favor.[28] As was so often the case with appointment lists, the faculty's actual favorite was in the number-two position, because the top choice, typically a renowned scholar, would be sought after by so many other institutions. They had opted for Lagarde's long-standing correspondence partner August Dillmann, who was introduced "as highly skilled in Chaldean." Among other things, the professor from Kiel was lauded for having "taught courses in Old Testament scholarship" to "high acclaim." Lagarde's name finally showed up in third position. And the language was substantially more matter-of-fact here: the former adjunct professor from Halle, who "is an expert in Oriental languages on a grand scale," was "mentioned in light of his teaching ability." When one considers that Lagarde had not delivered a lecture for many years, this judgment could hardly suffice for an appointment.

The progression of events offered few surprises, and Dillmann soon received the call to the city on the Saale. For Lagarde, his place on the list in Halle was at least a reasonable success. But instead of being pleased about the nomination, Lagarde had expected more and was disappointed. When Dillmann anticipated turning down the offer, Lagarde again believed he might have a chance. He immediately intervened with the Philosophy Faculty so as to underscore the seriousness of his intentions. But this was foolishness of the highest order. To begin with, the Halle faculty did not at all have it in mind to appoint the Berlin schoolteacher, whom they had placed on the list as a courtesy. Second, they saw Lagarde's behavior as meddling. The historian Heinrich Leo, Lagarde's champion in Halle, had to backpedal. He sent word to Berlin on June 19, 1862, that the faculty would not officially take steps to respond to the statements of a "private citizen." Outwardly, Lagarde played it cool. On July 20, he wrote to his wife, "To my mind, it is far preferable to have people ask why I am not a professor, rather than to ask why I am one." But Lagarde seethed inwardly. He lost his composure when his old schoolfellow Richard Gosche was short-listed. Lagarde could not accept the idea that an authority on Moorish culture, who was already an associate professor in Berlin, would be favored over him. As he understood it, a chair in Old Testament studies was involved, and this was not exactly among the ambitious literary critic and Arabist Gosche's preferred fields of research. On April 9, 1863, after Gosche had actually received the professorship in Halle, Lagarde wrote to Ewald in a rage: "Envy and nastiness have thwarted my appointment in Halle." Just how greatly Lagarde was caught up in the matter can be seen in his making what was, at best, a formally proper statement. His pronouncement that the Halle Philosophy Faculty had "recommended him as Rödiger's successor" implied that there had been an actual nomination, which the third-place listing had not really bestowed on him.[29]

Meanwhile, further misfortune had befallen him. The University of Giessen had also considered whether to appoint Lagarde in 1863.[30] The university, in Hesse-Darmstadt, was less important than Halle and mainly known as a "springboard" to higher positions. Since Lagarde had already been short-listed in Prussia, an outside appointment was not at all unrealistic. But it now came up for discussion in Giessen that the Orientalist had wrongly boasted about having been recommended as Rödiger's successor. The committee promptly took the ambitious applicant out of the running. Lagarde was beside himself and requested that the Giessen faculty provide him with the name of the person who had slandered him, but received no response. With Heinrich Leo's help, he obtained an official statement from the University of Halle concerning his placement on the list and, on May 7, 1865, went directly to Ludwig Lange, the rector in Giessen: "I have the honor of advancing official proof that will exonerate me entirely." At the same time, he demanded that the document be presented to the Giessen Senate, as well as "the name of the professor from Halle," so as to begin "disciplinary proceedings." Lagarde added melodramatically: "I believe that an honorable man owes it to another to stand by him in the fight against such egregious carelessness and perfidy."

In his written response of May 21, 1865, Lange proved to be an experienced university policy maker. He told Lagarde that he was obliged to refrain from presenting his letter to the Giessen Senate. In this instance, the informant in question, Giessen theologian Wilhelm Gass, would have been exposed in the most unpleasant way, as the breach of an official secret was no small matter. Furthermore, no one in Giessen had "accused" Lagarde "of lying." The combative Orientalist showed good judgment in this instance and refrained from taking further steps. The extent to which he had brought these problems upon himself through his impatient behavior may not have been clear to him. Lagarde had meanwhile become accustomed to attributing the more sincere feelings to himself, while assuming the other party had base motives. This attitude was hardly beneficial to his clarity of mind. On February 2, 1864, he informed Carl Hase in Jena that he had been rejected in Giessen, as well as in Prussia; neither did this statement open the door to a realistic option for him at the university in Thuringia (Jena).

The reasons for Lagarde's troublesome career start cannot be determined with absolute certainty. As a grammar school teacher, he was pretty far removed from the world of the academy, and he was not always a realistic judge of its idiosyncrasies. In any case, philosophy faculties in no way appreciated meddlers. An adjunct professor had to wait to be nominated, and Lagarde didn't even have recent teaching experience at the university level. His loud complaints of affronts and injustice would hardly have impressed established academicians. As stark as differences in status within the university were, most full professors didn't want to know about any grievances, as the entire system was tailored to these figures' full rights and prestige.[31] Moreover, if one counts how quickly news of Lagarde's behavior must have circulated among the small community of Orientalists, it is rather amazing that anyone would have considered the difficult Berlin schoolteacher for a professorship. One reason was surely his outstanding linguistic abilities. But these alone would not have been enough to generate broader interest in him. Rather, it came down to a mixture of his positivistic scholarly credo and his belief in traditional consensus-seeking.

Lagarde never entirely distanced himself from the romantic ideas of his youth, but he was a skeptical positivist in his approach to philological editions. Over the years, his prevailing self-image was that of a "laborer" in the service of knowledge who would only reap his true reward at a future time. This interpretation offered Lagarde great "psychological rewards"—namely, delight in being subservient to a powerful idea and the concurrent elevation of his own obsession with work. In addition, this view legitimized powerful attacks on all those who did not share his scholarly ideals. The price Lagarde paid for his approach was that his epistemological position showed signs of "intellectual encrustation" early on and could not be further refined. Yet as it happened, it was the very dogmatism of his commentaries that opened up new opportunities for him. The radical biblical criticism of the Tübingen School had shed serious doubt on the philological basis of biblical texts. For many theologians, there was an urgent need to clarify the question of authenticity without falling short of the preestablished scholarly level of Ferdinand Christian Baur and David Friedrich Strauss. At the same time, they had to draw a clear line between themselves and the atheism of the Tübingen School.

Lagarde was a first-class philologist with unshakable religious convictions. The inheritance from his adoptive mother allowed him to travel to the most famous libraries in the world, where the biblical record could be studied. Over time, his main objective of locating the original versions of biblical texts found an appreciative audience. An 1863 review appeared in the highly respected *Neue Evangelische Zeitung* (*New Evangelical Journal*) that reflected his growing reputation. In covering two of Lagarde's recently published writings, *Constitutiones Apostolorum* (*Apostolic Constitutions*) and *Anmerkungen zur griechischen Uebersetzung der Proverbien* (*Commentaries on the Greek Translation of the Book of Proverbs*), the anonymous reviewer had high praise for his expertise: "Of all present-day academic theologians [. . .] who have made sifting through the sources of ancient Church history their life's work, we would be hard-pressed to name a single one whose papers have as much right to be regarded as genuinely enriching our knowledge of those largely dark times as those of this author." Furthermore, the reviewer judged Lagarde's intention to establish the "probable original form" of biblical texts as fruitful and forward looking (*weiterführend*).[32] In the mid-nineteenth century, philology had not yet lost its aura. To many people of that time, it represented nothing less than the restoration of the true biblical message that lay hidden in the old manuscripts.

In the case of a number of texts, including the *Constitutiones Apostolorum*, Lagarde applied his historico-critical method to the time of the gospels. But the wish among the wider public for the discovery of an original version of the gospels did not come true.[33] Meanwhile, Lagarde resumed work on a subject in which he could best use his linguistic abilities: the Greek translation of the Old Testament. The impetus came from without. In 1861, Oxford University presented him with the Holmes and Parsons edition of the Septuagint so that Lagarde, who was highly respected as a scholar in England, might resume his study of the Old Testament historical record. And Lagarde took the university up on it. He, therefore, had his wife create an index that contained 42,116 Bible quotations by St. Augustine. His study, *Anmerkungen zur griechischen*

Uebersetzung der Proverbien, contained far more than simple commentaries on the Book of Proverbs; it concerned the establishment and effective use of critical principles for the Septuagint edition. On May 3, 1863, Lagarde sent a sample of his work to Jacob Grimm, and the doyen of *Germanistik* (German philology) was full of praise. In his response of July 3, 1863, Grimm told Lagarde pronouncedly: "The writing is so erudite and terse that I am astonished at your linguistic talent."[34] Jacob Grimm complied with Lagarde's request and appealed to the Prussian Academy of Sciences regarding a subvention to cover printing costs for Lagarde's edition of a Viennese manuscript containing the Arabic Gospels. Unsurprisingly, given Grimm's renown, his request was granted. Lagarde gradually made a name for himself in the academic world, not only because of his numerous text editions but also because of his exceptional knowledge in the area of Septuagint research.

Lagarde was much too skeptical not to have known that an "untainted text" was more of a heuristic assumption than a philologist's everyday reality. His correspondence is filled with comments to the effect that Oriental studies should protect itself from bold speculation. On that note, he remarked to Adolf Hilgenfeld on June 8, 1863: "I set very little store by internal reasons, as long as external ones can be utilized." On the other hand, Lagarde showed hardly any intellectual restraint toward the wider public. Rather, he argued that an authoritative edition of the Septuagint could only be expected from him if he were able to concentrate entirely on scholarship. In his 1864 edition of the Arabic Gospels, he exhibited extreme self-pity when he said: with the workload that a teacher carries, he "can only live from hand to mouth as a scholar and must be satisfied if, with tired limbs of evening, he is able to drag over building blocks that others are not using to build anything."[35] Lagarde, who grappled with philological details in a self-sacrificial manner, knew better than most that blowing one's own horn was part of scholarship. Since he didn't suffer from false modesty, he approached the most important men of his time with his vision of a unified Septuagint edition. Thus, on October 25, 1864, he asked Theodor Mommsen the rhetorical question, "Who would blame me if I [. . .] were to work in total silence on my LXX, to which I have given my all and from which other work is always dissuading me anew?"[36] At that time, Lagarde still fostered modest hopes that he could find enough spare time for the Septuagint while teaching school. But when the restructuring of the Berlin school system was completed, these hopes also turned out to be a chimera.

On March 1, 1865, the authorities informed Lagarde that they had provided a single schoolmaster position for him at the newly furnished, second vocational school. Considering that he could hardly employ his linguistic abilities there, the pay raise he had been promised was practically of no consequence. That same day, Lagarde notified the Berlin school board, "An assignment such as the one earmarked for me is not at all desirable, because I am too much of a philologist to give instruction in subjects other than the three ancient languages, except in the event of a dire emergency."[37] His refusal meant that he not only gave up a higher salary; it also ensured that he would be assigned to the Friedrich Werdersches Gymnasium for the foreseeable future. But the Orientalist was not prepared to peacefully accept the situation. On April 2, 1865, he appealed directly to the Prussian king with an account of his scholarly plans, and this petition would change his life.

5 Finally a Professor

In the spring of 1865, Lagarde wrote a petition to the king that underscored the urgency of his situation. He had befriended a general who helped ensure that the document reached King Wilhelm I of Prussia posthaste. And speedy delivery fit in well with the unusual nature of the dispatch. Written in a personal tone, it attested to Lagarde's distress about his stagnant occupation. At the same time, it gave insight into the serious Prussian attitude toward the cultural ideal of scientific objective understanding (*Wissenschaftsverständnis*). Although support for education had been fickle since the days of Wilhelm von Humboldt, there was no doubt as to its widespread acceptance in Prussia. And this was also true of the Crown. Even if the majority of Hohenzollerns were skeptical about the ideal of presuppositionless research, their commitment to science took precedence in the public domain. In looking back on the heroic Wars of Liberation of 1813–1815 against Napoleon, the prevailing consensus was that, in addition to a powerful military, a modern state needed good schools and universities. If someone was a major participant in the scientific discussion, his chances of being heard were fairly good. Lagarde believed in the importance of his request and adopted a sincere tone in his petition to the king.[1]

He referred to the support he had already received, as well as his copious London research findings. But due to the burdens of the teaching profession, he had only been able to have them printed, and a systematic analysis of the sources he'd compiled had not been possible. Additionally, he no longer had the "strength to lead a double life, such as I have done until now." His painstaking acquisition of Near Eastern languages and the historico-critical method were only preliminary steps to the real work ahead. With great intensity, Lagarde drove home the point that he was on the brink of fulfilling his scholarly life's work, yet was powerless in the face of adverse circumstances: "I cannot bear the thought that everything I have consistently worked for in a goal-oriented way over twenty years and have gained by relinquishing everything people call the enjoyment of life [. . .] would be of no use to science, simply because I could not find the support that would put me in a position to attain the goal that I am within sight of." Lastly, he put it to the king that he would like to find a reasonable means of implementing his carefully laid plans. Along with an edition of patristic texts, Lagarde promised a "critical edition" of the Septuagint. This was an audacious promise and hardly realistic in light of the profuse amount of source material the task would have required.

Among Lagarde's supporters was Justus Olshausen, himself a noted Orientalist and the acting councilor in the Ministry of Education and Cultural Affairs. Lagarde could not fool him. On April 14, 1865, when the granting of a two-year research period was up for debate, Lagarde expressed himself to Olshausen in a distinctly humble tone. A complete Septuagint edition would be impossible within the existing time frame: "You are able to judge it well enough, so there is no need for me to say another word about it. I will do all I can: I will not reach the goal, however." A single detail reveals that Lagarde had a really good hand to play at this point: he specifically addressed how a replacement for his teaching position could be found without causing any problems for the City of Berlin. Lagarde received the good news on August 19, 1865. He was granted a three-year leave of absence with full pay and the prospect of a professorship.

The official records do not reveal why Lagarde's bold petition met with success, but his project was no doubt given high priority. As great as public interest in a "nontheological investigation of religion" may have been, ideological reasons and Lagarde's high degree of expertise most likely played a role at the center of power. And the Orientalist's conservative political convictions were as indisputable as his religious seriousness. In any case, there was great joy in the Lagarde home. On the day the couple received the news, Anna de Lagarde told her parents that the king's decision meant "the beginning of a new life."[2] Of course, it took some time for the details to be worked out. Lagarde did not say farewell to the teaching profession until Easter 1866. This step was a turning point for the ambitious researcher and was accompanied, among other things, by Rückert's death. The man who had decisively supported Lagarde's interest in Orientalism could no longer share in the success of his difficult star pupil.

Like Rückert before him, Lagarde was drawn away from the Berlin metropolis to the peaceful countryside. He soon moved into a new apartment in the small Thuringian town of Schleusingen, where he could devote himself entirely to the Septuagint project. On June 8, 1866, he told the Jena theologian Adolf Hilgenfeld that his first loyalty was to Wilhelm I. As Lagarde stated solemnly, "I owe my salvation to our king. May he live to see at least one volume of my LXX."[3] Lagarde promptly completed one volume of his *Gesammelte Abhandlungen* (*Collected Essays*) in 1866. They were intended to publicly document the end of his school-teaching years. He dedicated the book to the person who had sent his petition on its way: "To His Excellency, the Royal Prussian General of the Infantry, Herr Doctor Heinrich von Brandt." In the preface, Lagarde spoke downright euphorically about the "matchless good fortune of being able to pursue his work in complete leisure."[4] For the first time in his life, he regretted having conducted many of his scholarly arguments in an overly harsh tone. But Lagarde wouldn't have been Lagarde if this charitable mood had lasted for long. He soon complained about the dreary life of a hermit in provincial Thuringia and stressed the opposition he encountered to his Septuagint edition.

Adjusting to the new situation was harder than Lagarde had anticipated. He had recently taken a cure in the Waldeck spa town of Bad Pyrmont, but his nerves soon failed to cooperate. Even after he received the imperial stipend, Lagarde continued to experience self-doubt. He knew better than anyone that he was under a great deal of pressure with the Septuagint project. While nothing distracted him from his scholarly duties, he was plagued by insomnia and reacted irritably to the slightest disturbance. The cramped conditions of his apartment and the alleged noise of the lumberjacks outside bothered Lagarde. He was particularly incensed about the "constant aggravation from the landlord who lives above me: his persistent noise, his mental and physical filth, and that of his daughter, who is just like him." In addition to his private sensibilities, there were publishing problems. Lagarde's works were difficult to sell, and he had either published them himself or through Brockhaus in Leipzig. But he was dissatisfied with Brockhaus's sales and marketing. Now that he was a scholar with imperial support, he toyed with the idea of switching to Wilhelm Hertz in Berlin, but could not make up his mind. The correspondence with Hertz shows that Lagarde had worked himself into a veritable state of misanthropy.[5]

Lagarde was mostly angered by the fact that many of the important manuscripts he needed for his Septuagint edition had not been sent to Schleusingen. This really should not have surprised him. After all, a half-timbered house posed a fire risk and was certainly not a suitable place to store valuable manuscripts. But this problem escaped his attention when he moved out of Berlin and into the Thuringian provinces. The situation also shed light on Lagarde's extremely fragile sense of self-worth. Until recently, he had seen Wilhelm the Great's decision as a turning point in his life, but he now abandoned himself to dark musings. He did not mince words with Hilgenfeld, to whom he confided on October 21, 1866: "It has been a real disgrace to our guild for a very long time that I am not a professor and don't even have a doctorate in theology." Full of bitterness, he continued: "More and more, I sing the old song of my difficult childhood."[6] Lagarde's critique of the present once again knew no bounds. Even though he suffered from terrible headaches, he commented on his daily vexations in a general way. For example, "cannibalistic tobacco smoking [. . .] always" reminded him "of just how far Germany had declined." In contrast to the Nachmärz world, however, politics were on the move and offered quite a bit of hope to dyed-in-the-wool nationalists like Lagarde.

Bismarck's *Konfliktpolitik* (policy of conflict) stood at the center of the discussion about German unity. The Lagardes also repeatedly questioned the Prussian chancellor's risky course of action. In principle, Lagarde felt no sympathy for the unscrupulous power seeker Bismarck, whose Borussian calculations fit poorly into the ideal of a Greater German Reich. He was nevertheless impressed with how energetically Bismarck went about enacting his plans, coming ever closer to German unity. Lagarde's view of Bismarck vacillated during these years. He hoped that Prussia would be militarily strong but feared its tyranny. In a July 26, 1865, letter to his wife, he bleakly divined: "Bismarck does not have the guiding religious and ethical principles that pertain to being a great statesman. I trust that the prize he will offer France is the annexation of Belgium, whose king must surely die within a short time."[7] Lagarde's tendency to interpret the German unification process as divine providence grew stronger over time. As his theological interpretation of world history increased, his moral reservations about Bismarck's policies decreased in equal measure. Lagarde's evaluation of the Schleswig-Holstein question was characteristic of this attitude. On May 2, 1866, he unequivocally told his father-in-law: "We will only get the duchies if we take more [of them]. Conservative politics are German politics. God means well by us, in that he compels us to act as we are doing now." On May 15, he wrote to his wife in the same vein: "World history is Prussia."

The approval of violence was an integral part of Lagarde's ideology. Because the kingdom had the necessary military power at its disposal, Lagarde had already emphasized Prussia's role in German history in his first political tracts of 1853. Yet his rejection of the Prussian bureaucratic state should also not be underestimated. Lagarde was basically like many others who longed for national unity: he got sucked into Bismarck's policies because they placed unity within reach. A prime example would be Theodor Mommsen, a confirmed left-wing liberal who initially expressed grave reservations about Bismarck. When it came to the conflict with Austria, however, he stood unreservedly on the side of Prussia. On July 18, 1866, the otherwise highly skeptical ancient historian advised his brother Tycho: "It is a wonderful feeling to be present when world history turns a corner. It is no longer simply a hope, but a fact and a heroic one for all time: Germany has a future, and that future will be determined by Prussia."[8] What is more salient in Lagarde's case is that, at the very height of national euphoria, he was still spouting culturally pessimistic remarks. On the occasion of the failed assassination attempt on Bismarck, he wrote to his wife from Bad Pyrmont on May 9, 1866: "I have surely heard fifty notables speak about it, and everywhere the same criminal views shouted openly across the street! We have sunken so low that even assassination is not too base for us." His indignation incited him to this cri de coeur: "One must live among such rotting carrion!"[9] In light of such rigid opinions, it is hardly surprising that Lagarde was taken for a Prussian officer.

Lagarde did not feel at home in Schleusingen either. He could not relate to the townspeople, who were preoccupied with their own concerns and rejected Prussian power politics for the most part. The period in Schleusingen was also much more turbulent than anyone could have anticipated. Bavarian troops needed billeting at first, and subsequent military events kept everyone in suspense. But the victory at Königgrätz on July 3, 1866, was highly gratifying to Lagarde, who felt vindicated in his "belief in his country."[10] He even helped transport the wounded to Dresden in September of that same year. After the military defeat of Austria, Lagarde didn't want to stop at half measures. He longed for war with France so that Germany would be unified under Prussian leadership. He stayed in constant contact with several of his Berlin students who shared his political views. On May 23, 1867, Jakob Vogel wrote him these youthfully animated lines: "Nothing has come of the war. I would hardly concede Alsace-Lorraine to the French, and I think that forbearance is no acquittal." With martial abandon, Hans Wegschneider remarked on October 31: "Perhaps Prussia will speak very soon with 600,000 men on the way."

Two letters to the young Semitist Eduard Sachau characterized Lagarde's own frame of mind. In the first letter, of December 10, 1867, Lagarde gave a derogatory assessment of contemporary university life. Since "so few private persons in Germany [. . .] are truly interested" in it, one could hardly suggest that a young man devote himself to scholarship. With regard to his colleagues, he advised the junior scholar "to develop the conviction early on that at least ninety out of one hundred are rascals or utter scoundrels, and to act accordingly." On December 19, Lagarde's mood had not lifted. He discussed at length why a talented Orientalist had no prospects in Germany. Nonetheless, he flatly remarked that, due to patriotic considerations, immigration was a dubious matter. Lagarde boastfully recalled that he had been offered a theology professorship in North America back in 1846. When one considers that he was only nineteen years old at the time, even a scholarly novice would hardly have been convinced by such a claim. But Lagarde saw it differently: "At such a critical time for the Fatherland," he did not have "the right [. . .] to give his best years to foreign countries." When nationalism was in its prime, these kinds of acknowledgments could be heard everywhere. But Lagarde went a crucial step further when he declared that, "science is not cosmopolitan." With this equally self-evident and casual statement, Lagarde fundamentally challenged the universalist orientation of human perception.[11]

The argumentative Orientalist seems to have had enough of the classical system in which knowledge was organized (*Wissensordnung*), widely accepted in Germany since the days of Kant. He stressed unequivocally that "Jacob Grimm was only possible in Germany, Newton only in England." He wrote in the album of a young colleague that he hoped he would develop "into a *German* man of letters." When one considers how international the tiny community of Orientalists was and how often Lagarde had gotten help in foreign libraries, these judgments were truly drastic. They suggest that he now considered the German nation the ultimate value (*Letztwert*) and was furthermore convinced of the supremacy of German culture. His apparently robust statements may possibly contain an additional compensatory element. From the perspective of his Septuagint research, his stay in Thuringia had not gone very well thus far. Lagarde was unable to live without scholarly work and, since he lacked access to important manuscripts, he leapt at an abundance of other projects. These disparate undertakings would soon divert him from his actual duties.

First of all, Lagarde wrote a family history in Schleusingen and dedicated it to his brother Hans on his wedding day in 1867. The scholar was filled with great pride, for Hans had served as a captain in the "war of reconciliation" and been honorably wounded in the process. The well-documented work was rich in material and bore the modest title *Nachrichten über einige Familien des Namens Bötticher* (*Information about Several Families Named Bötticher*). The content actually amounted to more than a mere genealogy, offering many historic excursions and personal commentaries. Lagarde presented his father as a man with a short fuse who never really learned to control his temper. It also included clear value judgments about Jews, who had been disagreeable to the Germans since time immemorial. This was also true of Jews' given names, which had only gained a certain currency because of scholastic theology.[12] Lagarde's *Beiträge zur baktrischen Lexikographie* (*Articles on Bactrian Lexicography*), published in 1867, exhibited extraordinary linguistic skills. But the world of the Upper Oxus River in Central Asia really had nothing to do with the Septuagint project.[13]

Even his *Materialien zur Kritik und Geschichte des Pentateuchs* (*Materials on the Critique and History of the Pentateuch*), published in 1867, was not exclusively devoted to the Greek versions of the Old Testament. But it did involve an ambitious scholarly task whose thematic commonalities with the Septuagint edition were apparent. In Lagarde's opinion, "early Christian history" had taken place in the countries east of the River Jordan, and that was where the "birthplace of the church" was to be found.[14] He also reiterated his thesis that, in the second century A.D., a single version of the Old Testament must have existed. This belief placed Lagarde in a minority position, yet he was not alone among theologians. Still, his archetype theory that an authoritative codex of the Old Testament existed around 130 A.D. has proven too simplistic. His source-critical position toward the Pentateuch was more seminal, although he had little regard for its Mosaic content.

Because it was linked to the reasonable prospect of a professorship, the imperial grant definitively increased Lagarde's scientific and political ambitions. Still lacking power of his own, he sought allies to enlist in his impending professional conflicts. On July 15, 1866, he swore his friend Hilgenfeld to an intergenerational battle in the field of Orientalism, but carefully avoided naming names: "Science is now in the hands of young men who, at all events, had to stick together in opposition to the leaders of the thirties and forties, who frequently and unjustifiably had all the say," he stated, remaining vague in terms of information and emotional content.[15] Lagarde also did not lose sight of the need to maintain ministerial support. In his letters to the minister of education and cultural affairs, Heinrich von Mühler, he repeatedly stressed the difficulty of his work on the Septuagint. A particularly impressive letter of March 31, 1868, reported on the status of his research. Time considerations had caused him to focus on the Pentateuch, but it had been impossible to analyze all the relevant manuscripts. Moreover, there was no way he could continue to work at this tempo: "The result would not be an edition of LXX. I would be admitted to an insane asylum instead or, at the very least, to an institute for the blind." Lagarde certainly knew that, in order to legitimize his research project, he had to produce genuine results. He published an edition of the Greek version of the Book of Genesis in the spring of 1868. The question he faced in *Genesis graece* was which manuscripts could form the basis for improving the Oxford edition by Holmes and Parsons.[16] But it was a first step toward Lagarde's Septuagint edition, and the academic world he so often reviled reacted immediately.

On August 1, 1868, the Old Testament scholar Eduard Riehm confidentially told Lagarde that the Theology Faculty in Halle would like to award him a doctorate. They had entertained the idea for a long time and, now that the Genesis text had come out, a welcome opportunity was at hand. This was a special tribute and a high honor for Lagarde, who began his academic career in Halle and had primarily thought of himself as a theologian for many years. On the one hand, the Orientalist's endeavors on behalf of God's teachings were considered historical scholarship; on the other hand, he had always placed high value on his interpretive expertise in the field of theology. Once again, he saw the state of theology as an indication of a nation's religious stance. He wrote to the Prussian Ministry of Education and Cultural Affairs on September 2, 1866, with these notions in mind: "The Fatherland depends on theology, because it needs religion as much as man needs air to breathe. A poor state of theology always proves that religiosity is nonexistent or unwell." On August 2, 1868, Lagarde sent his reply to Halle. He candidly disclosed that he had "long wished for a theological mortarboard" but also believed that he "had earned it" through long years of scholarly activity. The feeling now crept over him, however, that he was perhaps unworthy of the award. He lightheartedly pointed out that his Genesis edition was only "the work of a handyman and errand boy." But his biblical motto—the steward must be true to God's mysteries—would ultimately permit him to accept the award.[17]

Riehm, a tenured professor since 1866, took care of the rest. He had been among the first to hear Lagarde's lectures. On September 21, 1868, Lagarde was ceremoniously presented with a doctoral diploma.[18] His carefully formulated thank-you letter of October 14 shows just how much this honor meant to him. In it, he expressed the conviction that he would have gladly worked at Halle as a theologian and that the surrender of his teaching position had once been "especially painful." He promised to apply himself fully in the service of theology, and closed with the assurance that the honor bestowed on him "had been and would remain a comfort and encouragement in my less-than-joyful life, which is often replete with battles with Satanic powers masquerading as figures of Light." The solemn phrasing was not without a tinge of bitterness. From an outside perspective, however, there was hardly any doubt that Lagarde's appointment to a professorship was imminent. A glance at his correspondence with the Prussian Ministry of Education and Cultural Affairs shows how energetically he pushed ahead with getting established.

Thanks to imperial backing, the Septuagint edition had become a prestigious venture. Lagarde knew that he was irreplaceable and did not shrink from the limelight. On March 26, 1867, he asked Minister Mühler for a professorship so that he would be able to concentrate entirely on his research. On May 27, 1867, he presented the principles of his Septuagint edition to his mentor, Olshausen. Lagarde had decided in favor of a maximalist approach. All later versions would be replicated in the text, since "all versions" were nothing more than "new renderings." He commented disparagingly on the achievements of Jewish scholars, whose "truly frightful and unholy noncriticism" had already done considerable damage. As a concession, he offered praise and gratitude to the ancient Masoretes for their meticulous handing down of the Old Testament. Lagarde generally expected his Septuagint studies to give "insight into the historical development of Judaism, both before and after Jesus." He combined his methodical explanations with an urgent request for a professorship and even submitted a concrete suggestion: "I would like nothing better than to go to Göttingen, since [. . .] the character of the people in Lower Saxony is most agreeable to me and the big library in Göttingen offers so many advantages." He commented immodestly on his own list of publications: "These are the carefully constructed works of a handyman. But, then again, what have Prussian Orientalists achieved?" And with muted resentment, he pointed to younger scholars in his field who had already gotten a chance.

On March 31, 1868, Lagarde let the Prussian minister of education and cultural affairs know that it would be "a point of honor" for him "to be in a post from which I was excluded on insufficient grounds in the spring of 1854." If one considers how very important "honor" was to nineteenth-century bourgeois culture, then this statement well-nigh amounted to a demand. No academician who cared about his reputation would ever compromise in matters of honor, and Lagarde's conservative convictions and admiration for the military made him particularly sensitive in this regard.[19] At the same time, he had a marked sense of practicality. Without observing any of the usual courtesies, he brought forward how important it was for the ministry to "support" his "productivity" over the long haul.

And it finally came down to that: on February 27, 1869, the Prussian king appointed Lagarde as a tenured professor of Orientalism at the University of Göttingen. The salary of 1,200 talers turned out to be rather modest. But the chair was all the more prestigious because it had belonged to Heinrich Ewald, who had been dismissed for political reasons after the annexation of Hanover. The confident "Guelph" had refused to swear an oath of allegiance to the Prussian king in 1867. The designation of the chair turned out to be matter-of-fact: "to fill the existing opening created by the absence of lectures given by the former professor, Dr. Ewald, for courses taught at the university."[20] Naturally, this formal wording could not conceal the controversial nature of Lagarde's appointment. Because the opinion of the Göttingen faculty had not even been solicited, it is actually possible to allege that it was imposed on them. As a consequence, the reactions were emotional and politicized.

Ewald had acquired many a cranky idea in his old age and consciously ratcheted up the conflict with the Prussian king, but his supporters were in the minority. On May 26, 1868, the Munich Sanskrit scholar Martin Haug gingerly advised Ewald that a change of location might be in order. After all, from what one heard, his successor had already been found. He also added sympathetically: "Any honest and honorable person can only regret the way in which you have been treated."[21] The Ethiopia expert August Dillmann still sent his letters from Tübingen to "Göttingen/Hanover" in 1872. He thereby emphasized his sympathy for the Guelph contingent, which prompted an armor-clad statement from Lagarde. Lagarde's heretofore friendly contact with Dillmann did not survive this political difference of opinion. But most scholars sided with the Prussians and found Lagarde's appointment entirely in order.

The Bonn theologian Adolf Kamphausen expressed firm approval. In his letter of July 20, 1869, he stressed the importance of the Septuagint project, which Lagarde "had furthered [. . .]" already through considerable "preliminary work." Kamphausen had once worked as Bunsen's private secretary. Although he had never come into close contact with Lagarde until now, he added flatteringly: "You must surely have more silent admirers already than it has been possible to acknowledge publicly." Among the first to congratulate Lagarde on April 1 was Abraham Berliner, the head of the Gesellschaft für Talmudstudium (Society for Talmudic Studies) in Berlin. He pointed out that Lagarde truly deserved the professorship, because he was among the few Christian scholars who dealt intensively with Jewish sources. Berliner closed his appreciative comments with the wish "May God bless you in your noble task." In Halle, Eduard Riehm reacted euphorically, writing to Lagarde on August 21: "It has been a long time since I have greeted an appointment with as much joy and satisfaction as I have yours. Not only your own wishes, but those of many others, have been fulfilled. This is the final dispensation that you [. . .] have deserved for so long." He wished Lagarde a fresh new beginning in Göttingen and a most harmonious relationship with his colleagues. Of course, his letter also intimated problems had already arisen. Good relations with Ewald could not be achieved for long, so it was fortunate that "his strangely brusque behavior has made for conflict from the outset."

And the conflict was actually sparked by a clash between Lagarde and Ewald during the initial visit. The pugnacious Guelph factionalist threw Lagarde out of his apartment for not expressing outrage over his dismissal. Many Göttingen scholars shared Ewald's opinion, so they gave his successor a frosty reception. Lagarde certainly also spoke frankly and strongly emphasized his nationalist beliefs. He even plotted against his new colleagues behind their backs. On July 18, 1870, for example, he told Olshausen "confidentially" that there was no reliable candidate for the Göttingen prorectorate. He expressed this view in conspiratorial language: "Whether secretly or openly, the upper and especially the lower ranks here are nearly all traitors. That's why the king can only use officials who are the most trustworthy of men." This claim was surely an exaggeration, but it vividly illustrates the degree to which Lagarde was seized by a sense of mission. No matter how much he emphasized nationalism, he never lost sight of his own interests. And his conflict with Ewald did not simply result from differing political views, not by a long shot: Lagarde intentionally used the opportunity to harm Ewald's reputation and to increase his own options as a newly tenured professor in the process.

Lagarde immediately informed other Orientalists that Ewald had greatly mistreated him, or so he alleged. In his characteristically volatile style, he wrote to the eminent Arabist Theodor Nöldeke on March 15, 1869: "I have been received in a most friendly manner. Only Ewald was horribly rude [. . .] and, needless to say, I responded."[22] Lagarde even pulled the rug out from under his predecessor. In 1872, an inquiry from Cambridge professor William R. Smith presented a welcome opportunity to shed light on the power structure. Smith wanted to know whether Arabic could be studied on a very private basis in Göttingen and whether "Ewald still worked there." On January 20, Lagarde told Felix Klein, the dean of the Philosophy Faculty, that he was prepared to give private instruction, but Smith had to make a clear choice "between Ewald and me." As justification, he cited differences in their scholarly positions and emphasized how "loutishly" Ewald had behaved. It was therefore impossible "to let someone visit my home, who also goes in and out of Ewald's." The dean informed Smith of Lagarde's uncompromising position, and the English scholar decided to take instruction with the new tenured professor.

Even when Ewald lay dying, Lagarde did not tone down his rhetoric. On January 30, 1875, he wrote these merciless sentences to the Leipzig Orientalist Heinrich Fleischer: "Ewald is suffering from heart trouble and, as a consequence, now has edema. They expect him to die. In his day, he used me for his—intrinsically worthless—review. Since Easter 1869, he has harmed me as much as he possibly could. The scholarly world will soon forget him." One can only speculate over the persistence of Lagarde's ungrateful and disrespectful behavior. Lagarde rarely disclosed his real motives in his letters, and he did not keep a diary. The intellectually volatile and self-aggrandizing Ewald was certainly not easy to deal with. And Lagarde was personally indebted to him, which would have made contact more difficult for a scholar like himself, who always had honor in mind. In terms of demonizing their opponents, both mavericks were certainly a match for each other. But Lagarde's harsh rejection of his predecessor was more than psychological: it offered him the chance to show the Prussian government that he loved the Fatherland and gave him the space to make a fresh start academically. Many young Orientalists considered Ewald a cantankerous and unique genius whose time had long since passed. The young Julius Wellhausen wrote a dismal sentence from the Book of Genesis on a photo of Ewald. It is about Abraham's outcast son, Ishmael, and says: "his hand against every man and every man's hand against him."[23] Lagarde wanted to be seen as part of the young generation of Orientalists who replaced daring speculation with the scientific method. He consistently emphasized how systematic his own course of action was in comparison with Ewald's associative publications.

One should not overestimate the importance of professorial traditions in the history of scholarship. Even if ideas of reliable continuity dominated university rhetoric, loyalty and gratitude were usually no more common at institutions of higher learning (*Hochschulen*) than at other institutions. Most professors did remain loyally devoted to their predecessors for their entire lives. But fierce conflicts that could be used for self-dramatization, political positioning, or new beginnings were in no way unusual in the history of scholarship. Lagarde seized the opportunity, at any rate, and did his best to spirit away any recollection of the long-standing support he had received from Ewald. Moreover, he commented on his predecessor in such a pejorative way as to approach *damnatio memoriae.*

Ewald's death also had no effect on Lagarde's attitude. In his correspondence, he undauntedly belittled the reputation of the man who preceded him in his chair, a man who had been celebrated for his political stance in the Vormärz period and was once considered among the greatest in his field. In his letter of January 14, 1876, to the Strasbourg bookseller Karl Trübner, he refused to do anything to help with the sale of Ewald's library. In reference to Ewald's rejection of the Prussian king, Lagarde described him as an "old cretin" whom only his wife still adored. On July 7, 1878, Theodor Nöldeke let Lagarde know that Ewald, along with another Göttingen professor, Heinrich Karl Brugsch, had defamed him as an "uncouth ignoramus." And on December 23, 1882, he complained to the Oxford religious historian Max Müller about Ewald's "proverbial disorderliness," which had rendered his legacy practically worthless. Even Lagarde's opinions of Ewald that appeared in print were rather drastic. Lagarde commented disparagingly on his style: "To me, even Ewald's German is dreadful. The little that is witty in Ewald's books swims in such a sea of nothingness that I have never been able to read more than a few pages of any of them. And I have never read a single one in its entirety."[24] But Lagarde also used the vilification of his predecessor for purposes of generating and establishing an intergenerational, historical memory.

He affectionately contrasted the "hubristic Ewald" with the "modest Rückert," who had always been interested in purely scientific problems. As early as 1844, Rückert had allegedly mocked Ewald's "despicable posturing in the bitterest terms," a charge that, in light of Rückert's admirably reserved manner, was not very probable. Rückert would more likely have shunned Lagarde's unkind words about the "loud, hysterical" Ewald.[25] Shortly before his own death, Lagarde greatly distanced himself from Ewald's "German chauvinism." In his view, the "daunting influence [. . .] that supposedly fundamental yet opaque signifiers like *Daseynswort*, *Begriffswort*, *Dingwort*, *Selbstwort*, *Standwort*, *Nennwort*, *Sachwort* must have exerted on every healthy mind" was unmistakable.[26] One would be hard-pressed to find Lagarde's critique entirely unfounded, although it was not without piquancy. After all, Lagarde expended a lot of energy on the cultural roots of Germanness, and when it came to patriotism, he did not like to be outdone.

During the Franco-Prussian War of 1870–1871, Lagarde followed political and military events with great interest. He kept in touch with various Berlin students, who in turn told him of their experiences at the front. His wife's brothers' service on the Prussian general staff filled him with pride. He was excited about student patriotism in Göttingen, which in his estimation "seven eighths" of young people were caught up in. He was equally excited about the upbeat mood in the country and traced it back to the unified stereotype of the French enemy.[27]

As German weaponry proved successful, Lagarde's political ambition came alive. On August 20, 1870, he published an article in the *Magdeburger Zeitung* in which he called for the annexation of Luxembourg: "After the untold sacrifices the German people have made and still must make in this war, they are fully entitled to lay claim to their outstanding property. A plague on those who would hinder the German people therein!"[28] Lagarde thought the German name Lützelburg seemed appropriate for the new imperial lands, whose integration would be facilitated by the founding of a university. He published his article anonymously because he thought it "tactless [. . .] for people with French names (from Lorraine) to have an *independent* say in German affairs before Lorraine had become German again."[29] Lagarde was not the only one to have these kinds of views. In France, his friend Ernest Renan pled in favor of the annexation of Luxembourg, which Napoleon III had sought as the price for tolerating Prussian policy. In his famous open letter of September 13, 1870, to David Friedrich Strauss, Renan classified the annexation of Luxembourg as a "minor concession" that would not harm Germany.[30] Theodor Mommsen in turn demanded the forcible annexation of conquered territories, because the people of Alsace-Lorraine were not part of the "German race."[31] One should nonetheless draw careful conclusions about the political views of boastful, crowing scholars. There was widespread fear that a triumphal victory would encumber future peace. With an eye to the present, Mommsen recalled that, ever since the Battle of the Teutoburg Forest in 9 A.D., retreat had not defamed the Germans. At the same time, his Göttingen colleague indulged in more intrepid historical visions.

Lagarde's political white hope was the king of Bavaria. On September 4, 1870, just three days after the Battle of Sedan, which practically decided the war in Germany's favor, he sent an urgent appeal to Ludwig II. Since Bismarck lacked a sense of nationalism, Lagarde personally urged him to work toward the annexation of Luxembourg.[32] He pointed out that his family origins were in Metz, which enabled him to understand the suffering of "Luxembourgers who identified with Germany." He emphasized Luxembourg's essentially German character by referring to the crusader Gottfried von Bouillon, who had once fought for Henry IV. The historical basis of Lagarde's argument essentially boils down to an apotheosis of power. He implored Ludwig II to "seize" this great opportunity "with both hands" and trust in the future: "Like people everywhere, the vast majority in Luxembourg are followers. Once the leaders there come to believe that we are thinking of them and value them, the people will want to be German." He expressly thanked the Bavarian king for demanding the unification of north and south Germany, which had "given the entire war its character." The anticapitalist and antisemitic notes in Lagarde's letter were of secondary importance at this historic juncture. Nevertheless, his suggestive formulations show that he was emotionally involved. Lagarde warned the German people about the "evil" of succumbing to pure greed and "selling their German souls to the Devil." He contemptuously attributed Reichstag president Eduard von Simson's antagonistic position toward annexation to his Jewishness, and an accusatory note of "Jewish cowardice" vibrated along with it. His budding nationalistic dreams actually only came true in part. The annexation of Alsace-Lorraine put an enormous strain on Franco-German relations. Luxembourg remained independent, and Lagarde saw this as a loss for the "kingdom of God."[33]

In addition to his nationalistic visions, Lagarde was caught up in sheer scholarly ambition during the war with France. As far back as 1866, he was angry that he did not get the requisite Parisian manuscripts for his Septuagint edition. For this reason, he intervened at the Prussian Ministry of Education and Cultural Affairs. So as to obtain the valuable manuscripts, he even appealed twice to the French Emperor Napoleon III and reminded him of his friendship with Renan. Now Lagarde falsely assumed that his time had come. On September 10, 1870, he asked Minister Mühler "for permission to take all of the manuscripts that I need for my Septuagint edition out of the French National Library in Paris for an indefinite period with the Prussian state as guarantor." His request included five hundred manuscripts that would be stored "in the university library in Göttingen" for his "unrestricted use over approximately fifteen years." He impatiently proposed that he "set out for Paris immediately with the go-ahead and suitable accommodations." He received no response. The Prussian Ministry of Education and Cultural Affairs must have had better things to do in those eventful days than respond to the wishes of an inordinately ambitious Orientalist.

All the same, one must not forget that the Septuagint project was a matter of prestige for the Prussian state. In addition, Lagarde had promised to contribute to the sense of national meaning by providing a scientifically sound basis for theology. Very few scholars seriously doubted that God had given the victory to German weapons in advance of Sedan. Lagarde's request for the ministry to reserve the essential French manuscripts for him on a long-term basis was ultimately a sign of nationalistic ardor and sound realism. With exclusive access to the crucial originals, any competing interests could easily be put in their place. The freshly appointed professor wanted to seize the opportunity to do research. His excessive desire for recognition is reflected in a letter of January 2, 1871, to Adolf Hilgenfeld. The letter called for Paris to be razed to the ground. In the interest of science, however, the Bibliothèque Impériale should be spared from attack.[34]

Lagarde had gone out on a limb by committing himself to Prussian nationalism. For this reason, it must have affected him all the more deeply when he was personally accused of being unpatriotic. Letters of a flattering or pleading nature written by Germans to Napoleon III were found in the Tuileries in 1871. Henri Bordier immediately published a selected edition that was intended to illustrate the obsequious attitude of German scholars.[35] The *Deutsche Allgemeine Zeitung* (DAZ) was the first to react to the news by publishing a distinctly malicious article. The article directly quoted Lagarde, who asked for permission to wear the "insignia of the *Légion d'honneur*" because he was a relative of the Corsican king.[36] His letter finished off with the subservient apostrophe: "Your majesty understands what it means to have a famous relative." The DAZ article's purported intention was to strengthen patriotic morale by educating the public, but this was little more than a pretext for carrying out targeted disclosure. The journalist, who remained anonymous, called the person under attack "unprincipled and servile" and entirely discounted the fact that Napoleon III had quite recently been a recognized figure in European politics. He proclaimed "a court of remorseless public opinion" that would lead the way to a new era. The article was directed at academics who had been especially vocal in their nationalism in recent months. Besides Lagarde, Theodor Mommsen was also a target. Of course, Mommsen had more flair in handling public controversy than Lagarde and treated such accusations with contempt.

But Lagarde's response to the exposure was extremely thin-skinned. Shaken to the core, he even contemplated immigrating to England. On April 14, 1872, he contacted Friedrich Zabel, the editor-in-chief of the *National-Zeitung*, about whether a correspondent's post was open in London. He also pointed out that an untimely article involving him had come out. He admittedly "hated the name Bötticher today, just as he had twenty-five years ago." But he would like "to protect it from dishonor [. . .] for the sake of his half-brother." Lagarde did not bring up any political or ideological reservations he may have had about the liberal paper. He briefly mentioned content-related differences and simply added: "In reporting the facts," the only thing that matters is "for the reporter to be accurate." This approach was conscious on his part and intentionally covered up the crisis mood in the Lagarde home. A letter of April 12, 1872, from Anna de Lagarde to her sister, Hedwig Böhmer, clearly shows the prevailing shock and commotion within the family. She stressed that Lagarde's peculiar request from 1851 had been a youthful indiscretion, which should make it easier for him to be accepted into the diplomatic service. She referred with great pathos to the fact that "by dint of the most selfless, self-sacrificing hard work," her husband had "grown old before his time."[37] Anna de Lagarde felt that the scandal was entirely unfounded and unjust, and it even affected her religious views. With bitter disappointment, she told her sister that she "was not presently able to see the hand of Providence [. . .]" in the course of events. Her husband submitted his letter of resignation, combined with a plea on his behalf, to the Prussian minister of education and cultural affairs that same day.

Lagarde took a strong stand against the accusation that he lacked patriotic conviction. He believed at the time that he had a claim to the Order, but far be it from him to engage in any type of "servility."[38] His life of service to scholarship was proof of his independent disposition. His students, who numbered "in the hundreds," could certify that he had never failed to be patriotic. "A lesson in *Weltverachtung*" (pious rejection of worldly things) would be unnecessary, because he had long since gotten over the romantic perceptions of his youth. Although he had a clear conscience, his resignation was unavoidable, because this was the only way he could make "amends" to the University of Göttingen. To underscore the seriousness of his intentions, he pointed out that he would sell his newly built home. He closed with the following: "The proceeds will ensure that I won't have to work so awfully hard for my bread."

The resignation touched off an immediate frenzy of activity in Berlin.[39] Lagarde's ally Justus Olshausen made every effort to dissuade the valued researcher from his plans. Lagarde's resignation would have done lasting damage to the Septuagint undertaking. As a scholar and Orientalist, Olshausen was genuinely interested in the project. Since he knew how testy Lagarde could be, he approached him carefully. On April 17, 1872, he merely sent a letter to Göttingen and said it would not occur to him to accuse Lagarde of "servility or a lack of patriotic conviction." Fully aware that Lagarde's moods oscillated rather quickly between euphoria, tearful sentimentality, and the blackest doubt, he closed with these words: "By all means hold your head high, as in the past when times were bad!" Just two days later, Olshausen was able to report that the new minister of education and cultural affairs, Adalbert Falk, would do all he could to persuade Lagarde to withdraw his resignation. Falk, a left-wing liberal, had no reservations concerning the archconservative Lagarde. He gave Adolph von Warnstedt, the university trustee in Göttingen, full authority to retain Lagarde at Georgia Augusta University (as the University of Göttingen was also known). In light of Lagarde's "firmness of character," Falk anticipated that it would take considerable effort to convince him, but his fears turned out to be unfounded. Warnstedt was able to smooth the waters in a private conversation with Lagarde, as the trustee reported in his letter of April 20 to the Ministry of Education and Cultural Affairs. Warnstedt noted matter-of-factly: "It was easy to persuade him to stay."[40] But what else could the Orientalist have done? The faculty and university administration stood behind him, and the ministry showed unequivocal support for his research. Help from official sources certainly did not mean that he could easily come to terms with the public scandal. Lagarde tended to remember traumatic experiences for a long time, and that would certainly be the case here.

He withdrew his resignation on April 25, 1872. As his official letter to the Ministry of Education and Cultural Affairs shows, Lagarde was deeply affected by the matter. He brought up his desire not to tarnish the honor of the Göttingen municipal authorities by wrongfully resigning. He expressly stated that his colleagues were convinced of the rightfulness of his conduct and did not fear any "damage to the university." In addition, the generous state support he had received obligated him to complete the proposed project. He phrased everything in a somewhat artificial way, but the tone was almost conciliatory. Even so, Lagarde closed his letter to the ministry with bitter words: "I will never get over this incident. But perhaps my work will gradually enable me to calm down a little, since work is the only ethically permissible narcotic that I have known and used for many years." Lagarde struck an even darker tone in the letter he sent just one day later to his trusted friend Olshausen: he believed that "twenty years of the most serious life and work" had been "obliterated by half a line of newsprint." Lagarde recalled the 1870 suicide of the highly gifted document researcher Philipp Jaffe: the disapproval of his colleagues in the wake of a widely circulated rumor had driven him over the edge. For a devout person like Lagarde, suicide was not an option. But he saw "a difficult and dismal life" before him.[41]

He had just been appointed to the professorship he had longed for, yet he saw his life in tatters. This seems typically melodramatic, but one should not view his response to the scandal as a mere idiosyncrasy that merits the ridicule of future generations. From early childhood on, Lagarde was a psychologically unstable and vulnerable person who longed for the recognition of his contemporaries to an unusual degree. He also developed an ideology early in life that allowed him to confront the world as a victim and persecutor alike. This mindset developed a dynamic of its own, such that he increasingly experienced the present as alien. A letter of August 8, 1871, to his wife illustrates how his views had already come full circle and were resistant to any sort of criticism.[42] Lagarde saw "three old Hessian peasant women" at the train station in Kassel. "Tanned and wrinkled from sorrow and work," they looked to him like the very embodiment of "misery and pain." Without speaking to them, he concluded they were "on an exodus from this new Germany," which was liberal and powerful but nevertheless "entirely un-German." Lagarde concluded his free associations with the aphorism "We pray to foreign gods: that is our misfortune." He would stick to this dark point of view until the day he died.

6 A House Like a Fortress

Göttingen has often been extolled as a city of science and learning. Ever since its founding in 1737, Georgia Augusta University has been considered a modern institution. Generously endowed and furnished with a fantastic library, it has attracted scholars and students from all over Europe. Ulrich von Wilamowitz-Moellendorf was full of praise for Georgia Augusta, and universities in small towns like Greifswald did not escape his ridicule. He gushed in his memoirs: "A professor who comes to Göttingen is prepared to stay." Professors who were appointed after the annexation of Hanover must surely have had to adapt to the defensiveness of the populace. When the Egyptologist Heinrich Brugsch bought a house in the inner city, neighbors spread yellowish-white sand in front of his door. The colors were a reminder of continued loyalty to the Kingdom of Hanover, which had perished in 1866. Most of the dismayed scholars responded by criticizing the backwardness of Göttingen residents from their ivory towers. Brugsch, for example, condescendingly emphasized that landlords on the Leine River were solely interested in renting to "an affluent scholar in front, facing the street" and "a horribly stinking swine in the rear courtyard."[1]

Paul de Lagarde also suffered from the reticence of the populace and derided their ostensibly backwoods attitude. But he basically knew that he had done well with his appointment. There was a great Orientalist tradition in Göttingen, and the library was outstanding for his scholarly purposes. Precisely for these reasons, he had pressed the Prussian Ministry of Education and Cultural Affairs for an assignment in Göttingen. As was fitting, he built a home soon after his arrival so as to underscore his intention to stay. He did not have to struggle financially, because the inheritance from his great-aunt Ernestine de Lagarde was sufficient to provide him with a spacious property. The freshly appointed professor opted for a massive stone structure. It was situated above the city on Friedländer Weg and completely tailored to his needs.

Lagarde's house was primarily dedicated to research and provided space for his colossal library of more than three thousand volumes. Like many scholars in the period of the German Empire, he preferred to work within his own four walls and owned practically all the important works in his field. Unsociability was not the only reason behind this practice, for he was firmly convinced that a professor had to form independent judgments about scholarly problems. With this in mind, he once phrased it incontrovertibly: "There can be no scholarliness apart from those who always have their own books on hand at home."[2] To spare his back, Lagarde worked mainly at a stand-up desk. But he often sat in a saddle while engaged in scholarly study, a habit adopted by Wilhelm II himself, bizarre as this may seem today. Surely there must have been more behind the preference for saddles than a penchant for extravagance. The unusual seating arrangement presumably signified respect for the aristocratic lifestyle that, ironically, was widespread at the culmination of bourgeois Romanticism.

To most outsiders, the strictly functional way in which Lagarde's house was furnished felt anything but hospitable. It even seemed to Ludwig Schemann as "if someone were being led through the rooms of a deceased person while he was still alive."[3] And Schemann was among Lagarde's most devoted followers! The residence was decorated with steel engravings. These were portraits of people to whom Lagarde felt a special connection, including Jean Paul, Fichte, Rückert, and Jacob Grimm. The small bedroom was rather more personal. Three pictures hung over Lagarde's bed that hinted at the important role of women in his life. They were: "a picture of his great-grandmother, a picture of his adoptive mother, and a picture that his real mother loved." At first glance, this choice seems to conflict with Lagarde's self-styling as an emphatically masculine scholar and critic of his times. Upon closer inspection, however, much of the contradictory nature fades away. Lagarde developed close attachments to the women in his family who were sympathetic toward him when he was a little boy. And the mother who died when he was born became the antithesis of his father's world, which he experienced as brutal and bigoted. His extremely close relationship with his wife was also not exceptional in any way. In fact, there was an abundance of carefully balanced marriages within the male-dominated academic culture of the German Empire period. Among the most important wifely duties was the thoughtful support of her husband, who concentrated entirely on his scholarly work and its public presentation. The renovation of the couple's home at the end of the 1880s illustrates how close Lagarde felt to his wife. The man of the house not only set up his study so that there was room for four standing desks on which he could examine various manuscripts; he also had a "speaking tube" installed so that he could converse with his wife at any time.[4]

Lagarde hated to perform meticulous scholarly tasks in the restless atmosphere of public libraries. And that is why his stone home with a minimal risk of fire was supposed to facilitate the storage of manuscripts from other parts of the country and abroad. Since these were valuable originals, however, repeated confrontations between Lagarde and the responsible librarians came up. Because he insisted on working within his home, Lagarde pulled out all the stops in his broad correspondence on this topic. He emphasized the prestige of the Septuagint edition; he flattered himself and ranted, and often overstepped the bounds of propriety in the process. On March 6, 1876, he threatened to return manuscripts to the Bodleian Library at Oxford if he only had permission to read them in the Göttingen Library. Lagarde was absolutely up in arms when Lieber, the head librarian in Basel, insisted that he must not study the codex he had requested at home. Lagarde called in his friend, the theologian Rudolf Smend, and Smend promised to persuade the librarian to change his mind. But even Smend's efforts came to naught. The Old Testament scholar lacked the requisite forcefulness to press home Lagarde's wishes.[5]

In the summer of 1880, a fire in Mommsen's villa destroyed not only the historian's library but two old manuscripts as well. Domestic and foreign donations helped the famous scholar recoup his losses, but libraries had no more patience with eccentric researchers.[6] More and more institutions refused to send their manuscripts on dubious journeys, no matter how well known the recipient may have been. Lagarde had been generously allowed to receive valuable, one-of-a-kind documents for almost a decade, but he now received more and more negative responses. The tireless Orientalist read this as a decisive impediment to his Septuagint project and would blame Mommsen personally for his difficulties for the rest of his life. It is also noteworthy that Lagarde never reconsidered his position: for instance, he could have requested that a reading room be set up in the Göttingen Library for the supervised study of manuscripts from outside sources. But he undauntedly demanded instead that they be loaned for use in his solid-stone house with the notation "Göttingen conditions." Over time, his correspondence with the librarians in charge took on the nature of an open conflict. Regardless of his professional stature and state patronage, the researcher did not have the upper hand in these clashes. Still, one should not paint too grim a picture of Lagarde's professional world, not even after the fire in Mommsen's library. The solitary philologist did not shy away from speaking frankly in public debates. He also had scholarly admirers, and many librarians did their best to accommodate Lagarde's requests. A good example would be a letter of November 26, 1884, from Laubmann, the director of the library in Munich. The top official of the Royal Court and State Library not only sent the eagerly awaited manuscript posthaste; he also stressed that he "had always revered [Lagarde's] accomplishments" and promised to support his research to the best of his ability. Lagarde's demands were so high, however, that even the most well-intentioned officials had a hard time solving all the world's problems, so to speak.

Lagarde mainly used the freedom of professorial life to cultivate habits he'd grown fond of, rather than to form new professional associations. His misanthropic traits became increasingly entrenched. Rarely did he invite guests to his home, and he did not even feel safe there. He feared that his conservative views would surely arouse open hatred in predominantly liberal Göttingen. And he must have felt vindicated in 1876 when two shots with live ammunition were fired into his bedroom on Pentecost. He immediately complained to the police authority that it did not understand how to control the "liberal riffraff which, unchallenged, smashes the lantern across from my house nearly every week." If the situation did not improve, he announced, he "would ruthlessly make use of a weapon himself" and "enter into the Kulturkampf on his own." This was certainly masculine posturing, as well as a bizarre interpretation of events. The Kulturkampf, a state campaign launched by Bismarck during the 1870s and 1880s, was directed against Catholics and not against politically liberal trendsetters. But Lagarde was serious and warned the police authority one year later that it should make certain "the people's Christian festival celebrations did not take the form of pistol shots and rocks that threaten and harm the lives and property of peaceful citizens."[7]

Lagarde was a person who loved to complain, and his wrath was mostly directed at everyday occurrences. In 1879, he wrote an angry article for the *Göttinger Zeitung* that was directed against making music with the windows open. The noise-sensitive scholar saw it as an objectionable form of "modern educational barbarity," and urged "the authorities" to impose fines to protect him from it.[8] Lagarde readily pointed to the common good in justifying his grievances. On October 20, 1880, he asked the police to make salon music off-limits to a Jewish family. "Religious services and confirmation classes," the nervous scholar emphasized, "are most unpleasantly disturbed by clattering and rattling noises." On June 28, 1882, Lagarde asked the adjunct professor of history Ernst Bernheim to act jointly with him against "inconsiderate piano playing" in the neighborhood. He emphatically swore solidarity with all "hardworking people," who didn't happen to live outside of town, against the "scourge" of uninhibited music making. The fact that he avoided festive occasions whenever possible was symptomatic of Lagarde's increasing rigidity. Neither his colleagues nor his students were able to win him over when it came to most lighthearted celebrations. On March 25, 1887, he explicitly summed up why he couldn't come to young Julius Oppenheimer's wedding: "Anyone as rightfully involved in the past and future as I am in my life must stay away from the present, particularly from the marriage circle which, in terms of the present, is happier than any other." The phrasing was impressive and had a certain logic, but it still sounds like a rationalization of his own fears.

Lagarde became increasingly dissatisfied over the years. He was exhausted by the breakneck work tempo and morose about the supposed cultural decline, and the meaning of scholarly activity seemed questionable to him. As far back as November 13, 1875, he described himself to his friend, the Latinist Richard Schöne, as "a mistrustful, shy, badly wounded man." Concerning the times, he predicted darkly: "Everything, everything is going downhill, and swiftly at that." In the last years of his life, Lagarde had a simple life in mind and seriously contemplated selling his house, despite being very attached to it. Even the library that he had painstakingly assembled over many years felt like a burden. And so he charged the former Göttingen adjunct professor of Assyriology Paul Haupt with selling it. Haupt had meanwhile established a new professional life in Baltimore. Lagarde's plan was not able to be carried out, but it definitely sheds light on his attitude toward life. Göttingen flourished during the period of the German Empire and was among the most attractive German university towns. Yet Lagarde felt uncomfortable there, as did Kierkegaard in Copenhagen. Lagarde made scores of statements in which he mocked the intellectual mediocrity of his colleagues and the dull-minded Lower Saxons. Although tolerance for professorial oddballs was fairly high at the time, such comments made him increasingly unpopular. Lagarde also externalized many internal issues and was not sparing in his outlandish recommendations for improvement.

In an 1877 edition of the *Göttinger Zeitung*, he criticized the "very considerable monotony" of local "intellectual life" and the "lack of a strong taxpayer base." His proposed solution was an improvement in housing conditions that would precipitate the greatest possible influx of cultured, educated, and well-to-do families. Notably, this was entirely along the political line adopted by the long-standing lord mayor of Göttingen, Georg Merkel, who belonged to the hated Nationalliberale Partei (National Liberal Party). Moreover, he had driven up the municipal debt, which Lagarde considered entirely unacceptable. The same was true of the increase in taxes on brandy and beer, which were Merkel's attempt to climb out of the financial hole.[9] Lagarde's own approach was to disparage Göttingen, while simultaneously hoping for an improvement in the situation. But such reasoning was neither consistent nor promising. Disrespectful judgments about Göttingen were met with surprise and displeasure. In 1880, he described his hometown to Karl Frenzel, the editor of the *National-Zeitung*, "as a dreadful wasteland [. . .] that people call Athens on the Leine." It goes without saying that such statements did not win him any friends at Georgia Augusta University, where good town-gown relations were essential.

Miserliness was among Lagarde's most prominent character traits. He saved on everyday items in order to finance the costly self-publication of his writings.

He often paid bills at the last minute and was generally difficult when it came to business matters. He repeatedly adopted a harsh tone with the Kästner firm, which was his Göttingen book publisher for many years. He pointed to his own scholarly obligations, in particular, and urged the publisher to hold to strict deadlines, yet often made last-minute changes to his manuscripts. Lagarde gave the bookseller Ernst Kamlah one of his works on approval and it came back with an "ink spot." On October 12, 1887, Lagarde angrily informed him: "I refuse any further association with you, because I do not wish to again fall victim to your lack of knowledge of your customers. As can be seen from this example, there are some truly modern and fashionable rogues among them." In 1882, he refused to provide an obligatory copy of his text *Aegyptiacorum libri sex* (*Six Books of the Egyptians*) to the royal library in Berlin. He justified this by pointing to his allegedly low salary and the fact that he "printed everything at his own expense." As if this were not enough, he also criticized the library's lending policies, which were not at all friendly to patrons.[10]

Over time, Lagarde became obsessed with the printing of his own writings. While it was obvious that his highly specialized works had a small readership, he placed great hope in sales. Printing occupied an ever-increasing portion of his time, leaving less of it for his own scholarly work. On April 17, 1875, his friend Georg Hoffmann, an Orientalist in Kiel, imploringly remarked: "You will, of course, always have to bring money to the table. But must you subject yourself to all the aggravation that goes with bookselling? I don't see how it benefits an idealistic scholar to also take on the martyrdom of an idealistic bookseller." Lagarde remained obstinate, however, and diligently continued to self-publish his editions. Information about the author and place of publication were often missing from his unadorned volumes, making it noticeably more difficult to order them. It almost seems as if Lagarde saw the failure of his scholarly writings as a positive thing, because it allowed him to continue complaining about the ignorance of his contemporaries. On October 19, 1884, he wrote to William R. Smith in Cambridge in a patronizing tone: he was certainly prepared to recognize that Smith was carrying out a difficult scholarly task, but at least Smith was compensated for it by the recognition of the English scholarly world. Lagarde's own works, on the other hand, were geared toward German theologians and might just as well be thrown in the garbage. Not only that, he had to bear the burden of printing costs.

In many respects, Lagarde's behavior was that of a malcontent. He repeatedly protested that his early writings appeared under the name of Bötticher in library catalogues. He even asked the British Museum to correct these listings. In light of existing bibliographic rules, however, such changes were not within the realm of possibility. Hidden behind Lagarde's complaints was the conviction that he had begun a new life when his great-aunt adopted him. But a great deal speaks for the assumption that he was embarrassed at having assumed the name of his wealthy aunt. In his personal dealings, Lagarde was extremely rigid on this topic. When the Göttingen Latinist Hermann Sauppe cited his early work *Arica* under the name of Bötticher in 1871, the combative Orientalist took it as "a personal insult."[11] On June 26, 1886, Lagarde made this imperious statement about the editing of the *Deutsche Enzyklopädie* (*German Encyclopedia*): it would be just as appropriate for him "to be featured under the name of Bötticher [. . .] as to speak of Voltaire as Arouet." Lagarde's efforts in this direction were ultimately successful and, even among historians, his birth name faded into obscurity. In one of the most important works of recent German historical scholarship, Lagarde is listed as "Böttcher," but the critics do not seem to have noticed.[12]

Lagarde not only became embroiled in numerous conflicts; he also became increasingly lonely. He was incapable of making eye contact with other human beings and only tolerated those in his immediate proximity who submitted unconditionally to his views. Among these few persons was his student Georg Hoffmann, who provided the Göttingen faculty with the *venia legendi*, permission required to lecture at the university, at Lagarde's request in 1870.[13] Just one year later, Hoffmann, an expert in Classical Syriac, could rejoice over an appointment at the University of Kiel. Hoffmann was certainly a diligent and rather important scholar, but he was no match for the strong-willed Lagarde. He admired the comprehensive linguistic skills of his academic mentor while also valuing his contributions as a poet and political writer. Lagarde's dependency on Alfred Schöne was even more apparent. The Latinist lost his professorship in Erlangen because of a faux pas and had to urgently rely on Lagarde's intercession. Schöne approached the famous scholar submissively and endeavored to validate his views.

The high praise for Lagarde that is woven into his correspondence is nothing short of astounding. In November 1880, the Catholic theologian and Semitist Gustav Bickell expressed outrage at the fact that Lagarde was forced to wait for his professorship for so long. Bickell considered Lagarde's employment as a grammar school teacher to be "an assassination attempt that was just as scandalous as if a despot had ordered Raphael [. . .] to sweep the streets or Newton to copy documents." Surely this was a great exaggeration but, as far as we know, the Göttingen Orientalist did not object to such laudatory statements. Yet no amount of praise could give Lagarde the self-confidence that he had lacked since early childhood. A letter he wrote to Franz Overbeck in 1874 clearly shows that Lagarde's attitude toward life had not changed much since his first trip to London. "As unlikely as it may seem, I am," he remarked, "an extraordinarily shy person who would prefer to live in a cloister on some high mountaintop and to leave the world to itself."[14]

As happy as Lagarde had been about the appointment in Göttingen, he soon found everyday life at the university equally intolerable. He had nothing but disdain for most of his colleagues, and his correspondence with the Prussian Ministry of Education and Cultural Affairs is full of disparaging assessments. On February 21, 1875, he described the situation in Göttingen to his sponsor, Olshausen, as "disgusting." He deliberately avoided visiting the common room so that he would not run into a colleague whom he "had caught in a barefaced lie." But despite his misanthropy, he still had some friendliness left in him. Hardworking scholars like Ulrich von Wilamowitz-Moellendorf treated Lagarde with polite respect, and Lagarde carefully cultivated his personal contacts of many years. The practical value of flaunting his position as an outsider should also not be underestimated. His brusque manners sometimes helped him achieve his objectives and, beyond that, he gained valuable time for his many research projects. His wide-ranging scholarly correspondence proves that he could strike very different chords in pursuit of his goals.

Whether on the road or in Göttingen, Lagarde was nearly always busy and his wife played the key role in managing his affairs. As his "private secretary," she organized his appointment calendar and decided which letters would be forwarded to him while he was away. She even gave him advice in scholarly matters on occasion. Thus, she consoled Ludwig Stern in 1885 when the directorship of the Berlin Museum of Egyptology went not to him but to the younger Adolf Erman. This was a delicate matter, because Stern was one of Paul de Lagarde's most trusted correspondents, whereas the ambitious Erman was likewise among the few scholars that the Orientalist treated with ongoing respect. The question of seniority also came up: Prussians in general and the Lagarde home in particular attached great importance to this system, according to which it was not uncommon to promote young scholars from whom one expected great things. Anna de Lagarde was entirely familiar with the academic landscape and advised Stern to resign himself to the situation.[15] But she always left the decisive steps to her husband. In Stern's case, Lagarde called for a statement that he would be employed in Göttingen under the same financial arrangements as those for Erman and then successfully campaigned for Stern to get a librarian position at Georgia Augusta University.

Research trips on behalf of the Septuagint edition became more burdensome for Lagarde as he got older. He rarely found relaxing diversions or trusted contacts in foreign places, so he worked indefatigably and yearned for home. A letter of August 26, 1882, to his wife from Florence illustrates just how terribly homesick he could get. Lagarde emphasized how the Laurentian Library made him long for a "cool forest" and described Florentine women as "pretty, but nasty *animals* for the most part."[16] He talked about how much he would enjoy reading Dante in Göttingen, exclaiming at the end of his letter: "But how I long for Germany, for rest, for fresh air, for You! Only I know the sacrifices I have made for my entire life. Visiting strange places is not my forte." These lines certainly show a degree of self-pity. But Anna de Lagarde would still have been delighted with this covert declaration of love. For her part, she always worried when her husband traveled. She knew he was inept in everyday matters and was afraid that something might happen to him.[17] She often sent letters on ahead to his new destinations so that he would feel at home there. And she drafted letters that asked his hosts to make allowances for their shy guest's idiosyncrasies.

Lagarde's travel correspondence clearly shows his inability to enjoy the world very much. His tendency to automatically associate modernity with evil also increased. In a letter of August 14, 1874, to his wife, he called London's Crystal Palace a "[t]asteless glass box." He indeed viewed the daring glass-and-iron structure as a "real Temple of Baal, anti-Christendom, as it were."[18] His fierce hatred of Jews added to his abhorrence of the present. He criticized the Moorish architectural style of Jewish synagogues by means of the usual stereotypes. As Lagarde traveled, he observed the wealth of individual Jews and their public influence. But he also bristled at encounters with the opposite, so he spoke disdainfully about the unfinished synagogue in Turin: "The wanglers were too poor to finish it! The city will now complete it at its own expense. No consideration for the royal house."[19] Lagarde was particularly interested in the political sphere, which he looked at with the eyes of a cultural critic. He was in Rome when Benjamin Disraeli died and wrote contemptuously about the happening to his wife: "The world is so wretched that even a tightrope-walking creature like him could play a role in it!"[20] Anna de Lagarde supported her husband in nearly every sphere, including his hatred of Jews. She was full of admiration for his alleged moral fiber and was happy to take a backseat in ideological matters, which was surely conducive to domestic harmony.

Their contemporaries believed the Lagardes had a good marriage. These two lonely people had an unusually close relationship based on mutual responsibility. To a considerable extent, their lifelong union was about well-honed teamwork. Anna de Lagarde read out loud to her husband during revisions so that he could rest his worn-out eyes. She worked "for the Lord's sake," he told Olshausen on May 27, 1867. From early on, Lagarde took work to well-nigh spiritual heights. In a letter of June 3, 1860, to his wife, he boldly asserted: "I think that human beings are *only* happy when working. Work also shapes people and, to the extent that it is successful, improves them. Successful work is always a measure of the maker. For the two of us, work signifies respectability and faithfulness."[21] Lagarde's praise was surely well intended, but it also covered up the simple fact that he'd been denied the fame he sought as an author. There is hardly any doubt that Anna de Lagarde relieved her husband of the bulk of life's burdens. In many respects, she made his scholarly existence possible. But the officer's daughter benefited from her marriage to the eminent professor as well. She occupied a socially prestigious position and had a man at her side who discussed all his concerns with her whenever possible. He also gave her a great deal of attention, which was not the rule in the male-dominated university world of the German Empire.[22]

Their carefully balanced marriage also offered Anna de Lagarde a great deal of "symbolic capital." This stemmed mainly from the unusual position of trust that she occupied vis-à-vis her husband. On March 6, 1885, she confidently told the practically "all powerful" Prussian ministerial official for personnel matters, Friedrich Althoff:[23] "I am always authorized to accept and open postal items that arrive for my husband in his absence, wherein Your High Well Born may rest assured of the utmost discretion on my part." On October 12, 1890, she even gave the Wilstedt pastor Stakemann a glimpse into her identity as the trusted partner of a famous professor: "You hopefully know, of course, that keeping silent is not impossible for us—I happen to know many rather talkative *men* and would not entrust them with any secrets I might have. If I simply introduce myself as Lagarde's wife and privy secretary, about whom he has never had a complaint, I believe this will suffice to reassure you. I have also learned to quickly recognize—even if "Confidential" is not expressly stated—whether it concerns something that he *must* read. That same year, she explained to an acquaintance why her husband had to contend with so many difficulties: while his efforts always "aim toward the kingdom of God, that is [to say] the Gospels and the person of Jesus himself," an inimical bureaucracy has done its best to frustrate him.[24]

His wife's protective love confirmed Paul de Lagarde's tendency to divide the world into friends and foes. Once someone had forfeited his goodwill, that person could hardly count on a change of heart from Lagarde. But it appears that Anna de Lagarde did not take a backseat to her husband in her inclination to demonize. On October 10, 1890, she explained to Pastor Stakemann, whom she had befriended, that even after thirty-six years of marriage, she trusted her husband and his sense of justice. She said in a confessional tone: "I do not believe that love is blind; on the contrary, it sharpens the senses. One would like to be rid of every mote." Paul de Lagarde's clashes were never about personal vanity, for, according to his wife, "it was always" a matter of "the fight for God against the Devil." This was a noble assessment that, nevertheless, says more about the unconditional loyalty of the professor's wife than it does about her ability to explain his many conflicts.

Anna de Lagarde's few extant letters prove just how much her husband's love meant to her. On September 4, 1879, following the deaths of many family members, she reflected on the impermanence of human existence. In hindsight, she wished her relatives an easy death, but declined the same for herself. When her husband was away, all her thoughts were focused on the next *Wiedersehen*. But if she should die unexpectedly, he must never forget "that all my thoughts and sentiments are only thankful—thankful that God has placed me in your hands and in your love, and thankful that you have gladly held me therein." She also cautioned him against excessive fear of people and being too stern with himself. She knew what had plagued him "all his life" and had not lost faith in his goodness.

A day later, Anna was caught up in thoughts about her husband's death and promised to visit the places that "had been dear" to him and had "done him good." On September 7, she finally studied her husband's earliest essay, felt "life flowing through her," and read it through "in a single sitting."[25] She praised his "belief in our *Volk*" and his faith in a better future that, above all, required a solid childhood education. As no other, he had been called to summon the German *Volk* to return to the true and authentic values of bygone days. Anna de Lagarde closed by moving boldly from the wished-for to the possible. The "seeds of the future" would bear fruit. Otherwise, "God might not have given you the ideas or the artistry to express them. Now that they are here, they must also take effect." We do not know how Paul de Lagarde responded to this letter. But we cannot deny that his wife was highly attuned to his political and religious visions. The round of private letters concluded on November 2, 1879, with a birthday greeting. Anna de Lagarde spoke about a festive new dress that she would like to wear if it "meets with your approval." And she encouraged her husband to face life "with new courage." As a birthday gift, she enclosed a first edition of his favorite book, Jacob Grimm's *Deutsche Mythologie*.[26]

Although the professor was bitter in many ways, he always adopted a respectful, affectionate, and loving tone with his wife. When he traveled, he made an effort to entertain her with lively narratives and, more important, to allay her fears. The couple, each of whom had few friends, grew closer over the years. Paul de Lagarde displayed a fearful tenderness that many acquaintances of the gruff scholar would not have guessed existed. In 1887, he called his wife "my dear flower."[27] And he described to her with great interest how delighted he had been over little children playing in Rome. In 1891, when he sent her the text of an epitaph from London that made a deep impression on him, he seemed almost to be offering a premonition of his own death:

A tender partner I have been
And many troubles have I seen.
My conflicts they are gone and past,
And I have gained the rest at last.
I'm free from sorrow, grief and sin,
With God eternally shut in.[28]

But this is probably a backward-looking projection. In the Lagarde home, death and impermanence were recurrent themes that urged the couple to live piously. And the Orientalist's comment that he "now had something meaningful to put down on paper" points more to a happy discovery than to dark forebodings.

But Lagarde paid a high price for his wife's warmhearted support. He was totally dependent on her in practical matters and never really learned to endure periods of loneliness. A poem in which he imagined life after his wife's death illustrates just how attached he was to her. It is titled "Lord, Help Me" and shows that he knew just how psychologically and emotionally vulnerable he was. The last verse reads:

But fully I must needs despair,
if the angel of death would drive,
my dear beloved from my side,
I would alone in woe abide.
Lord, help me, for I must needs bear.[29]

We should certainly not read Lagarde's verses as a mere expression of psychological sensibility. His love for his wife had its limits, and these were closely connected to his own state of mind. Anna de Lagarde also had something of her husband's grim sense of reality. As she noted on the cover sheet of her excerpts from his private testimonials that she drew up after his death, her husband's letters had "always been written cursorily."[30]

As intimated thus far, Paul de Lagarde never came to terms with his mother's death. In his poem "Rückblick" (Reflections), lines turn up that even suggest he interpreted his hatred toward his surroundings as a legitimate attitude based on personal fate:

Now we have loved sufficiently:
today our hatred catches fire.
Who ere faces eternal death,
may do what he desires.[31]

His sheerly unbounded loneliness may have even better characterized his attitude toward life. Lagarde almost always took disappointments personally and was terrible at dealing with them. Many of his personal relationships crashed and burned over minor matters, and were never rehabilitated. Even in old age, Lagarde remembered how lonely he had felt as a child. The following verses from "Rückblick" seem to prove that he experienced his mother's puerperal death as a narcissistic wound:

Mother has abandoned me,
and made off for her grave:
Alas! The child, no love had he,
by his bed at end of day.
Alas! The child, no love had he,
on his aimless way.
He wandered, lonely, through the maze,
and no one helped him when he strayed.

As harshly judgmental as Lagarde could be about the weaknesses of his fellow man, he also sensed the enormity of his own brokenness. His letters to his wife contain many indications of his self-hatred. And he suffered from depressive states of exhaustion from an early age that caused him to see death as a means of deliverance. Just as he linked his childhood loneliness to his mother's death, he traced his limited emotional maturity to the same source. These verses from his poem "No. 11" vacillate between tearful sentimentality and self-hatred, and have been cited repeatedly for good reason:

Oh mother, child yourself like you have borne.
Why didn't you remain to play with me?
I did not dare to grow up, for then with whom?
And so I've aged, but have remained a child.[32]

One rarely gets the impression that Lagarde made a serious effort to cultivate his own happiness. He loved music and learned to play piano as a boy. Yet he nearly gave up music altogether for the supposed good of his scholarly work. More and more, he came to resemble the figure of the "deaf violinist" who was the embodiment of an unhappy life in the poem "No. 11."[33]

The Lagardes had a childless marriage, something that was unquestionably stigmatized in their day. The sources remain silent as to the reasons for this outcome. It cannot have been that Paul de Lagarde didn't love children, for his letters to his wife clearly show that they gladdened his heart. He also had good relationships with his students when he taught school, and they remembered him fondly later on. There are two other possible explanations for the lack of children, assuming there were no medical reasons to take into account. The first was that Paul de Lagarde needed a great deal of love and comfort, so his wife had her hands full with "mothering" him. She might not have been all that excited about raising her own children. For her husband's part, he must have feared the loss of his spouse's undivided attention. In any case, the Lagardes apparently did not exceed a certain level of intimacy in their personal relationships. When Georg Hoffmann suggested that they serve as godparents to his daughter Irmengard, the Lagardes did their best to turn him down. Above all, they countered the threatening personal commitment on religious grounds. On August 13, 1873, Anna de Lagarde explained to Hoffmann that, in her opinion, she did not have the "*right* [. . .] to take on such a duty and honor," given her undoubted distance from the church as an institution. But their colleague in Kiel did not so easily admit defeat. He told Anna de Lagarde on September 9 that the Protestant Church "did not excommunicate anyone who did not renounce the Church himself." On September 29, he chose a softer tone with her husband and hoped for a private talk about "Canon Law in the Protestant Church." But none of these efforts did any good: the Lagardes stood their ground, and Hoffmann had to find other godparents for his daughter. The second, possibly more obvious reason for not having children was Paul de Lagarde's love of scholarship. The Orientalist put such ceaseless energy into his many projects that children would only have disturbed his daily routine. And the importance he attached to Bible study was something he only questioned at times of complete exhaustion.

Whenever Paul de Lagarde contemplated childlessness, it was mainly in relation to his own mortality. He had already lamented the passage of time when he was in Schleusingen. Shortly after his professorial appointment, he felt that he was finally an "old man." When he intended to resign his professorship in 1872, the crisis reinforced his conviction that he could expect little more from life. At a time of existential gloom, he adopted a bitter tone in writing to an Orientalist with whom he had a rather distant relationship: "But, one day, children turn a blind eye to you. I must die a lonely man, since my unsold Chaldean prophets and companions are of no use to me."[34] Lagarde was not even convinced of the ultimate value of scholarship.

The Orientalist led a harried academic life. He sensed that the Septuagint edition was bound to exceed the limits of his ability. And maybe that was why he started many other projects that, needless to say, kept him from his life's work. Lagarde had hoped to arrive at the pinnacle of his scholarly generation, but soon found himself surrounded by younger colleagues. In the left-wing liberal "Falk era," referring to the Prussian minister of education under Bismarck, Adalbert Falk, Prussia saw the purposeful expansion of university education. Mostly younger scholars were appointed to the new chairs, and they were expected to play a key role in German progress and the establishment of the German Empire.[35] The majority were just over thirty at the time of their appointments. In 1869, a rare talent like Nietzsche was appointed in Basel at the tender age of twenty-four. Lagarde had waited more than fifteen years for a professorship. The biblical scholar felt old by comparison to the emerging generation, and there was envy in the Lagarde home. When Georg Hoffmann gingerly brought up the harsh behavior of the Göttingen professor, Anna de Lagarde responded unequivocally: "Your path through life has been very smooth as compared to that of my husband." Therefore, Lagarde could not expect "to gain complete understanding for his views and, in many cases, for his conduct."[36] This was probably an accurate assessment, but it also discloses a questionable tendency to belittle the success of others. In addition, Paul de Lagarde's résumé contained fewer signs of martyrdom than he claimed and forcefully brought up time and again. At the age of forty-two, he had a prestigious chair that was very satisfactory by the standards of his generation. Many of his contemporaries had waited in a long line of appointment seekers.

In many respects, Lagarde's house symbolized a fortress against the approach of old age. He left it reluctantly and, when he did, it was mainly to take books out of the library. He usually kept the few students he had at a distance and focused entirely on his scholarly work. In his communications with the Prussian Ministry of Education and Cultural Affairs, Lagarde stressed the enormous time pressures he faced. When it came to the tiresome question of access to manuscripts in his home, he told Undersecretary of State Sydow on September 3, 1878: "I am more than fifty years old and have absolutely no time to lose if I wish to complete my important life's work." Lagarde was almost pathologically shy when it came to being photographed. In the few photos he saw of himself, he detected signs of aging and felt compelled to work even harder. When Eugen Wolff, an adjunct professor in Danzig, asked him in 1890 to contribute to the series Deutsche Schriften für nationales Leben (German Writings on National Life), Lagarde's response was friendly but firm: "When I was in Sylt for three weeks, a dear, former student photographed me. The picture arrived with his letter, and it showed me how old I am and how little time I have left. [. . .] It's impossible: I cannot promise anything, because I am sure that I wouldn't be able to deliver it."[37] An incident in Rome from that same year shows the degree to which the aging scholar was fixated on work. He told his wife in great detail about the explosion of a powerful bomb that led to numerous injuries and major property damage. The force of the blast also destroyed the windowpanes of his pension, and shards of glass were still lying around when he returned to his room. But neither his own survival nor the misery before his eyes moved him in earnest. His letter only referred back several times to his "poor work," which had suffered as a consequence of the disruption.[38] Even in the heroic age of scholarship at the close of the nineteenth century, this reaction would have been peculiar.

In his biography of Hitler, Joachim Fest painted an impressive portrait of German professors in the period of the German Empire: their "facial expressions blended so much idealistic sternness and loyalty to principles with brooding intensity, and their conventional attitudes were not without their dark side." He emphatically highlighted the cloistered "domesticity" of those thinkers, whose works tried to encompass an entire world. He approvingly quoted Paul de Lagarde, according to whom "books and dreams [. . .] were their basic principles."[39] And there is certainly a lot of truth in this statement. But the question still arises as to whether the unsociable Orientalist was more of a prototypical professor or an outsider in the world of the academy. The ambitious scholar was a notorious lone wolf in Göttingen and was seen carting his "heavy folios" through the city.[40] In the rest of Germany, people saw him as so confrontational that this assessment found its way into the lexica. No matter how outlandish Lagarde's intensity about his work may appear from a modern perspective, it was not at all unusual in the nineteenth century. Work practically became "the new shrine, a type of myth that held society together."[41] The number of scholars who literally worked themselves to death in the service of knowledge is legion. Many of their proposals amounted to "gigantomania" and took decades to complete. Yet even in the era of networked research and its apparently synergistic effects, one is humbled by the lifetime achievements of these scholars.

Lagarde's peculiarity consisted less of his identity with a professorial position or his enthusiasm for research and more of the specific content of his work. His scholarly activity was infused with private matters and politics, the religious and the profane, in a uniquely intensive way. For the very reason that his ideological writings were so widely disseminated, his scholarly practice is worthy of a closer look; it also contributed to the establishment and reinforcement of his worldview.

7 An Established Outsider

Paul de Lagarde has mainly been portrayed as a solitary scholar who constantly feuded with his colleagues and clung doggedly to his life's work, a complete edition of the Septuagint. This is most certainly a distorted perspective, but the degree to which it complies with Lagarde's heroic self-fashioning gives pause for thought. He was fond of depicting himself as a "guild" outsider whose love of truth elicited responses that pretty well encompassed the entire spectrum. In point of fact, many colleagues judged him difficult. But neither Orientalism nor theology ignored him, as the sheer number of reviews reveals.[1] There was a certain inclination to regard the holder of a renowned professorship as an outsider plagued by envy and resentment. Yet emphasis on idiosyncratic characteristics like mistrust, cantankerousness, and oversensitivity is hardly adequate for an overall picture of the man. At any rate, a primarily psychological explanation runs the risk of discounting Lagarde as a consciously calculating, single-minded scholar. Like practically all tenured professors, he fought for the validation of his ideas, purposefully nurtured and supported his students, and endeavored to maintain good relations with state ministries. He carried on extensive correspondence with Prussian ministers, and the unusually influential advisor Friedrich Althoff even visited him in Göttingen. All this leads to skepticism concerning Lagarde's melodramatic self-portrayal, while giving rise to a more levelheaded description of his scholarly practice.

Lagarde was minimally present in the everyday life of the university. He repeatedly asked the Göttingen trustee to release him from his teaching obligations so that he could leave early on his research trips for the Septuagint edition.[2] Since he worked at a breakneck pace with no regard for his health, he suffered from recurrent states of exhaustion, so he also made visits to spas. There were essentially two reasons why Lagarde's requests for time off were always approved without hesitation: First, the Septuagint project and any related proposals that could contribute to its success were given high priority in Berlin. Second, so few students attended Lagarde's courses that it was easy to find ways to prepare or catch up on coursework.

The Ministry of Education and Cultural Affairs offered to arrange for Lagarde to teach regular courses in Hebraic studies, a proposal the scholar found unappealing but agreed to do anyway. But he soon noticed how much effort it took to give instruction in something that interested few students. On January 26, 1871, he informed Minister Mühler that he would like to disband the recently founded Hebrew Society. He also returned part of the grant money "because, with a single exception, student performance did not meet the most basic requirements." In the years that followed, Lagarde held his students to rigorous standards. Since he assumed that students had acquired the requisite linguistic basis for his courses, he generally dispensed with introductions. He familiarized them with grammatical subtleties and honed their translation skills. In the process, he became convinced that there was inherent ethical value in all true work. An account given by his star pupil, Alfred Rahlfs, spelled out the moral imperative that dominated Lagarde's private rebukes. He was not fully prepared on one occasion, and the student's oral translation from the Syriac text came to a halt. Lagarde consequently asked him to stop speaking and paid no attention to him for the rest of the hour. Rahlfs was so ashamed that, from then on, he always prepared the texts with utmost care.[3]

Lagarde didn't much value the large survey courses that characterized academic instruction in the period of the German Empire. Given the many knowledge gaps, he thought it presumptuous to provide his students with a definitive historical overview of Orientalism. Armed with nothing but a notepad to deliver his lectures, he instead chose to confront these gaps by means of special examination and research questions.[4] This method certainly helped acquaint budding scholars with the distinctive features of their discipline. Many researchers emerged from Lagarde's courses, including the well-known New Testament scholar Eberhard Nestle, the Assyriologist Paul Haupt, as well as the Egyptologist Wilhelm Spitta and Alfred Rahlfs, a Septuagint specialist. The opportunity to offer reliable guidance to students in other disciplines went unused, of course, and Orientalism in Göttingen remained the specialized discipline it had been in Ewald's days.

Lagarde fulfilled his faculty duties at first, but not later on. He found administrative tasks more burdensome over time and tried to pass them on to colleagues. On May 5, 1878, he beseeched Minister Falk to permit him to decline his appointment to the postdoctoral committee. He movingly described his secluded life: "I need no companionship, no pub, and live as a recluse. No one needs to know anything about me, other than that I work every single day." Since scholarly activity was his only joy, he would not allow his valuable leisure time to be "spoiled by things that bear no relationship to my life's work, which is to impart knowledge and to expand its limits." With such an attitude, it is no surprise that he won few friends on the faculty. But Lagarde was not aware that he was culpable in any way. From his point of view, a professor had to focus entirely on scholarly tasks, and routine business had to take a backseat. On June 24, 1876, he told the Berlin classical scholar Richard Schöne: "I am on friendly terms with a number of colleagues, and there is no antagonism with anyone other than [Albrecht] Ritschl. I exist as little for most of them as they do for me." This was a sugarcoated view of things, however. Not only did Lagarde argue with Ritschl, a theologian whose optimistic reading of Protestantism he found intolerable; by virtue of his rigid adherence to principles, he also came to blows with other colleagues. Lagarde had a low opinion of the philosopher Hermann Lotze and called him the "most second-rate epigone of epigones."[5] This was certainly an unfair assessment of an accomplished methodologist and rather significant thinker. Moreover, Lotze's overt communication conflicted with Lagarde's views on collegiality. Yet the Orientalist repeatedly insisted on confronting students with his own opinions. His assessments were as personal as they were principled, and clearly did not fit in well with the demands of everyday university life.

Lagarde took the firm position that the university had to limit the number of full professorships. On August 5, 1875, when chairs in astronomy, art history, and history of German literature were about to be established in Göttingen, Lagarde cast a "dissenting vote" at the Ministry of Education and Cultural Affairs. With typical directness, he took the position "that the vitalization of scholarly meaning in the nation" did not depend upon "establishing and filling as many university professorships as possible." He put forward a similar argument when the Old Testament professorship opened up. On May 18, 1888, he wrote pointedly to Friedrich Althoff: "Since so many professorships exist in duplicate and triplicate, Göttingen was not ailing in the least."[6] In both instances, the vital interests of the other faculty members ultimately proved more compelling. Yet even as Lagarde's position did not win majority support, the inner consistency of his reasoning cannot be denied. The idea that only one full professor at each university should be granted responsibility for a particular discipline fit well with his elitist understanding of scholarship. His late-Romantic desire for freedom was adamantly opposed to the increasing bureaucratization of the educational system. For its part, the tenure system was not easily reconciled with the requirements of the modern mega-universities that had already begun to appear at the close of the nineteenth century. The system hampered new areas of research, resulted in great misery among adjunct professors, and, most notably, was less and less able to accommodate the demands of university teaching. In terms of efficiency, Althoff's espoused "principle of organizational minimum" could not be easily dismissed. And Lagarde was among those who subscribed to it.[7]

Lagarde always placed special emphasis on the well-being of scholarship and did not dignify social motives. He even brought up physical disabilities as a means to keep "unsuitable" applicants away from Georgia Augusta University. He attached great importance to the idea that everyone was responsible for his own life and, therefore, had to make timely provisions for potential misfortune. When the mathematician Alfred Clepsch died in 1872, leaving behind a wife and four children, the Philosophy Faculty was eager to help out. But on January 10, 1873, Lagarde cautioned against providing too lavishly for the needy family. After all, the salary of the deceased had "always been on a par with, if not better than, that of his colleagues." If the faculty did not do as he wished, he threatened that he would inform the Ministry of Education and Cultural Affairs. But, despite the generous support the widow received, it apparently never came down to that. Yet many a professor must have shaken their head at Lagarde's behavior, particularly since he had just built a large house and could not have been considered poor by any means.

Lagarde also had an aversion to promotions within the university. When the ancient historian Otto Gilbert was to be appointed *Professor Extraordinarius*, Lagarde turned to Richard Schöne, who had good contacts at the Prussian Ministry of Education and Cultural Affairs in Berlin. Lagarde told him that the minister must not do anything "until he had heard from the faculty." In a cautionary tone, he then added: "You will prevent a great deal of embarrassment if you push through this assuredly loyal request."[8] On November 30, 1879, Lagarde wrote directly to the Prussian minister of education and cultural affairs, Robert von Puttkamer, who was among his most ardent supporters. (As interior minister, Puttkamer would subsequently lead a feared regime.) Lagarde shared the politician's conservative values and absolute rejection of liberalism. And Puttkamer was particularly convinced of the importance of the Septuagint project.[9] Lagarde expressly emphasized how poorly Gilbert had performed at his habilitation colloquium. In principle, he considered it dubious for a university library official to receive permission to teach at all, since his post did not allow him to conscientiously engage in any lecturing activities. And Gilbert's reading of seven different subjects in seven consecutive semesters simply proved his intellectual dishonesty. Finally, he was not authorized to administer the grammar school teaching examination and would, therefore, have hardly any students. So the establishment of a secured professorship in the history of antiquity would only mean "throwing away the state's money." This very negative attitude suggested personal reservations. The fact that the fledgling adjunct professor, Gilbert, was striving to teach a broad range of courses would also allow for other possible interpretations. In any case, the former grammar school teacher from Hameln did not have a powerful advocate in Berlin, so the professorship remained nothing more than a fond wish for the time being. But Gilbert went on with his work undeterred and was awarded a professorship in Greifswald in 1886.

Needless to say, opposition to Gilbert's appointment as *Professor Extraordinarius* was more the exception than the rule. In looking over Lagarde's employment of more than twenty years at Georgia Augusta, one almost gets an impression of normalcy. Like many of today's scholars, he lived for research and avoided teaching duties whenever possible. Lagarde also had no particular interest in academic self-government, but he faithfully executed his deanship in 1882–1883. He addressed the condition of old records that urgently needed to be bound, recalling the former solidarity with the Göttingen Seven.[10] Without reliable support from the Philosophy Faculty, however, his carefully crafted yet somewhat marginal initiatives had little effect. Nor did his radical views ruffle many feathers. But, time and again, the German academic world had to respond to sensational publications coming out of Göttingen, and how it saw Lagarde was another matter entirely.

Among Lagarde's most conspicuous behavioral patterns was his outspoken handling of internal matters. He cared little for the social customs of the German academic system, which were strongly geared toward containing conflict and safeguarding social prestige. The scholar, highly sensitive himself, repeatedly brought his colleagues' embarrassing habits and mistakes before the court of public opinion. A particularly sensational instance was the sale of valuable earthenware vessels and images of the gods that allegedly came from the ancient kingdom of the Moabites. In 1868, a German missionary to the area formerly known as Moab discovered the world's oldest Hebrew inscription, dating back to the time of King Mescha in c. 850 B.C.E. The Prussians didn't show much interest in the discovery, but when the missionary publicized it in Paris in 1870, it soon came to be regarded as a national disgrace. The scandal subsequently generated enormous interest in additional finds from the area comprising modern-day Jordan. A Jerusalem atelier took advantage of this enthusiasm, producing terra-cotta pottery and other antiquities on a grand scale and offering them for sale. Distinguished scholarly experts like the ancient historian Theodor Mommsen and the Arabist Heinrich Fleischer were every bit as caught up in the matter as was the Orientalist umbrella organization, the Deutsche Morgenländische Gesellschaft (German Oriental Society, DMG). For patriotic reasons, the society had recommended the acquisition of the "Moabite antiquities"[11] and, following the arrival of the crude forgeries, was disgraced to the core. Since he was not involved in the sale, Lagarde repeatedly added fuel to the fire. He regularly updated the editor-in-chief of the *National-Zeitung*, Friedrich Dernburg, on the latest developments in the story. Lagarde rejoiced greatly when the Prussian Landtag (legislative assembly) got around to debating the "Moabite antiquities" in 1876. Mommsen was the only one at the hearing who was capable of preventing further escalation of the scandal and employed the full force of his reputation to that end.

Lagarde was extremely dissatisfied with an outcome that entirely conformed to the interest of the DMG. On June 11, 1876, he wrote to the society's chairman in Leipzig, Otto Loth, that Mommsen's flimsy defense could not possibly resolve the matter. So as to prepare fully for all eventualities, he drew up a precise list of Mommsen's errors.[12] On March 25, 1878, Lagarde wrote a letter of complaint to DMG board member August Müller in Halle. According to Lagarde, Johannes Gildemeister, Georg Hoffmann, Theodor Nöldeke, and Johann Gottfried Wetzstein had "never" doubted "for a moment that the rubbish was fake," yet, like "all German Orientalists," they now stood disgraced. It is significant that the scholars involved were close associates of Lagarde and, as a result, his call for new board elections was pushed aside. Once again, the Göttingen Orientalist had gotten the short end of the stick. But this did not deter him from taking additional steps. He published a polemical article in the April 1880 edition of the *Protestantische Kirchenzeitung* (*Protestant Theological Journal*) that portrayed the sale of the "Moabite antiquities" using antisemitic undertones.[13]

The maxim "live and let live" was foreign to Lagarde's nature. After he was appointed to a professorship, consideration for others became even less important to him than it was before. In 1877, he planned for a collection of his polemical essays under the title of *Symmicta*, a collection that threatened to embarrass him in specialist circles. But he later withdrew the volume on the advice of Georg Hoffmann. On April 9, 1887, the Orientalist from Kiel had warned him that he was taking his "personal and vigorous deductions" much too far. In the process, he was forfeiting the advantages of a morally spotless position. Lagarde had already revised the book once and had deleted several passages that struck a deeply personal note. The original preface ended with a dark statement about the value of human life that didn't belong in a collection of academic essays: "Life," he put it categorically, "is a terrible burden anyway, and one cannot understand its purpose from an earthly perspective." Concerning life, he continued in drastic terms: "If I were to merely to contemplate it with respect to those with whom and for whom I have to work, or if I were to find it as some abandoned object lying in excrement on the street, then I would certainly not bother with it."[14] In rejecting the academic establishment, Lagarde also made reference to personal motives and reported unpleasant details of his colleagues' lives. It was nevertheless apparent to him that private matters did not belong in academic publications, so he decided to undertake an additional revision.

The new version of *Symmicta* appeared that same year, but the content was not substantially different from the previous versions. Lagarde inveighed against his colleagues and attested to their arrogance, ambition, and lack of veracity. He aired suspicions that eminent professors were guilty of plagiarism or, at any rate, of malevolently overlooking his writings. He accused Jewish and Protestant scholars alike of habitually distorting the facts.[15] The Lagardes turned a deaf ear to the objections of well-meaning friends. On March 31, 1878, Anna de Lagarde justified her husband's recent publication to Georg Hoffmann by comparing his love of truth to that of Lessing. In this instance, her loyalties would later be revealed by the absence of the applicable Hoffmann documents from the Lagarde estate. But even Hoffmann had proceeded tactically, pointing out the merits of the revised manuscript to the domineering Lagarde. Once the second volume of *Symmicta* appeared in 1880, however, such concessions were futile.

The tone of this essay collection is so vitriolic that words almost fail. Lagarde began in the foreword by pointing out that the behavior of the Prussian educational administration had made him into "a cripple."[16] His rebukes against his colleagues were exceedingly blunt and, by the standards of the day, unquestionably defamatory. In an embittered and one-sided way, he depicted the ignorance of the various appointment committees that had judged him unfairly every time. And he showcased embarrassments surrounding the "Moabite antiquities." As he put it—that is, disparagingly but with a grain of truth—the best thing for a scholarly career was to be just "a skosh above mediocrity." Lagarde's image of scholarly expertise bordered on paranoia and was typical of how he assessed the academic establishment. Under German law, "a man" was judged "by his peers," whereas mediocrity held sway in academia. Its peculiarity lay in the fact "that five, ten, twenty times per year, academia speaks with flylike tenacity—one Semite god is rightly called Beelzebub—in some newspaper about trying to establish a reputation for expertise and about bringing knowledge to the many Philistines."[17] Even scholars who had been on good terms with Lagarde were not safe from caustic value judgments. A long-standing opponent like the Berlin senior professor Albrecht Weber could read the following statement about himself: "He [Albrecht Weber] understands no Armenian, yet he critiques a manuscript that deals with Armenian, even as he vents hatred on this occasion and thinks he can commit murder."

Hoffmann, a peaceable man who was not only friends with Lagarde but also with many of the professors under attack, responded immediately. On June 17, 1880, he wrote these imploring words to Anna de Lagarde: "If only I were able to dissuade my dear friend from going further down *this* path! It comes from overworking to a degree that is beyond anything I have known him to do. Lagarde was not like *this* before." Similar opinions were widespread among scholars who were well disposed toward Lagarde. On August 28, 1880, Wilhelm Spitta hit the nail on the head. Without mincing words, he told his former teacher: "I believe that all those who have done you harm could not have damaged you as much as your own book will surely do." But Lagarde had already decided to throw down the gauntlet to his colleagues.

In the fall of that same year, he published a pamphlet, *Aus dem deutschen Gelehrtenleben* (*From German Scholarly Life*) that added a political component to the by-now familiar injuries presumably suffered by Lagarde: liberalism was responsible for the meager scale of truthfulness in Germany. Its followers represented an atomistic worldview that was entirely unsuited to the understanding of historical connections. He couched this argument in terms as defamatory and oppressive as those directed at his colleagues: "Liberals of our day always stick to one thing: to a liberal, neither the past nor the future counts, but only the present."[18] On the other hand, Lagarde attested to his own devotion to truthfulness, as well as his ability to see things holistically. There could be no more debate over scholarly matters, and Lagarde no longer really cared whether his colleagues approved of him. Rather, he fashioned himself as an original thinker who felt that the grunt work of everyday scholarly life was beneath him. In keeping with this self-styling, he developed an aesthetic of spitefulness with which to attack his personal and ideological opponents.

The "boundaries of disgust" played a major role among the bourgeoisie, which held rigid beliefs about cleanliness. Differences between different social and religious milieus, in particular, were dramatized by means of these boundaries. Ideas of cleanliness were a unifying factor within one's own social milieu and added noticeably to the vehemence of political clashes.[19] In Lagarde's case, it is striking that he not only stirred up prejudice against individual groups within society, such as "Jews" and "liberals," but also denigrated his own profession. Thus, on April 29, 1884, he wrote to Georg Hoffmann about his colleagues: "I am much too disgusted by these guttersnipes to pay them any heed." And there are an increasing number of similarly drastic quotes. Most served to immediately reduce psychological tensions and, at the same time, tended to underscore his own greatness.

In the course of his highly personal scholarly disputes, Lagarde declined to refute criticism of his stances. On the contrary: the stubborn professor interpreted the objections of the fraternity, about which he harbored distinctly monolithic ideas, as confirmation of his own views. After publishing his collection of essays about the academic establishment, he told the young Orientalist Emil Dillen in St. Petersburg on December 20, 1880, that, "for a time," he would "be the most hated and slandered scholar in Germany." Lagarde had already explained his criteria to Theodor Nöldeke on June 26, 1878: there was no way he would debate his personal views; he had simply published too much for that and, moreover, had far too low an opinion of his contemporaries. Rather, he feared for "the Fatherland and scholarship," both of which were in grave danger, "if [. . .] rogues and bunglers were the leading authorities."

To him, the military was the measure of all things: "If an officer were guilty of forging documents, he would be expelled from his regiment within twenty-four hours," and scholars who plagiarized should not be dealt with any differently. This was, of course, a highly idealized image of the Prussian military that, precisely because of its honor code, covered up its members' offenses time and again. Lagarde's scholarly understanding was also alarmingly rigid. He nearly always characterized the sciences by a multiplicity of positions that could not easily be sorted according to standard criteria. And Lagarde's forceful positivism and firm honor code were a combination that was excellently suited to an era in which Scholarship—capital S intended—was very exclusively conceived. Lagarde's drastic judgments about differing approaches or "misguided" colleagues sometimes even produced an unintended favorable outcome for the objects of his attacks. Neither did Lagarde keep quiet when it came to his opinions of very young scholars. Especially critical of the intellectual mediocrity and inadequate philological training of German professors, he complained about their costly consumption of beer and tobacco, at the expense of book sales, and the overall corruptibility of critics. Even when it came to third parties, Lagarde did not shrink from contemptuous judgments. Thus, he warned the Strasbourg student Wilhelm Nowack against reading Hermann Hupfeld, the theologian and Orientalist who had made a name for himself as a Psalms researcher. Irrespective of his merits, Hupfeld could only be studied with the utmost care, because he was "a glaringly ignorant Philistine who didn't really understand any language."[20] On the one hand, statements such as this can be understood as "blowing off steam." The overworked scholar vented his displeasure without worrying about professorial collegiality. On the other hand, this is how Lagarde disseminated his beliefs, and he would not have expected young scholars or students to contradict him. Given the difference in status, a considerable number must have been flattered that he even deigned to address them personally.

Lagarde paid even more attention to scholars who had just earned their stripes and were waiting for a professorship. In doing so, he did not limit himself to the field of Orientalism. He supported the conservative-minded economist and jurist Franz von Liszt, and gave him insight into the specifics of the "appointment merry-go-round." In order to improve Liszt's chances of an appointment, he concurrently lobbied for him at the Prussian Ministry of Education and Cultural Affairs. On December 1, 1878, he informed the important ministerial official for personnel matters, Heinrich Göppert, that Liszt was a very talented scholar who had "been warmly devoted" to Germany "since time immemorial." But he admonished Liszt, who was Austrian, to exercise utmost caution in dealing with faculties. When his appointment prospects in Breslau went up in smoke, he advised Liszt "to be very wary and discreet." In his letter of January 9, 1879, Lagarde affably advised him to accept every job, "even a Swiss one." In closing, he implored Liszt to "never show your feelings! There will be plenty of time for that later on." But Liszt had enough self-confidence to go his own way. On November 13, 1881, he was in a position to tell Lagarde that he had been offered, and would accept, an appointment in Marburg. His life's work, the standardization of international criminal law, bore megalomaniacal and illusory traits similar to those of the Septuagint edition. In his tome, Liszt responded to the fast-growing economic integration among the states, the same integration that the cultural pessimist Lagarde either ignored or condemned lock, stock, and barrel.[21]

Lagarde came right to the point in his letters of recommendation, and it appears as though he mainly had the welfare of those he was supporting in mind. He gladly wove in confidential information that was intended to inspire confidence among recipients. For example, his letter to Otto Benndorf played a role in the appointment of Gustav Bickell to a theological chair in Vienna. Although the letter contained a few criticisms, it ended on a positive note: when Bickell's "heart speaks, he listens to it and goes confidently on his way."[22] One can infer from a letter to Paul Haupt, dated October 9, 1880, that Lagarde attached great importance to supporting the new generation of academics. Lagarde made a highly egotistical statement that was, nevertheless, somewhat appealing to the young scholar: "Seldom has a scholar been so frequently or so wickedly lied about as I have. For this reason, I have the worst possible opinion of the fraternity. But I see no reason to somehow obstruct those who are freshly entering the field. On the contrary, I am always at pains to make things easier for them. And I have only one condition: unconditional sincerity." But if one takes a closer look at Lagarde's relationship with the talented Assyriologist, one realizes that this was not the entire story.

Paul Haupt's academic career got off to a rough start. In 1878, he finished his doctorate in Leipzig at the tender age of twenty-one. His dissertation, *Die sumerischen Familiengesetze* (*Sumerian Family Laws*), was published the following year and caused a sensation in the field of Assyriology. A student of Friedrich Delitzsch, Haupt had turned to Lagarde that same year and presented him with his very first work.[23] A friendly correspondence developed between them and, in 1880, Haupt considered doing his postdoctoral lecturing qualification in Göttingen. The linguistic researcher and Orientalist Archibald Henry Sayce from Queen's College, Oxford, spoke on his behalf. On October 16, 1880, he informed Lagarde, whom he knew personally, that Haupt was the most promising young scholar among those who were currently entering the field of Assyriology. Nevertheless, the habilitation process was not enjoyable for Haupt. Lagarde apparently had no interest in competition in the field of Semitics, a fact he did not hide from Haupt's dissertation supervisor. On November 27, he told Delitzsch that his student must prove "that he could sight-read idiomatic, unvocalized Arabic and Aramaic prose texts." In a seemingly patronizing manner, he added: "At one Assyriology colloquium, the entire procedure was hardly more than a formality"—which allowed him to conclude with the innuendo-charged and unequivocal statement "unlike on another occasion." Delitzsch must have quickly understood the threat this message contained. At any rate, Haupt refrained from traveling across the Bodensee, which would have meant taking a Semitics exam administered by an angry Lagarde. Acquisition of the *venia legendi* (permission to teach) did not present any real problems, but it was narrowly limited to the field of Assyrian, which substantially reduced Haupt's prospects for a professorship in Orientalism.

Character issues also entered the picture. Haupt assumed that he could storm Mount Olympus and thus acquired an attitude of superiority early on. He did not sidestep controversy, nor did he spare the greats in his field from criticism. In many respects, he resembled the young Lagarde, who had also believed that his outstanding linguistic talents would quickly earn him the necessary recognition. Although the Göttingen Orientalist tended to harshly criticize his colleagues, with Haupt he adopted the attitude of an established scholar. Lagarde was not at all pleased that Haupt got into an argument with the Parisian scholar Julius Oppert, so he prompted him to end the conflict. Oppert had been the first in the world to be awarded a professorship in Assyriology. But Lagarde unreservedly represented Haupt's interests, vis-à-vis the Ministry of Education and Cultural Affairs. In December 1881, he got Haupt a travel grant to London and Paris. His letter of recommendation ended with these words: "He [Paul Haupt] is unquestionably a very talented and astute scholar, whom one can more reliably train by helping him and placing him in the company of colleagues than by ignoring him."[24] But the problem of finding a professorship for Haupt in Prussia had still not been solved.

With the narrow wording of the *venia legendi*, Lagarde had seen to it that the talented young scholar was barely placeable. In Göttingen, Haupt lectured on his specialty areas, Babylonian, Assyrian, and Sumerian, and also offered courses in Ethiopic. Lagarde went outside the university to gain additional support. On September 28, 1882, he told Prussian governor Otto Theodor von Seydewitz that Haupt was "the only German" who "held the promise of achieving anything substantial" in Assyriology. But efforts to keep Haupt in Germany proved fruitless. At the beginning of 1883, he received an offer from Johns Hopkins University in Baltimore to set up an Oriental seminary. There was no doubt that Haupt had to accept the offer, yet Lagarde made hay while the sun shone. He persuaded the minister of education and cultural affairs, Gustav von Gossler, to arrange for an associate—albeit unsalaried—professorship in Assyriology in Göttingen. In his letter to the minister, dated February 2, 1883, Lagarde did not mince words: "I will not refrain from expressing myself as to what it means with respect to foreign countries when the only Assyriologist with a future—not just in Germany, but in all of Europe—is forced to earn his bread and butter outside of his Prussian Fatherland." Haupt was granted leave for three years, but always returned from Baltimore at the beginning of May to teach at Georgia Augusta.

Even in the New World, Haupt kept faith with his teacher. On April 12, 1884, he apodictically told Lagarde: "I am going to 'stand by you even more openly' from now on, since I no longer need to fear that well-meaning persons will ascribe my devotion to overambition." Haupt's academic interests increasingly shifted from knowledge of cuneiform to the same issues of Old Testament text criticism that occupied Lagarde. For his part, Lagarde did what he could on behalf of the young Assyriologist, who was unhappy with his new place of employment and would have liked to return to Germany. In 1886, Lagarde even supported Haupt's plans for an expedition to Mesopotamia. But, here again, he could do little for his protégé. Haupt lived too far away from the center of things and tried in vain to get official backing for his daring enterprise.

In a letter of January 5, 1887, to Haupt, Lagarde made the brutality of academic life clear. In no uncertain terms, he brought it to his protégé's attention that people in Berlin expected a more substantial work from him than he had yet produced, and "a compendium of Assyrian grammar" would be best. On November 4, 1887, he issued a dark warning: "It's now raining adjunct professors in Assyriology who want to outdo you. So be careful." Six months later, Lagarde approached Althoff directly as to whether he would be able to establish a professorship in Assyriology in Göttingen.[25] In his correspondence, he repeatedly alluded to Haupt as a first-rate academic force in an expanding research field that would be a credit to the German nation. But no such efforts helped. Lagarde was neither an Assyriologist, nor was he so well connected that he could seriously help Haupt. Moreover, his fierce polemics had earned him numerous enemies, and the self-aggrandizing Haupt was too much like him in many ways. While Haupt established himself as a leading authority in his field, his scholarly ambitions were far too bold. He tended toward erratic trains of thought and precipitous judgments, and advanced his political views in his scholarly oeuvre. The same was true of his antisemitic convictions. On December 28, 1886, he told Lagarde that only the betrayal of Jewish "clerics" made possible the Persian King Cyrus's conquest of Babylon. After his victory, Cyrus rewarded Babylonian Jewry by allowing them to return to the Promised Land. Underlying the Persian king's facilitation of Jewish return to Palestine was not any theological respect for Yahweh but rather his desire "to be rid of these unreliable followers." In 1889, Haupt gave up his dream of a German professorship and applied for American citizenship.

At first glance, the negative influence that Lagarde exerted on Haupt's scholarly advancement seems indisputable. This is especially true of the latter's unrealistic project, a complete critical edition of the Old Testament, which never got out of the starting gate.[26] Nevertheless, one should not underestimate the degree to which Haupt's scholarly beliefs were inspired by Lagarde. He worked with great concentration on his cuneiform edition of the *Epic of Gilgamesh*, which was dedicated to Lagarde and appeared in 1891, the year of Lagarde's death. Even if the edition was written in the Delitzsch tradition, the dedication was no small matter. The work has remained significant to this day and is still cited in the relevant literature.

Lagarde's longtime friend and correspondence partner Alfred Schöne was almost the polar opposite of Paul Haupt. He contributed very little to the science of classical philology, and worked for nearly his entire life on a monograph about the Greek historian and author Thucydides that never should have appeared in print. Schöne had a friendly, if slightly superficial, disposition and was very fond of the gentler sex. Lagarde's eulogy even diplomatically mentioned the personal magnetism of his charming friend. Even "younger women, who confided in this venerable man until he reached a ripe old age," had been able to understand his "awe of the hallowed."[27] Yet his passion for women had been Schöne's undoing. As a young professor in Erlangen, a respectable career had seemed to await him, until he became the subject of a scandal.

In early December 1874, Schöne molested a floral shop assistant who was just sixteen years old.[28] His strained marriage had already been the talk of the town. The press didn't respond until two weeks later, but the reaction was harsh in the extreme. The *Nürnberger Anzeiger* alluded to the fiasco and the punishable nature of the university professor's behavior. The Bavarian Ministry had no choice but to react. Just three days later, Minister Lutz made inquiries in Erlangen as to whether the article "was based on actual facts" and what steps were being taken. When confronted, Schöne confessed to the deed. As a result, the official documents speak rather euphemistically of "importunate advances." But the mere fact that Schöne voluntarily gave up his chair says a lot about the seriousness of the offense. Moreover, senior professors very rarely felt compelled to take such steps. Universities usually protected their own to the extent possible.

Although he otherwise attached great importance to codes of honor, Lagarde doted on Schöne, of all people. He immediately helped the classical philologist search for a new place of employment, which, in light of his meager oeuvre and miserable reputation, was anything but easy. Schöne knew that he would have a hard time finding any other advocates and showed a high degree of adaptability in his dealings with Lagarde. In his letters, he paid scrupulous attention to Lagarde's sensibilities and validated his worldview to the best of his ability. On April 25, 1876, he gave Lagarde a detailed account of his "deeply wounded spirit," which darkened the world for him. After finding work with Theodor Mommsen, he hardly ever missed an opportunity to vilify Mommsen's despotic character. Schöne portrayed Lagarde's increasing isolation from professional circles as the inevitable consequence of a heroic life. During a yearlong correspondence in 1876–1877, he wrote to him in a sympathetic but rather Byzantine manner: "You are feeling lonely. But your self-awareness will tell you that the higher you climb, the fewer companions you can expect to have."

Schöne even supported Lagarde in his conflicts with the Berlin establishment and, despite Lagarde's self-styling as "a fearless warrior on the side of truth," he surely could have done with words of encouragement. Schöne praised Lagarde's unfailing creative energy and compared him to the Roman historian and author Livius, even though Lagarde outclassed him in his focus on essentials.[29] Lastly, Schöne shared Lagarde's pessimistic view of contemporary culture. On December 28, 1882, he painted a grim, fatalistic picture of big-city life in Paris that could just as easily have come from Lagarde: "The situation here is truly repulsive. I get the impression that we are witnessing a slow disintegration. Nothing is certain anymore, least of all the banks and the big financial houses, which God in his wrath has allowed to become too large."

For Lagarde, restoring Schöne's honor and finding him an appropriate position were the central matters. With this in mind, he wrote on September 17, 1876, to the Leipzig philologist Friedrich Ritschl, who had once taught Nietzsche and was among the greats in his field. Lagarde felt that Ritschl ought to provide Schöne with a professorship at the Moscow Lyceum and chose a military metaphor to underscore the seriousness of his request: Schöne's "friends should not rest until he stands among the rank and file again." Ritschl expressed interest in the proposal, but the matter petered out after Ritschl died unexpectedly that same year. In February 1877, Lagarde organized a Göttingen signature list on behalf of their dismissed colleague. Twenty-three scholars signed the document aimed at getting Schöne hired in Prussian higher education. The petition did not argue the matter further on legal grounds, but essentially emphasized the core idea "that the Fatherland could not afford to lose any available employees, period."

In support of the petition, Lagarde asked the Bavarian Ministry for information. Officials in Munich were cooperative, informing the senior professor on February 8 that "early dismissal" of the matter had failed, because Schöne's marital problems had caused feelings to run high at the time. (The marriage later ended in divorce.) When Lagarde inquired as to whether the Erlangen Philosophy Faculty would object if Schöne returned to his old position, officials responded with even greater benevolence. Dean Eugen Freiherr von Gorup-Besanez also responded on February 8. He made it quite clear that people in Erlangen had nothing against a Schöne appointment and, in fact, believed he would "be a credit to any German university." People in Middle Franconia apparently wanted to let the dust settle on the matter.

Nevertheless, a professorship for Schöne remained out of reach. So Lagarde had to accept that his protégé was entirely at the mercy of Mommsen, who was a strict and often temperamental employer. Lagarde held the famous professor responsible for the fact that a professorship in Prussia did not materialize for Schöne. He angrily called Mommsen a "permanent shadow government" in professional matters and was convinced of his ruthlessness.[30] On February 10, 1878, he urged Richard Schöne to merely show important documents regarding his brother's professional advancement to Mommsen, but on no account to hand them over. Lagarde underscored his mistrust with this unrestrained statement: "I will only talk to this [particular] 'subject,' if at all, by means of a riding whip."[31] Needless to say, Lagarde's drastic formulation was not well received. He had to backpedal, but left the difficult task to his wife. Anna de Lagarde's response of February 14 was the height of academic diplomacy, but still could not hide a certain animosity. She expressed regret that "unpleasant and painful feelings" had been "caused," and referred to her husband's spirited disposition. But it wouldn't do Mommsen any harm to admit his mistakes from time to time. As harshly as those in the Lagarde home judged Mommsen, they were equally lax with regard to Alfred Schöne's misconduct. In a letter of December 6, 1880, to privy councilor Heinrich Göppert, Lagarde used Schöne's fate as an opportunity to complain about bourgeois double standards: "The spotty virtuousness of the world totally infuriates me. With one person, people overlook everything, while they persecute someone else mercilessly over a single problem." But it wasn't only his past that mitigated against Schöne's placement at a German university; it was also his scholarly mediocrity.

It is truly amazing how generously Lagarde overlooked Schöne's intellectual mediocrity. One should bear in mind that Lagarde had hardly any friends and was essentially a lonely man. But he knew that he couldn't get much professional capital from his involvement with the Latinist, so he mainly played up Schöne's unfortunate situation or his personal qualities. On December 23, 1877, for example, he told the renowned Parisian Assyriologist Julius Oppert that Schöne was "a very shy, thoroughly decent and good person." But friendly rhetoric did little to change Schöne's profile. If he wanted to accomplish anything on Schöne's behalf, then he had to depend on Göttingen. In 1877, he couldn't even get Schöne on the list for an associate professor of philology. When Georgia Augusta was looking for a Hellenist in 1882–1883, Lagarde failed again, because Schöne couldn't even run a distant second to the faculty favorite, Wilamowitz.[32] But, in 1884, the school managed to provide him with a librarian position in Göttingen. Three years later, a miracle happened: in faraway Königsberg, Schöne was appointed to a professorship in Latin grammar. As expected, Lagarde had been pulling strings behind the scenes. As soon as the opening in Königsberg came up, he approached Althoff to get the green light for the appointment.[33] Lagarde was even more emphatic with the Königsberg Sanskritist Adalbert Bezzenberger: "Jump at the opportunity. You cannot find a more knowledgeable, more cultivated, more reliable, more conscientious man than Alfred Schöne." On May 2, given the interest in an established grammarian, Lagarde also pointed to Schöne's ability to acquaint himself with unfamiliar subject matter. No doubt about it: to find a professorship for a librarian who had already turned fifty-one was an achievement of the highest order.

In Lagarde's scholarly dealings, however, Alfred Schöne was more the exception than the rule. The Orientalist knew all too well that his own scholarly reputation depended not only on his publications but also on the quality of his students and the trustworthiness of his personal recommendations. As much as he may have been at variance with the fraternity, this did not mean he no longer wanted to have any influence on it, not by a long shot. That's why he stuck to the rules in most internal matters and cultivated an outsider position in public. But Lagarde's international standing was another matter entirely. In England, France, and Italy, his wide-ranging editions were more highly regarded than in Germany, and people had great respect for his knowledge of Middle Eastern languages. He was also one of the few German scholars of his time who was conversant in modern foreign languages. Lagarde read Chaucer and Shakespeare in the original English. He communicated with the outstanding Italian and French Orientalists in their native tongues. But he also successfully used his command of ancient languages in his scholarly correspondence. So he wrote to the responsible Vatican officials in fluent Latin and occasionally socialized with the tiny research community of Coptic scholars in Coptic.[34] His English-language skills were of primary importance to his international reputation. Admittedly, he liked to imitate German thought patterns and figures of speech, and his papers therefore lacked a certain Anglo-Saxon elegance. But he was able to say whatever he wanted to, and that was more than most university professors in the land of Humboldt could claim in those days.

Lagarde had reliable contacts at Oxford and Cambridge who thought highly of him as a biblical researcher and rigorous philologist. In spring 1879, the prestigious Trinity College, Cambridge, purchased part of his library and paid for an extravagant research trip to southern Europe in the bargain. Lagarde was by no means so altruistic as to silently offer up a sacrifice. On December 30, he reminded Olshausen, his long-standing supporter at the Prussian Ministry of Education and Cultural Affairs, how disappointed he was with the government. Olshausen knew that Lagarde was quick to take offense and hastened to dispel his doubts. As always, the Septuagint edition took high priority in Prussia, even if the Foreign Office could not get hold of each and every manuscript. Furthermore, he expressed the hope that he would at least be allowed to see the first volume of the Septuagint, although that was "in God's hands." But Lagarde's travel activities had reached critical mass, and he could be glad that the expenses for his research trips to Rome and London in 1881, as well as those to Turin and Paris in 1882, were covered by English patrons.[35]

Lagarde's reputation in England was also due to his willingness to help. On March 19, 1876, he asked the principal librarian for London, Oxford, and Cambridge if he would be interested in receiving scripts from Prussian universities that were nearly impossible to procure via the book trade. The Orientalist didn't require any acknowledgment. He simply wished for his efforts to be seen as a token of his "gratitude for the wonderful hospitality that I, and many of my scholarly associates along with me, have enjoyed for all these years in

England and at English academic institutions." Lagarde's initiative was aimed at increasing scholarly exchange between Germany and England. On May 14, he proudly reported to Minister Falk that his idea had been greeted warmly. All three universities that he'd approached had accepted the "offering with the liveliest gratitude." Finally, this was an expression of the high regard in which German scholarship and the ideal of presuppositionless research were held at England's elite universities.[36]

Lagarde's international prestige was also seen in the Netherlands' offering him, in 1885, its very first professorship in the English language. The historic University of Groningen had decided to take this step, and Barend Sijmons, the philologist in charge, made every effort to win Lagarde for his alma mater. He couldn't promise Lagarde a student following, of course, so he stressed the prospect of "gaining the success due to him through teaching and other productivity in a new field."[37] The job understandably did not entice the frequently overworked Lagarde, and the university had to go in search of another candidate.

Lagarde belonged to that group of scholars who mainly experienced the world from behind their own writing desks. Even in the heyday of nationalism, the type of researcher who put the intellectual map before the geographical one was fairly common. We need only recall the important Oxford religious scholar Friedrich Max Müller, who, like Lagarde, had been promoted by Bunsen. As much as he loved India, he focused entirely on old manuscripts and never set foot on the subcontinent. He justified his approach as follows: "My India lay not on the surface, but many centuries beneath it."[38] A respect for language and history was hidden behind this statement that, regardless of any positivistic influences on scholarly practice, had its roots in Romanticism. Old manuscripts were the main scholarly sources, and close study of them was supposed to provide insight into the state of the world and the distinctive characteristics of religion. Lagarde was a passionate philologist who, despite his criticism of the academic establishment, retained a considerable amount of enthusiasm. This applied in great measure to his love of Coptic. Here, he believed he belonged to an elite group of researchers that had a multitude of important tasks before it. It suited him fine when his colleague Adolf Erman wrote to him from Berlin on December 22, 1881: "The righteous will now be recognized by whether they practice Coptic. The vast majority of Egyptologists will certainly not decide to do it, as it is not 'interesting' enough to them." But, time and again, Coptic had to take a backseat, because work on the Septuagint and a host of other projects demanded his time. Since the beginning of the 1880s, Lagarde had been saddled with a *Bibliotheca syriaca* (*Syriac Collection*), a *Bibliotheca aegyptiaca*

(*Egyptian Collection*), as well as an edition of collected writings that circulated under the name of Clemens Romanus. This almost boundless number of projects must surely have exceeded the capacity of a lone scholar.[39]

During his research trips, Lagarde put blinders on and concentrated entirely on the manuscripts. As expected, his accounts make for dry reading and mainly served to confirm his preconceived ideas. But even a workaholic philologist like Lagarde occasionally succumbed to the fascination of the Orient and tried to take advantage of the possibilities it contained. And so he responded with great interest when his student Wilhelm Spitta informed him on March 3, 1887, that, on account of national bankruptcy in Egypt, old manuscripts were being offered at bargain prices. He immediately brought this item to Minister Falk's attention so that he would take the appropriate steps.[40] In view of the uncertain situation, people in Berlin remained cautious, and Spitta avoided more substantial purchases as a result. Overall, Lagarde was quite interested in the widely traveled scholar, but he couldn't get him excited about German academic life. On August 30, 1878, Spitta told Lagarde that he would definitely consider whether to quit his job in Cairo "in order to begin the fight for a no-win, penniless existence as an adjunct professor." Nor did Spitta get ahead in Egypt. Like so many Europeans, he left the country four years later in the wake of the Alexandria massacre. He was forced to leave behind "all the books, manuscripts, papers, notes—in short, everything that I have worked on for the past twelve years"[41]—and was happy to have escaped with his life. However, such episodes were exceptional in Lagarde's correspondence. He usually corresponded with scholars who pursued their assignments in private studies or in the reading rooms of great libraries.

Scholarly jubilees were among the most important events in Lagarde's life. He was filled with pride when, in fall 1875, he was invited to the inaugural celebrations at Franz Joseph University in Czernowitz, the capital of the Austrian duchy of Bukowina. In his celebratory address of October 4, Lagarde solemnly stressed: "Divine Providence—who would wish to deny it?—has seen to it that Germans are born with the desire for truth and scholarship." Filled with idealism, he continued: "Germany is on good terms with scholarship by birth and, as it has learned from foreigners, has a closer relationship to it than other countries. And that's why Germany has friends in every place where scholarship is loved."[42] Lagarde thereby picked up on Fichte's idea that, because of their intellectual depth, Germans were especially predestined to study science. He also held the nationalistic belief in the greatness of the German people, a belief that had become all the more pronounced in late nineteenth-century thinking. Significantly, people on the northeastern periphery of the Habsburg

Empire had chosen German as the only language taught in schools and selected Lagarde as their speaker. He retrospectively told the university administration in Göttingen about the attitude of the citizens of Czernowitz: "Germans are thought of here as sensible, talented older brothers, so to speak. Their younger, less intelligent siblings follow them eagerly, because they realize how advantageous it is to do so." As narrow-minded as this statement sounds and as arrogant as it presumably was, Lagarde appears to have been genuinely pleased with the welcome he received in Bukowina. When his hosts wanted to print his celebratory address, he immediately wrote it down from memory.[43]

But Lagarde kept his distance from big celebrations at the University of Göttingen. It is not easy to judge whether this was more an expression of reservations about persons or the events themselves. A key player on two occasions was the theologian Albrecht Ritschl, whom Lagarde considered an exemplar of shallow academic optimism. In fall 1883, people on the Leine River and in every corner of Germany observed the four hundredth anniversary of Luther's birth. Lagarde had brought up Luther's alleged narrow-mindedness in a host of publications, so the celebration was problematic from the start. Lagarde viewed Luther as little more than a power-hungry champion of the people who was swept up in the general outrage at the beginning of the sixteenth century.[44] In his eyes, a Luther celebration was not in keeping with the interdenominational character of the university, whose sole purpose was to serve scholarship. With this in mind, he drafted a letter to the Göttingen pro-vice-chancellor, Consistorial Councilor Hermann Schulz, on November 9, 1883, arguing that Luther's importance had been barred from discussion and that people were deliberately mistaken about contemporary piety. It was precisely because people knew about the religious indifference of their contemporaries that they shied away from any form of public debate. On the basis of this double standard, Lagarde concluded that he was not required to attend the festivities. But he refrained from sending the letter, as it would have constituted an affront, and the Luther celebration at the university took place without him, all the same. For Lagarde, not showing up was a matter of conscience. But, needless to say, his actions had no political impact. They merely increased his isolation from the faculty and ensured that the strained relationship with Ritschl, who gave the official address, turned into out-and-out rancor. The famous theologian contemptuously informed a friend that Lagarde considered Luther a "completely insignificant man," because he hadn't "sifted through any versions of the Septuagint."[45]

Lagarde also stayed away from the 250th anniversary of the university in 1887. Albrecht Ritschl was still considered the defining figure in Göttingen. Although his Kingdom of God theology had seen better days and, even at Georgia

Augusta, the call for a systematic historicization of biblical sources had grown louder, it was still beyond question that the theologian would give the anniversary speech. In grand style, he invoked the nobility of classical university education, which had to be preserved during the contemporary "overcrowding crisis" at German universities.[46] Such a view was not so far removed from Lagarde's own. In that more than one thousand students were already enrolled in Göttingen, he also felt that the elite character of scholarship was at risk. But, in contrast to Ritschl, he considered Humboldt's ideas just as utopian as they were deleterious, because an excess of general education would in no way lead to a better understanding of the present. Nevertheless, the event garnered empire-wide attention and was rather meaningful for Lagarde, as well. The Prussian Ministry of Education and Cultural Affairs awarded him the title of privy councilor, which included an appreciable increase in salary.[47]

One year later, the Göttingen Gesellschaft der Wissenschaften (Society of Sciences) nominated Lagarde as its emissary to the eight-hundredth anniversary celebration at the University of Bologna. Lagarde was beside himself with pride. He immediately requested that the trustee grant him leave for at least one week. By way of explanation, he not only pointed to the travel time but also to the need "to introduce" himself to "the top people in Bologna." In Bologna, he was particularly impressed with the hospitality of the Italian people. He sang the praises of the student fraternities from Germany, which had held back from arrogant behavior toward the French in attendance. As nationalistic as Lagarde was, he knew how to observe etiquette when traveling abroad. In Italy, his dealings with German colleagues were appropriately friendly, even if they were frequently trying and conflict-ridden back home.[48]

Lagarde's self-image as a scholar is not easy to describe. From early on, he felt that he'd been treated unfairly, truly discriminated against. But, in spite of everything, he held on to the scholarly ideals of his youth. Even his vehement attacks on university life should not obscure his close identification with his social role as a professor. Like many senior professors, he managed to make an art of seeing himself as an outsider even after he was firmly established in academia. Personal idiosyncrasies were behind this practice, but so was a goodly dose of calculation. Lagarde knew that the "outsider" aura was especially attractive to young scholars. At the same time, he banked on the prestige of an esteemed professorship. The language of his scholarly texts is strangely dazzling. Sweeping generalizations and stark judgments stand alongside dry passages that are limited to a philologically ascertainable series of facts. Lyrical turns of phrase sometimes appear, used by Lagarde to point out unexpected opportunities for research or luck in finding sources. But, for the most part, his style alternates between quasi-know-it-all pedantry and airs reminiscent of a prophet.

Lagarde felt that decisions made by the academic establishment set the course for the entire nation. Since everything was black or white with him, with no shades of gray in between, every decision carried enormous weight. He rarely took the trouble to understand his opponents. So it is certainly no coincidence that this fateful sentence is found in the second volume of *Symmicta*, of all places: "I am an extraordinarily serious person whose good fortune and misfortune lie in the fact that I take everything—without exception—seriously."[49] Lagarde was inspired by the belief that, by means of royal support, he had triumphed over a host of enemies. Surely this was a romantic idea and, in light of the single-mindedness with which he sought to advance his career, more than a little complacent. But one also cannot deny how indebted he was to Wilhelm I for his immediate support. On October 2, 1883, he turned directly to the German kaiser and presented him with his scholarly convictions.[50] Lagarde introduced himself as an honest laborer in the vineyard of the Lord, whose efforts were aimed toward "gaining recognition for theology as a branch of historical scholarship." He played up his groundbreaking scholarly ventures and expressed the hope of "winning more laborers for a field that will bear fruit a hundredfold, the same field in which I must cease to be active within a short time."

The melancholy tone of this document illustrates that scholarship meant a great deal to Lagarde, but was certainly not everything to him. The letter indeed held the promise of certain progress, but only indirectly touched on the ultimate question of human existence. In his view, religion was responsible for the answers, and every action had to be aligned with religion. He attached vital importance to Germany's role in the salvation of mankind. And it was for this very reason that he found the state of the Bismarck empire intolerable.

8 Future Conspirators

In 1871, it seemed as if the bourgeoisie had reached their much longed-for political goal of a unified German Empire. When newspapers announced the impending French surrender on January 27, the eminent historian Heinrich von Sybel wrote a deeply emotional letter to his friend Hermann Baumgarten: "By what means did we earn the grace of God that has allowed us to see such great and powerful things?"[1] Now that Germany had attained its most important goal, he truly questioned whether he would be able to find a new mission in life. This view of things was not at all atypical. The German bourgeoisie as a whole felt in harmony with history and interpreted the victory over the French "enemy" as a sign of God's favor. An economic boom also took place in the wake of unification. The upswing was powerfully fueled by five billion francs in French reparations, more than three times the hard currency available in Germany at that time. People everywhere established joint-stock companies that, in turn, fueled feverish speculation. Berlin real estate reaped profits of up to 600 percent. But high market prices were as short-lived as the enthusiasm for the foundation of the empire.

The downturn arrived overnight. On May 9, 1873, dubious speculation caused the Vienna Stock Market to collapse, dragging the entire world economy from Berlin to New York into the maelstrom. Overheating of the German economy had particularly terrible repercussions. Between 1872 and 1874 alone, stocks lost approximately 50 percent of their value, and the surplus of available capital dwindled into a shortage. Countless firms proved financially insolvent. By the beginning of 1874, sixty-one banks, 114 industrial concerns, and four railroad companies were forced to declare bankruptcy. In the building industry, not more than seven of the fifty-five firms founded during the period of rapid industrial expansion from 1871 onward survived. Contemporaries saw the events as a "Great Depression" and backed up their perception with a meaningful sense of the deflationary crisis. The economy ended up suffering from extreme weakness for nearly two decades, and a decrease in real wages and high unemployment were among its consequences.[2]

There was great disappointment among small shareholders, in particular, and many professors fell into this category. They had invested in technologies of the future and in the railroad, having been promised a high rate of return. The majority of these investors were victims of unscrupulous businessmen and felt betrayed by the political system. Very few considered that their own unbridled pursuit of profits had played a certain role in their losses. In lieu of this recognition, cultural criticism took on a life of its own, and the "spirit of the founding of the German Empire" was maligned as superficial and unbearably greedy. The idealistic philosopher Rudolf Eucken, more of a moderate in his critique of the present, was a prime example of this way of thinking. Eucken was chiefly bothered by the value placed on money. He thought that politics had moved toward greater and greater dependence on the economic system.[3] A growing number of voices, from Jacob Burckhardt to Richard Wagner, predicted an overall cultural decline. In early 1873, Lagarde dispatched his first political treatise into this dark atmosphere. Awkwardly titled "Ueber das Verhältnis des deutschen Staates zu Theologie, Kirche und Religion. Ein Versuch Nicht-Theologen zu orientieren" (On the Relationship of the German State to Theology, the Church, and Religion: An Essay Addressed to Nontheologians), it picked up the thread of a lecture from 1859 that raked contemporary Protestantism over the coals.[4] In addition, the question was now where Protestantism stood on religious substance and the future of the German Empire.

At the center of Lagarde's critique was the Christian concept of religion, which primarily reflected the Apostle Paul's views and had almost nothing to do with Jesus or his disciples. This viewpoint was by no means original since, in a work that caused a sensation back in 1869, Ernest Renan had already separated the world of Early Christendom from Pauline "falsifications."[5] In keeping with those of the Parisian Orientalist, Lagarde's source-critical arguments emphasized the time gap between Jesus' lifetime and the writing of the Gospels. The same is true of the distinction Lagarde made between Jesus and the Jewish tradition. And he gave antisemitic prejudice free reign in the process. Like Renan, he strongly emphasized the Pharisees' "arrogant *Lebensferne* [alienation from reality]." But the rigid way in which Lagarde turned against the Apostle Paul has a meaning all its own. Suggestively and just as incontrovertibly, he said: "No people crucifies its ideals, and someone who a people crucifies absolutely does not correspond to the people's ideals" (p. 58). This statement had multifaceted implications, but Lagarde's lips were sealed as to how he wished it to be interpreted. He merely made reference to a forthcoming paper that was supposed to deal with Jesus' relationship to the Jewish people. It never actually appeared in print, however.

Lagarde was generally skeptical about existing Christian dogma. In essence, he felt, it had been passed down through history and barely still contained any ideas from the Gospels. Like all true religions, Early Christendom had been filled with God's presence. The Early Church did not concern itself with problems of dogma. In Lagarde's opinion, this also held true for the central theological elements like the doctrine of the Trinity. His estate contains a note in which he addresses belief in the Trinity as follows: "The church—that is to say, the true church—would always refuse to answer such questions, since the ability to answer them does not improve the human condition, and it all comes down to betterment alone."[6] At first glance, this may appear to be a purely historical statement. But, in fact, it contains the normative belief that any religion worth its salt must be attentive to the perfectibility of mankind.

Despite the earlier significance of the historical Jesus, Lagarde did not attach any importance to this question, because a living religion was never the result of fundamentalist belief. The meaning of historical events did not consist of "becoming knowledgeable" but of providing "the nation in which they occurred with the basis for a new existence" (p. 60). In principle, this was a functionalist view that judged religious myths according to their value to the nation. But, with a clever sleight of hand, Lagarde pushed these thoughts into the background: the very uncertainty of historical reports proved the earth-shattering power of the events that underlay them. So the difficulty of saying something certain about Jesus simply proved how much he had changed Jewish life. Complete renunciation of an archival-critical understanding of history was in harmony with a heroic view of Early Christianity. The worship of historical fact was nothing more than a kind of "fetishism" (p. 65) that was intended to mask the inner emptiness of the present. For the existential character of religion—that is, the "personal relationship of a devout person to God, living in him" (p. 65)—was beyond question.

The transformation of religious life stood at the center of Lagarde's expositions. If it was seriously intent on survival, then the newly founded German Empire needed a spiritual core. Due to their dogmatism, however, Protestantism, Catholicism, and Judaism had long since ceased to matter. No religious community was entitled to state support, because it could not seriously claim to represent the entire nation. Lagarde therefore concluded that existing churches should be declared sects and theological faculties disbanded. The future belonged to a new religion, one that would give the nation a spiritual center. Finally, unification of the empire entailed a redemptive component from the perspective of national history as sacred history, because "nations were not born in the physical sense, but by means of historical events. But historical events were subject to the workings of Providence, which showed them the way and the goal" (p. 72). However, it was not within the power of the state to create a new religion; states could only establish certain parameters. Lagarde understood these to include the establishment of public school education that refrained from all burdensome knowledge and, instead, fostered children's powers of imagination. The merits of university theology were also introductory in nature (lit. propaedeutic—providing introductory instruction). Theology's role was that of a "pathfinder of German religion" (p. 73). In that comparative religion encouraged a "certain polytheistic attitude" (p. 74), Lagarde attached considerable importance to this endeavor. The study of other religions showed "that God had willingly revealed himself at all times to all peoples" (p. 74). But the type of Protestantism that dominated university lecterns was far removed from such an unbiased view. For more than a hundred years, this Protestantism had been characteristically weak-willed and ambitiously denominational. Meanwhile, it was in such an advanced state of dreariness "that it was no longer possible to make rhyme or reason of this mess" (p. 74). Since Protestantism offered no help on the path to a religion of the future, one had to regard the support it received from the state as a grave error. The ideal of general education was similarly misguided and mainly paid homage to liberals. The number of school dropouts was an unmistakable sign of where today's youth stood on the subject of idealism. For half of them, it was simply a matter of obtaining authorization for the yearlong, voluntary military service that ended with the title "reserve second lieutenant," an enticing entry ticket to refined society. A corrupt authorization system had eroded the moral substance of German society from within and could be seen as a counterpart to the halfhearted religiosity of the Evangelical Lutheran Church. Lagarde thereby addressed a theme that had been a topic of public discourse for some time.[7] But, for him, the matter was not so much the future of the German educational system; he was more concerned with the soundness of his conclusion that contemporary religious life had no prospect of success.

Lagarde argued that, due to its transpolitical importance, the state mustn't get sucked into partisan battles. Its most important duty was to create an intellectual climate in which a national religion could thrive. Lagarde held those who set their hopes on the kingdom of God to a radical morality in which "tolerance" and "compromise" had no meaning because every action was either "a duty or a sin" (p. 81). Since the religious forms of the past were used up, the only hope for a born-again people lay in radical transformation. The new religion urgently needed to be developed, but the form it would take lay hidden in the womb of the future. And so the treatise ended with the vague appeal for people to behave in a way that would allow for the emergence of a national religion. Lagarde cleverly adapted the closing words to the visionary content of his religio-political message: "We should not be human, but God's children; not liberal, but free; not conservative, but German; not religious, but devout;

not Christian, but evangelical; the divine incarnate, living in each of us, and all of us coming together in a complete circle; no one like another, and no one unlike another; really growing in love without envy. For on the upward path to God, one person comes ever closer to another, yet the one never obstructs the other's path. Amen to that" (p. 83). This was no longer the polemical language of the contemporary critic, but the diction of a prophet.

Lagarde's treatise consequently aimed to delegitimize Protestantism, which, at the close of the Franco-Prussian War, had the upper hand in matters of religious interpretation. Members of his own family even took up the challenge. It is significant that Lagarde's polemical statement "no people would crucify their ideal" sparked the argument. His brother-in-law, Wilhelm Berger, noted that Jesus had been sentenced by the Pharisees, not by his own people. Lagarde defended his assertion with typical brusqueness, and his claim represented a long tradition of Christian antisemitism: "Jesus' judges and executioners were the leaders of the Jewish people, the Pharisees and the Sadducees."[8] By reason of expertise alone, there was no debating Lagarde's authority within the family. But how the public at large would respond to this peculiar mixture of religious and political opinions was entirely uncertain.

Representatives of the Evangelical Lutheran Church expressed great reservations about Lagarde's treatise. Even his colleagues in Göttingen distanced themselves from it. Only the guiding intellectual force of liberal Protestantism, Albrecht Ritschl—irrespective of his fundamental differences with Lagarde—expressed interest in Lagarde's ideas.[9] But this self-confident, systematic theologian was the sole person at Georgia Augusta who did. People elsewhere were also surprised at the radicality of the polemical paper. A close acquaintance like David Hilgenfeld was of the opinion that Lagarde had gone too far in his criticism of the church. On February 6, 1871, he told him "that it was not necessary to separate the Gospel from Christianity, to look upon the Apostle Paul as an unauthorized intruder, or to declare that Protestantism is unimportant and outmoded."

But, on the whole, a deafening silence prevailed.

Johannes Wedde, a poet from Hamburg, was the only one to respond in print. He complained in the weekly paper *Die Literatur* that Lagarde had gotten caught up in the "doubtful aura of the Protestant Association." This was certainly not an accurate assessment: the Deutsche Protestantenverein (German Protestant Association), founded in 1867, was situated within the broad spectrum of religious liberalism that Lagarde rejected. But the review illustrates how easily people could rank the religio-historically schooled author among powerful reformers, due to his critique of the academic establishment.[10]

Surprisingly enough, Lagarde's reaction to the review was anything but dismissive. On February 20, 1874, he thanked the author for having broken "twelve months of strict silence" about his treatise. Although he cannot have overlooked Wedde's interpretational problems, he closed his letter with the lofty sentence: "May truth lead the way!" Apparently, what mattered most to Lagarde was to provoke some sort of public response.

Lagarde also withheld criticism regarding Catholics at this point. In 1873–1874, he wrote two letters to the centrist politician Peter Reichensperger, whom he had met on a train trip. He forcefully promoted his religio-political views and presented himself to this member of the Reichstag (German parliament from 1871 to 1945) as a "recluse" and "loyal opponent."[11] But it is not known how the matter-of-fact politician reacted to Lagarde's overtures. In light of the 1872–1887 Kulturkampf pitting church against state in Prussia, it does not exactly stand to reason that a Catholic would have shown much support for the ideal of a "national religion." In general, Lagarde was in danger of isolating himself. Even a close friend like the scholar Georg Hoffmann couldn't handle the situation. On March 17, 1873, he admitted to Lagarde that he could find no bridge to his worldview, because Hoffmann had lost his way when it came to belief in a personal God. Other readers felt similarly. While Lagarde's political conservatism appealed to them, they did not share his religious beliefs. Although he was usually quick to take offense, Lagarde seems not to have taken this type of criticism personally and continued to send his polemical paper out into the world undeterred. Approximately sixty copies were distributed in all.

One of the most important addressees was Heinrich von Treitschke. The nationally minded historian was considered a first-rate scholarly authority, and his opinions in both political and moral matters carried a lot of weight. Treitschke expressed complete agreement with Lagarde's criticism of the academic establishment. With his own brand of pathos, he said in his response of March 29, 1873: "We are threatened by a weakening of spirit and mind, a barbaric system of superficial education that has such a horrendous impact for the very reason that it is enamored of itself and pretends to be on the side of humanity." Treitschke was much more skeptical about Lagarde's image of Paul, but he refrained from an explicit response, because he didn't think he had genuine knowledge of theology. So he passed the treatise on to Franz Overbeck, a young theologian who was teaching in Basel. Treitschke promised an in-depth response from Overbeck, who had been inspired by the essay to a theological confession of his own.

But Overbeck had already written to Göttingen by that time, and his letter could not have been more enthusiastic: "What could be more desirable at the present time than to be fortified by such a treatise, from which a cornucopia of truths spill out with triumphal clarity over a field in which one is confronted with public opinion, both scholarly and unscholarly, and from which one turns away in disgust, often disheartened?"[12] Overbeck was more moderate in his assessment of the academic world, however. He argued in favor of the widespread reform of theology but was opposed to its complete elimination. And Overbeck remained skeptical about Lagarde's "differentiation between the Gospel and Christianity."[13] He expressed reservations about Lagarde's image of Paul in the form of a shrewd question: "What do we retain of our ideas about Early Christianity if we adopt this view?" Regardless of such critical objections, the temperamentally reserved Overbeck was without question impressed by Lagarde's apodictic train of thought.

In the very first sentence of his discourse *Ueber die Christlichkeit unserer heutigen Theologie* (*On the Christian Spirit of Our Current Theology*), Overbeck stressed how thankful he was for Lagarde's inspiration. By this, he especially meant Lagarde's critique of the spiritual emptiness of the Gründerzeit, an emptiness that no "general education" could cover up. Overbeck also judged the church as urgently in need of reform. But there were still major differences separating Overbeck's worldview from that of Lagarde. A more detailed description of Lagarde's treatise as a "polemical and peaceful paper" suggests that Overbeck considered Lagarde's fundamental rejection of theology excessive. At the same time, he thought the idea abstruse that the comparative history of religion, of all things, could provide help in normative matters. He felt even more strongly that theology would not be helpful on the path to developing a "national religion." As he stated with remarkable clarity and directness: "Theologies have always been guided by their respective religions; in fact, the later the initial driving forces of the religion, the more energetic and undisputed they were."[14] The Basel theologian was skeptical about Lagarde's idea of a "German religion" to about the same degree that he was disconcerted by Treitschke's glorification of Hegel's *Machtstaatsgedanke*, the powerful national state as embodying "the Divine Idea as it exists on earth." Nevertheless, Overbeck recommended Lagarde's treatise to his friend Friedrich Nietzsche, with whom he had been intensively discussing the condition of the educational establishment in recent days.

Nietzsche was also impressed with Lagarde, whose position as an outsider seems to have attracted the classical philologist. Since his show of support for Wagner and his bitter quarrel with Wilamowitz, Nietzsche himself had been eyed with suspicion in his own field. In any case, Cosima Wagner noted in her journal entry of April 8, 1873, that Nietzsche told her Lagarde had been ostracized.[15] In addition, the two men held many of the same views: like Lagarde, Nietzsche did not believe that Germany's victory over the French constituted proof of spiritual superiority, and he regarded excessive historical literacy as an impediment to any new cultural beginnings. Moreover, he was convinced by Lagarde's sharp distinction between Jesus' message and Paul's ideas, a less radical form of which he already knew about through his familiarity with Renan. So the assessment of the enthusiastic reader (i.e., Nietzsche) was correspondingly positive. On January 31, 1873, he described Lagarde's treatise to his friend Erwin Rohde as "a little, highly remarkable text that says fifty false things, but fifty more that are true and right."[16] On the other hand, Nietzsche, like Overbeck before him, had great reservations about Lagarde's integration of "church and state." He judged Lagarde's idea as similarly high-flown to that of the left-leaning Hegelian David Friedrich Strauss, who wanted to endow the German Empire with a "new faith."[17]

At any rate, Nietzsche grappled with Lagarde in the period that followed. He occasionally cited Lagarde's scholarly oeuvre in his lectures and studied his political *Streitschriften* (polemical writings). But benevolent interest gradually gave way to scornful detachment. That the Orientalist from Göttingen styled himself a prophet seemed especially disconcerting to Nietzsche. In 1880, he wrote of Lagarde in *Rede und Schrift der Religiösen* (*The Rhetoric and Writings of Religious Persons*): "If a cleric's style and expression, both spoken and written, do not indicate that he is a *religious* person, then his beliefs about and on behalf of religion no longer need to be taken seriously. Those beliefs hold no *power* for the person himself: as his style indicates, he is just as ironic, presumptuous, malicious, fussy, and moody as the most ungodly person."[18] In light of this damning judgment, it is astounding that Nietzsche had anything more to do with Lagarde. Yet Nietzsche's works clearly indicate that he read him. For example, his formulation of the word *moralin* is reminiscent of Lagarde's polemic formulation *judainfreies Judentum* (Jewless Judaism). Lagarde's conviction that the Apostle Paul was completely opposed to the Gospel and had systematically reinterpreted it may have been even more important. This conviction was an integral component of Nietzsche's book *Der Antichrist*, which the philosopher considered his most important work.[19] The same can be said of the importance that Nietzsche attached to the person of Jesus. It led him to the trenchant pronouncement: "In essence, there was only one Christ, and he died on the cross." Lagarde put it less elegantly in his treatise "Ueber das Verhältnis des deutschen Staates zu Theologie, Kirche und Religion," but the content is strikingly similar: "Jesus proclaimed and stood for the Gospel which, in a certain sense, died with him" (p. 80). If one considers how much

Nietzsche loathed crypto-theological figures of thought and false prophets, then this reference cannot be easily explained.

Although Overbeck intensively promoted Nietzsche's ideas, Lagarde expressed no curiosity about them. The professor from Göttingen was solely interested in the social impact of his own religio-political concepts. He published his *Politische Aufsätze* (*Political Essays*) in 1874. But the volume contained only one newly written text, which appeared along with "Ueber die gegenwärtigen Aufgaben der deutschen Politik" (On the Contemporary Role of German Politics) and "Ueber das Verhältnis des deutschen Staates zu Theologie, Kirche und Religion." The new text was ambitiously titled "Diagnose" (Diagnosis) and described the German state as a provisional arrangement that lacked inner and outer unity. In particular, the expansion of the state had been a "stopgap measure," since neither Austrians nor Luxembourgers had been assimilated.[20] In any case, Lagarde adopted no particular line of reasoning, and wasted his time on numerous matters of church history and constitutional law intended for specialists, at best, but of no interest to a wider readership. A few turns of phrase, such as his critique of the "parasitic nature" of grammar schools or the "viscous slime of educational barbarism," were the only signs of his usual rhetorical power. Even though Lagarde was not terribly satisfied with the third essay, he and his opinions were thrust into public view.

Lagarde sent his *Politische Aufsätze* to a host of recipients, including the German ambassador to Paris, Prince zu Hohenlohe-Schillingsfürst, the chief of staff of the military, Earl von Moltke, and the bishop of Mainz, Freiherr von Ketteler. In order to allow for the preferences and idiosyncrasies of the addressees, he tailored his approach to each recipient, and this seems to have worked well. Field Marshal Moltke sent a friendly reply, saying that he had already read twelve pages and hoped "to study" the treatise "in more detail" soon.[21] Lagarde attached a great deal of importance to the historian and author Thomas Carlyle, whom he admired for his radical critique of the present. On December 4, 1874, precisely one day after Carlyle's eightieth birthday, Lagarde sent a copy of his *Politische Aufsätze* to London and added this expectant comment: "I apply to you, who know that a warrior life is the best of all lives." Lagarde had to wait a long time for an answer from the "apocalyptic Scot" (Huizinga), but it turned out to be all the more effusive. In his multipage letter of May 20, 1875, Carlyle stressed that he agreed with Lagarde on all essential points.[22] He called the Pope "an absolute nothing" and praised the "satirical" portrayal of Jews. He highlighted Lagarde's central idea: "without the restoration of true religion, there can be no real profit for a people."

Lagarde was delighted with the verdict. He was simply euphoric when he wrote to London on June 1 that he and his wife, Anna, saw themselves—and Carlyle as well—as "future conspirators." Lagarde did not elaborate on what he meant by this. But it makes sense to assume that he saw the state of the German Empire as so disappointing and messed up that he focused his hopes entirely on the future. Lagarde had also believed in the elitist character of devoutness from early on. On April 19, 1853, he wrote to the woman who would later become his wife: "To think of Christianity as a religion of the masses is entirely wrong. Its basic principle is noble and aims to create an aristocracy among mankind, a community of silent conspirators."[23] A letter of July 31, 1853, to Anna Berger may make a stronger impression with regard to the Heilsgeschichte aspect of his worldview. In an absolutely positivistic line of reasoning, he spoke about the life of the new religion he longed for: "Heathenism only fell into decline after Christianity already existed. And so the mere fact that Christianity is falling into decline is proof enough for me that the religion of the spirit is already known to a small, oppressed community somewhere in the world." In any case, Lagarde proudly showed Carlyle's letter to Georg Hoffmann and informed Franz Overbeck about the "letter I can truly call enthusiastic."[24] Nonetheless, Lagarde was not really satisfied with his *Politische Aufsätze*. According to his evaluation of current circumstances, in particular, he felt as though he hadn't struck the right note. So he took the book out of circulation then and there.

Just two weeks later, from August 31 to September 12, 1875, Lagarde again wrote down his political ideas. The text bore the austere title "Ueber die gegenwärtige Lage des deutschen Reichs. Ein Bericht" (A Report on the Current State of the German Empire) and was anything but a lackluster commentary. On the contrary: it took an offensive position with regard to the controversial issues of the day.[25] In terms of content, the paper can be divided into two categories. In the first section, Lagarde presented his assessment of the current political situation, as well as its value system. Its focal point was the relationship among state, country, and people, a topic that occupied many scholars after the founding of the empire. The second part analyzed the state of contemporary theology after the early years of the Kulturkampf. At the same time, Lagarde considered how Germany could arrive at a national religion.

Lagarde began his inquiry with the statement that the German Empire had no secure borders and, for this reason, faced the threat of being surrounded on two sides. He especially believed that conflict with Russia was inevitable, because the German hinterland was in need of the coastal region between Danzig and Königsberg in the long term, while the region was also of economic and military interest to the Czarist Empire. The main objective of German policy must be the "gradual Germanization of Poland" (p. 109), a goal with which Russia would also have to reckon. Moreover, the Czarist Empire could not be seen as an ordinary opponent. By dint of its huge population alone, which reminded Lagarde of the biblical plague of locusts, it was exceptionally dangerous. The primary justification for actions taken by the state would remain the security of the German nation. In any case, such a justification would be brought forward more than sixty years later, in 1940, for the annexation of Belfort in the west. In this later instance, the annexation was dignified by the claim that the Germans were a young people with a future, whereas the French or Hungarians were comparatively worn-out and stale. This idea did not originate with Lagarde, of course; it was a concept that enjoyed widespread popularity in the age of the nation-state. Within the Bismarck empire, Treitschke was its most efficacious advocate. He deduced that the distinctive character of the German nation made an aggressive foreign policy necessary.[26]

Lagarde's economic ideal was autarky. Germany had to be completely independent from imports so that it could pursue a powerful foreign policy in the interests of its own people. Lagarde's criticism that assembly-line production undermined all sense of patriotism was connected to the concept of autarky. As with Karl Marx, the debate centered on rejecting the division of labor: "No one should be required year in, year out, to do nothing other than to put a machine in place and look after it, a machine that folds and glues envelopes or drills eyes in needles. Such things do not satisfy the heart: human beings want the whole experience" (p. 115). But Lagarde's train of thought was an entirely religious one. He wasn't interested in the suffering of the workers per se, but in the fact that the industrial world led to "apathetic, brooding doubt or wild gorging," which, in either case, was an impediment to spiritual contemplation.

Lagarde considered ongoing emigration a serious problem for the German nation. This was because "farmers were" not "the true foundation of the state" (p. 118). There were too few people who, in accordance with Germanic tradition, owned their own land. The best remedy would be for Germany to colonize Austria, whose people only had importance as "material for Germanic regeneration" (p. 121). The moment he spoke about the peoples of Eastern Europe, Lagarde's diction took on an aggressively colonialist character. It was therefore the task of German farmers "to show the Magyars, Czechs, Ruthenes, Hannacks, and Slovaks who the better man was, and who, as the better man, had the right to rule" (p. 122). Lagarde's political objective only partially fit this nationalistic worldview in which armed farmers would prevail against the original inhabitants. A peaceful Central Europe under German leadership would "extend from the Ems to the mouth of the Danube, from Neman to Trieste, from Metz to the Bug" (p. 123).[27]

Lagarde had a romantic, conservative understanding of the state. As a consequence, citizens were "organically integrated members of a polity" (p. 125). He argued in favor of the simplest, most direct tax system and neighborly responsibility. He disapproved of political parties as decision-making organizations, because they were necessarily "partisan" and could, therefore, never represent the will of the entire people. Instead of average politicians, the state needed prophets who would replace "old, worn-out ideas" (p. 130) with sustainable, new ones. In general, one must refrain from parliamentarianism, because it was nothing more than the organized abandonment of personal responsibility. With pointed intensity, Lagarde talked about the disastrous "political priesthood" of parliamentarians, likening its impact to that of the "ecclesiastical priesthood" (p. 131). He placed his hope in boosting Germanic values, for which mutual trust between the people and their rulers was constitutive. On the other hand, the state's current access to all areas of the polity was a crisis symptom that pointed to the weakness of national power in Germany.

Many of Lagarde's invectives were directly aimed at Bismarck, whose policies prevented the Germans from becoming a people "of nothing but free men" (p. 133). His critique of Bismarck applied particularly to the undue influence of the press, which had made public opinion into the plaything of political calculation. His government symbolized Germany's lack of a true ideal. There wasn't even "a secretly open alliance" (p. 136) of people who believed in the nation's future and were ready to work toward it. This was a suggestive image, but it also hinted to the reader that he could have belonged to the chosen few who would one day determine the future of Germany. Lagarde's assessment of the present was extremely pessimistic, however. Since the founding of the empire, Germans were farther than ever from the development of their Faustian character, and the educated classes were not in a position "to even miss the most essential possessions: freedom, unity, religion" (p. 138).

In many respects, the second part picks up the thread of the treatise "Ueber das Verhältnis des deutschen Staates zu Theologie, Kirche und Religion." As in the previous case, Lagarde now spoke as an intimate connoisseur of contemporary theology, predicting its speedy end. His principal opponents were those scholars who propagated a "moral world order" or "universal love for mankind" as the core of Christianity. Such a stance was entirely ahistorical because, when the church was founded, the end of the world and the Last Judgment were expected to occur within a short time. A proper understanding of the Gospel embodied the diametrical opposite of dominant liberal values: "In the Gospel, love for mankind comes from above, from joy and humility. In liberalism, it comes from below, from fear and a guilty conscience. There, one loves because he is alive; here, because he will die" (p. 144).

Since the Catholic Church could only emerge stronger from it, Lagarde considered the Kulturkampf a foolish undertaking. It had acquired a vibrancy from the political confrontation that, in other respects, it had almost completely lost. Furthermore, the state lacked the will to "fight" Catholicism "on principle, i.e., the desire to destroy it" (p. 146). The church was even harder to target because the Pope could not be regarded as its head, but only as a "puppet" of the Superior General of the Society of Jesus (p. 149). Lagarde thus employed a starkly anti-Catholic thought pattern whose violent and latently paranoid character is obvious. He assigned positive value, however, to Catholic institutions that contributed to the preservation of "culture," and "whose moral failings" had "broken the back of Protestantism" (p. 166). Generally speaking, the power of "historical religions" was judged as "used up." In fact, this was true "not only in Germany, but in all of Europe" (p. 149). According to Lagarde, the rapidly increasing lack of faith was a sign of the times. And this lack of faith was undermining the moral standards of individuals and nations alike. He spoke almost imploringly about the danger of universal nihilism: "We are standing at the abyss. Whoever thinks the precipice is less of a precipice because it is veiled in mist may keep his opinion to himself" (p. 150). Educating people in a humanitarian fashion did not get us any further along and, upon further examination, only produced "midgets" (p. 154).

What surely must have surprised many of his contemporaries was that Lagarde considered science the most reliable ally of religion. One could learn from science that true faith neither needed nor tolerated any state guidelines. Furthermore, scientifically based theology taught people how rotten the foundations of contemporary religious communities were. Not even the textual bases of the Old and New Testaments could be considered reliable. All of this would only be remedied if people learned to understand theology as a "branch of historical scholarship" that saw Christianity as a "historical fact" (p. 161). Along with comprehensive philological abilities, a capable theologian had to "possess" a feeling for "great historical events," which according to Lagarde "dated back to a celestial power" (p. 163). The science of comparative religion could even teach people how God had worked throughout history. But Prussian universities were a far cry from any of this. As an investigation into the laws enacted in May 1873 governing state theological exams clearly showed, the tests had placed excessive demands on students. The students had to acquire immense amounts of historical knowledge and, as a result, would "become even more anemic, superficial and untruthful [. . .] than they already were" (p. 170).

Hegelianism had dominated university lecterns for a good fifty years. Lagarde now pointed to it as the cause of the excessive demands placed on students by these learning requirements. This was a direct consequence of Borussian hubris, which held that academic training was complete, while progress in all empirically strategic disciplines like "philology, comparative linguistics, chemistry, physics" (pp. 173ff.) was indisputable. The disastrous Prussian school authorities had teamed with Hegelianism and caused knowledge for its own sake to lose all meaning. Only its despicable usefulness had any value: "To be a teacher and go to school today is a business" (p. 178). A person's true obligation to honorably practice his profession was no longer within the purview of the Prussian educational system. For his purposes, Lagarde took advantage of current themes. Over the decade-long founding of the empire, for example, Hegelianism had long since passed the zenith of its popularity and was far from determining the curriculum in schools. This was even more true of the university world. Neo-Kantianism in universities owed its triumphal progress to the dependence of the success of the natural sciences on a methodology that would receive unqualified, energetic patronage.[28]

The recognition that Germany urgently needed an ideal was crucial to the solution of future endeavors. It was all too easy for outward success to obscure a polity's lack of substance. "The Reich is not a unity" (p. 182), Lagarde stated apodictically. And one must keep in mind here that Germany was more to him than an empirical fact of history. Like Fichte, Lagarde understood "Germany" in terms of the "notion of the ought." Unlike Fichte, however, he concentrated his energies on the inner, rather than the outer, enemy. "Germany," he concluded both affirmatively and evocatively, "is the sum total of all German-feeling, German-thinking, Germanically inclined Germans. Every one of us who, in light of this, does not consider himself personally responsible for the existence, the good fortune, the future of the Fatherland at every moment of his life is guilty of treason; everyone who does so is a hero and a liberator" (p. 182).

Antisemitic motifs did not play a central role in Lagarde's train of thought, but neither were they marginal. As a religion, Judaism was just as outmoded as Protestantism and Catholicism. But its danger lay in the great influence it exerted on the European press. At the same time, Jews were a factor in national disintegration. Countries that had been subjected to strong Semitic influences, such as Spain, could not "be considered [. . .] European" (p. 111). When speaking about the sinister influence of "liberal, neo-German, Jewish [. . .] journalists," Lagarde fused antiliberal and antisemitic enemy stereotypes to some extent. But, for the most part, Lagarde argued along traditional antisemitic lines. He reproached Jews for their backward-facing outlook, which did not suit the demands of the new era. But the eagerly progressive outlook of liberal Protestants was even more ruinous, because its superficial optimism prevented pursuit of the most important goals: spiritual rebirth and the national unity that would result from it.

A bit more about Lagarde's use of language: his diction is a remarkable blend of matter-of-fact passages and powerful, often crudely pejorative imagery. With regard to the possibility that Austria could be governed by Hungary, for example, he stated: "Things have not gone so far downhill in the birthplace of the Nibelungenlied and German literature that one must eat goulash or dance the czardas in order to govern them" (p. 112). The images Lagarde used to evoke the magnitude of the contemporary cultural crisis were particularly intense. From the very outset of the treatise, readers were sworn to unconditional love of truth: "Even in the case of a hopeless illness, it is better to know where one stands than to hope for blue skies while the coffin is all but ordered and the grave dug" (p. 106). What's significant is that, whenever he intended to depict contemporary religious life, metaphors of death would appear. Lagarde not only used them to dramatize his critique of religions, which had descended to the state of mere cults, but to sanctify his idea of nationhood as well.

Lagarde's diction was at its most impressive when he described the horror of life in a godless world. The following statements deserve to be read very carefully. They not only show the extent of Lagarde's despair about the present but also the profoundness of his cultural pessimism. They are reminiscent of Heidegger's famous comments on "the One" in *Sein und Zeit* (*Being and Time*): "If anything is characteristic of our time, it is the brutal tyranny of generality, which the old church called the world, whether this world comes in the guise of habits, fashions, customs, societies, states, or churches. All other suffering is infinitesimal as compared with the pain of being a Helot, never to be allowed to belong to oneself, not even for half a minute" (p. 172).[29] Unlike Heidegger, however, Lagarde presented his stance from the perspective of the history of philosophy. Given that all institutions had become washed up due to the homogenizing forces of modernity, Lagarde still retained hope that the onset of mass production would not stifle life altogether. The choice lay with "individual persons," who were entrusted with the "future of earthly affairs and the future of Germany" (p. 172).

These were solemn words. But, once again, the public response to Lagarde's paper was not encouraging. The *Neue Evangelische Kirchenzeitung* described his worldview as plain over-the-top. The *Merkur* (*Mercury*) doubted whether "a thinly populated country without industry could become thickly populated." The verdict of the *Protestantische Kirchenzeitung für das evangelische Deutschland* (*Protestant Church Newspaper for Evangelical Germany*) was even more negative and accused Lagarde of "boundless arrogance and dogmatism."[30] Even Franz Overbeck expressed reservations. On January 14, 1876, he raised doubts over why Lagarde, given his fear of the "omnipotence of the state," expected so much of the German Reich, which is why Overbeck himself warned against "driving out the Devil with Beelzebub."[31] Overbeck refrained from offering explicit criticism, but indicated to Lagarde that people in Bayreuth were interested in his ideas. The politically ambitious professor responded immediately.

On January 16, 1876, Lagarde sent a copy of his treatise *Ueber die gegenwärtige Lage des deutschen Reichs* to Cosima Wagner and stated conspiratorially in the accompanying letter: "May I ask you to read my work yourself and to circulate it among your friends? The press is sure to address it with profound silence." Cosima and Richard Wagner set to reading the treatise immediately. They approved and were downright enthusiastic. Cosima phrased it this way in her response of February 6: "The task you assign to Austria, your proposals regarding the schools, the evidence you provide that a people lives solely through its ideals, the attempt to save the core of Christianity for us, all of these points [. . .] have captivated us and filled our consciousness." She invited Lagarde, together with Overbeck, to Bayreuth. But the professor, always mindful of his independence, turned down the invitation. In 1878, Lagarde responded similarly when Richard Wagner invited him and Constantin Frantz, the second most important Bismarck critic in Germany, to shed light on the question Wagner posed in his essay "Was ist deutsch?" (What Is Germanness?).[32]

Despite his great determination to have a political impact, Lagarde was rather shy, and his scholarly projects took up nearly all his time. On November 30, 1880, he explained to Hans von Wolzogen that his time was filled "for years to come." Moreover, Lagarde revered Bach and Beethoven but didn't care at all for Wagner's operas. After seeing a performance of *The Flying Dutchman* in 1881, he wrote to his wife from Munich: "I am completely cured of Wagner and will not voluntarily sit through such torture again. And Wagner is a *world* apart, a yawning chasm between me and all those empty, ostentatious goings-on."[33] A few days later, he sent these disparaging comments from Rome: "The overall result is that, for the price of two talers, I have learned that my instinctual aversion to Wagner was entirely correct."

Although many were given the brush-off, people in Bayreuth remained stubbornly interested in Lagarde. This attitude could not merely be explained on the basis of common ground with the Wagnerian worldview, despite manifold points in common that extended from admiration for the king of Bavaria to the rejection of metropolises and marked antisemitism. Within a short time, Lagarde had become the subject of fierce debate in intellectual circles. The concept of a "national religion" took center stage. He also occupied himself with a topic that was otherwise largely ignored in the educational and socio-critical discussions of the 1870s. And one should not be led astray here by the objections of exceptional thinkers like Nietzsche or Overbeck. Many people felt the meaningless void in the German Empire was so great that they longed for a spiritual answer for the German people as a whole. The state and church were under pressure to modernize, and modernization did one more thing: it made radical voices heard.[34]

Even Ernst Schmeitzner, Nietzsche's publisher since the summer of 1874, showed interest in Lagarde. He intended to develop his publishing house in Chemnitz into a center for cultural criticism and wanted to sign a contract with the professor from Göttingen every bit as much as he did with Overbeck or Richard Wagner. On March 2, 1875, the businessman obsequiously told Lagarde that he "would do everything possible in order to fulfill his wishes." Even though he was dissatisfied with the Diederichs Bookshop in Göttingen, which handled his political treatises, Lagarde did not respond to the offer, and his reasons remain obscure today. He most probably wanted to avoid the effort it would have taken to change publishers. In light of Lagarde's combative temperament and the great reservations that Schmeitzner's "house author," Nietzsche, would later have about Lagarde, it is likely that the new relationship would not have been a happy one.[35]

At Eastertide 1878, the fifty-year-old Lagarde published a book that would soon make him famous. Even the title, *Deutsche Schriften* (*German Writings*), was programmatic. It also reminded Lagarde of Jacob Grimm's *Deutsche Mythologie*, which his great mentor had likewise published at the age of fifty in 1835. The *Deutsche Schriften* were essentially a loosely connected group of essays and poems, yet they seem to have given the predominant impression of homogeneity. This is even more surprising since the texts in question were written for very different purposes. What may also be responsible for the perception that the *Deutsche Schriften* were an integrated whole was Lagarde's declamatory rhetoric. He emphasized in the preface that, for him, it had always been about "truth and the Fatherland."[36] And he presented his main purpose as the development of a religious community. The contemptuous picture Lagarde painted of his opponents stood in stark contrast to his noble goals. In keeping with their dispositions, his opponents had confined themselves to slinging mud at him and suppressing positive responses. He styled himself an infamous author, but this certainly does not suffice to explain why Lagarde struck a sympathetic chord with readers. The deeper reasons for his success can only be seen in the message itself and the way it was expressed linguistically.

The *Deutsche Schriften* covered a wide spectrum of subject matter, ranging from disappointment at the defensive foreign policy stance in the Bismarck era to criticism of assembly-line production to lamenting the state of the church and the indolence of its representatives. Lagarde touched on styles that ran the gamut from cynical commentaries to atmospheric idylls. From a purely chronological perspective, a quarter century lay between the first essay about conservatism at the beginning of the Nachmärz period and the final two papers, "Zum Unterrichtsgesetze" (On Teaching Laws) and "Die Religion der Zukunft" (The Religion of the Future), which Lagarde wrote especially for his magnum opus. The elegiac tone of the several poems Lagarde incorporated expresses how greatly the author suffered in the present and how much he longed for better times. Generally speaking, Lagarde's nationalistic-religious semantics tie together an astounding number of topics and assimilate biblical motifs to a larger extent than his critique of the philological state of the Holy Scriptures would lead one to assume. At the same time, one should not disregard his political purposefulness. The ideological writer knew exactly whom he was attacking. On April 6, 1879, he wrote emphatically to Gustav Bickell: "My mission is to destroy Protestantism and the neo-Prussian school system." And Lagarde went to considerable effort to achieve his purpose. For example, he asked the Office of Statistics what kinds of financial aid were available for students in Prussia. When it came to student alcohol and nicotine consumption, he was not content with hearsay and requested the numerical data.[37] Lagarde willingly informed his readers about these statistics, as well as other data that substantiated his reasoning. And so there is an evidently positivistic streak in the *Deutsche Schriften* that, on the face of it, does not gel with its religio-political thrust. Yet the obviousness of its highly normative judgments may have actually enhanced its appeal.

The essay "Zum Unterrichtsgesetze" contains a wealth of opinions about the two institutions that decisively shaped Lagarde's life: schools and universities. When it came to schools, he claimed to speak from his own intimate, twelve-year experience on the job and, as a tenured professor, his authority in matters of grammar school politics was beyond question anyway. He chose to start with German universities' continual need to discuss how dreadfully incapable their students were of independent thought. This pointed to the grave weaknesses of the school system, which was incorrectly considered exemplary on the whole. Overloading the students with material had particularly disastrous consequences. When confronted with such quantities of superfluous knowledge, no young person could be expected to hold personal opinions. Finally, Lagarde repeated his criticism of the "authorities," who placed some sort of monetary value on every school-related qualification. This linkage inevitably had a corrupting influence on students and their parents. Overcrowded classrooms and overtaxed teachers added yet another layer that made a farce of school teaching. His demand for "thirty students at most" to be "taught in one and the same classroom" (p. 203) may seem moderate by today's standards, but it was bold for an era when classes commonly had more than fifty students. Lagarde used his own workload at Berlin grammar schools to underscore the danger that, under the current circumstances, teachers would become "burned-out slag" (p. 204). He cited grading 212 to 239 assignments per week. Only the receipt of a royal stipend, he pointed out powerfully, had saved him from physical collapse in 1866.

There was an abundance of hard laborers in the nineteenth century, and Lagarde was among the hardest workers in the academy. So the fact that he, of all people, championed increased leisure time in the educational system was not without a touch of irony. Sufficient time for continuing education was of primary concern for teachers, as continuing education was the only way to counteract ossification within the profession. But this measure would only succeed if the state were free to promptly dismiss incompetent teachers. Students, on the other hand, should concentrate on no more than a few subjects in which their intellectual discernment needed sharpening. Lagarde also argued in favor of establishing elite boarding schools where, away from the destructive impact of big cities, a small number of students could acquire crucial life skills. The English public schools may have served as a model for the Anglophile scholar. But German boarding schools like Schulpforta in Saxony-Anhalt had such excellent reputations that they could easily have served as models for the future.[38] Lagarde showed no support for the education of girls, of course. In keeping with his archconservative understanding of society, elementary knowledge was sufficient to prepare female students for their future roles as housewives and mothers.

Universities had to provide such a large number of educational services that there was barely enough time to teach the essentials. For this reason, saddling them with the additional burden of research was entirely out of the question. He proposed assigning research to academies and developed detailed plans to reform them. Universities would have to get over the lack of outstanding scholars, because the idea that important scholars would necessarily be convincing teachers could only be regarded as a myth. For the simple reason that doctorates could be reserved for future scholars, university standards would not be lowered. While the "current practice" made the problem worse "by allowing attempted deception, if it was discovered, to remain within scholarly circles that soon forgot about it" (p. 215), future cases of academic fraud would be the concern of the public prosecutor. The urgent exhortation to only fill positions for which a suitable candidate could be found was also along these lines. Against the backdrop of his own life experiences, Lagarde considered it a sure thing that "not only ideas, but also nonentities kept company with one another" (p. 222). This led to the regrettable mediocrity in recruiting, and one was hardly ever called to account for the social consequences of this phenomenon. Lagarde recommended free competition instead, which, in a poor country like Germany, would lead to an improved situation in the foreseeable future. Further, it was urgently necessary that universities strengthen their regional sense of rootedness. As soon as the provinces were responsible for them, many financial and administrative difficulties would take care of themselves. Since people were mainly interested in situations that had unmistakably personal relevance to them, private support would then be easier to come by.

Some of Lagarde's proposals for reform must have seemed bizarre to his contemporaries. In order to boost book sales, he wanted to forbid Prussian libraries from loaning out all books printed after 1520 (!). The wish to minimize the scholarly print media that harmed authors was hardly more realistic. At least such ideas clearly show that Lagarde's scholarly ideals were properly conceived. Since the Middle Ages enjoyed increasing popularity as a conservative alternative to the imagery of the liberal era, they were the height of fashion.[39]

The scholarship program was something close to Lagarde's heart, and his introductory comment could still be valid today: "No one in Germany knows what all is available or where to find it" (p. 227). He condemned the misuse of scholarships by the well-to-do and called for the social significance of scholarly funding to be strictly observed. Lagarde's ideological rigidity certainly led him to strange conclusions. For example, he considered it "absolutely out of the question for people who participated in the usual tavern scene, smoked tobacco, had dogs and indulged in other so-called pleasures to receive one red cent of scholarship money" (p. 228). However, our removal in time should not prevent us from seeing that many of Lagarde's ideas would successfully have taken hold in the reform movements at the turn of the twentieth century. And it is truly remarkable that, during the decade of the Reichsgründung, he deemed the victory over nicotine ten times more important than the victory at Sedan.

The meaning Lagarde attached to schools and universities shows up in the figures of thought that lend historico-philosophical dignity to an educationally skeptical train of thought. Lagarde took the view that people lived "in the midst of civil war" (p. 187), by which he primarily meant the aftershocks of the Kulturkampf. The emptiness of contemporary culture manifested itself in people's inability to describe things precisely. Lagarde, like Confucius before him, considered questionable means of expression a symptom of cultural decline. In Lagarde's Germany, one noticed "a way of speaking in which people no longer spoke, but shouted; no longer said things nicely, but charmingly; not greatly, but colossally; in which they no longer found the right word, because the word no longer stood for the thing itself, but for an echo of some talk about the thing" (p. 189). Lagarde considered moral decline, such as could be seen in the growing numbers addicted to drugs, a temporary phenomenon. He imploringly exhorted his readers: "Make no mistake about it: a stone rolling downhill does not stop by itself—it must be stopped" (p. 230).

Germans had sold their souls to an insipid *Gemütlichkeit* (geniality, coziness) induced by alcohol and nicotine, rendering schools powerless to exercise pedagogical authority. Lagarde expressed the helplessness of teachers in an equally emphatic and momentous way: "We cannot educate, because education must be for all time. And the parents of the children sitting before us don't think about eternity, but strictly about whatever is current" (p. 190). Unfortunately, the basic conditions required to change parents' behavior were missing. Yet it was advisable to prepare for the ideal future that one aspired to, a typically conservative, traditional future that would be a "union of free clans under a strong kaiser" (p. 221). The immediate purpose of Lagarde's conservative utopia lay in the rejection of the present, which was the result of political and pedagogical "fraud in the founding of the empire." He hoped for a time when Germany's future would no longer be determined by despicable utilitarianism, but by true religiousness. He put his faith in young students who, as soon as they "sensed [. . .] war or a coming storm" (p. 234), would show plenty of idealism.

Antisemitic motifs did not play a quantitatively important role in Lagarde's politico-educational remarks, but these remarks' inner content was highly significant. His argumentation aimed to delegitimize liberalism, an ideology that displayed Jewish influences. He placed special emphasis on the core dishonesty of liberal Judaism, which only appeared willing to acculturate and conflicted with the uniformity of national culture. At the same time, hatred of Jews was essential to the idea of "German religion." According to Lagarde, the contents of the Old Testament were without a doubt morally corrupting and alien to the Germans. With true biblical wrath, he said: "If ye want no orthodox statutes and notions, ye German forefathers, then first get ye rid of Old Testament biblical history, and do it so thoroughly that their names may never be mentioned in the presence of your children" (p. 200). In the harshest terms, Lagarde repudiated the idea that the content of the New Testament was already laid out in the Old Testament: "The biblical history of the New Testament is only tolerable on the condition that Jesus, whom it is about, is the Son of God, as the church claims he is: the rabbi of Nazareth is extremely boring" (p. 200). With this statement, Lagarde not only apodictically separated Jesus from Judaism; he also expressed this point with harmful intent. This was no longer just the antisemitic scholar speaking, but the antisemitic pamphleteer as well.

From among the essays in the *Deutsche Schriften*, the last one attracted the most attention. Its title, "Die Religion der Zukunft" (The Religion of the Future), is programmatic and suggestive in equal measure. But the title is misleading. While Lagarde took a detailed look at events in Christo-Judaic religious history, he had very little to say about further developments. From biblical criticism to clashes with the Prussian school system, he picked up on familiar motifs and tried to make the best possible use of them for his new main theme, the development of a national religion. Lagarde's understanding of God took the perfectibility of man as its starting point, and the ethical character of that understanding is clear. He categorically emphasized: "One only reaches God [. . .] by endeavoring to become a better person, because only effort can arrive at goodness, and goodness and God are one and the same" (p. 236f).

Lagarde generally stuck to the idea that only knowledge won from intensive source study could help in theological matters. With this in mind, he defined theology as "the knowledge of the history of religion" (p. 240f). There were two pitfalls to avoid in solving religio-historical problems. One was that myths were anything but original religious phenomena: "They were the cultic and interpretational materials of a priesthood" (p. 238). The second was that one could not impose present-day ideas on the past, as was the rule for research in comparative mythology and its penchant for "dirty business" (lit. unethical behavior) (p. 240). As a result, Lagarde implicitly turned against the religio-historical models of progress that had flourished since the Age of Enlightenment. In analyzing the past, he mainly identified periods of decline that were well suited to the culturally pessimistic framing of his arguments. At the same time, his orientation toward a future religion required a cyclical perception of time that was in turn connected to the vitalization of nationalistic mythic traditions. The intellectual inconsistencies and contradictions resulting from the use of both linear and cyclical concepts of time do not seem to have bothered Lagarde. Rather, the ambiguity of his perception of time served to push forward the timeless and genuinely historical character of religion, as the need arose.

Lagarde's idea of religion was comparatively down-to-earth and focused on the cohesion of human society. In almost sociological language, he said: "Religion never has a relationship to nature: it develops and operates within the human community" (p. 238). But since genuine human society depended on inwardness, the decidedly soulful Germanic past had special meaning. In his approach to *Volkstum* (popular customs and traditions), the scholar from Göttingen proved to be an out-and-out nationalist. According to Lagarde, only historical (i.e., great and powerful) peoples could be considered "healthy," whereas noble savages, wrongfully described as "primitive," were "the consequence of disease" (p. 239). He blended the already highly problematic doctrine of "young nations" with antisemitic views and identified the Jews of Eastern Europe as its clearest expression. One example of his pejorative language should suffice: "Today, ten- and twelve-year-old Jewish parents in a Hungarian *puszta* beget microcephalic half-men, half-beasts that are of pathological and not physiological import" (p. 239). One would nonetheless be in error in proclaiming Lagarde a biologist straightaway. From Lagarde's perspective, even the nation, the epitome of true community, could only be understood as a spiritually elite phenomenon. "The nation does not consist of the masses, but of a spiritual aristocracy," he phrased it emphatically. Unequivocally, but just as open to additional layers of interpretation, he continued: "The nation does not live in the past, but in the future" (p. 245).

Lagarde approached biblical history as a cultural nationalist and found it wanting. He only attributed high moral character to future-oriented, patriotic prophets: "The prophets had an instinctive feeling for ethics and for Israel. For the first time in history, the flame of love for the Fatherland burned in them with the purest light: a love for the Fatherland that did not see in the Fatherland the old habit of a pleasant life, but that bore a great mission, the earthly embodiment of an idea" (p. 244). In this case, however, one must also consider that the image of the prophets shone so brightly in order to further darken the Pharisees' Judaism and its alleged arrogance toward other peoples. In a strikingly judgmental tone, he spoke about the sinister influence of this priestly caste: "The nation was essentially pharisaical and, since becoming so self-righteous, has been an object of scorn and loathing to all who come into contact with it" (p. 245). Lagarde judged monotheism an already ubiquitous religio-historical phenomenon that had been wrongfully monopolized by liberal Judaism. At the same time, he allowed himself to make value judgments containing no trace of scholarly skepticism. The following exemplary passage admittedly doesn't allow for precise historical classification. But the preponderance of relevant references can already be seen in the choice of words: "Even in those days, many a comfortably retired *Biedermann* (petty bourgeois) thought that Jewish monotheism was a religion, that Plato—without revealing the source of his wisdom—was only a student of the marvelous Moses, and so accorded the keyword Judaism the same benevolence that equally high-minded souls grant nowadays to no less worthless terms, such as liberal and nationalist" (p. 246).

Lagarde considered Jesus the decisive break in continuity with the history of Judaism, comparing his importance to that of Copernicus in the field of astronomy. In lieu of unworldly sophistry, Jesus had preached "repentance" and "new birth." The religio-historical importance of Jesus was less apparent in the specific form of the stories told about him, and lay more in the fact that these stories could be told at all. In some ways, his death was related to the myths of the Levant, but "[he] transposed these old *Weisen* (ways, tunes) into a higher key, from minor to major" (p. 248). The church soon distanced itself from the poetic aspect of faith. In doing so, it had failed to fulfill its most important task, to create space for religious experiences. Lagarde saw the decisive influence of Judaism as the main cause of this undesirable development. And so "the Jewish way of dealing with the Holy Scriptures was passed on to the church" (p. 249), and the church had not resisted it sufficiently. Presently, the hypertrophic preoccupation with history showed a strong Jewish influence. But since taking stock of the past was not an approach that furthered the development of a new religion, one had to outgrow this attitude, regardless of any liberal clichés like "culture" or "making the world a better place."

The main task facing "Germanic peoples" was "to establish a link between their nationality and religion." Ecclesiastic dogmas could only be taken into consideration if the "Jewish poison" were to be completely removed from them (p. 254). Lagarde's nationalistic view of religious life was strictly opposed to the philosophical theory of historicism: "Apart from those things that can be repeated at any moment, nothing is of benefit to mankind" (p. 254). Lagarde was very moderate in his critique of the sacraments, however. He only wanted to change the Eucharist so that it more strongly emphasized the impermanence of human life. Lagarde placed the salvation of individual human beings alongside the fate of nations and, in doing so, was solely interested in Germany. The "future church" must be an expression of "the natural Germanic predisposition" (p. 254). Just what this consisted of was never concretely explained, because the Germans had never found their place in history. But Lagarde left little doubt that he—like Jacob Grimm before him—saw a solitary life that was close to nature as appropriate for Germans. This pastoral idyll also served a dual function: it delegitimized Christo-Judaic priestly supremacy as unrealistic, indeed hostile to life, and simultaneously conveyed the fundamental principles of social conservatism. As did many other nationalists of his time, Lagarde formulated his idea of the nation as a religious community, emphasizing its exclusive character. And the success of the theologically knowledgeable cultural pessimist in politically activating the stock of religious symbols is noteworthy.[40] The historico-philosophical priming of his thinking, which was mainly directed against the liberal belief in progress, also appears striking.

Lagarde countered the liberal concept of history with romanticized ideas whose roots lay in the period of the Befreiungskriege (Wars of Liberation against Napoleon: 1813–1815). Only when a people recognized its true nature would it decisively gain strength. For this reason, victory on the battlefield showed that a particular people took part in God's plan. Lagarde put forth a similarly teleological argument for the immortality of the human soul: "The actual proof of the immortality of the soul does not lie in ideas, but in the plan that becomes visible in the life of every person who treads the path of goodness. To recognize this plan, to ponder it and devote oneself to its realization, is to be pious and guarantee eternal life" (p. 257). The counter-Enlightenment thrust of this statement is obvious because, since Kant's *Kritik der reinen Vernunft* (*Critique of Pure Reason*), ontological proof of the existence of God or the eternal soul was no longer taken seriously. Lagarde's Christian scholarship pointed to metaphysical self-evidence that Kant would have simply considered inconceivable. But Lagarde did not acknowledge or further engage problems of logical inconsistency, paradox, and mixing of philosophical categories. He automatically jumped from historical debates to judgments about the current social situation, and only his religio-political metaphors connected these heterogeneous topics.

Despite any outward success, the state of Bismarck's German Empire seemed desolate to Lagarde. Germans had to understand that they were Europe's "most hated nation" (p. 259), because they had still not found their identity. The cause of this unfortunate conclusion was easy to determine: "What is called German nowadays is as much of a synthetic product as Judaism or Jesuitism. Foreigners do not know the real Germans at all" (p. 259). In a harsh tone, Lagarde condemned the excesses of contemporary culture. His hatred of intellectuals led to draconian visions of annihilation: "Literati float on the surface of the new German Empire; namely, those who are literary figures openly and those who are secretly led by some party head or other. These invasive weeds must be purged from our rivers and seas, and the political system without which they could not exist must be destroyed" (p. 260). The actual political intention of this statement lay in declaring the hated liberal intelligentsia an enemy. But the historico-philosophical implications went way beyond that. As in Wagner's

Ring des Nibelungen (*Ring of the Nibelung*), the *Untergang* (decline) of the morally corrupt present was a prerequisite for the regeneration of a better world. Accordingly, Lagarde tied the condemnation of his contemporaries to chiliastic premonition of a better future. And so our quotation about the destructive effect of "literati" ends with these words: "All flowers on the shore and all stars in the heavens will be reflected in the pure mirror. The old gods will disappear from the waters, and no one will bear a grudge against us" (p. 260).

Lagarde used impressive imagery to lament the Germans' estrangement from their spiritual roots. They neither appreciated their true poets nor recognized the holy places of their faith: "Woden[41] had to disguise himself as a felon, and no one in Gutenswegen, Wunstorf or Rodenstein recognizes him any longer. Gnomes' caves, if they happen to lie near a coffee garden, are occasional strolling destinations for cigarette-smoking pithecoids (creatures related to apes). But beech trees and oaks along the way tell the strollers nothing about German faith" (p. 261). In direct connection to Fichte's famous seventh "Rede an die deutsche Nation" (Address to the German Nation), Lagarde underscored the normative character of his own concept of Germanness, which was grounded in the "infinite improvability" of the people. He cited Madame de Staël's famous statement according to which "three qualities" explained the Germans' superiority to the French: "independent spirit, love of solitude, and the uniqueness of individual persons" (p. 262). With a mixture of self-assurance and maudlin sentimentality that was so characteristic of his style, Lagarde commented on this assessment from the time of Goethe: "Anyone who knows the characteristics of the new German Empire will know, as soon as he has read this, with tears in his eyes, just how German this Empire is" (p. 262).

Lagarde judged the political culture of the Gründerzeit to be substantially misguided. Universal suffrage favored mediocre careerists, and parliamentarianism only pretended to have fair decision-making processes. Parliamentarianism was actually subject to the dictates of the time and had to be considered a modern form of "jungle law" (p. 263). Politicians lacked all understanding that the true meaning of the nation was religious in nature. The upcoming problems required larger time horizons than was usual in the day-to-day business of politics. They would surely not be solved for centuries, because "a Fatherland was only a step on the path to eternal life" (p. 264). Only individuals, not associations or parties, played a role in the creation of a national religion, and that was why all support of politics must belong to them. But one couldn't even begin to talk about this prospect in Germany, because the principles of 1789 and their advocates, the liberals, dominated the discussion instead. Seen in that light, political conditions had not changed at all for at least a century. Those who set the tone were still "officially addressed as *Wohlgeboren*," the form of address for members of the lower nobility (p. 267), whereas the people themselves were barred from the real business of government.

Lagarde's text began as a religio-philosophical essay and ended as a political treatise. Textual nuances and carefully considered trains of thought played almost no role in it. Rather, it was dominated by striking value judgments and hidden appeals that were supposed to induce readers to agree on an emotional level. Liberals and ultra-Montanists (the conservative Catholic movement that placed Papal authority over all others) were not opposed on the basis of their universalistic views, but were utterly condemned as "prophets of foreign gods" (p. 268). The idyllic characterization of Germanness mainly provided contrast to the enemy stereotypes that came from the arsenal of contemporary nationalism. Crudely, yet also in good conscience, Lagarde committed his readers to his aggressive ideology: "We want our own nature to be acknowledged, nurtured, transfigured. But we do not want to be driven by a Russian coachman on a French leash or beaten with a Jewish whip" (p. 268). The real point does not lie in the assessment of the prevailing political situation or in the petrification of nationalistic stereotypes. What's decisive is that the spiritual elevation of Germanness turned into a political agenda, the end goal of which was a united Europe under German leadership. An excellent example of the metahistorical character of his arguments turns up in the final sentences of the essay: "In 1878, we are sick from the necessity of carrying out what should have happened in 878. Of course, the problem was not presented so as not to be solved: The first step to overcome it is, at any rate, to recognize the problem and the difficulty it entails" (p. 269). In the hands of the strict antihistoricist Lagarde, history had become an incantation for a better future that promised a genuine, religious life. As the widely favorable response showed, he had touched on themes that many people felt were pressing, and chosen language that political and religious dissidents identified with.

Significantly, people first heard about the *Deutsche Schriften* by word of mouth. On December 30, 1879, Lagarde informed his academic patron, Olshausen, about a sideswipe by journalists in Bismarck's employ: "The reptiles were ordered to hush up my political works. Nevertheless, they have found their way to enthusiastic readers."[42] Hidden behind this statement was a typical mixture of conceit and fear of persecution. But its actual content was even more important. Lagarde's drastic critique of modern alienation had struck the right note and produced a lively response from the educated bourgeoisie. His correspondence mainly attests to how often the *Deutsche Schriften* were read as a spiritual confession of faith. A typical reaction was that of the philosopher

Paul Natorp.[43] After intensively reading Spinoza, the young scholar doubted the existence of a personal God and the immortality of the soul. His state of unemployment made Natorp feel even more unsure of himself, and he saw the *Deutsche Schriften* as an important means of dissociation from the materialistic culture of the Gründerzeit. He particularly shared Lagarde's assumption that the German Empire would only be capable of surviving if it countered moral decline with its own religion. Natorp approached the venerable author with extreme caution. In his letter of January 24, 1879, he asked where things stood regarding the acceptance of pantheists in the new German Empire. He also expressed the longing for a helping hand in his life. Like many members of his generation, Natorp thought it wise to overcome the idealism of the 1840s through a new kind of realism. But he didn't even know how to get started with his own life, and so he asked Lagarde to lead him in the right direction.

On February 2, 1879, Lagarde answered from his customarily lofty standpoint. He advised against pointless intellectual speculation and praised the merits of radical self-criticism in religious diction. A fundamentally changed approach to one's own soul was at the epicenter of a new beginning. Although his rejection of the present was abundantly clear, Lagarde avoided genuinely political statements: "Anything is now useless that aims at the Great or the Whole," he phrased it solemnly. He then carried on emphatically: "Nowadays, Jesus would end up in one of Berlin's prisons, Hausvogtei or Plötzensee. The same goes for Zoroaster, the Buddha, and Confucius." He advised Natorp to let all ethical behavior begin with himself. This was certainly ambiguous and, furthermore, limited in a political sense. But it placed all responsibility for the state of the world on the individual. It nevertheless took into account that the young philosopher wanted to find his own way and that he also felt strongly obligated to his Protestant parents. Whatever the possible risks, Lagarde's patriarchal advice did not entirely miss its mark. Deeply moved, Natorp wrote to Göttingen on February 4, 1880, that he wanted to be worthy of the kindness shown to him and had decided to pursue a life of scholarly work. He hoped to gain additional spiritual direction from the *Deutsche Schriften*. And he asked for permission to turn to Lagarde again in case of emergency. It never came to that, however. Natorp, a friend of the Jewish philosopher Hermann Cohen, became one of the most important scholars of the late nineteenth century. He was a cofounder of neo-Kantianism in Marburg, and supported young people with advice and assistance. But his early encounter with Lagarde had positive consequences: questions about the essence of true community and religion would occupy Natorp all his life.

The reaction of the Berlin Egyptologist Adolf Erman to Lagarde's magnum opus is also telling. On July 7, 1880, he reported to his friend and Göttingen colleague that, in reading the *Deutsche Schriften* with his brother, he had found it a welcome relief from "the repulsive stale air of modern life." There were "so many in the younger generation" who were among Lagarde's "not-so-secret admirers." And so Erman decided in favor of Lagarde's worldview, a path that enjoyed widespread popularity. Many readers of the *Deutsche Schriften* saw themselves as part of an elite that, given the prevailing political climate, had been sworn to silence. Totally different viewpoints were united in the conviction that they were members of a Lagardian "association that was an open secret." For example, Erman swore by Kant and Goethe, neither of whom Lagarde held in particularly high regard. If he was not sure of a reader's overall approval, the powerful cultural pessimist usually ignored these kinds of "trifles." His response to Erman was both friendly and self-confident: "I am glad that my *Deutsche Schriften* did not seem strange to you. Thankfully, they have received a certain amount of enthusiastic approval: officially, they must be ignored."[44] From then on, the *Deutsche Schriften* were a kind of self-help book that the Egyptologist consulted time and again. He even took the volume with him on vacation. On April 30, 1886, Erman told the much-admired author that he had gone to great effort to understand the world "but finally realized that everything of this sort was best read about in your work."

But Lagarde was aiming more for political goals than for success as a contemplative writer. In the second volume of *Symmicta*, he put it programmatically: "I have absolutely no feeling for theoretical truth." With his fondness for paradoxical figures of thought, Lagarde continued: "I want to bind and free my *Volk*. Every thought that goes through my mind aims to do this in the right way."[45] But the ambitious scholar was smart enough to reasonably weigh the importance of fame in the achievement of political goals. At the same time, he attached great importance to being properly understood. Many of his letters are classic examples of careful guidance to readers. Lagarde repeatedly gave the impression of being a shy recluse with the soul of a prophet, whereas he was, in fact, energetically and persistently expanding his flock of followers. The Orientalist succeeded in creating an aura of heroic isolation. Nearly all his closer associates were convinced that he had been silenced by malevolent opponents and Bismarckian journalists. But the facts did not bear this out, as the response to the second volume of *Deutsche Schriften*, published once again by Diederichs, clearly shows.

An increasing number of those in the academic world were convinced that an idealistic approach to the problems of the time was a must, and they responded in this spirit. Friedrich Paulsen, a young senior professor in Berlin who embodied the future of educational theory, admired the basic principles behind Lagarde's thinking. The Kiel scholar Ferdinand Tönnies, whose fame as an authority on Hobbes preceded him, hoped that Lagarde societies would be formed in Germany during his lifetime.[46] On March 4, 1884, Heinrich Freiherr von Stein, one of the most enthusiastic worshippers at the Wagner "shrine," underscored the inspirational effect of the *Deutsche Schriften*. The young scholar, who considered aesthetics the heart of philosophy, also hoped that his literary efforts partook of the Lagardian spirit.

Treitschke gave the *Deutsche Schriften* a favorable but appropriately detached review in his personal mouthpiece, the *Preussische Jahrbücher*. He emphasized Lagarde's originality in connection with the crisis of contemporary education but criticized his "puritanical severity," which "did little to combat the harsh reality of life." His criticism was aimed mainly at Lagarde's assumption that only boarding schools were in a position to educate the future elite of the German Reich. Significantly, Treitschke placed the Göttingen scholar in close proximity to Fichte, to whom he also attributed "exaggerated idealism."[47] In the eyes of his followers, Lagarde's importance lay precisely in the uncompromising sincerity with which he championed his views. They saw his love of truth as entirely indisputable. The mere fact that he involved himself in many unpleasant debates only strengthened their opinion that he valued hard-won realizations over shabby compromises.

Lagarde's claim that he could elicit no response lost much of its plausibility over time. But the actual correspondence between Lagarde and his followers is what effectively established his image as a despised prophet. Lagarde had become embittered early in life, yet he longed for validation. In trying to convince him of his own importance, many of his correspondents basically wrote exactly what this pied piper wanted to hear. A letter of November 3, 1884, to Lagarde from Franz von Liszt illustrates just how taken his followers were with him. As for Lagarde's effect on young people, he said almost evocatively: "You have found *more* than a *circle of readers*; you have sown a seed in a great many hearts that *will* sprout, even if not today or the day after."

Readers' interpretation of Lagarde's work as the expression of a self-contained worldview was vital to its reception. The cultural critic had to work hard to create this impression. After all, he suffered from extreme mood swings that caused him to make many impulsive statements. He was also prone to erratic and contradictory judgments in political and cultural matters. Nevertheless, the seemingly impossible happened: with the aid of beseeching appeals, as well as patriotic and religious semantics, Lagarde earned the reputation of a self-assured author who was true to his principles and could show the German people the way to a better future. Among the enthusiastic commentaries found in his estate, just one statement from the Jewish Wagnerian Max Koch will be quoted here. After reading the *Deutsche Schriften*, Koch turned to the esteemed author on July 4, 1884, and said the following: "In contrast to the stereotypes that confront us everywhere at present, I sensed here a great, self-contained nature. [. . .] Released from the chains of conventional lies that threaten to smother our entire existence, a truly German desire for truth and freedom blows refreshingly and vigorously toward us from your words." As a scholar who worked positivistically, Lagarde turned almost pedantically against any form of value judgment, yet gladly accepted this kind of effusive praise. He answered Max Koch that same day: "I am always happy when I learn of a new comrade."[48]

Alfred Schöne went exceptionally far in his admiration for Lagarde. Moreover, he was diligent in his efforts to provide reviewers. In his letters, he repeatedly stressed Lagarde's powerful personality and his gallant love of truth. On August 22, 1878, he even felt compelled to explain the essence of the *Deutsche Schriften* to Anna de Lagarde: "It comes from an entire person, is the work of and testament to a great and cohesive worldview and, like all that is great and wonderful, is sovereign, masterful, and exclusive." This statement was fairly convoluted and may well point to Schöne's personal dependency on the easily enraged Lagarde. But it would be too simplistic to merely explain Lagarde's aura of "heroic isolation" in terms of individual psychology and to thereby spirit it away as an aesthetic phenomenon. The scholar from Göttingen really did send a myth out into the world that finds its way into the history books even now. Very few readers, other than Friedrich Nietzsche, were truly skeptical as to what Lagarde's religiosity and disdain for his contemporaries were all about. Of course, Nietzsche knew exactly what he was talking about: despite his radical self-criticism, his oeuvre contained numerous passages that served the general bourgeois principle of the unity of life and work. Among the main things he called for was "to make a whole person of oneself,"[49] a demand that was excellently suited to covering up Nietzsche's own inconsistencies. But Nietzsche, who found religious surrogates dishonest and despised dependence on authority, scoffed heartily at faithful disciples. Lagarde took a different position, and his plea was for an authentic life that encouraged people to follow good examples.

Over time, Lagarde won more and more followers who spread his message. In the Netherlands, a middle school teacher originally from Weimar named Wernicke authored a laudatory review of the *Deutsche Schriften*. It focused on Lagarde's political agenda and described his critique of the German Empire as entirely legitimate.[50] As he proudly informed Lagarde on April 26, 1883, the poet Siegfried Lipiner made sure Lagarde was well received in Vienna. One gathers from the same letter that Lipiner had a revelatory experience upon first reading Lagarde: "A few words about the Gospel appear in your *Schriften* that hit me like a bolt of lightning in a dark and doubtful time. Ever since I saw the way and found my bearings, I have been going forward undeterred." A letter from Lipiner, dated March 15, 1884, illustrates just how much he admired Lagarde. He asked him for a few personal lines, because "the person and love for same is the highest and most beautiful." Bearing in mind that the author of the poem *Der entfesselte Prometheus* (*Prometheus Unbound*) was himself quite accomplished, Lipiner's voluntary recognition of Lagarde's authority may be seen to carry additional weight.

The aesthetics of the *Deutsche Schriften* even spoke to readers who were skeptical about or even rejected Lagarde's worldview. On October 22, 1879, for example, the Berlin legal historian Felix Liebermann told Lagarde that the *Deutsche Schriften* had affected him like a "rich, tangy, and wonderfully authentic" wine. The prominent Jewish academician spoke almost effusively about the merits of Lagarde's book: "Freedom from the influences of everyday surroundings, the fervent love of truth, the willpower to research, the abundance of knowledge, the astuteness of the final conclusions, the selfless purity of the publication—how powerfully attractive I find all of this!" Liebermann judged Lagarde's attitude toward Judaism entirely unacceptable, however. Precisely because he shared Lagarde's identification of Jewish religion with "liberal humanitarian ideals," yet appraised it entirely differently, their stances could not be reconciled. Liebermann closed his letter rather ironically with the words that he would "gratefully [. . .] appreciate it" if Lagarde "could continue to respect" him "just a tiny bit." It seems, however, that the self-assured cultural critic did not answer him.

Lagarde's followers argued over whether Germany had enough spiritual energy left to develop a national religion. In Cairo, Wilhelm Spitta expressed particular skepticism and found many of Lagarde's ideas overblown. On December 29, 1878, he explicitly told his former Göttingen teacher: "I consider it impossible, and believe that I can prove it historically and psychologically, for a people as culturally advanced as the Germans to still be capable of creating a religion." Even a nonconfrontational scholar like the Kiel Orientalist Georg Hoffmann expressed muted criticism over the idea of the new religion and noted that he found the socio-critical aspect of the *Deutsche Schriften* more convincing.[51] Lagarde's call for inner reflection and a serious approach to life likewise reached people who did not agree with every implication of his national mysticism. The ascetic ideals that Lagarde preached, in sharp contrast to superficial contemporary life, were not the least of these. Hoffmann proudly sent word to Göttingen on June 18, 1879, for example, that his friend Scheppig had stopped smoking after reading the *Deutsche Schriften*. Lagarde's rigid moralism was even held in high regard among students, who became increasingly conservative in the early 1880s. Such rigidity promoted separation from the allegedly complacent Gründerzeit. At the same time, it harmonized superbly with the students' own elitist self-image.

Although Lagarde's oeuvre had been highly regarded in England until now, the message of the *Deutsche Schriften* fell flat. His solemn cultural pessimism must have been too far removed from the careful skepticism and resigned empiricism that the British appreciated in his scholarly works. Even so, a review in *The Academy* stressed that Lagarde's idealism was beyond debate. But the unknown critic wanted his recommendation of the *Deutsche Schriften* to be limited to university reformers and students of Oriental philology.[52] The desire for national religious transcendence was considerably greater in France. Ernest Renan, with whom Lagarde had been in contact since the 1850s, gave his famous lecture "What Is a Nation?" at the Sorbonne in 1883. In language reminiscent of his Göttingen colleague's, he said: "A nation is a spiritual principle that results from profound historical connections, a spiritual family."[53] One might argue over whether and to what extent Renan's famous definition of a nation as a "daily plebiscite" points to common ground with the voluntarism of Lagarde's worldview. Whatever the conclusion, the similarity of the idealistic imagery is indisputable and shows Fichte's formative influence. Lagarde and Renan also shared the belief that, when times were bad, true thinkers were doomed to obscurity. Certainly this view was excellently suited to styling oneself an ostracized scholar, but it also contained the seeds of arrogant conceit. In any case, a central problem with Lagarde's worldview lay in its harsh decisionism, which, practically by itself, led to the abhorrence of ideological opponents.

Lagarde's political understanding was essentially religious in nature. As far back as June 20, 1861, he had written to his wife "that the real objective of politics was for people to be reborn."[54] Lagarde held fast to this idea for his entire life. As a consequence, he never attributed any true significance to the field of Realpolitik. In the aforementioned letter, he also stated apodictically that God's spirit was essentially hostile toward "the natural world." Social circumstances and political constraints really didn't play an important role as far as Lagarde was concerned. He took the metahistorical certainties he derived from the German national character and the overall cultural situation much more seriously. He thereby developed a preference for dramatic images that had very little to do with people's daily lives. Lagarde's political thinking was substantially based on upgrading the people's value and, as a countermeasure, devaluing the state, an inflexible institution that seemed primarily interested in maintaining the status quo. As Fichte once had done, Lagarde assigned his own nation a special role in spiritual renewal, because "Germany is the heart of humanity."[55] The way in which he included religious symbols made Lagarde one of the most successful authors of the Bismarck era. But the drastic metaphors that he favored were in danger of being quickly worn out. In his dealings with enemy stereotypes, however, the cultural pessimist displayed not only ideological vehemence but rhetorical finesse as well.

9 Liberalism: Image of the Enemy

When Lagarde published the second volume of his *Deutsche Schriften* in 1881, liberalism had already passed its zenith. Shortly after the 1878 assassination attempts on Kaiser Wilhelm I, Bismarck decided to dissolve the Reichstag. He also campaigned against liberals and the Social Democratic Party. Although liberals decidedly opposed terrorism, the angry public accused them of being unpatriotic. Conservative parties came out ahead in the parliamentary elections of July 30, 1878, and liberals lost a good one-fifth of their votes. This was a political attempt to further divide the liberal movement that, prior to the founding of the empire, had already split into national and left-wing liberal camps. The Nationalist Liberal Party (NLP) soon fell in line with Bismarck's new course, which included strict protective tariffs and ratcheted up the conflict with the Social Democrats. Whereas the Progressive People's Party and centrists emphasized the tyrannical nature of this decision, the NLP agreed to the "socialist law" that banned the organized workers' movement on October 18, less than three months after the parliamentary elections. The liberals' fate was thus sealed, and the split permanently diminished their power. But Bismarck continued to work with conservatives, who shared his main social and economic ideas. Whether and to what extent the crisis of 1878–1879 changed German nationalism has long been debated among historians. It has thus been pointed out that liberal ideas of nationhood were always exclusive in nature. On the other hand, it would be difficult to dispute the significant advances made by the political right after Bismarck turned toward nationalism as the preferred ideology of integration.[1] At any rate, Bismarck's contemporaries vividly experienced how politically effective nationalistic feeling could be. Most of them expressed approval for the "inner Reichsgründung" that was allegedly taking place.

Lagarde gloated over the weakness of the liberals' position and felt vindicated in his negative attitude. The period of *Honoratiorenpolitik* (rule by the most deserving) was ending, and the elections unequivocally proved how effectively one could garner votes with prejudice and handy slogans. In Berlin, the court chaplain Adolf Stoecker successfully won over his followers with a mélange of social romanticism and antisemitic convictions.[2] He handled his petit bourgeois audience in a calculated way and demanded submissive integration of the Jews: otherwise, *Ausnahmegestze* (exceptional laws, e.g., those enacted by Bismarck that banned many different groups) would be inevitable. Stoecker, a key player in the Christian Socialist Party, had held a parliamentary mandate since 1881 and could easily fill huge lecture halls. New chances for an impact opened up for Lagarde in the early 1880s as well. Of course, there was great rivalry among ideologues on the political right, and the professor from Göttingen faced the task of creating a unique image. Like so many others, Lagarde used the prefaces and forewords of his publications for publicity purposes. He also wrote a preface to the second volume of the *Deutsche Schriften* that summed up and furnished commentaries for his previous political writings. This idea has a rather stilted effect from a literary perspective. Lagarde referred to familiar topics in very abbreviated form, such that new readers would have found much of what he said incomprehensible. But this approach gave him a chance to pointedly lay out his views and to promote himself. Lagarde had a great many rhetorical means at his disposal and took full advantage of the opportunity.[3]

The preface begins with image creation: Lagarde stressed that he had refrained from holding public office in the early 1850s because of the political standstill that already prevailed. But the facts in no way support this contention. Bunsen could have opened the door for Lagarde to a career with the Foreign Office. But Bunsen mistreated his scholarly assistant when he was in London and expressed no real personal interest in him. This opener, therefore, not only shows how cleverly Lagarde could fabricate his own past; it was also highly useful for his entire line of argumentation. A jet-black image of the intellectual atmosphere in the Nachmärz period created the perfect, negative backdrop upon which Lagarde's political ideas could unfold. The era had a distinct lack of inner vibrancy that was shaped by Hegel's scholastic philosophy and King Frederick William IV of Prussia's indecisive temperament. Lagarde considered Bismarck the era's most important representative. Bismarck had fulfilled the desires of liberalism, and the magnitude of his popular mediocrity was comparable only to Luther. To portray the *Reichskanzler* (chancellor of the Reich) as an agent of liberalism had little basis in fact. But an objectively balanced opinion may not have been what Lagarde was after. It was more a question of packaging enemy stereotypes so that he could totally condemn the time in which he lived.

In 1872, Lagarde had already seen that the days of liberalism were numbered and cited this as his motivation for writing the *Deutsche Schriften*. The founding of the German Empire required a deeper sense of meaning, and liberals were in no position to provide it. If a united Germany intended to flourish as a polity, then it needed a greater sense of purpose. Germany's mission was to colonize Austria, which again needed a "race of rulers" (p. 90). In order to legitimize colonization, he pointed out that a "nation of farmers" (p. 90) like the Germans depended on expansion. This combination of racial and imperial ideas was entirely suited to positioning Lagarde in the political sphere. However, his intellectual world derived its special character from his belief that foreign policy ideas would only need to be fulfilled in the distant future. The German people were not yet prepared for war, so the most important duty of patriotic scholars was to prepare them for the coming engagement. Lagarde's argumentation acquired a utopian foundation that freed him from descending into the "dregs of Realpolitik." This also left open the possibility for him to verbalize radical opinions of contemporary culture that carried few political obligations. Education, as earlier chapters have intimated, was Lagarde's favorite area of contemporary criticism.

As could be seen in the domination of the natural sciences, the German nation lacked inner substance. This was because the arts and humanities had lost their essential, professional core and now argued over nothing but *quisquilia* (Latin: trifles, minor details). Behind this view were Lagarde's positivistic convictions that every area of scholarship involved cumulative scientific progress and only one generally accepted point of view. Concerning the alleged excess of contemporary historical approaches, he stated pointedly: "One would like to live somewhere beyond the reach of people and their anguish. And one does not care for history if it's a matter of Catholic, Protestant, not to mention Jewish history" (p. 91). The prevailing mood directly reflected the inner crisis of the German Reich. It was no coincidence that Schopenhauer, whose theories exhorted people to comfortable resignation, was the new idol of philosophy: "The lives of the best people now had but one refrain: everything was to no avail" (p. 92). This attitude was unacceptable to Lagarde, because everyone was obliged to use the life God had given him to the best of his ability. With individuals standing at the center of his political ideas, the main matter was to protect them from the paternalism of presumptuous institutions. The Prussian educational system had to be eradicated because its alignment with outmoded educational materials stood in the way of national rebirth.

Lagarde's sharp criticism of his own time was shaped by the strongly religious emphasis that still informed his political message. The short text ends with a revealing description of a funeral at which Lagarde, in lieu of a clergyman, recited the last words for a deceased student. Deeply moved and with a great deal of self-stylization, he said: "I thought and said nothing bad. Yet shame burned in my soul concerning all that I thought and said. Who was I to presume—in the face of deep pain, under God's heaven in the twilit, still bitter spring—to address eternal matters?" Lagarde continued in a similar tone: "Every time I try to express myself on matters of patriotism, I am in a far more serious and sad mood than I was on that occasion. Back then, every word fell on fertile soil: may that now also come to pass" (p. 94). An air of religious seriousness shielded Lagarde's thoughts from criticism and lent them a certain sanctity. At the same time, his attitude was characterized by considerable aggressiveness. He even viewed liberals with a secular orientation as opponents of the yearned-for national religion.

Lagarde hated liberals from early on and saw them as the embodiment of irresponsible living. Their spiritual indifference destroyed the nation's inner cohesion, while their need for the mere accumulation of knowledge made it decisively harder to impart historical meaning. Overly critical handling of sources undermined faith in prehistoric myths and sagas, without which no nation could survive. Lagarde was also convinced that liberals were responsible for the repression of his scholarly oeuvre and for the difficult start of his career. After Adalbert Falk became minister of education and cultural affairs, Lagarde seriously considered pressing for the liberal politician to be removed from office so as to prevent something worse from happening. But he soon realized the illusory nature of his plan, which only served to strengthen his rejection of the political establishment.[4] Lagarde's attacks on liberalism applied equally to the press, schools, and academia. He viewed the burning down of Mommsen's house and its effect on access to old manuscripts as the number-one cause of the slow progress on his Septuagint research. He attacked liberal educational policy as the main cause of overriding student helplessness. And the press of his day was nothing more than a "funneling system" that offered corrupt journalists a lucrative income.[5]

Given that liberals were Lagarde's main political opponents, it was hardly coincidental that he dedicated a passionate essay to them in the second volume of the *Deutsche Schriften* with the suggestive and defamatory title "Die graue Internationale" (The Gray International).[6] Lagarde was working with paranoid ideas that were widespread during the decade-long founding of the empire. In December 1874, the journalist Otto Glagau published a series of articles in *Die Gartenlaube* (*The Arbour*, an illustrated family paper) to unmask the "Jewish stock market swindle." The unpretentious paper had a respectable circulation of 460,000. The articles painted a grim picture of overall corruption and disseminated Glagau's theory that the social problem was nothing more than the "Jewish problem." The municipal court judge Carl Wilmanns spread the crazy idea that a "Golden International" of Jewish millionaires was responsible for the collapse of the German economy.[7] The organized workers' movement and political Catholicism had to endure similar smear campaigns about their alleged lack of patriotism.

Lagarde concocted the liberal "Gray International" as an analogue of the Red, Black, and Golden Internationals, and made it responsible for Germany's demise: the reasons for its success were hardly impressive and consisted of "indolence and the desire to shine" (p. 337). But the consequences of the liberal mentality had to be regarded as dreadful. Above all, the maxim underlying every culture contradicted this mentality: "Everything of use to a person is the result of his own effort" (p. 337). That's why French war reparations would inevitably deliver negative consequences for the German people. They had a "decaying" effect on a disoriented polity that, up to this very day, had not recovered from the *Gründerkrach* (stock market crash of 1873). For many of Lagarde's contemporaries, this must have been an attractive way of looking at things. It offered an easy-to-understand interpretation of highly complex economic processes and, at the same time, moralized about the economic malaise. Moreover, his readers' self-perception as victims of an overpowering Zeitgeist made it easier to understand Lagarde's idiosyncratic train of thought, which oscillated between harsh accusations and self-pity.

As with nearly all his essays, Lagarde allowed himself to digress historically on numerous occasions. Although they may sometimes appear quite peripheral, these digressions served a unified purpose, which was to prove that the German past was a tale of woe (*Leidensgeschichte*). Twice, in the Thirty Years' War and during the Napoleonic era, the nation had barely escaped a doomsday scenario, yet had never been granted the good fortune of "manly reform": "A botch-up happened after 1648, botch-up after 1806" (p. 338). A sharp critique of education accompanied his incontrovertible view of history: one could place little hope in the younger generation, because it had been spoiled by an overly regulated school system. And scholars paid homage to a disoriented collector's passion that even found satisfaction in genuflecting before every scientific fact. Lagarde's stocktaking of the inner substance of contemporary culture yielded a disastrous conclusion: "Three things are the fruits of our educational system: bad eyes, vast revulsion at all that was, and no capacity for the future" (p. 344).

In general, one needed to spell out how ubiquitous liberalism had become. Whenever Christian orthodoxy defended an isolated scientific fact, it was under the spell of liberalism and "didn't even properly understand the concept of the church" (p. 340). In deliberately prophetic diction, Lagarde pointed to the upcoming spiritual tasks: "How often people have been disinclined to revive religion. But religion is not revived: it awakens. I have suggested that its still-glowing coals be collected and heaped up on top of one another: no one may recommend anything else, and no one may long to do anything other than this—the mouth of man does not blow breath into these coals. If we have arranged the dying embers that He is to bring to life, then the breath blows from the heights or from the depths, as it pleases God" (p. 340). True religious life admittedly lay in the distant future. Frantic activity reigned all around and was the enemy of inner contemplation. Scholars themselves had been heavily influenced by liberal arbitrariness and no longer had a stable, religious ideology. "Having grown up in an atmosphere without religion" (p. 341), they lacked the requisite adherence to principles to advocate a better life and true community in the face of opposition.

Lagarde, like many of his contemporaries, interpreted both assassination attempts on the kaiser as signs of overall moral decay. The assassination attempt on which he focused, however, was astonishing. Max Hödel, a former Socialist Workers Party member and journeyman metalworker, failed in his attempt to assassinate the kaiser with a pistol on Unter den Linden. He had aroused universal shock and indignation by wishing "to go to the scaffold with a cigar in his mouth" (p. 343). But Lagarde judged this tasteless behavior trifling as compared with the lapses of contemporary priests. Hödel's "smattering of education" was far more serious, since it had imparted no moral standards to him. This was not an original point of view. Yet the second assassin, Karl Nobiling, had a doctorate in economics, and people repeatedly brought up the uselessness of his university education. At any rate, it is remarkable that Lagarde, a fierce critic of the "horde of doctoral candidates," rejected this argument. He instead defined education as the rare ability "to distinguish the essential from the inessential and to take the essential seriously" (p. 343). He simultaneously attacked the state and society for not having changed substantially since the attempted assassinations.

The remarks of the cultural critic Lagarde were accompanied by strikingly displayed hatred of Jews. This fit in well with the times, because Bismarck's changes in domestic policy favored an upswing in the antisemitic movement, as demonstrated by the emergence of a new concept. The term *antisemitism* was bandied in the social circles of the journalist and agitator Wilhelm Marr in fall 1879 and was immediately taken for granted in large parts of Germany.[8] The neologism offered a pseudoscientific basis for the rampant hatred of Jews. Because of its vagueness, it could be used as a springboard for various political themes. Moreover, it served as a badge of the new anti-emancipationist movement. That same fall, Heinrich von Treitschke questioned whether Jews were part of the German nation.[9] His clearly delineated alternatives were emigration or complete assimilation. Naturally, these options were unacceptable to the highly acculturated German-Jewish bourgeoisie. The self-aggrandizing historian even had student followers who, given the crisis of overcrowding at

German universities in the 1880s and 1890s, increasingly embraced his strident nationalistic mind-set. However, many of his colleagues found the functionalization of antisemitic judgments just as unacceptable as the endangerment of academic harmony. Rudolf Virchow and Theodor Mommsen, two figureheads of liberalism, headed up a broad alliance in opposition to Treitschke. Following an intense journalistic controversy that stretched far beyond Berlin, they finally succeeded in isolating Treitschke and extinguishing the antisemitic wildfire.[10] For his part, Lagarde was of the opinion that Treitschke had framed the questions under discussion with needed clarity and an uncompromising attitude. He said correspondingly disparaging things about Treitschke's left-wing liberal opponents and cast doubt on their political expertise (p. 344).

Nevertheless, the main thrust of his argumentation was still religious in nature. Lagarde enjoyed presenting himself as a theologian and firmly challenged the "Jewish character" of monotheism. Without Platonic elements, monotheism would have gained absolutely no importance within the history of philosophy, which overflowed with abstract speculation as it was. Lagarde also reiterated a sharp distinction between Jesus and Judaism, a manifestly empty religion of laws. Moreover, the attitude of Jews to the Gospel was an unpardonable sin. Lagarde emphasized strongly that, precisely because of their impenitence, history had nothing to offer Jews or Muslims: "There are persons and peoples on whom Jesus, as he himself said, came to pass judgment" (p. 346). Lagarde's assessment of postbiblical Judaism was predictably contemptuous. He denigrated the Jews as "impotent enviers and loudmouths" (p. 346). Even in sentimental passages that lament the lack of a future for modern Judaism, the brutality of the Lagardian interpretation of history is clear: "Behind them is a history that is not a history: parasitism and small-scale marketing of goods purchased from other peoples, hatred of the human race, an existence without goals or content. In front of them are animosity and scorn. The heart of every feeling person will bleed when he considers the Jews" (p. 347f). In the guise of empathy, Lagarde cemented prejudices that had always belonged to the core of antisemitic ideology. The massive employment of enemy stereotypes, as well as their dazzling ambiguity, was among the specifics of his texts.

Lagarde's audacious figures of speech blended his critiques of Protestantism, liberalism, and Judaism. Each suffered from an excess of printed words that prevented all forms of living spiritual encounters. "Original sin," he said in deliberately solemn language, "wanders with the Jews, the same sin that weighs heavily on Protestantism and liberalism. A book or books are the existential focus of all of them" (p. 348). These were astonishing words for a scholar who had a vast library of his own and, at one time, had wanted to establish the basis for a new faith by philological means. Since then, however, the welfare of the German people was at the center of the Lagardian worldview, and the nation had the ultimate value for him: "The highest praise the German people confer is that of authenticity: if one considers how the people think about those who face them as refined persons, if one considers what the people's feelings about the condition of our state, schools, and churches are, then one will realize just how German the new Reich appears to Germans" (p. 349).

On the surface, these statements had to do with a vague rhetoric of identity that Lagarde tried to plug in to the nationalistic discourse. Upon closer examination, however, one detects an independent, ideological agenda. The powerful cultural pessimist was spreading normatively loaded ideas of Germanness. Against such a backdrop, contemporary culture must have seemed empty and trivial. This went to the heart of his critique of liberalism. Lagarde used sharp contrasts to play off the distinctiveness of the German people against contemporary liberalism. To him, it was not at all about clarifying his key concepts, such as *Volk*, nation, or Germanness. All the imagery aimed to denigrate liberalism as a meaningless ideology: "These liberals," he said, alluding to the famous tale by the German poet Adelbert von Chamisso, "are the opposite of schlemiels: they have a shadow, but no body" (p. 338). Just as unequivocally, Lagarde wrote: "Jews and liberals are natural allies, since the former and this one are not natural but rather artificial products" (p. 349). In marked contrast, he attributed a "substance" (*Wesen*) to the German people that would determine their actual sustainability. Lagarde pushed his essentialistic view almost to the point of needless repetition. So that "German unity" could finally be achieved, he called for sweeping reform of the Prussian school system, "since this can only rest on actual substance, never again on apparent substance" (p. 339).

The content of Lagarde's metaphysics of Germanness invited a multiplicity of projections and was, therefore, ideologically accessible. But whether it was decisive for the history of ideas may be another matter. By denying his ideological opponents their own "substance," the cultural pessimist helped fuse and energize enemy stereotypes. As the need arose, the dominance of Protestantism, liberalism, or Judaism threatened to bring about the ruin of the German Reich. In those days, many attempts were surely made to delegitimize liberalism as an un-German worldview.[11] Judaism and liberalism were not equated only within political antisemitism: this identification had been widespread among rightists ever since May 1875, when the far-right newspaper *Kreuzzeitung* had made Bismarck's Jewish banker, Gerson von Bleichröder, responsible for the wretched state of the German economy. The primary objective, of course, of most argumentation schemes was to establish interpretational sovereignty over the idea of the nation. Politicians involved in policy debates gave substantial consideration to their own clientele, which naturally did not make a very convincing impression. Lagarde, on the other hand, refused to accept any substantial definitions of Germanness. As a result, his ideas acquired a forward-looking aura, while the radicality of his enemy stereotypes appeared to prove the authenticity of his thinking.

The second volume of the *Deutsche Schriften* even impressed the skeptics among Lagarde's followers, those who viewed his religion of the future as unrealistic or illusory. On February 5, 1881, Wilhelm Spitta emphasized Lagarde's "holy and patriotic seriousness." And on March 25, Georg Hoffmann praised the "beauty, power, and originality of the style." The violence and virulence of Lagardian antiliberalism did not bother either of them. But not only Lagarde's bourgeois admirers thought highly of his radical rhetoric; it also awakened interest on the extreme right. For example, the June 19, 1882, edition of the *Deutsche Tageblatt* expressly cited Lagarde in pointing out that the ideas of 1789 had begun their triumphal progress with the liberals. The paper also praised his idealism and contrasted him with the insincerity of contemporary parliamentarians.[12] On July 20, 1883, the Viennese journalist Engelbert Pernersdorfer asked Lagarde for permission to print the entire article "Die graue Internationale" in *Deutsche Worte*. This magazine, with its revealing subtitle, *Politische Zeitschrift für das deutsche Volk in Oesterreich* (*Political Magazine for the German People in Austria*), was of considerable interest to the cultural critic. Even if they greeted his plans for Central Europe with mixed feelings, Austrian antisemites were still among the most important addressees of his *völkischer Botschaft* (nationalistic and racist message). Lagarde gave immediate permission and only requested "a copy of the applicable issue" from Pernersdorfer.[13] Upon the piece's publication, the editors noted the fine collaboration with the professor from Göttingen, on whom they "had" frequently "relied for assistance." And they urged their readers to study the *Deutsche Schriften*.[14] Lagarde had used the opportunity to spread his political ideas throughout the "monarchy on the Danube." Among the most politically charged questions for Lagarde was what would effectively oppose the political power of liberalism.

Lagarde had been a political outcast since his break with conservatives in December 1849. As a man of passionate, principled ethics, he considered it unforgivable that Prussian conservatives had tied the protection of their own best interests to the public welfare. He summarized his critique in an undated note: "Advocates on the right," he said categorically, "are advocates for the *entire* right: otherwise, they are defending rights and not The Right, freedoms and not freedom itself."[15] Yet Lagarde did not stop dreaming of an ideal conservatism that would look respectfully upon tradition and protect the common folk. In that regard, his social ideals were geared more toward the idea of a national religion than they were toward political reality. At the same time, he hoped for changes in the balance of power and the founding of an independent, truly conservative party. Alfred Schöne, who knew precisely what Lagarde was yearning for, wrote this clear message to him on March 13, 1877: "Our current political situation doesn't make one very happy. It seems we are now drifting toward a crisis that could become serious enough." And, in closing, he expressed this desire: "We lack a truly conservative party that ought to be made up of right-wing nationalist liberals and Free Conservatives." Lagarde placed his greatest hope in the aristocracy, whose political importance could be deduced from English society.

Lagarde wrote a rather formal article, "Die Reorganisation des Adels" (The Reorganization of the Aristocracy), for the second edition of the *Deutsche Schriften*. In response to social and ethical challenges, he wanted to expand the hereditary nobility by means of an elite meritocracy that would mainly comprise civil servants.[16] Lagarde set up a host of requirements intended to govern membership in the aristocracy. They underscored the importance of national affiliation, as well as the profession of Christian faith, and assigned increased importance to the king in the "court of honor." All this was largely illusory, because the ideas did not correspond to any real interests or political contacts. Lagarde's rhetoric was intended to underscore the future sustainability of his reform ideas and turned out to be equally unrealistic: "The German people will gladly relinquish national and provincial parliaments, liberalism, progress, and a few handfuls of coronets if they could finally be assured of a tailor-made political and social system" (p. 314). The defiant closing statement did not open new horizons, but simply emphasized his own resoluteness: "It would be better to chop wood than to continue living this contemptible, civilized and cultured life: we must go back to the source, aspire to that secluded mountain where we are not heirs, but spiritual forebears" (p. 314).

Lagarde doubted that the aristocracy would become a socially decisive power that could rival liberalism. Although he trusted the German people in principle, for the time being he rejected plebiscites in any form. On December 2, 1883, he wrote resignedly to the political scientist from Berlin, Hans Meyer, who had just returned from a two-year trip around the world: "An old man no longer expects much: liberalism has been mollycoddled for too long to be capable of defeat by anything short of a royal decree and, given how things stand, I don't expect to witness such a thing." In the same letter, he characterized the political situation of his day in somber terms: "We have no conservative party, no developmental continuity, no lineage, no administrative districts, no communities. May God make amends!" But, as intensively as Lagarde indulged in doubts about his own time, this outlook alternated repeatedly with euphoric faith in the future and bustling activity. In order to eliminate what he saw as the most significant flaw in the political system, he published "Programm für die konservative Partei Preussens" (Agenda for the Prussian Conservative Party) in the fall of 1884.[17]

Lagarde was convinced that the most important characteristic of true conservatives lay in their adherence to principles. The existing conservative parties had not earned their names, because they had linked their political existence to Bismarck's success and had to go along with his whims unconditionally. Lagarde's theologically based skepticism about the state is possibly the most conspicuous aspect of his conservatism. He clearly expressed his rejection of the Hegelian view of the state as an end in itself: "Everything that exists serves the development of the human soul: as soon as it ceases to permanently serve in this capacity, it becomes an idol. No trace of the state is present in eternal life. In the event that public prosecutors, mayors, tax collectors, or ministers get into heaven, they will not enter as public prosecutors, mayors, tax collectors, or ministers" (p. 353f). Furthermore, the combative essayist considered it an established fact that an excessive state presence led to mediocre government. It was necessary to bolster the people against a constantly status-quo-oriented state. The revival of German law would serve this purpose, as it was equally directed against revolutionary threats and the despotism of bureaucratic power. Lagarde even found anarchy more appealing than all-too-powerful officials who, as far as he was concerned, were nothing but "servants of the nation" (p. 361). In any case, the reputation of the Prussian Landtag (legislative assembly) suffered from the large number of elected state civil servants whose only claim to productivity consisted of a host of senseless or harmful laws.

One could see just how low the Prussian state had sunk from its handling of tax revenues. There was no longer any sense that this money belonged to the taxpayers and was only allowed to be spent "on the common good" (p. 362). Lagarde thereby took up a theme to which he had already devoted a lot of space in the second volume of the *Deutsche Schriften*. At that time, he had fundamentally opposed a higher tax burden and the sinister power of money. A state that was primarily financed through excise taxes on tobacco and alcohol encouraged its population's dependency on narcotics and, therefore, lacked any sense of true idealism.[18] Lagarde's polemics were aimed at rejecting protectionism while strengthening communal and regional institutions. In the interim, he and many other critics of Bismarck had to accept the irreversible nature of setting the economic agenda. So Lagarde ramped up his critique of journalists in Bismarck's employ and their lack of character instead. He considered it a top priority of the yet-to-be-created conservative party "to finish off reptilianism" (p. 374). Lagarde looked upon journalism with great skepticism. In his view, it offered manifold opportunities to irresponsibly express opinions. He interpreted liberal support of press law as an expression of will to power and as anything but the genuine profession of universal values.

All in all, Lagarde deemed the situation in Germany so precarious that dictatorship seemed like a reasonable form of government. On account of the disappointing economic and political situation, it was no coincidence that many people had decided to emigrate. Indeed, approximately three million Germans left the country during the Kaiserzeit (period of the Second German Empire, 1871–1918), and the vast majority of them immigrated to the New World. Emigration reached a high point in the 1880s, when a dramatic drop in prices led to mass unemployment.[19] It was not without self-styling that Lagarde recalled how, at the tender age of twenty, he developed a plan to settle the "southern tip of South America" (p. 338) and sent it to the Department of Commerce. Meanwhile, the shortage of farmland in the German colonies had become apparent. If things in the Kaiserreich did not change quickly, one would soon find graves in southwest Africa with this inscription: "In Germany, he loved German ways and laws. He also hated injustice, which is why he died in Africa" (p. 392).

If one considers how strongly Lagarde wanted to see the salvation of the human soul become the focal point of politics, it was remarkable that he sided with colonialist ideas. But his type of conservatism did not want to be measured by whether what existed was preserved, but by whether people were enabled "to be themselves" (p. 398). The precise reason for Lagarde's rejection of the ideas of 1789 lay in their nature as equalizing and, therefore, inevitably false. In lieu of "*liberté, égalité, fraternité*," the German people should focus their attention on three other principles: "The right to become what God intended us to become; dissimilarity, which alone makes polyphony possible; God's children" (p. 400). These were high-flown and ambiguous words that actually called for a closer understanding of Lagarde's theological ideas. But even the uninitiated reader easily understood the cultural pessimist's opposition to the ideas of the French Revolution and their liberal offspring.[20] But "Programm für die konservative Partei Preussens" makes one thing abundantly clear: responsible politics had to be modeled on religious goals and not on economic interests. "Ethics versus money" (p. 403) was the bold formula that Lagarde saw as the summation of conservatism's future conflicts. To his followers, the future viability of this approach was beyond question. On November 1, 1882, Georg Hoffmann expressly thanked Lagarde for "finding fault with the entire world and, at the same time, having so much faith in its rebirth." Furthermore, the scholar from Kiel voiced his satisfaction that, through the new party manifesto, "German politics" would come to know "a means of uprightness and justice."

In 1886, Lagarde published an expanded version of his *Deutsche Schriften* that figured as the definitive edition. Meanwhile, he had become accustomed to his role as a prophet and, therefore, ended the preface theatrically: "It is the forerunner's lot to be forgotten when what he preached has come to pass. I will thank God if I am quickly forgotten as a politician, for then the great future that I now proclaim and call for will have arrived."[21] Lagarde's changes to the already well-known essays amounted to a few formalities. He added a new version of his "Programm für die konservative Partei Preussens," as well as an essay, "Über die Klage, dass der deutschen Jugend der Idealismus fehle" ("Concerning the Lament that German Youth Lack Idealism"). It contained his assessment that the culture of Bismarck's empire was both weak and antiquated. This was how he tried to tap new followers. The professor emphatically represented himself to young people as an exponent of an ideal worldview that, despite all opposition, was the wave of the future.

The final discourse in the book was directed at liberalism and bore the title "Die nächsten Pflichten deutscher Politik" ("The Future Obligations of German Politics"). Along with familiar attacks on the liberal press and the alleged foolishness of parliamentarianism, it contained a lengthy defense of war. But that was not its antiliberal feature, as very few liberals cherished the hope for "everlasting peace." In the era of nation-states, the vast majority of bourgeois politicians welcomed an aggressive foreign policy.[22] The specifics of Lagarde's argumentation consisted of the importance he attached to the *Raum* (category of space). In view of the apparent overpopulation of the German Empire, he regarded it as a given that areas of Russia would be acquired for German settlers. If the Czarist Empire could not bring itself to "oblige," then Germany would be forced to proceed with "expropriation" (p. 422).

Lagarde came to speak about Eastern European Jews in connection with his colonization plans. As things stood, they would be "gotten rid of and sent to Palestine or, better still, Madagascar" (p. 423). He linked authoritarian utopian ideas that were already under discussion in the Vormärz period (before the March 1848 revolution) to the resolution of the "Jewish question." He simultaneously referred to the latest political opportunities that the French protectorate in Madagascar, founded in 1885, appeared to offer. The research literature then repeatedly emphasized Lagarde's importance to the so-called Madagascar plan. But one should not overestimate the political significance of what was most likely a passing remark, and the corresponding prospect that the deportation plans under discussion in the Third Reich were strongly inspired by Lagarde.[23] But there is also no reason to deny that his political ideology showed contempt for humanity. With the greatest of ease, he emphasized how it was different from previous diplomatic practices: "This policy is somewhat Assyrian, but it's the only one there is" (p. 423). Behind the policy was the conviction that it was Germany's mission to establish the kingdom of God. But the unctuous rhetoric cannot hide the exorbitance of the demands. Significantly, Russian rights were never talked about, and the praise of German culture was directly associated with the desired conquests: "Germans are a peaceable folk, but they are convinced of their right to live as Germans. And they are convinced that they have a mission on behalf of all nations on earth. Should anyone prevent them from living as Germans, prevent them from pursuing their mission, then they are authorized to use force" (p. 423).

Lagarde's dream of unlimited farmland in the East was incompatible with the commonly accepted maxims that a war of limited objectives needed to be fought and its true success would depend on the solidity of the peace treaty concluded thereafter. A war of conquest in Eastern Europe was not only too risky for liberal politicians but for conservative military officers as well. And winning it was highly questionable. When the possibility of war with Russia suddenly appeared in 1878, Helmuth von Moltke's attitude typified those reservations. He told the Prussian chief of staff in emphatically plain terms: "The Russians are disagreeable neighbors. They have absolutely nothing that one could take from them following a victorious war—they have no gold, and we cannot use more land."[24] Lagarde saw it differently and linked his Fichte-inspired idea of a "German mission" to dreams of conquering Eastern Europe. The scenario of a colossal German-Russian war also influenced Lagarde's vision of a united Central Europe under German leadership. Neighboring countries like Poland and the Czech lands were chiefly considered potential allies against Russia and were, therefore, evaluated on the basis of their military usefulness.

In habitually striking language, Lagarde gave free reign to his anti-Slavic prejudices. Although he had never dealt intensively with Eastern Europe, he regarded Germans' hatred of Slavs as an established fact. He made this bold generalization: "They all hate us, because they know that our life is their death, and because they know that, without us, they are totally incapable of spiritual existence. Nevertheless, they do not want to recognize our superiority" (p. 428). Time and again, Lagarde casually slipped pejorative value judgments into the text. Cited here as a typical example of his contemptuous diction are his words to describe Slovenians: the only ascertainable talent they had was "for selling mousetraps, graters, and sieves" (p. 429). He generally considered the little Slavic peoples so futureless that there would be no better destiny for them than Germanization.[25] On the other hand, he saw potential allies in King Carol I of Romania and Prince Alexander of Bulgaria, both of whom were threatened by the "Muscovite giants" (p. 431). The idea that Bulgarians were not ethnic Slavs, but Finns, was behind this strange belief. In line with this hypothesis, Lagarde considered Prince Alexander von Battenberg, chosen as the Bulgarian ruler in 1879, one of the few shining lights of southeastern European history.

Lagarde sided with Prince Alexander in the Serbo-Bulgarian War of 1885. He sent him "twenty marks to help wounded Bulgarians" and hoped that the "small sum" would "suffice as an expression of support." On April 6, 1886, Lagarde sent a package of books to Sofia that contained his poems and the *Deutsche Schriften*. He obsequiously assured the prince that he did not expect any thanks. For him, it was enough "to have gladly presented the valiant and prudent prince with a small gift."[26] Lagarde described his major work in a comparatively reserved manner as resistance to a "failed attempt to teach Germans to make an inherently foreign culture fit them." Nonetheless, the aggressive nature of what he had in mind for Eastern Europe could not be doubted. So he entrusted the ecclesiastical training centers "on the borders of the Reich [with . . .] laying out where the Germans needed a foothold" (p. 433). Meanwhile, he thought of the name Germania (p. 448) for the united Central Europe that would take shape after the dissolution of the Austrian multiracial state.

Lagarde was especially sympathetic toward German nationals living abroad, who, in his opinion, were making irreplaceable cultural contributions in Eastern Europe. For this reason, they deserved the complete support of the German Reich. On November 14, 1884, he sent a collection of his theological writings as moral support to the state consistory of the Augsburg Confession of the Evangelical Lutheran Church in Hermannstadt. With a typical mixture of idealistic and conspiratorial language, he requested that "[you] see in this donation an expression of my conviction that Transylvanian Saxons must not be allowed to be forgotten by Germany and are, indeed, not forgotten. We shall wait for better times to speak more loudly and to take action." So as to strengthen Transylvanian love for the German Fatherland, he enclosed "volumes of the *National-Zeitung* in which they reported on the Wars of 1870–1871 and the already scarce, complete lists of our losses." As if this were not enough to emphasize his own patriotism, Lagarde described himself as "the last representative of a Metz family that, between 1865 and 1870, had hoped for the German free city of Metz to again become part of the Reich." He had faith in the "coming of God's spring" for Transylvanian Saxons.

Lagarde liked to adopt a patronizing posture in his correspondence with Eastern Europeans. To Poles and Czechs, he suggested an alliance against Russia. But he also let it show through that he was not convinced of their equality. On December 27, 1886, he wrote to the Polish student society member August Maczkowski: "The Poles have exactly the same right to be a nation as the Germans; yet they don't have it in opposition to the Germans, but alongside the Germans. All the more so, as Poles are, to the best of my knowledge, dependent on German culture as a source of spiritual life and will remain so for quite some time." Lagarde cared little that such statements were offensive. He affably told Maczkowski that "an orderly Pole who doesn't ask the impossible is no real enemy of Germans." In this context, he referred to Alexander von Battenberg, who had "served" Bulgarians "with his whole heart and been of great benefit to them."

The acceptance of Lagarde's ideas among Eastern European intellectuals was quite limited. Even positive opinions like those found in his correspondence were written in such a way as to leave the door open to a change of heart. After the publication of the second volume of the *Deutsche Schriften*, a shrewd fellow like the sociologist Tomáš Masaryk reminded Lagarde that he had "not spoken in an adequately factual" manner about the Czechs.[27] Needless to say, Lagarde was not prepared to revise his opinions. On November 6, 1886, he responded to the liberally minded professor from Prague in language that brooked no contradiction: "The Czechs have the same right to exist as every other nation, yet not against us, but along with us. And as long as Germany is not certain if Czechs are helpful to Russian plans, and as long as it is not certain if Poles will become Jesuit lackeys, then we will be enemies of Czechs and Poles." It is hard to imagine a mediatory response to such statements and, in fact, this letter ended Lagarde's correspondence with the future president of Czechoslovakia.

The aggressive features of Lagarde's nationalism are plainly visible today. Even Vincent Viaene, who put forward the theory that Lagarde's thinking lacked brutality, noted that his expectant idealism ended at Germany's borders.[28] Statements that show contempt for human beings surely point to character defects in the chronically overworked scholar. At the same time, two factual associations should be considered. On the one hand, his dichotomous worldview had always tended to demonize ideological opponents, whether liberals, the Protestant church, Jews, or Slavic peoples. On the other hand, Lagarde had to hold his own against a multiplicity of competitors in the journalistic mass market. As controversial as his aggressive rhetoric was, it still ensured him of considerable attention, especially since his followers could always point to sentimental passages and claim there was another Lagarde. And it can hardly be denied that the radicality of his proposals appealed to the disillusioned of every stripe.

Lagarde showed great energy in spreading his ideas. He personally saw to the circulation of the *Deutsche Schriften* and sent out a huge number of complementary copies into the world. He had no fear of important persons. On April 6, 1886, immediately following the publication of the single-volume edition, he sent a copy to the hated Bismarck and presented himself as a fighter for the "eternal honor of the German Fatherland."[29] That same day, another volume went out to the Prussian finance minister, Adolf von Scholz. In contrast to the *Reichskanzler*, who was content to send a formal word of thanks, the minister responded very personally to the surprising gift. On August 5, 1886, Scholz informed the author that he had read the book and praised Lagarde's poetry, in particular. With regard to the impact of the *Deutsche Schriften*, he thought not only of the present but also of the future at all times. On April 6, Lagarde also sent a copy of the book to Prince Wilhelm of Prussia, who would later become the German kaiser.[30] The carefully worded cover letter exalted the heir to the throne as the "born leader of today's youth." Lagarde stressed that his critique of education had been met with across-the-board approval among German students. At the same time, "mature men [. . .] like Heinrich von Treitschke, Karl Hillebrand and Friedrich Paulsen" would support him—all and sundry scholars who had fiercely fought left-wing liberalism and written with a skilled, journalistic pen. Lagarde outlined the future of the nation with this statement: "Little Germany may only be considered one perhaps unavoidable, perhaps necessary step on the march to a Greater Germany, just as the North German Confederation had been a step in the direction of today's German Reich." So the future German kaiser knew of Lagarde's imperial agenda that disregarded existing borders because it considered the mission of the German people the highest value. On June 24, 1886, Chamberlain Eduard von Liebenau expressed thanks on the prince's behalf for the "honorable token of appreciation."

In his letter to the Prussian heir apparent, Lagarde had a reason for bringing up the respect he enjoyed among students. The *Verein deutscher Studenten* (Union of German Students), founded in December 1880, agitated against Jews and liberals in equal measure. He advocated the strictly nationalistic agenda that had already set the tone at universities for years and looked for intellectual "straight men" among the professoriate. It was as if Lagarde were predestined for this assignment. On September 28, 1885, the editor of the *Deutsche Studenten-Zeitung* (*German Student Newspaper*), Eugen Wolff, turned to the professor from Göttingen. He would like to found a "union of minds": in the

Deutsche Schriften, Lagarde "had called" such a union "a necessity." The objective the young official had in mind was no less than "protecting young students from decadence." And he solicited Lagarde's signature on the appeal for the planned organizational meeting. But the senior professor kept his distance. Lagarde severely criticized the vague meaninglessness of the proclamation and in no way considered its consequences desirable: "I am certain that associations which meet for such purposes lead to talk, not to action. We don't need conspiracies, but conspirators, and conspiracies that are organized by the press can help us least of all."[31] He was equally severe when it came to the future prospects of student politics: "We have no church, no aristocracy, no conservative government: they cannot contribute in a place where no one is active."

But as much as Lagarde liked to appear in the role of the experienced man who knew what was good and right for everyone, he hardly ever spoiled his chances for acceptance. He advised Wolff in a patronizingly friendly manner: "Given his place, everyone does his very best in his own way. And everyone connects with his neighbor, who does the same thing, from person to person, not in a union." The Orientalist was always under time pressure and had no interest in long-lasting contacts. When Wolff implored him to please finally write an article for the *Deutsche Universitäts-Zeitung* (*German University Newspaper*), Lagarde answered him unequivocally in the negative on November 8, 1885. Referring to an upcoming research trip, he asked Wolff "not to continue mailing packages. They would only lie around unread for months." Lagarde could not permit himself to take such an attitude toward his scholarly creations, which for the most part had a small circle of readers. This was also true of his complete edition of the works of Giordano Bruno, in which he had placed great hopes.

Lagarde had undertaken extensive preparations for his edition and even looked through the trial records of the Italian philosopher, who was finally burned at the stake in Rome around 1600. He didn't have the slightest sympathy for the former Dominican monk, even though Bruno was convicted of heresy for his pantheistically inclined thinking by the tribunal of the Inquisition. His Bruno edition, published in 1888–1889, had a strictly antiliberal thrust. Lagarde spoke boldly in introducing his work. As he so often did, he used the literary and review journal *Göttingischen gelehrten Anzeigen* for this purpose: "My task serves scholarship, not any party, least of all the godless, history-denying party of liberalism."[32] Lagarde judged the philosopher, who was plagued by inner doubts, on strictly moral grounds and found him too lightweight. Bruno's extensive religious speculations, in particular, were not accorded any ethical dignity. In evocative style, Lagarde said: "I cannot get away from the fact that, in such surroundings, a man, so long as he was young, would not rather have built barricades and grabbed a gun or a dagger and, when he got older, would not have preferred to found a poorhouse, a hospital or, as far as I'm concerned, a school, rather than to dream up metaphysics that drew on astronomy."[33] This statement not only implied a projection of his own standards onto the late sixteenth century, a tie that could scarcely be convincing in the age of historicism; it also spirited away the fact that Lagarde himself was neither a revolutionary nor a social reformer but simply a Prussian civil servant.

But what is even more unnerving is the political meaning that underlay the senior professor's Bruno edition. He took the philosopher from Nola for a troublemaker who was "the diametrical opposite of Dante." One can hardly imagine a greater reproach coming out of Lagarde's mouth. After all, he considered Dante the paragon of pious, medieval life. His glorification of Dante as the "first Italian" bore signs of veiled self-identification at the very least.[34] In turn, the image of Bruno as the "sea [. . .] from which the water driving the mills of our liberalism flows toward us"[35] was unsurpassed in its stridency. Contemporaries were anything but convinced by the stylization of Bruno as a secret source of contemporary liberalism. Indeed, this view had no basis in source material and bore all the signs of a trumped-up conspiracy theory.

In any case, the success of the *Deutsche Schriften* did not carry over to the Bruno edition, in which Lagarde had invested considerable sums of money. Hardly any critics expressed interest in the work, and the books lay like deadweights on the shelves. In a correspondingly sullen mood, he wrote to the Prussian minister of education and cultural affairs, Gustav von Gossler, on August 31, 1889, that not more than "127 copies" had been "sold: 60 in Italy, 30 in England, 37 in Germany and non-Italian, non-German, non-English Europe." Lagarde could not see any plausible reason for the disastrous sales. But he had largely dispensed with advertising, and the circle of readers with an interest in the Italian first edition of Giordano Bruno must have been rather small. He instead pointed out to Gossler that the Bruno edition would be "hushed up everywhere because I am not a Jew." On January 18, 1890, he told the Parisian bookseller Klincksieck: "I intentionally do not belong to any party or coterie and will not be reviewed for that reason." Lagarde had been in the practice of assigning blame for his own failures in this way for more than three decades. But the extent of his bitterness had increased, as had the intensity with which he felt threatened by enemy "cliques." The violent fantasies that increasingly appeared in his late works reflected his fears and also allowed for an almost physical release of strain. Surprisingly enough, Lagarde's persecution and doomsday scenarios seem to have fostered his acceptance more than they harmed it.

Grave cultural pessimism prevailed in the 1880s, particularly in academic circles. Many people believed that European civilization was rushing headlong toward disaster and felt that Lagarde validated their worldview. After receiving the single-volume edition of the *Deutsche Schriften*, for example, Adolf Erman advised Lagarde on April 26, 1886: "I still often draw analogies as to how things could well go on, and the same dire thoughts always occur to me: Europe will come to a slow materialistic and spiritual death, a gradual dying out, and then some external catastrophe will put an end to it." In contrast to many cultural pessimists, however, Lagarde's apocalyptic thinking offered an important advantage. As in the case of Richard Wagner, the dawning of a better day presupposed the end of the despicable present. Thus, the end of the modern world could also be celebrated as the beginning of a new era in which mankind had learned to focus on the essentials and its relationship to God. An admittedly important difference from Wagner was that Lagarde repeatedly developed his doomsday scenarios against the backdrop of entirely real historical conflicts.

So Lagarde considered French revanchism an incontrovertible certainty. Shortly before his death, he wrote to his wife from Paris on September 4, 1891: "All Frenchmen, even those who are on the friendliest of terms with Germans—I am sure of it—long for war."[36] Precisely because of the tragic inevitability of the conflict, however, people have to stand by their respective fatherlands. Lagarde sometimes entertained ideas of out-and-out annihilation. In a second letter of September 4, 1891, to his wife, he called for the total destruction of Paris: "No stone may be left standing there if we want peace." A few lines later, after recalling friendly associations with Frenchmen, he brooded over what "a terrible world" it was.[37]

Haunted by extreme mood swings, Lagarde eased the burden through violent fantasies that he sometimes softened afterward with sentimental remarks. While he energetically underscored the homogeneity and inner uniformity of his worldview, his thinking was actually shaped by a large number of inconsistencies. They not only reflected his inner conflict but also expressed both his over- and underestimations of his ideological opponents. And Judaism aroused the greatest anger in Lagarde.

10

The Camel Sparrow

We have already learned something about Lagarde's hatred of Jews. He thought of his nationalism as internally homogenous and looked upon every form of collective Jewish identity as hostile. In the tradition of Fichte and German Romanticism, Lagarde believed that a Jewish state-within-the-state was deadly. But he also vehemently attacked Christian denominations for not offering any real resistance to growing secularization. And he saw the distinguishing weakness of Protestantism in its close relationship to "Jewish literalism." In many respects, Lagarde's orientation was close to that of ecclesiastical antisemitism. But his rejection of Judaism went far beyond the cheap sensationalism of the usual prejudices. He separated the world of the Gospels from Judaism and emphasized Paul's fateful role in church history. He considered postbiblical Judaism a fossilized phenomenon, the remnant of a distant, bygone era.

Lagarde went to great effort to make his *Deutsche Schriften* accessible to the antisemitic movement. In later editions, he intensified his attacks on Jews. His fusion of antisemitic and antiliberal enemy stereotypes was particularly effective. By adding just the right amount of spiciness to his critique of self-satisfied, bourgeois society, he made it attractive to outsiders and victims of modernization. But Lagarde also found followers among middle-class conservatives. The conservative bourgeoisie rejected liberalism and appreciated his pessimistically colored social criticism, since radical criticism of contemporary life afforded an easy link to the protection of a noble self-image and societal claims of supremacy. Lagarde brilliantly activated biblical imagery for use in the latest political and ideological conflicts. And he did it in such a way as to make his thoughts appear innovative yet tried and true.

But all this information tells us very little about the concrete aspects of Lagarde's antisemitism, which was certainly not limited to the confines of his study or the writing of brochures. As a professor of Orientalism, how did he view Jewish scholars? What ideological concepts determined his actions? To what extent did he collaborate with key figures in the antisemitic movement? Lagarde did not fully express his antisemitic resentments in a vacuum: he insulted fellow human beings and provoked responses. His prejudices took a specific form that reflected not only the Zeitgeist but were also part of his conflict with a milieu in which he felt ever-increasingly misunderstood.

In the early years of his professorship, Lagarde was respected and sometimes even admired by Jewish scholars. He was considered one of the few professors who had the requisite linguistic skills and a serious interest in Hebraic literature. In 1880, the highly respected *Monatsschrift für die Geschichte und Wissenschaft des Judentums* (*Monthly Journal of Jewish History and Scholarship*) sang his praises: "Hardly anyone can compare with him in his command of an enormous quantity of linguistic material, which may well comprise all Semitic languages and most Indo-Germanic ones."[1] From time to time, Lagarde spoke quite frankly and expressed his antisemitic views in a surprisingly curt, abrupt manner. But people were used to this sort of thing from German Orientalists and, in comparison to his predecessor, Ewald, Lagarde seemed almost restrained. The eminent businessman from Lemberg, Salomon Buber, exemplifies someone who showed considerable respect for Lagarde. An indefatigable collector of old manuscripts from the nonlegal portions of Talmudic literature, Martin Buber's grandfather was practically unequaled in his knowledge of Jewish intellectual history. He valued Lagarde's expertise, as well as his unselfish advice. When a private tribute to Salomon Buber was about to take place in 1882, people naturally brought it to Lagarde's attention.[2]

This attitude was in no way unusual. Lagarde's correspondence contains many statements from Jewish scholars who ungrudgingly recognized him as a talented Orientalist. The opinion of the Hungarian rabbi Immanuel Löw was typical. On January 7, 1880, Löw sent Lagarde his "first work, which is about Aramaic plant names." Following a friendly response from Lagarde, Löw spoke candidly on February 25 about how much courage it took "for a person to defend his work before the most competent judge." His fear was not unfounded: Lagarde's correspondence with Christian colleagues shows that, even at the beginning of his tenure, he was extremely critical in assessing Jewish scholars. His comments mainly included a strong dose of traditional hatred for Jews, accompanied by a firm belief in the superiority of his own scholarly education.

Lagarde exhibited particular skepticism in the case of young rabbis who sought doctoral degrees in his area of study. He actually credited them with sufficient knowledge of Oriental languages, but not with mastery of the scientific method. In 1876, he firmly turned away the rabbi from Erfurt, Adolph Jaraczewsky. And, in 1877, the outcome wasn't any better for the Russian Jew Albert Scheinin. Among his usual criticisms were overemphasis on content and the neglect of source-critical issues. His friend Georg Hoffmann had similar views. On January 6, 1874, Hoffmann told Lagarde that, on the Kiel Fjord, one couldn't "make sketchy deals in the doctoral ordination of Polish or Hungarian rabbis." The very nonchalance of such statements shows that the value judgments behind them were largely taken for granted.

On October 21, 1881, Lagarde wrote a letter to the Königsberg philologist Adalbert Bezzenberger that typifies his ambivalent assessment of Jewish scholars. In it, he discussed the application of David Kaufmann, a professor at the Budapest Rabbinical College who enjoyed a certain amount of respect in the scholarly world: "Everything he [Kaufmann] wrote is outstanding. He knows Hebrew and Jewish Aramaic, but he's only interested in facts and not at all in language." With a gibe at contemporary theology's lack of philological orientation, Lagarde continued: "It certainly wouldn't hurt theologians in Königsberg to hear how he deals with the Old Testament. He will not exactly do the Good Book justice for the reason that he is a Jew." This was an attitude that one could hardly contest through argumentation, because the accusation of ideological narrowness threatened to turn even the highest praise of Jewish scholarship into its polar opposite. In this instance, Lagarde advised his colleague that "Kaufmann may possibly wish to see his appointment as a triumph of Judaism." It is no surprise that, under the circumstances, the highly qualified candidate did not make the final cut at the East Prussian university in question.

But Lagarde occasionally proved benevolent. This was the case, above all, when Jewish scholars behaved very modestly and worked in fields that were important to him. On January 25, 1878, he recommended the philosopher Jacob Freudenthal to the Prussian Ministry of Education and Cultural Affairs for a special professorship in Breslau. In a patronizingly friendly manner, Lagarde said that Jews could ideally be integrated into German society. The ministry had done an outstanding job of ignoring the Jewish extraction of some professors in Göttingen. He characterized his position to the expert counselor for university affairs, Heinrich Göppert, with this bold statement: "In any case, we will only overcome this very annoying, very talented nation-within-a-nation through helpfulness and love, not by rejecting their best and brightest, one of whom is most certainly Freudenthal." This is a remarkable opinion, since the number of Jewish university lecturers in Göttingen was higher than average. Between 1866 and 1918, no fewer than forty-one Jewish scholars worked at Georgia Augusta, but very few of them held senior professorships.[3] As irritably as Lagarde responded to the advancement of Jewish scholars in general, specific instances seem not to have concerned him. He was interested in Freudenthal's philosopho-historical work, particularly in his studies of the Arab response to Aristotle. He hoped that Freudenthal might be able to devote himself entirely to scholarship without material concerns. And his wish came true: Freudenthal got the coveted position in Breslau in 1879 and was even appointed to a senior professorship in 1888.

Lagarde was especially supportive of Moses Samuel Zuckermandel, a rabbi from Pasewalk. On April 22, 1876, he recommended the reserved scholar for the directorship of the Breslau Jewish Theological Seminary. Lagarde was not sparing in his praise. Above all, he emphasized the rigorous objectivity of Zuckermandel's work. He pled for the rabbi to receive a guaranteed position for life so that he "would provide an essential service to the Jewish nation and world literature alike" by means of respectable scholarly editions. That opportunity came to nothing. Later that same year, however, Lagarde energetically took steps to ensure that Zuckermandel was given access to valuable manuscripts in Erfurt that were indispensable to his critical edition of Tosefta (supplementary materials not included in the Mishnah that were redacted by the third-century C.E.). Behind his efforts was the conviction that the compilation, comprising sixty tractates, was a source of inestimable value to Jewish intellectual history. Lagarde considered it a "parallel law book of the synagogue" (i.e., rabbinic Judaism) that, due to its heterodox character, had been "suppressed" by the most powerful Jewish groups. In 1880, he got Zuckermandel a Parisian grant and secured support from the Prussian Ministry of Education and Cultural Affairs for the printing costs of the Tosefta edition.[4]

Lagarde took his commitment to capable Jewish scholars for granted. He felt that the strict objectivity and hard work of scholarship were suited to overcoming traditional prejudices and to fostering the integration of Jews into German society. On December 4, 1880, he explained his motives to Zuckermandel. He openly admitted "that I do not look favorably upon a separate nation of Jews and their presence in Europe." He referred to an ancient parable to justify his friendliness toward the nearly penniless rabbi. He was of the opinion "that the sun more easily gets the wanderer out of his coat than a storm, and that's why I have always treated individual Jews as lovingly as possible." This was an exceptionally smug statement, considering how uncompromising Lagarde could be in speaking out against Jewish scholars in the daily routine of the academy. But there is something else that may well be more important: he differentiated between Jews who sincerely tried to integrate into German society and those who only pretended to do so or were completely "obdurate," a cause of deep structural inequality between Germans and Jews. The inhumane statement "I choose those who become Germans" was clearly as dangerous as his generally arrogant, haughty attitude toward Jewish scholars. Lagarde justified his support for Freudenthal to the Prussian Ministry of Education and Cultural Affairs by stating that Jews "must entirely join with Germany or get out of

Germany. Since the latter is not possible, the first must be contemplated in all seriousness."

Lagarde was convinced that safeguarding Jewish identity was impossible for real scholars. On the one hand, Judaism and its multifarious laws were part of an outgrown phase of human history. On the other hand, Judaism contained opinions that were not compatible with strict standards of objectivity. Such reservations about Judaism were widespread at German universities. When the brilliant Jewish medievalist Harry Bresslau complained to Leopold Ranke about persistent unfair treatment in the academic world, Ranke answered him unsympathetically: "But Bresslau, you're stepping over the line here."[5] Jewish scholars were well aware that the path to one of very few permanent positions would be facilitated by baptism into the Christian faith. The number of scholars who converted was considerably high, a fact that was critically debated among German Jewry time and again. Influential Jewish intellectuals like Hermann Cohen and Moritz Lazarus even considered baptism an act of dishonorable self-surrender.[6] Of course, every conversion also held an aspect of personal fate. Sometimes scholarly enthusiasm was a top priority, while in other cases it was burning ambition or the desire to leave the confines of one's own background. Some Jewish scholars believed that a professorship justified practically any sacrifice; others simply resigned themselves to the existing power structure. In any case, distinguished professors like Ulrich von Wilamowitz-Moellendorf left their students in no doubt as to how greatly they valued conversion to Christianity. When concretely faced with this problem, Lagarde behaved similarly.

In spring 1882, the young Egyptologist Georg Steindorff was recommended to him by his longtime friend Adolf Erman. Like Lagarde, Erman did a lot to advance the careers of his prize students and, to Erman's satisfaction, Lagarde took Steindorff under his wing. On December 31, 1882, he substantiated to Steindorff the virtues that were especially prized at the height of the Age of Positivism: "labor of love and healthy skepticism." Steindorff was, in fact, a passionate researcher who put all his energy into university education. He realized early on that powerful advocates were important to a successful career. Steindorff showed great admiration for Lagarde and was prepared to discuss the topics he brought up with no ifs, ands, or buts. On November 11, 1883, he wrote to Göttingen in an almost subservient manner: "My only wish is that you, esteemed teacher, may one day be satisfied with your pupil." Steindorff gave up Assyriology and, so as to share in Lagarde's research interests, concentrated on Hebrew in addition to Egyptology. Moreover, he focused his thoughts more closely on the significance of spiritual rebirth.

On December 24, 1884, after Steindorff got his doctorate in Berlin, he presented Lagarde with his wish "to convert from Judaism to Christianity and agree to be baptized." At the same time, he hoped that the professor from Göttingen would review his doctoral thesis. Lagarde's extremely friendly response came quickly by return mail. He regarded a review as impossible, because he had not mastered hieroglyphics and could not ignore the existing teacher-student relationship. But Lagarde looked so favorably upon the idea of conversion that he offered to act as godfather to the talented young scholar. The senior professor stated emphatically: "Inwardly, you have not been a member of the religion of your forefathers for a very long time." Now it was a matter of "committing" himself to "the development of world history." Lagarde also stressed that Steindorff would "naturally have to fight battles" and solemnly advised the young scholar: "Refrain from speaking for the time being; such personal matters are profaned by words." Finally, he counseled: "You are now entering into freedom, not into slavery. A free man has the law within him, because he has the love of all that is good within him."[7] This statement was entirely well meant but also illustrated Lagarde's strongly negative image of "Jewish legalism."

Steindorff felt encouraged by Lagarde's friendly words and gladly accepted his offer of godparenthood. On January 15, 1885, he also asked if Lagarde would "stand [. . .] by his side [. . .] as a *Führer* [guide]" during the planned conversion. Steindorff needed advice and help in matters beyond questions of faith. On February 19, 1885, he admitted to his mentor that he had accomplished very little so far that year. By way of explanation, he said he had "gotten so physically tired from the inner battles that I have fought on the path to my new life" that he "very often lacked the strength to do scholarly work." Behind this apology were the professional possibilities that had opened up to Steindorff with Erman's appointment as director of the Egyptian museums in Berlin. The personal and professional turbulence soon subsided. On April 20, 1885, the young scholar was able to tell Lagarde of his upcoming christening, as well as his impending appointment. He also thanked him for his "fatherly care." Within a short time, he advanced from the position of assessor to Erman's personal assistant, which meant he could look forward to a carefree future. Steindorff was absolutely euphoric about the new course his life had taken. Alluding to Schiller's *Der Ring des Polykrates* (*The Ring of Polycrates*), he wrote to Lagarde on November 13, 1885: "I almost dread the Gods' envy! All of my fondest hopes have been fulfilled this year. My inner person has become someone else; my outer life seems quite secure. From a scholarly standpoint, I want to do all that is within my power."

In the period that followed, Steindorff gave Lagarde detailed reports about his professional and private affairs. The ambitious Egyptologist married Elise

Oppenheimer, a woman from a prominent Jewish family. He lived for his research and waited for a professorship. To Lagarde's great delight, he not only worked on hieroglyphics but applied himself intensively to Coptic as well. Steindorff was appointed associate professor in Breslau in 1893 and was given a chair in 1904. His letters to Lagarde express his happiness with the decision to be baptized and his growing circle of Christian friends. He and his wife read the *Deutsche Schriften*, and he held Lagarde's poetry in especially high regard. On July 4, 1889, he asked the Orientalist to be godfather to his son, Ulrich. Lagarde, however, shied away from close personal relationships and, as he had once done with Georg Hoffmann, declined the offer. Steindorff's baptism was apparently the only thing that could move Lagarde to assume the obligation to godparenthood, and it is hard to imagine more convincing proof of the importance Lagarde attached to conversion from Judaism to Christianity. In Lagarde's view, of course, there was no fundamental right to inclusion in the German nation, and the Orientalist's goodwill was admittedly hard-earned. His position in response to the widespread ritual murder accusations of the late 1800s illustrates that his opinions of Judaism could turn out to be very divergent.

In Europe, 1881 was a year of antisemitic violence. A multitude of antisemitic riots broke out in the Russian Empire after Czar Alexander II was assassinated. They mainly took place in the Ukraine, where rioters could count on the benevolent approval of powerful figures. That was because the new monarch, Alexander III, and his chief procurator of the Holy Synod (the top official in the Russian Orthodox Church), Konstantin Pobedonostsev, were convinced that baneful Jewish plundering was responsible for Russia's fate. Abetted by the failure of police to restrain rioters, no fewer than 259 pogroms took place by year's end.[8] But antisemitic unrest was not limited to the Czarist Empire. The discontented populations of Pomerania and West Prussia also rebelled against the ostensibly superior position of the Jews. The magnitude of the violence, which ranged from arson to pillaging, showed that the emancipation laws had in no way led to full equality or even to the acceptance of Jews.[9] The utopia of liberal middle-class society had never actually reached the rural areas and seemed increasingly antiquated in the urban strongholds of liberalism as well. The Jews in rural areas found themselves confronted with accusations that clashed with the progressive optimism that the Jewish bourgeoisie so dearly wanted to hold on to.

Spectacular events took place in Tisza Eslar, a small town in northeastern Hungary. When, in 1882, a Christian maid disappeared, strange rumors circulated and the uneasy population soon spoke of ritual murder. They were stirred up by antisemitic agitators who saw an opportunity to spread their ideology. The trial, in which a thirteen-year-old testified against his own father, developed into a media circus. Journalists came from far and wide, and catered to a craving for sensationalism that they had largely created themselves. But the charges proved unfounded. And it was not only Hungarian Jews who greeted the acquittal of all fifteen Jews on trial with relief.[10] But hopes that people would finally see the accusations of ritual murder as medieval were not fulfilled. On the contrary, it became apparent that Central Europeans were extremely interested in demonizing Jews.

The star among antisemitic "experts on Jewish superstition" was the Catholic theologian August Rohling. Since 1877, the former priest had held a professorship at the German University in Prague. His inflammatory pamphlets had been translated into six languages and reached a mass audience. At the same time, he became entangled in clashes with rabbis and Protestant theologians who didn't go along with his drastic, moreover dilettantish, interpretations of Hebrew texts. When Rohling got into a fix because he attacked Franz Delitzsch for his allegedly Jewish background, he sought Lagarde's help on January 24, 1881. But Lagarde kept his distance and advised Rohling to exercise restraint: "Do not allow present achievements to seduce you into forgetting your priestly honor. Be as keenly objective as you wish, but make no remark that goes beyond the objective facts."[11] Lagarde was even less prepared to argue openly in favor of Rohling's assertion that Jews had a tradition of human sacrifice.

In response to the inquiry of the Budapest rabbinical conference on the purported Jewish tradition of ritual murder, Lagarde answered unambiguously. On October 7, 1882, he stated that the religious and legal writings of Judaism "had never demanded the use of human blood for religious purposes." Just as the superstition of individual Jews had little to do with Judaism, "the superstition of individual Christians" could not be brought forward "against Christianity." This clear statement was not to be taken for granted. The theological faculty in Marburg, for instance, decided in favor of a noncommittal report that Hermann Cohen found deeply insulting.[12] In December 1882, Moritz Lazarus, a widely recognized ethnopsychologist and an intellectual guiding force within liberal Judaism, sent Lagarde a copy of a work hot off the press in Berlin, *Christliche Zeugnisse gegen die Blutbeschuldigung der Juden* (*Christian Testimony against Jewish Blood Libel*). Lagarde himself had helped bring about the work. Along with statements from theological faculties and ecclesiastical dignitaries, the publication contained those of outstanding Old Testament scholars and Orientalists. Among those who openly opposed the ritual-murder myth were Franz Delitzsch, Theodor Nöldecke, Eduard Riehm, and Paul de Lagarde.[13] Regardless of their widely differing scholarly and political positions, all agreed that the documentary sources contained absolutely no support for the idea of Jewish ritual murder. After all, Mosaic law prohibited the drinking of blood, so the accusation that Jews needed the blood of Christian children in preparation for religious ceremonies was not even remotely plausible. But Rohling persistently sought to establish contact with Lagarde, who, unlike himself, had comprehensive linguistic knowledge and solid academic training.

Although the Prague professor had offered his expert services in Tisza Eslar, he never got the chance to use them. In the summer of 1883, at the trial's height, he published an inflammatory pamphlet instead. It was eloquently titled *Die Polemik und das Menschenopfer des Rabbinismus* (*The Polemics and Human Sacrifice of Rabbinism*). Rohling tried to substantiate his bizarre opinion of rabbinical "bloodlust" by providing a wealth of evidence.[14] But after the acquittal of the accused in August 1883, he got into his own legal troubles and had to answer for his attacks on Judaism before a court in Vienna. He wanted Lagarde to draw up a legally watertight defense and, on March 4, 1884, sent him the second edition of the controversial leaflet for that purpose. Rohling determined that his sorry effort had provided a "sufficient, albeit anything but complete, compilation of bloody episodes" to prove the barbarity of Judaism.[15] But Lagarde showed no inclination to go before the court on behalf of his colleague's careless quotes and sweeping generalizations. His response of March 15 admittedly contained antisemitic undertones but was *nevertheless* entirely clear on the matter: "I am not willing to argue in court with a Chasid from Lemberg over the interpretation of this book, which I have never studied in depth." Lagarde was referring here to Rohling's assessment of the Zohar, which he saw as entirely incorrect. Without much ado, he advised his scholarly counterpart: "You are way off base, and the sooner you turn around, the better." Lagarde was not only convinced that Rohling's position was untenable; he was also of the opinion that the "Jewish question" could never be solved by exegetic pedantry.

As early as March 8, however, Lagarde had told Rohling his own opinion of Judaism, expressed in the form of a parable: "The Persians, like the Greeks, called ostriches 'sparrow camels' and asserted that, if one bade the animal to fly, it would say, 'I am a camel,' and if [one bade it] to run, it would invoke its avian nature. It is similar with the Jews: either they are a race or a religious community, whichever they think accords with their intentions." As amiable as this image may appear upon first glance, it nevertheless has grave implications. In essence, it contains the rejection of all forms of collective Jewish identity. This was right in line with the view advocated by Lagarde as early as 1853: the Jews had to completely assimilate if they wanted to be integrated into the German nation. As Treitschke said, if the alternative was exclusion (*Ausschluss*) from the German nation, then one could no longer speak of any other option for the Jewish population.[16] However, the judgment contained in the parable yields another point for consideration. Lagarde was convinced from early on that true piety was impossible without community. With this in mind, he made a somber and categorical notation: "Orthodoxy without a church is like a flying fish or a bat—not at home in any element. Only he who believes in community is orthodox. And who believes in fellowship with others nowadays?"[17] If one takes this assessment into account, then Judaism's persistent rejection of "German religion" would almost necessarily appear godless. And the choice conceded to Jews with respect to the nation and religion acquires a diabolical aspect. In any case, the dazzling image of the sparrow camel was not capable of laying the foundations for a principled stance on Judaism.

On April 7, 1889, Lagarde again entered into a discussion of events in Tisza Eslar, this time with Prussian minister of education and cultural affairs Gustav von Gossler. Lagarde now emphasized that, in general, he had never disputed the guilt of the accused. One could not allow oneself to be blinded by numerous Jewish demonstrations of solidarity. At stake was Israel's reputation "of being the most enlightened people on earth," a reputation Jews did not want to lose for political reasons. In alluding to his own theory of a liberal-Jewish conspiracy, Lagarde ended with these bitter words: "Liberalism and humanity [*Freisinn und Humanität*] are the two braided loaves on which the German people are chewing at this time." Toward the end of his life, Lagarde entered a world of hatred that was completely resistant to reality checks. He barely still allowed statements that he would have once used to distance himself from antisemitic phantasmagorias. But Lagarde's view of Judaism exhibited strong stylization from early on that was hardly compatible with his intimate knowledge of the Hebrew sources.

Lagarde liked to contrast specifics of German and Jewish national character, and this typically meant invoking violent content. A particularly striking example is found in his *Gesammelte Abhandlungen* (*Collected Essays*), published in 1866. He juxtaposed what Germans and Jews would consider a meaningful life and an honorable death. The latter yearned "to sit under grapevines and fig trees in the land where milk and honey flow," while "our forebears" had bellicose virtue in mind: "They fancied Norse sagas of the god Odin, battles, eating meat and drinking mead. They scoffed at the land of milk and honey and [lounging on] bearskins."[18] Lagarde, the poet, was also moved by essentialist convictions. So he worked for a long time on his theater piece, *Rispa*, which was supposed to illustrate "the contrast between German and Jewish character." In order to bring the inherent antagonism to light, he gave Saul the "German slave" Rispa.[19] But Lagarde seems to have sensed that this approach was much too daring. Today there is no trace of the unfinished manuscript.

Lagarde's essay "Die Stellung der Religionsgesellschaften im Staat (The Status of Religious Communities within the State)" was programmatically far-reaching. The piece, which first appeared in 1881 in the second volume of the *Deutsche Schriften*,[20] emphasized that the existing religious creeds were "altogether undesirable" (p. 273), as was the case throughout the decade of the Reichsgründung. But Judaism was clearly the main focus of his critique. He strongly emphasized the cultural stagnation that had characterized it since the days of Ezra. Since their return from Babylonian exile, the Jews had consciously distanced themselves from and become strangers to all other peoples. Lagarde combined his strongly judgmental assessment of Jewish "separatism" with invectives from the arsenal of political antisemitism: "The Jews, who despite wishing to be treated as the equals of Germans, emphasize their foreignness every day in the most conspicuous way through the architecture of their synagogues. What does it mean for someone to lay claim to being called a German and to build his most holy places in the Moorish style so that he does not forget he is a Semite, Asian, alien?" (p. 275). In his typically coarse way, Lagarde allowed himself to make apodictic statements that clearly indicated his low opinion of Jewish religious traditions. Yet the decisive factor lay elsewhere. He aggressively stigmatized Jews as the inner enemies of the German nation: "Every alien substance in a living body creates feelings of unease, illness and, frequently, even suppuration and death. The foreign body can even be a precious stone. The result would be the same as if it were a little piece of rotting wood. Jews are foreigners in every European nation and, as foreigners, are no more than carriers of putrefaction" (p. 278). In view of this brutal characterization, it hardly mattered anymore whether Lagarde still believed it would be possible for Jews to become part of the German nation "by being born anew, of the spirit" (p. 278).

Surely, to state flatly that Lagarde had been a biological determinist since 1881 would be going too far. As always, he prided himself greatly on his idealism, and many passages can be found that attest to his rejection of racial theories grounded in materialism. But one should not overlook the fact that Lagarde presented his worldview in biologistic terms. Among his papers, there is an undated note in which he called Jews the "bacteria in intellectual creativity."[21] Lagarde presumably sought to enter into the late nineteenth-century biologistic discourse, in which it was customary to speak of a "war of extermination" against deadly diseases. The dynamic content of his radical nationalism may be even more important. Fichte had already underscored the close relationship between Germanness and Christianity. And he saw both ideologies as an expression of an "enhanced life."[22] At the same time, he tended to categorize everything that was foreign to the nation as moribund or already dead. Picking up on the essence of this idealism, Lagarde developed a fondness for dichotomous figures of thought. In terms of pure semantics, he favored expressions and, above all, images that allowed the German nation to look like a vulnerable collectivity.[23] This led to the abhorrence of national enemies and lent his writings a radical aura, without which he would have had to substantially revise his late-Romantic, organological worldview. The cultural pessimist loved to present himself as the seal-bearer of tradition. Yet he saw to it that his type of national religion did not make an antiquated impression, but instead remained suitable to modern advances. This also meant, of course, that his negative image of Jews was increasingly derived from his rigid understanding of national purity. Proof for this can be found in his "Programm für die konservative Partei Preussens," published in 1884, which, among many other things, decidedly represented the relationship between Germanness and Judaism (Deutschtum und Judentum).[24]

With exceptional malice, Lagarde picked up on the opinion of his archenemy, Theodor Mommsen, that Jews had always been carriers of "decomposition" (p. 396). Although Mommsen had energetically defended the Jews against Treitschke's invectives, even he exaggerated the special historical role of Jews and tended toward questionable value judgments. And, in an era of unbending nationalism, this perspective tended to marginalize Jews. Unlike Lagarde, however, Mommsen always kept an eye on the creative contributions of Jews to cultural history. And he knew the importance of "functional elites" to transnational empires.[25] Within Lagarde's puristic understanding of the German nation, multiplicity and differences occupied exclusively negative positions. He expressed his concept of an ideal Germany in language reminiscent of the ancient Greek philosopher Parmenides, who had placed pure being at the center of his thought. In such a way as to permit no contradiction, Lagarde stated: "Germany must become full of German people and German ways [. . .] as full of itself as an egg, so that there is no more room in it for Palestine." In order to underscore the urgency of his concern, Lagarde chose an especially dark metaphor. With an exclusivity seldom heard since Fichte and Ernst Arndt, he said: "Germany is once again the heart of Europe. If [. . .] Prussian conservatives are able to solve the problem of destroying Judaism, then the problem will also have been solved for Europe. And it must be solved, or Europe will become a killing field" (p. 400).

Not all opponents of Judaism found Lagarde's radical semantics attractive or even politically feasible. An anonymous author sneeringly remarked in the *Neue Evangelische Kirchenzeitung*, for example, that the cultural critic had not taken concrete steps to carry out his ideas. It was not without a touch of irony that he reproduced Lagarde's ideas in his own words: "The German-Christian spirit shall grow stronger and, by means of the flame of enthusiasm, shall redeem the Jews from their unpleasant separate existence." And he commented on Lagarde's lack of pragmatism in a similarly pointed way: "He who walks the solitary path is a conservative. To him, the present-day Conservative Party is no conservative party, nor is the Evangelical Lutheran Church any kind of church. It's better for us to take things as they are and try to improve them. But politics can only be driven by reality, not by merely idealized powers."[26] However apt these comments were, a substantial critique would have looked very different. There was an increasingly urgent demand for a public response to the prominent professor's antisemitic remarks.

Just a few months later, Lagarde clashed with a leading representative of the Wissenschaft des Judentums (Movement for the Scientific Study of Judaism). The bone of contention was Ludwig Techen's dissertation, *Zwei Göttinger Machzor-Handschriften* (*Two Manuscripts of the Göttingen Mahzor*), published in 1884. Lagarde's student sharply criticized the liturgico-historical studies of Jewish researchers and the work of Leopold Zunz, in particular, a founding figure of the Wissenschaft des Judentums. This was very unusual behavior for scholarly novices, given that the person under attack was held in high regard and that the Jewish scholarly world had followed the celebration of Zunz's ninetieth birthday with great interest. Added to that was the specific character of a doctoral dissertation seen to reflect careful scholarly work and not meant to spread any kind of iconoclastic hypotheses. The assessments of the dissertation were correspondingly reserved, and it presumably bore the stamp of his doctoral advisor, Lagarde. An anonymous critic made a particularly clear statement in the *Jüdische Litteratur-Blatt* (*Jewish Literary Magazine*). Under the derisively intended title "Aus der Schule de Lagarde's (From the Lagarde School), he alluded to a wealth of technical errors on Techen's part and exposed him as a "young know-it-all."[27] At the same time, the critic stressed that the Göttingen Philosophy Faculty should never have allowed the inadequate study to be published.

As required by the academic code of conduct, Lagarde responded in the name of his students and the faculty under attack. In the essay "Lipman Zunz und seine Verehrer" (Lipman Zunz and His Admirers), he strongly emphasized the famous Jewish scholar's strange relationship to synagogal poetry.[28] With nearly unsurpassed rudeness, he said: "At least I have no doubt that most of this 'poetry' does not belong in a religious service, but merely in a comic newspaper. I think there is no place in Germany for people who admire this rubbish!" (p. 142). Even the title of the essay contains an insult. Lagarde included the given name, Lipman, that antisemites would have normally used to label Zunz insufficiently assimilated. Even if nineteenth-century scholarly arguments were frequently conducted on a personal basis, this response unquestionably went too far. Digressions and gaffes made Lagarde's text appear like an antisemitic lampoon, rather than a scholarly polemical paper.

Lagarde mainly expressed outrage at the insolent way that Zunz had read Enlightenment values into Jewish medieval poetry. He compared the followers of the Jewish scholar with "journeyman tailors who, on Sundays, paraded their large-checked pants, red neckties and tinsel watch chains in front of maids and, on Mondays, boasted that, yesterday, people everywhere had taken them for cavalry officers in civilian clothes" (pp. 144ff). He thus took advantage of antisemitic clichés that were successfully disseminated through popular prints to a growing extent.[29] Incidentally, he disputed the achievements of Jewish soldiers in the Franco-Prussian War of 1870–1871, achievements that became crucial to German-Jewish identity. Lagarde's remarks about the alleged "ethnic Jewish vice" (p. 143), usury, were particularly one-sided. He spoke in detail about conditions in eastern Pomerania and western Prussia, where the rural population was suffering as a result of the deflationary crisis. But economic issues did not interest Lagarde in the slightest. Like an antisemitic con artist, he compared "Jewish Shylocks" to "cross spiders" that had "spun their webs across those poor, unfortunate areas" (p. 151).

The attacks against Zunz were made even more volatile by the Jewish scholar's death shortly before the publication of the inflammatory pamphlet. However, someone like Lagarde knew no pity. He stated dryly and callously that he had arrived at an unflattering assessment of Zunz years ago. Time and again, he chose language intended to be offensive. Regarding additions to the translation of medieval texts, he commented that Zunz had "falsified and lied" (p. 141) and that, despite his broad knowledge, he was a "blockhead of the first order" (p. 142). In an era that placed scholarly honor very nearly above all else, invectives of this magnitude required an immediate response.

In early 1887, several Jewish scholars turned against Lagarde. David Kaufmann accused him of hate-filled attacks that were entirely inappropriate among academics. He interpreted this as a consequence of the Wissenschaft des Judentums' lack of rootedness at German universities. The absence of institutional anchoring left Jewish scholars open to being accused of insufficient methodological training, although they were brilliantly educated and knew how to work in a disciplined way. Kaufmann also harshly criticized Lagarde's pejorative use of the word Jew and stylized the grim professor a Prometheus whose "liver had been chopped to pieces by [. . .] the vulture of Jewish hatred."[30] Abraham Berliner struck an arguably more strident note. Berliner had once generously congratulated Lagarde when he took over Ewald's chair. But ever since Berliner had received support from the Berlin Academy of Sciences, he had been confronted with derisive remarks.

Berliner's polemical paper, "Professor Paul de Lagarde, nach seiner Natur gezeichnet" (A Portrait of Professor Paul de Lagarde according to His Character), stressed the Orientalist's envious nature above all. Berliner pointedly emphasized the senior professor's difficulty recognizing other people's accomplishments. "Mr. Lagarde can hardly write five lines without criticizing, disparaging, and scolding. Even when he feels compelled to offer praise, he immediately looks for a way to qualify whatever praise he gives by modifying it."[31] Such an assessment must have been a hard pill for Lagarde to swallow, given that he was thoroughly convinced of his fairness. But there was worse to come: Berliner referred to Lagarde's embarrassing petition of 1851 and scoffed at his command of the German language. The citation affirming Lagarde's statement that "a tree that is bent early in life will never grow straight and never be a joy to man" was anything but noble. For the Orientalist suffered all his life as a result of his joyless childhood, and he hated any public allusions to the experience. Lastly, Berliner implied that Lagarde had dubious motives for taking his mother's name. This did not really correspond to the facts, but it touched a sore spot. Only the substantial inheritance from his great-aunt had opened up the possibility of an independent scholarly life to Lagarde. And it is quite probable that, in academic circles, people may have spread rumors about what motivated him to arrange for the adoption.

What especially annoyed Lagarde was that the chief rabbi of Vienna, Moritz Güdemann, immediately discussed Berliner's polemical paper and also made sure that its contents reached a wider audience. He published his article in the decidedly liberal *Neue Freie Presse* in Vienna, which also had a big readership abroad. Ironically titled "Der 'deutsche Nationalheilige' Paul de Lagarde" (Paul de Lagarde: The German "National Saint"), Güdemann pointedly stressed that Lagarde could not be taken seriously as a "political writer." Like many before him, he had to recognize that a prophet had no honor in his own country. Güdemann expressly pointed to the Orientalist's letter in which he had once "begged" Emperor Napoleon III for the Legion of Honor medal. At the same time, he hinted at the questionable nature of Lagarde's patriotic convictions.[32]

Bearing in mind that, in 1872, Lagarde had been willing to give up his professorship in Göttingen over this very charge, one can hardly consider Güdemann's assessment accurate. But it spoke from the heart for all those who saw Lagarde's grandiloquent nationalism as self-righteous or even mendacious.

The Göttingen professor, who could dish it out but couldn't take it, was beside himself with rage. On April 6, 1887, he resigned from the Paris-based Société des Etudes Juives (Society of Jewish Studies) because an anonymous author from there had "dragged his name through the dirt." Lagarde stated from on high that he was "not used to being part of a society that allowed its members to be attacked by unnamed writers." It was not without justification that he felt like the victim of concerted action. But he had apparently forgotten that his own publications had actually invoked the collective protest of Jewish scholars. Occasionally, it even appeared as though Lagarde had fallen into the role of a martyr. Thus, he declined the support of his scholarly friends in this public dispute. On March 13, 1887, he wrote to the renowned Tübingen biblical researcher Eberhard Nestle, who had offered to help him: a person would have to wait until he was dead before being allowed to tell the truth about the Berliner "condottieri"—anything else would entail grave disadvantages. His latest publication was also aimed "against our lords and masters, the Jews. And, although I did not wish it, their comrades have naturally been scrutinized along with them." Through this statement, Lagarde made reference to his obsessive idea of a Jewish-liberal alliance.

Shortly thereafter, Lagarde struck back against his critics with a harsh polemic. The pamphlet was called *Juden und Indogermanen* (*Jews and Indo-Europeans*) and fit in well with the cultural, biologistic, and rampantly nationalistic conventions of the late 1880s. Lagarde presented Güdemann's article, as well as other publications that took aim at him. He also reprinted documents, such as his letter of resignation from the Société des Etudes Juives, and expected them to generate a positive public response.[33] Yet the pamphlet showed him at his worst. The professor from Göttingen ostentatiously backed up the study of his "young friend, Ludwig Techen" (p. 270) but declined to provide a detailed refutation of the accusations aimed against him. In lieu thereof, he gave his antisemitic prejudices free reign and made absolutely no effort to present a logical sequence of ideas. From the unpatriotic attitude of Jews to their greed, Lagarde made use of myriad clichés that shall not be laid out in extenso here. He saw the "stupidity" of Jewish scholars as an important reason why they bluntly revealed their true natures: "A clever person would [. . .] not let others see into his heart as deeply as these people do—not if his heart looked like theirs" (p. 301).

But let's look at the principal motive for this erratic argumentation. Lagarde fully defended his own positivistic scholarly ideal. Scholarly progress was only possible on the basis of self-sacrificial work with source material and absolutely objective judgment. On the other hand, the study of the Talmud and its countless exemptions undermined the readiness to work rationally, which was why Jews had to first learn methodology from the Germans. Rabbinical learning, which belonged entirely to the past, had no real scholarly worth anyway. Rather, it should be regarded as "*Judain*" (p. 272), which induced a kind of stupefaction and undermined all ability to form unbiased opinions. In making this statement, Lagarde recapitulated themes long in use against the Wissenschaft des Judentums. But he added a stridency that must have attracted attention, even in the heated climate of the 1880s. He indefatigably stuck to his position that Zunz's translations were "horrifically tasteless" (p. 283) and that those who admired them could not be German.

The matter-of-factness with which Lagarde handled Judaism as a religious denomination and delegitimized its tradition as "liturgy" (p. 273) is truly remarkable. At the same time, he decided in favor of a sharp dichotomy between Jewish or Semitic features, on the one hand, and German or Aryan on the other. So it was characteristic of Jewish academics to comment on their own works, whereas inherently tactful German scholars abhorred self-reflection (p. 286). Indo-Europeans generally tended toward a tragic worldview that was characterized by the relationship between "guilt" and "atonement" and their "benedictive effect" (p. 304). The Semitic worldview, for its part, was marked by lies and deceit, as signified by the "thousand pieces of silver" (p. 305). Lagarde expressed some reservations with regard to the term *antisemitism*. He considered it conceptually imprecise, because in his view it didn't apply exclusively to Jews. But far more important than this frequently voiced objection, Lagarde used the new term as a political buzzword and endowed it with a radicality that was missing from the conventional term, *Judenfeindschaft* (hatred of Jews). Moreover, like Treitschke, he stressed that "antisemitism" was not unknown to the German people but had arisen from the "national psyche" (p. 330).

According to Lagarde, Europe's problem lay in a whole series of backward peoples and, along with Jews, he counted Gypsies, Basques, and the Irish among them. Typical of all these peoples was their inability to accept modern advances and their holding on to their distinctive traditions. At the same time, it was a given for them to enjoy the full blessings of civilization: "They want to be foreigners and citizens at the same time, to hold views from centuries ago, yet to be granted all of the rights that modern people have" (p. 329). Lagarde was, in a sense, repeating the message of his "sparrow camel" parable, which stipulated that integration into a great nation had to exact a merciless price. In short, his new idea also contained a lesson in the meaning of "younger peoples," a concept that would quickly gain importance in the Age of Imperialism. In the vast majority of his diatribe, however, Lagarde pursued ideas that were commonplace among his antisemitic contemporaries. Yet this could hardly be ascertained from the drastic images with which he formulated his accusations.

Lagarde lost all sense of moderation, particularly, in his discussion of "Jewish usury." The misery of the rural population could be traced back to the activity of Jewish middlemen, whose immoral attitudes he strikingly portrayed. The cultural pessimist was disappointed in his contemporaries and let himself get carried away with a statement, the final sentence of which has become notorious as an expression of contempt for humanity: "It takes a heart as hard as crocodile skin so as not to feel pity for the poor Germans who have been bled dry and so as not to hate the Jews, which is the same thing, and so as not to hate and despise those who—for humanitarian reasons!—speak up for the Jews or are too cowardly to crush these profiteering vermin underfoot. One does not negotiate with trichinae and bacteria. Trichinae and bacteria are not cultivated; they are destroyed as quickly and as completely as possible" (p. 339). This passage illustrates the typical mixture of sentimentality and brutality that were increasingly emblematic of the Lagardian worldview. Its subtext implies the rejection of liberal values, while its main point can hardly be interpreted as anything other than an expression of the will to destroy. Lagarde's aggression was also directed at "stock exchange Jews," who had so many respectable people on their consciences. He declared the stock exchange a "bane to the people" because it "made the acquisition of previously undreamed-of wealth possible" without any obligation to society. There were unfortunately no goal-oriented policies, however, that could lead "orderly migrations" of the unemployed "to good colonies." For this reason, one should not be surprised if, given Jews' "speculative gains," the "desire to kill the Jews" were to be openly expressed.[34]

The inhumane character of *Juden und Indogermanen* is obvious. Lagarde consciously violated the standards of civil intercourse and even denied the opposing party the right to exist. At the same time, his desire to justify the antisemitic movement attracted attention. He provided it with key terms and exaggerated its political success. But it would be wrong to overemphasize the modern character of his views. Lagarde's popular nationalism and his fantasies of destruction were rooted in a religious ideology that bore unmistakably pietistic traits. He treated Jews and liberals accordingly, identifying them with each other in an irrational way. And he did not deal with them as true constituents of modernity. Their activity created discord and pointed to God's enemy, the Devil, who "was older than the world of man" (p. 345). To do justice to Lagarde's glorification of backward-looking values, one must consider the religious orientation of Lagarde's worldview.[35] The same applies to his appeal to male virtues, such as those that end the text: "The times are very serious, and call for [real] men" (p. 351). It was hardly coincidental that, in an era of politically fundamentalist creeds, vaguely general religious statements like these enabled him to count on widespread approval.

The conflict with Moritz Güdemann introduced Lagarde to one of the undisputed figures of the antisemitic movement, Georg von Schönerer. The leader of the Austrian pan-Germanist Alldeutscher party used massive force against his political opponents and advocated a strictly nationalistic mind-set. He rejected the Christian calendar and calculated the beginning of time according to the Cimbrian victory over the Romans in the Battle of Noreia in 113 B.C.E. Meanwhile, he stood for a rigid racial antisemitism that found clear expression in the All-German slogan "through purity to unity."[36] Schönerer informed Lagarde about the article by the chief rabbi of Vienna and made the party newspaper, *Unverfälschte Deutsche Worte* (*Unadulterated German Speech*), available to him for a response. The Orientalist made immediate use of the offer and defended himself against his critics in an open letter, dated February 20, 1887. He stressed that Friedrich Wilhelm IV had given him permission to use his grandmother's name. Even more important for Lagarde was the portrayal of his petition to Emperor Napoleon III as the "youthful indiscretion" of a "completely naive Romantic." In order to explain the indignation of Jewish scholars and their liberal "comrades" over this bygone event, he remarked "that the former did not yet see themselves, and the latter no longer saw themselves, as Germans." Lagarde looked at Schönerer as a potential ally. On May 19, 1887, he promised he would send the politician his essay "Juden und Indogermanen" as soon as it came out. He thanked Schönerer for the "masculinely sensible" way that he expressed his thoughts and signed the letter, "With unadulterated German regards."

Ruhler, the chairman of the Schulverein für Deutsche (School Association for Germans) in Graz, more-or-less simultaneously went about getting Lagarde to write an article. In his letter of April 30, 1887, he cited his organization's main goal as the "fight [. . .] against Semitism, which was ruinous to Aryans." And he flattered Lagarde as a "champion of our truly nationalistic thinking, every bit as intrepid as mentally strong." The senior Göttingen professor showed little interest in being published in a mediocre school calendar. But he didn't miss an opportunity to promote his own interests and sent a copy of "Juden und Indogermanen" to Graz. He recommended publishing Napoleon Bonaparte's speeches and decrees that had been printed in Graz, and people in the state of Steiermark gladly seized the opportunity.[37]

Lagarde was even in contact with the antisemitic soldier of fortune Bernhard Förster. As Lagarde had once done, Förster taught at a Berlin grammar school and prided himself greatly on his doctoral title. His fanatical hatred of Jews brought him into conflict with the authorities early on. In 1880, he picked a fight with Jewish passengers in a streetcar. While being interrogated by the police, he haughtily stressed the "Aryan" origins of his forebears.[38] The friend and future husband of Elisabeth Nietzsche (the philosopher's sister) was a subversive agitator with no sense of reality. Due to his antisemitic activities, he lost several lawsuits and, in the end, his teaching position. The antisemitic petition he initiated demanding special laws for Jews obtained at least 225,000 signatures, but Bismarck turned it down. Förster concluded that he had no future in the capitalistic German Empire, allegedly run by Jews, and decided to emigrate. He imagined founding a colony in Paraguay with the potential to become a "New Germany." On December 29, 1882, shortly before making his first trip to South America, he turned to Lagarde for money and a copy of the *Deutsche Schriften* to take along.

Even though Förster would subsequently find himself in constant financial straits, his relationship with Lagarde did not break down. The few surviving documents do not allow us to draw any conclusions as to whether Lagarde actually gave financial support to Förster's colony of Nueva Germania. In view of his cautious nature and pronounced thriftiness, however, it is unlikely that he did. On December 25, 1885, Förster asked Lagarde about the Jewish origins of the Prussian minister of education and cultural affairs, Gustav von Gossler, who had initiated proceedings against him. And, on May 14, 1886, he effusively thanked Lagarde for the new edition of the *Deutsche Schriften* that Lagarde had sent to him in Asuncion. Lagarde's remarks about the idealism of the younger generation of Germans and the need to colonize southeastern Europe met with Förster's unqualified approval. But the question remains as to how great a role tactical considerations played in the formation of Förster's opinions. At any rate, he only made general reference to Lagarde's ideas for colonization in his monograph *Deutsche Colonien in dem oberen Laplata-Gebiete* (*German Colonies in the Upper Rio de la Plata Region*). In view of the "terrible situation in the Russian Empire, where Jews and nihilists were systematically working to destroy what existed and, so it seemed, were succeeding; in view of the moral collapse of the Austrian dual monarchy and the disintegration of states within the Balkan countries," he warned against immigration to those areas recommended by Lagarde.[39] Förster's judgment was driven by his own predicament because, for a whole variety of reasons, he urgently needed more settlers.

On February 15, 1888, Förster and his wife sent Lagarde their final regards before departing for Paraguay, presumably for good. But their foolhardy project quickly foundered. The couple had lured German-speaking families to South America with lame promises, yet without any real contractual protection or a solid financial basis. When appearances could no longer be maintained and newcomers insisted that promises be kept, the splendor of Nueva Germania came to an abrupt end. At the beginning of 1889, Bernhard Förster departed this life under unexplained circumstances, and much circumstantial evidence pointed to suicide. He turned out to be bankrupt, which is what his brother-in-law, Friedrich Nietzsche, had thought about him from the start.

Another key figure in the nascent antisemitic movement, Theodor Fritsch, was also in close contact with Lagarde. After completing his engineering studies, this Saxon farmer's son took to writing and disseminating inflammatory antisemitic leaflets. And his tireless energy quickly earned him renown. The two men were first in touch in 1886. Lagarde sent Fritsch his essay "Die nächsten Pflichten deutscher Politik," which argued strongly in favor of German settlement policies in Eastern Europe. Fritsch enthusiastically expressed his thanks, saying that he "had seldom found such a wealth of stupendous ideas packed into such a small space." He also offered to publish a biographical article about Lagarde in the *Antisemitische Correspondenz* (*Antisemitic Correspondence*), which had a respectable print run of five to seven thousand.[40] As he nearly always did when it came to the dissemination of his own ideas, Lagarde kept his reservations in check. Fritsch published excerpts from the essay "Juden und Indogermanen" in a fall 1887 edition of his paper. And he gave them the title "Prof. Paul de Lagarde über die Juden und den Antisemitismus" (Professor Paul de Lagarde on the Jews and Antisemitism). But the collaboration did not always go smoothly. For legal reasons, Fritsch mainly used a pseudonym in publishing his hate-filled brochures. And he got on the professor's nerves with his lax work habits. On March 6, 1888, Lagarde urgently warned him about careless citations. Such behavior might call the public prosecutor's office to action and could never help "to win over waverers and cowards, although they really should be won over."

When Fritsch asked for a photo for the *Antisemitischer Volkskalender* (*Antisemitic People's Calendar*), Lagarde proved dismissive, informing Fritsch on July 8, 1888, of his unmistakable refusal: "I may not be seen, since the austere seriousness of my character is unhelpful and would only harm a good thing." Lagarde had, of course, no fundamental reservations against targeted publicity or the antisemitic movement. The aging scholar rejected on principle the idea of private photographs being made public. But Lagarde also kept his distance when Fritsch invited him to collaborate on an *Antisemitischen-Katechismus* (*Antisemitic Catechism*) in 1890. Fritsch was absolutely furious over Lagarde's refusal, because he not only lived for antisemitism but from it as well. His *Catechism*, which presented racist half-truths and statements by well-known Germans concerning the "Jewish question," was a commercial success, and Fritsch would have liked to expand it with Lagarde's help. On April 3, 1890, he sent an angry letter to Göttingen: "The people do not delight in such 'kings' [of scholarship]! The large coins that our antisemitic intellectual 'princes' strike cannot be used by the people as currency; they must be reminted into smaller, low-value coins. But if the people try to do so, then the proud 'lords' will loudly call them *plagiarists* and *scoundrels*." Lagarde answered him the very next day, purportedly willing to compromise: "You have no idea, my dear Herr Fritsch, how many deadly insults your [. . .] letter to me contains. I forgive all of these insults because, despite your anger, you write so kindly that I have not gotten cross with you." Lagarde still declined to concretely collaborate, of course. And he did not retract his criticism of Fritsch's citation practices.

One should not overemphasize the periodic friction between Fritsch and Lagarde because, in the end, they knew what they had in each other. Just as Lagarde depended on the support of publishers to further disseminate his ideas, Fritsch took conscious advantage of the Orientalist's standing. And the *Antisemiten-Katechismus* was successful without professorial support. In 1893, the handy treatise appeared in its twenty-fifth edition and promoted not only Lagarde but his friend Franz von Liszt as well.[41] As for its content, the work concluded that the "Jewish race" had a ruinous effect, and the Jews' differentiated scholarly world-picture certainly could not be brought into line. Despite his massive antisemitic judgments, Lagarde claimed he was a researcher who was under a strict obligation to be objective. He counterbalanced the quickly rising number of negatively rated Jews with a few shining lights. Salomon Buber was among them. During the culmination of his conflict with leading representatives of the Wissenschaft des Judentums, Lagarde told the scholar "how greatly" he "valued" his "abilities."[42] Kind deeds of this sort did nothing to change Lagarde's deep-seated antisemitism. But this is not at all easy to boil down to a conclusive formula: Lagarde blended Christian antisemitic, sharply nationalistic, hegemonic, cultural, and occasionally biologistic judgments in a highly unconventional way. And he held them together with a rhetoric that was rich in metaphors, yet light on reasoning. It was precisely this wandering lack of clarity that gave special potency to his polemical writings. They offered readers a multitude of opportunities for identification. At the same time, they included a historico-philosophical framework that allowed each instance to be interpreted as confirmation of the reader's own worldviews.

The Oxford doyen of research on antisemitism, Peter Pulzer, has rightly pointed out that, in the 1880s, those politicians and ideologues who "bet" only "on racist antisemitism" were marginalized. If they wanted to be successful in a climate of rapid social change, then "the politics of resentment needed multifarious enemy stereotypes."[43] And this was exactly what Lagarde offered, but he also offered a great deal more. The fusion of Judaism and liberalism provided apparently compelling justification for reservations about the modern age. His cultural pessimism corroborated many people's views on corruption and the emptiness of contemporary life; yet his vision was also not entirely without hope. His cyclical concept of history pointed to the corruption of his time but was not far removed from the dawning of a better day.

Simultaneously, Lagarde made his passionate commitment to the German nation accessible to the German bourgeoisie. His rigid rejection of cultural diversity and personal freedom of choice were, in a way, entirely modern. In late nineteenth-century Europe, less and less room existed for "religion and speech to be places of complex identity,"[44] and nation-states became the dominant reality. This shift ushered in hard times for minorities, including those in the German Empire, which took great pride in its constitutional character. The inability to achieve a positive understanding of cultural differences ensured that no ethnic or religious minority could fundamentally or fully overcome its precarious status. And this rule applied in spades to the highly gentrified German Jews. By reason of their upward mobility, Jews had to be constantly reminded of their origins. The academic world, with its rigid patterns of exclusion and crisis of overcrowding, was marked by numerous forms of class envy that illustrated the considerable extent to which antisemitism was a post-emancipatory phenomenon.

Finally, one should not forget that Lagarde articulated his hate-filled views about the Jewish people from the prestigious position of a German senior professor. That's why he claimed dual competency for his views' content. He saw himself as an Orientalist expert in the Jewish tradition while, as a theologian, he also claimed responsibility for the great religious questions. No other late nineteenth-century antisemite had a similar opportunity to lend scholarly dignity and religious significance to his value judgments. His response to the 1888 antisemitism trial in Marburg shows how Lagarde attempted to convert his scholarly aura into political capital.

11

The Talmud on Trial

The national electoral law was a two-edged sword. Universal, equal, secret, and direct male suffrage was, in fact, greatly admired for its modernity. And the law actually promoted broader participation across social strata. We need only recall that, prior to the First World War, the Social Democrats rose to become the strongest political party. But the election results did not represent any real share in the political process, which led to growing disappointment among the populace. At the same time, *Honoratiorenparteien* (liberal parties led by elites that had no fixed popular base) made a big deal of their members' status and trusted in personal arrangements, which made them seem increasingly antiquated. Given the conditions of the "political mass market" (Hans Rosenberg), parties soon decided on an emotional style of campaigning and backed the mobilization of their own voter constituencies. For example, Bismarck's turnaround in 1879–1880 encouraged conservatives to adopt a sharper approach. In 1881, they entered the Reichstag campaign with the slogan "Jews equal liberals and liberals equal Jews."[1] Against the backdrop of a domestic crisis that had only just been overcome, it was important to conjure up new dangers, because the "subdued" variety of antisemitism laid the foundation for more radical forms of hatred for Jews. The antisemitic movement quickly gained popularity, particularly in regions that were affected by the major agrarian crisis of the 1880s.

The people in North Hesse suffered to an exceptional degree from the globalization pressures that had become increasingly evident since the founding of the German Empire (Reichsgründung).[2] As a consequence of the centuries-long practice of dividing available land among all heirs, Hessian farms were unusually small. More and more grain and meat from overseas reached the German market, creating pricing pressures that forced economically unprofitable farms into bankruptcy. Even Bismarck's protectionist policies provided no tangible relief for farmers, who were still suffering the long-term consequences of Kurhessian (Electorate of Hesse, founded in 1803) stagnation. Many victims of modernization, including small farmers and portions of the old middle class, looked upon Jews as the main cause of their problems. Finally, Jews constituted 2.7 percent of the total population in the Prussian province of Hesse-Nassau, about three times the national average. Jewish cattle markets functioned efficiently, but the Jews were not to blame for the larger economic dislocations in the region. The disillusioned rural population was simply looking for a scapegoat and not for a sophisticated explanation of economic relationships. In the 1880s, antisemitic resentment was embodied in a man who, until then, had been unknown: Otto Böckel, an assistant librarian in Marburg.

Born in Frankfurt am Main in 1859, Böckel was the son of a building contractor. Like the young Lagarde, Otto Böckel suffered under the yoke of a father inclined to violence and retreated into a world of fantasy at a young age. He was apparently very linguistically gifted, and his devotees credited him with knowing sixteen languages. But, in contrast to Lagarde, no convincing proof of his talent survived for posterity. Böckel was keenly interested in folk song research from an early age. Supposedly following in the footsteps of the Brothers Grimm, he wandered from village to village, talked to simple folk, and dreamed of an academic career. But his aspirations proved too ambitious. After successfully completing his doctorate in Marburg in 1882, he had to settle for a deeply disappointing, subordinate position at the university library. In addition, he must have realized that his dissertation supervisor, the scholar of classical and Romance languages Edmund Stengel, showed no interest in his idealistic, but less-than-conscientious, work in folk song research.

So Böckel devoted himself halfheartedly to his professional work and discovered the world of politics instead. In the fall of 1884, he "experienced an awakening" when, at a public demonstration in front of the Marburg regional court, he delivered an emotional speech and saw that he easily attracted the listeners' attention. The demonstration concerned the blacksmith Konrad Hedderich, who was accused of murdering his Jewish debtor, the businessman Salomon Korn, and his wife in their sleep. Along with other antisemites, Böckel celebrated Hedderich's acquittal from lack of evidence as the victory of a just cause. He soon got extensively involved in political agitation, zealously spreading his message that interest-free credit and "Jew-free cattle markets" could remedy the plight of the rural population. Böckel often published his brochures under the pseudonym Dr. Capistrano, a Franciscan monk who had raged against the Jews during the Hussite Wars of the fifteenth century. In remarkable contrast to the brutal passages, Böckel occasionally gave voice to sentimental feelings. His elegy to spring, "Germania," was exclusively aimed at victims of libel and those deprived of their rights and ended with this verse:

A new spirit will blow,
And in Germany, every part,
A new race will begin to grow,
Young and fresh of mind and heart.

Aye, a new day dawns in German lands;
Aye, your savior is nigh.
Make the Jews into slave bands
You will be free—Germania![3]

No doubt about it: Böckel had far more talent as an agitator than a poet.

People in the antisemitic camp didn't give much thought to intellectual property. Böckel's most successful publication, *Die Juden, die Könige unserer Zeit* (*Jews: The Kings of Our Time*), borrowed its title from Alphonse Toussenel's *Les Juifs rois de l'epoque*, written in 1847. It basically consisted of an 1886 speech that Böckel gave in Berlin at the Bockbrauerei, one of the financial backers of the antisemitic movement. More than one hundred thousand copies of the pamphlet were printed up and sold for a song. Böckel, like the Austrian, Schönerer, stood for a racist worldview. And both men denied the religious dimension of the so-called Jewish question. On the basis of dubious statistics, Böckel also intimated that the integration of Jews would lead to the downfall of the German nation. In order to spread his political agenda, Böckel relied on catchy slogans like "Germany for Germans" that simple minds could understand.[4] He vehemently attacked "Jewish usury," in the process popularizing a code word, "Jewish usurocracy," an enemy stereotype that combined antisemitic and anticapitalist ideas. Moreover, it perfectly suited his culturally pessimistic rejection of modernity.

The agrarian crisis reached a climax in 1887, and parliamentary elections were simultaneously pending. With the financial backing of antisemites in Berlin, Böckel decided to run for office. He not only relied on his speaking abilities during the campaign but also employed a host of other devices. Since the conservative *Oberhessische Zeitung* (*Upper Hessian News*) would not allow him to advertise, he founded his own newspaper, *Der Reichsherold* (*The Imperial Herald*), which attained a wide circulation of 30,000.[5] Böckel wrote the majority of the editorials and convinced prominent antisemites like Theodor Fritsch to work with him. He also made a concerted effort to address his readers, allowing farmers, primary school teachers, and students to express their complaints and concerns. Böckel's organization, the Reformverein (Reform Association), was entirely tailored to his personality and introduced an aggressive campaign style in the rather sleepy rural district of Marburg. His supporters distributed a host of leaflets, pasted over the posters of other parties, and intimidated political opponents. A coalition of Conservatives, Free Conservatives, and National Liberals was formed to thwart Böckel. But the antisemitic agitator had already acquired a special reputation: many victims of modernization regarded him as a modern-day Robin Hood figure who openly expressed his concerns and defied plutocratic despotism. His Conservative opponent, Karl Grimm, was considered pale and not very assertive by contrast. And the Conservative motto, "For God, King, and Fatherland," appeared strangely antiquated in comparison to the antisemitic slogan "Germany for Germans." It is hardly coincidental that this motto was still effective on the eve of the First World War, when it was propagated anew by the chairman of the All-Germans, Heinrich Class.[6]

Böckel had an absolutely charismatic effect on people in the provinces. The "Hessian peasant king" rode into villages in a magnificent horse-drawn carriage with his hair flowing and a laurel wreath on his head. Epithets like "Savior of the Farming Community" and "the second Luther" show how greatly he was venerated. Even the sick were brought to Böckel's campaign events so that they could hear his antisemitic diatribes. When it came to intimidating his political opponents, the self-confident agitator used violence, mainly perpetrated by students, who were among his most loyal followers. His simple ideological message promised the elimination of Jewish competition, as well as the return of better times, and was particularly effective during the "overcrowding crisis" at universities. Students took care of distributing leaflets and other printed matter; they brought Böckel's views to the most remote villages. The agitator's efforts paid off in the end. Böckel received 56.6 percent of the votes cast in the February 1887 election, making him the youngest member ever elected to the Reichstag. In addition to his considerable demagogic abilities, Böckel owed his success to voter turnout, which soared from 49 percent in 1884 to 75 percent in 1887. Even in the province of Upper Hesse, the era of *Honoratiorenparteien*, which had no political apparatuses of their own, was apparently coming to a close.[7]

The aggressively fought campaign resulted in an abundance of lawsuits, and the action against the Marburg primary school teacher Ferdinand Fenner caused the greatest furor.[8] As with many others, Fenner's dissatisfaction with his own situation led him to politics. After retiring as a Lutheran pastor, his father had purchased a farmstead but was forced to sell it to a Jewish buyer during the economic crisis. Fenner was also dissatisfied with his own less-than-prestigious and poorly paid occupation. His extensive personal file also proves inappropriate professional conduct.[9] He incited his students to insult and mistreat the children at the Jewish school. Out of personal conviction, Fenner joined the Böckel movement in the fall of 1886. But his zeal was greater than his political skill. At his first electoral address, on December 5, 1886, he got into heated exchanges with the audience and went so far as to hurl invectives. He alleged that Jews had double standards and claimed that the Talmud exhorted them to swindle Christians. This was no small matter, given that the ethical substance of one of the main sources of Judaism was under consideration.

At the behest of the Marburg rabbi Leo Munk, a stenographer had attended the campaign event. Munk was among the avowed opponents of the Böckel movement, and the stenographer's notes prompted him to file a complaint with the school administration. In response, Fenner told the local school committee there was inherently grave danger "in the equality of international Judaism and homegrown Germanism."[10] The public prosecutor's office started an investigation. On January 18, 1887, charges were brought against Fenner for publicly slandering a state-recognized religion. Since the court did not feel competent to discuss the matter on its own, it decided to appoint scholarly experts. After rejecting Munk as a prospective expert witness on grounds of bias, the prosecutor's office nominated the philosopher Hermann Cohen. The defense nominated Paul de Lagarde as its expert, and no one raised objections to his antisemitic views. The esteem in which both scholars were held must have, in itself, caused a sensation. Along with the evaluation of the Talmud, a series of themes were up for debate that were of great importance to the appraisal of Judaism. As for the Talmud, August Rohling had achieved great success with his inflammatory pamphlet *Der Talmudjude* (*The Talmudic Jew*) in the early 1870s. And the denigration of the Talmud was a core element of antisemitic propaganda.[11] The extent to which the state was prepared to defend Jews as a religious minority was also implicitly up for discussion. As a consequence, people nervously watched the public hearing that took place on April 25, 1888.

The overcrowded courtroom of the Königliches Landgericht (Royal Regional Court) reflected widespread interest in the case, with journalists coming from near and far to report. Interest was stirred in part by a desire to learn more about Otto Böckel's election victory and the situation in Upper Hesse. Moreover, this was the first defense of Judaism in the context of formal court proceedings, a fact that attracted considerable attention. In order to get a detailed picture of Fenner's campaign speech, the trial opened with the examination of witnesses. Böckel firmly emphasized that his party fought against Jews for racial reasons alone. Since antisemites placed no importance on Jewish religion, Fenner's remarks about the Talmud must have been expressed in hypothetical form. This was, of course, an attempt to build a legal defense. But members of the antisemitic press reported that Böckel displayed the courage of his ideological convictions. Along these lines were reports in Theodor Fritsch's *Antisemitische Correspondenz*, which could rightly be called the antisemitic movement's most important source of information.[12] The *Westfälische Reform* (*The Westphalia Reformer*), published in Dortmund, also unequivocally took Fenner's side. It was typical of the publication's tendentious journalism to systematically call the philosopher Cohen by the name of "Cohn," a stigmatization that was apparently supposed to underscore the Jewish character of his thought.[13]

Lagarde decided not to actually appear before the provincial court in Marburg. Since the sources remain silent on this issue, one can only speculate why. His view of the Böckel movement does not seem to have been unreservedly positive. In his inflammatory treatise "Juden und Indogermanen," he judged the situation in North Hesse as intolerable. However, his characterization of Böckel's brand of antisemitism as "fanatical" also suggests reservations.[14] In the last years of his life, Lagarde had little time to spare for anything that threatened to take him away from the Septuagint project. In addition, he knew that antisemites frequently operated on legally shaky ground and that it did not further one's reputation to be too closely associated with them. But all this did not push Lagarde's desire for political effectiveness entirely into the background. His correspondence with confirmed antisemites contains a fair amount of advice on how one could ward off "Jewish-liberal attacks." The Marburg trial also offered a large public forum in which to discuss his belief in the ruinous influence of Judaism.

Lagarde's expert opinion had to be read in his absence. The court had bidden him and Cohen to answer two sets of questions. First, it wanted to know if the laws of the Talmud were legally binding for all Jews and if Fenner's name-calling was insulting to the Jewish religious community. Second, the court sought clarification as to whether, according to Mosaic law, the Talmud exhorted Jews to swindle Christians. Lagarde's statement began with a long *captatio benevolentiae*. The Orientalist stressed that any real understanding of the Talmud required an entire lifetime of scholarship and that he had only devoted a fraction of the necessary time to the work in question. Nevertheless, he felt able and entitled to give an advisory opinion because, unlike Jewish scholars, he had the necessary virtues for unbiased historical research: "intellectual sobriety, modesty, a calm-blooded temperament, and the ability to face unpleasant truths."[15] Lagarde had sung an impressive paean to intellectual discipline, but his official statement left much to be desired in terms of scholarly restraint.

In a coarse and judgmentally one-sided manner, Lagarde characterized the Talmud as "rubbish in which foolishness of the highest order stands alongside wise sayings, and pathetically absurd stories stand alongside profound or, indeed, illuminating sagas" (p. 6). Due to its heterogeneous content, as well as the multitude of interpretations, this work had no ethical relevance. Lagarde pulled out all the stops in contesting the overall intelligibility of the Talmud. He brought up the differences between the Jerusalem and Babylonian compilations, which occasionally contradicted each other. The Karaite sect, for its part, rejected the rabbinical tradition but believed firmly in its own brand of Judaism. But the judgments attached to Lagarde's religio-historical claims were even more problematic. Because the Jews had no uniform worldview, Lagarde concluded that they could not have any dogmatic theology. Those who thought otherwise had allowed themselves to be deceived by Jewish "national vanity," which led to involvement in the "prevailing philosophy of the day" (p. 7). "Slandering the Talmud" (p. 7) was no more disparaging to the Jewish religion than a comparable assessment of Luther's after-dinner speeches was to Lutheranism. This strange comparison was explained by Lagarde's hatred for the Wittenberg reformer, whom he considered a narrow-minded fanatic. Since his testimony was supposed to support Fenner's defense, however, he was careful not to make his depiction of Luther overly explicit.

Lagarde also exercised a certain amount of caution in discussing the second question, as to whether the Talmud exhorted Jews to swindle Christians. Armed with skilled source criticism and concealed scorn, he criticized the regional court's approach to the problem, which was an unmistakable product of the nineteenth century. He certainly reinforced contemporary value judgments by expressing his personal opinion that, after the founding of Christianity, Israel "had lost all right to exist" (p. 21). Even though Protestant university theology took the greater worth of the Christian faith for granted, it still did not deprive Judaism of all value. Within Lagarde's rigid system of historical thought, on the other hand, postbiblical Judaism was "nothing more than [. . .] dross, worthless, and therefore troublesome and repulsive" (p. 21). At least Lagarde conceded that Jewish religious sources contained no evidence to support the idea that the Talmud legitimized Jewish swindling of Christians. All the same, "Germans, lamenting the Jewish plague" (p. 22), had long since formed their own opinions on the matter. This statement touched on the theological question that was under discussion in the political world. Having come this far, he decided in favor of an equally apodictic and defamatory opinion: "The public in Germany, Austria, France, and Russia holds the opinion that, by and large, Jews [. . .] advocate those Talmudic views which look upon Jews as a superior race that is engaged in a real struggle of sorts with non-Jews" (p. 22). As powerful as this passage may have appeared from an antisemitic perspective, it was irrelevant in assessing the ethical substance of the Talmud.

Not only were Lagarde's historico-philosophical statements about Judaism and his political remarks extremely problematic; he was also skating on thin ice as regarded true scholarship. In forming his opinion, he drew extensively on Rohling's tendentious work *Der Talmudjude*. Lagarde had been well aware that

Rohling's scholarship was anything but solid ever since Rohling had defended the ritual-murder legend in Tisza Eslar, if not before. Following Lagarde's violent conflict with representatives of the Wissenschaft des Judentums in 1888, however, this was no longer an issue. Lagarde cited Rohling's shoddy work as if it were a serious historical source. This and other scholarly judgments by Lagarde were aimed solely at harming contemporary Judaism. And he knew exactly what he was doing. His official opinion on the Marburg case was intellectually erratic but exceptionally rich in material, and he worked on it for more than three weeks. The text offered a gold mine of antisemitic "arguments" for anyone who didn't have the time or didn't want to study Judaism in detail. And that's exactly what the text was taken for: a rich source of material.

Before the trial began, Lagarde sent his expert opinion to Adalbert Bezzenberger, the professor from Königsberg, who responded approvingly: "Your expert opinion is immensely important for anyone who, like myself, has an aversion to modern Judaism, yet cannot justify this aversion to himself on more than a practical basis."[16] Portions of the Lagardian view directly traced the latest political argumentation. He pointed to the disastrous influence of Jews in Spain and Poland, which could be seen in the backwardness of these countries, and also catered to anti-Catholic sentiments in the process. The subtext of the disparaging opinion "the Talmud sometimes exudes humanitarianism" (p. 21) was directed at liberals. Liberal buzzwords like *humanitarianism* and *education* were massively attacked in the 1880s, and their meaning became increasingly ambivalent. At the same time, Lagarde's expert opinion strongly emphasized the value of unbiased research. It may well have been the contrast between Lagarde's expectant scholarly rhetoric and his ruthless antisemitism that deeply outraged the second expert, Hermann Cohen.

As a Septuagint researcher and an outstanding authority on Oriental languages, Lagarde enjoyed considerable respect in the academic world, as did Cohen, who was the only Jewish scholar to hold a chair in philosophy at the University of Marburg. But Cohen's position within German Jewry was not undisputed at the time. He'd sought compromise in the "Berlin antisemitism dispute" and made too many concessions to Treitschke in the interest of reaching common ground. Cohen's idea of a German-Jewish cultural synthesis in no way signified the abandonment of distinctive Jewish characteristics. Rather, he emphasized Jews' value for the nation of Kant and Goethe. Cohen presented a correspondingly vigorous defense of the ethical substance of Judaism, which Lagarde had ridiculed. To Cohen, the philosopher, it was an incontrovertible fact that the religion of his forefathers was characterized by love of one's neighbor, "the original form of monotheistic ethics."[17] He did actually concede that, for devout Jews, not every statement in the Talmud was normatively binding. But there could be no doubt that the Talmud contained "the laws given to Moses on Mount Sinai," which is why its binding force was beyond question.[18] Therefore, "every Jew who was concerned with the honor of his faith" would interpret an attack on the Talmud as a slander against his religion.

Cohen was also unequivocal in his response to the second question. Judaism knew no double standards in its treatment of strangers. Within the rabbinical tradition, strangers were considered descendants of Noah and were protected under the Noahide laws. These laws would apply to all people and make the unequal treatment of non-Jews a punishable offense, proving sufficiently that the Talmud advocated not exclusive, but rather universal, ethics. Needless to say, this was an extremely normative argument that might not apply equally to all specific cases. On a purely factual basis, however, Cohen's train of thought had plausibility and inner coherence. For how could one do justice to the special character of a religion if one were to measure its moral substance by means of ephemeral phenomena, rather than in terms of its basic principles?

Cohen ended his expert opinion with a strong critique of Lagarde's methods. Questionable secondary literature like Rohling's *Talmudjuden* should simply be inadmissible in lieu of original sources. Lagarde's use of such sources showed a degree of dishonesty for which no excuses could be found. Cohen saw it as a consequence of antisemitism, which increasingly poisoned people's minds. He was also convinced that universities had to take a stand against ideologization of thought in general. "Where racial hatred and defamation rage, clichés abound," Cohen stated emphatically. He continued: "Clichés and judgments become epidemic and also unexpectedly infect rigorous scholarly work. Respect for the truth is equally essential to science and life."[19] Needless to say, Fenner's defense remained unimpressed with these arguments, pointing out, in its summation, that many Germans from Herder to Fichte had condemned the Jews and asked for an acquittal. The prosecution, meanwhile, criticized Lagarde's comparison of the Talmud to Luther's toasts, as well as the overall tone of his expert opinion.[20] The prosecution considered a prison sentence of at least six weeks to be appropriate. The trial was subsequently adjourned, forcing curious onlookers to wait a week before the verdict was announced.

On May 2, 1888, the court sentenced Fenner to two weeks in prison and required him to bear the total cost of litigation. The ruling concluded that the accused had actually made the statements of which he'd been accused. But, in view of his inexperience in political matters, the court considered a lighter sentence appropriate. Neither side was satisfied with the compromise. Cohen was disappointed that "the inner credibility of the two expert opinions" had played no role in the opinion issued by the court.[21] He immediately published his testimony in the form of a leaflet, which garnered national attention and went through three editions within a short time. But his factually compelling argumentation did not have a profound political impact. Conservative Lutherans still argued with it most intensively. The *Sächsische Kirchen- und Schulblatt* (*The Saxon Church and School Paper*) criticized Cohen's "overestimation of philosophy" and considered it generally inappropriate to try religious matters in court. Lagarde, for his part, took Fenner's final sentence as a personal affront. With the help of Theodor Fritsch, he organized the sale and distribution of his expert opinion. Despite its price of one mark apiece, however, the text did not seem to generate much interest. In the prestigious *Theologisches Literaturblatt* (*Theological Literary Journal*), the scholarly defects of Lagarde's opinion were even rated as an embarrassing faux pas on the part of the renowned professor.[22]

Nevertheless, the Böckel movement successfully capitalized on the Marburg trial. It styled Fenner a martyr who, in a world dominated by Jews, had been given an unjust prison sentence. It goes without saying that Fenner's antisemitic lawyer, Julius Martin, filed an appeal of the court's decision. Böckel also circulated a derisively annotated version of the ruling, whose twenty-pfennig price took the financial circumstances of his impoverished followers into account. A letter of May 4, 1888, illustrates the highly charged atmosphere in Marburg. Its author, the law student Carl Göring, angrily informed Lagarde that the Orthodox rabbi Munk had accused the scholar in the *Oberhessische Zeitung* of spreading falsehoods about the Talmud. A second letter let Lagarde know that Cohen had called him a "phrasemonger" and a "windbag" in his expert opinion. The anonymous author, who had chosen the pen name "G. W. Leibniz," added this rhetorical question: "Should the senior professor from Göttingen put up with something like this?" And he then answered, betraying his stylistic inexperience: "So fresh, pious, cheerful, and free, he campaigned against the Jew, Cohen."[23]

Lagarde didn't want to let the Marburg matter rest. Through Fenner's defense attorney, Martin, he inquired as to whether legal action against Munk or the responsible public prosecutor, Bertram, would be feasible. On May 7, 1888, he admonished Martin "to undertake nothing [. . .] unless success" was "assured." But he searched for Bertram's address with an intensity that, in and of itself, shows how seriously he took the matter. On September 1, 1888, the postal service notified him that it had discovered no fewer than "fifty-four persons by the name of Bertram" in Hanover and that it had asked every potential high school graduate if the enclosed letter was meant for him. Furthermore, the postal service had informed "all letter carriers" of Lagarde's request.[24] As it happened, the public prosecutor had died unexpectedly and, when Lagarde learned about this, he refrained from taking further steps. He had originally intended to demand "public satisfaction, of course" and had written a petition regarding the matter to the Ministry of Justice. The petition complained en passant about events in Marburg and "the Palestinization of universities, as well as the legal, medical, and acting professions."[25]

Meanwhile, Fenner's petition for appeal had failed, placing Lagarde in an awkward position. Before the trial began, Lagarde had agreed to receive an impressive fee of 150 marks for his expert opinion, and the destitute primary school teacher was now obliged to compensate him. Professor Lagarde, who was otherwise unyielding in financial matters, turned down the money because he saw Fenner as a victim of *Gesinnungsjustiz*, an illegitimate politicized application of judicial procedure and the law. At the beginning of October 1888, he asked Fenner's lawyer how the problem could be cleared up. Ultimately, Lagarde's wife took care of the restitution, which further reassured the nervous teacher.[26]

A letter of June 29, 1888, from his friend, the Germanist Edward Schröder, illustrates just how routinely people in Lagarde's milieu admitted to holding antisemitic views: he emphatically agreed with Lagarde in his dispute with Judaism. Schröder also expressed his view that one would "hopefully still be safe from [. . .] the Judaeophile index for a while." If one considers how precisely statements by the opposition were recorded in antisemitic circles, there can be little doubt that this assessment was a projection. In any case, Schröder considered the "Jewish question" an objective fact to which even his Jewish friends had to own up. And the certainty with which he presented this view suggests that he knew he was substantially in agreement with Lagarde.

Lagarde had fairly close contact with the antisemitic movement overall. In 1889, the Deutsche Reform-Verein (German Reform Association) even offered to run him as its candidate in the Reichstag elections. But he turned down the offer because he felt the prospects were much too uncertain.[27] Lagarde was not wrong in his assessment of the political potential of Böckel and his followers, who largely comprised farmers, tradesmen, and small businessmen. When antisemites in Berlin withdrew their support in 1890, Böckel could barely still afford the expensive campaigns. Moreover, he was accused of many legal violations and constantly in trouble with the authorities. The Verein zur Abwehr des Antisemitismus (Society for the Defense against Antisemitism), which was founded in 1891 and had branches in Frankfurt, Marburg, Cologne, and elsewhere, was a champion of political counter-agitation. Its members consisted mainly of left-wing liberal academics like Hermann Cohen and Böckel's dissertation supervisor, Edmund Stengel, who considered the organized hatred of Jews a disgrace to the constitutional state. These individuals' pointed assessment of antisemitism as a relic of the past significantly underestimated its ideological importance to the victims of modernization. In a reasonably stable society like the German Empire, however, the focused struggle against the antisemitic movement led to a reduction in its political effectiveness.

Böckel and other antisemitic members of the Reichstag found themselves isolated. And their failure to get a single bill through parliament may well be indicative of their isolation. Due to their blaring conduct and lack of expert knowledge, they were soon considered political opportunists with whom one could not seriously collaborate. In addition, their populist program had limited political feasibility, because they virtually ruled out coalitions with right-wing parties.[28] In North Hesse, Böckel's aura was tainted by his unstable private life, which earned him several alimony suits. Finally, his economic ideas resulted in a fiasco. Business stagnated in the "Jew-free cattle markets" and the so-called farmers' banks proved barely viable. When the cooperative banks offered good credit opportunities to the impoverished rural population, Böckel's influence was finally over with.

The reasons for Lagarde's political involvement largely remain a mystery. He certainly harbored considerable hatred for the Jews, and the bourgeois-saturated world in which he felt so alien induced him to engage in public confrontations. On the other hand, the semiliterate antisemitic agitators couldn't even quote material properly and would not have commanded his respect. And the Böckel movement cultivated a robust form of racism that did not at all fit his idealistic understanding of the German nation. Lagarde said in retrospect that he would never have agreed to testify for Fenner if he had been properly informed about the school teacher's conduct.[29] But this may well have been a half-truth that primarily reflected his disappointment at the trial's outcome.

As an Orientalist, Lagarde knew of how the Talmud had sparked anti-Jewish polemics for centuries. As a person with scholarly authority, he saw the Marburg trial as an opportunity to erase the unscientific reputation of antisemites and their ideology. Needless to say, this effort was not entirely successful. The religious importance of the Talmud clearly came to light during the proceedings, which ended with Fenner's legally binding sentence. Nevertheless, it would be too simplistic to consider events in Marburg as nothing more than a victory for the constitutional state. On the one hand, the antisemitic movement had gained a platform that it used to its advantage. So it was that Fenner's defense lawyer pointed to a long line of philosophical Jew-haters. Without inciting protest in the courtroom, he expressly named Herder, Kant, and Fichte as forerunners of the antisemitic movement. On the other hand, the Marburg events proved that scholarship was not in a position to bridge opposing ideologies. As energetically as Cohen pled for his universalistic version of Judaism, he could not sway the other side. His moral appeals only reached those who were already convinced and were simply interpreted as arrogance by his political opponents.

Lagarde also suffered from a structurally related problem, of course. In a nationalistic era, his view of the special meaning of Germanness admittedly had majority support. But his direct reference to Romantic thought frequently appeared antiquated or, indeed, out of place. He even utilized his expert opinion before the Royal Regional Court to propagate the ideas expressed in his *Deutsche Schriften*. He emphasized that the "Christian point of view" could only unfold in a "harmonic chorus" of the "great nations."[30] In addition to a desire for recognition that could make him difficult to bear, further problems entered the picture. Although Lagarde's treatment of his contemporaries was brusque and intolerant, he reacted most oversensitively to their criticisms. He was particularly hurt by his poor treatment by Jewish scholars in 1887. Of course, he gave as little thought to the fact that his invectives against Leopold Zunz had started the entire affair as he did to the increasing radicality of his choice of words. His behavior after the Marburg antisemitism trial also bore signs that he was losing control. The action he planned to take against the public prosecutor's office was unrealistic, and the language of the petition he intended to submit to the Ministry of Justice seemed querulous.

Lagarde had worked hurriedly, even feverishly, for many years with an eye to his great task, a complete edition of the Septuagint. When he realized toward the end of his life that he would not remotely reach his goal, this must have profoundly affected his self-image. He now looked to excuse an outcome that, even with respect to scholarship, he could only construe as a failure. And since he was blind to the exorbitance of his antisemitic claims, he became a slave to the very scapegoat images that had decisively shaped his political ideology.

12 Scholarly Failure

Lagarde was a man of enormous scholarly ambition. In his student years, he entertained the audacious hope of producing philologically precise editions of the Old and New Testaments. When this proved illusory, he discovered his scholarly mission in life, a critical edition of the Septuagint aimed at providing the key to the text of the Old Testament, which he saw as unsubstantiated and insufficient in many respects. As enthusiastic and highly educated as he was, Lagarde, over time, rallied other scholars, ministry officials, and even the Prussian king to his cause. The main reason he was given the chair in Orientalism at Georgia Augusta was so that he could devote himself without distractions to translating the Greek version of the Old Testament.

The Septuagint project was a high priority at the Prussian Ministry of Education and Cultural Affairs. Lagarde received generous subsidies and was given leave for research trips. The Ministry of Education and Cultural Affairs even wanted to provide him with a personal assistant, a rare exception in the Kaiserreich. But the notorious loner categorically turned down the offer, because he regarded close collaboration with an inexperienced scholar as annoying and objectively tricky.[1] During Lagarde's recurring disputes over permission to borrow valuable manuscripts, the ministry offered quite a bit of support. His mentor, Justus Olshausen, tried especially hard to ensure that the eccentric professor's idiosyncrasies did not jeopardize the Septuagint edition. Over the course of many years, however, Lagarde only delivered preliminary studies for the planned edition or busied himself with totally unrelated matters. If one also considers that, by means of complaints and threats of resignation, Lagarde succeeded time and again in compelling the state to fund him, then one could hardly count him a despised scholar.

Of course, Lagarde saw the world with different eyes. He bemoaned his colleagues' lack of support and became extremely angry that they rarely bought his books. He repeatedly enumerated to the Ministry of Education and Cultural Affairs how much money he lost in the self-publication of his books. And, in fact, the amounts Lagarde forked over for the printing of his works was considerable.[2] On the other hand, no one forced him to publish in this way. It hurt the reception of his scholarly ideas, while it offered the questionable advantage of reducing external considerations to a minimum. Yet however brusque his manner, he knew full well what his main task was. The scholarly world expected a Septuagint edition from him, and it would judge him by how he kept his promises. Although senior professors were held in high esteem during the Kaiserreich, a chair was no sinecure. A professor's position had to be justified by convincing scholarly achievements over a lifetime.

Signs already indicated at the beginning of his tenure that Lagarde sensed the boundlessness of his plans to compile a critical edition of the Septuagint on his own. Old before his time, he repeatedly suffered from nervous exhaustion that followed periods of intense scholarly activity. And he thought frequently of death. He was tormented by the idea that his efforts could have been in vain, owing to the incompleteness of his analysis. On February 19, 1879, he wrote darkly to William Aldis Wright in Cambridge: "Night is drawing near, and what is to be done, ought to be done soon." Paradoxically, the success of the *Deutsche Schriften* seems to have furthered his concentration on the Septuagint, although it actually represented a considerable distraction.

In early 1880, Lagarde published an article that laid out a schedule for his Septuagint edition, at the same time recalling his past twenty-five years of scholarly activity. He strongly emphasized the theological character of his publications, which had always been in the service of the Septuagint. Lagarde attached a double meaning to his political writings. In the first place, they had substantially altered public opinion and, in the second place, they demonstrated his contribution "to interpreting the prophets." Finally, after the many apt statements in the *Deutsche Schriften*, his "own ability to prophesy" could no longer be in doubt.[3] To many outsiders, this euphoric self-assessment may have seemed like hubris. But it also revealed Lagarde's desire to energetically promote the publication of the Septuagint edition.

On May 30, 1880, Lagarde informed the Prussian minister of education and cultural affairs, Robert von Puttkamer, that the period in his life for collecting information was finally over. From now on, it was a matter of "working on" the rich stores. He proudly wrote to Cambridge, where his research was met with particular interest, that the first volume of his Septuagint edition would come out in 1883.[4] On December 20, 1880, he solemnly informed Emil Dillen in St. Petersburg that the printing of his edition would "not allow him to breathe a sigh of relief [. . .] for five years." The reaction of the scholarly world to Lagarde's announcement was entirely positive, as typified by the words of the Basel theologian Rudolf Smend. On August 23, 1881, he expressed his "great joy" over the projected speedy publication of the Septuagint edition. But anyone hoping Lagarde would focus entirely on his main task from then on would soon be disabused of the idea. He turned to numerous fields of knowledge that stretched from Coptic to the Church Fathers, and he set aside only a fraction of his time for the Septuagint.

Lagarde had nevertheless placed himself under so much pressure with the aforementioned announcement that he was prepared to pay another researcher to collate the material. But his collaboration with the young Orientalist Gustav Meyncke, who was supposed to be in Rome on Lagarde's behalf, failed before it had really begun. On June 26, 1880, the mistrustful Lagarde asked for a written statement that Meyncke would not duplicate his transcript, "either for himself or for a third party." Although Lagarde had kept his letter emphatically impersonal, the precautionary measure was highly unusual and contained what nearly amounted to a defamatory allegation. So the indignant Meyncke immediately withdrew from the assignment. Now entirely on his own, Lagarde seems to have worked faster than usual, but at the expense of thoroughness. He first tackled the Septuagint edition of Lucian, which was an unusually difficult undertaking. The Greek version of the Old Testament had circulated in the area of Antioch and Constantinople around 400 C.E. and was, indeed, much less uniform than Lagarde had assumed. On account of this miscalculation, he did away with a detailed analysis of the various manuscripts, and this probably detracted significantly from the quality of his edition.[5] In the period that followed, Lagarde vacillated between various drafts of the edition, none of which truly satisfied him. But the Orientalist from Göttingen successfully managed to finish his project on time and, in late summer of 1883, the first volume of the Septuagint edition became available. It bore the title *Librorum Veteris Testamenti canonicorum pars prior graece* (*Books of the Old Testament Canon from the Original Greek*) and dispensed with all textual variants except for the Book of Esther. In spite of this very puristic approach, the first responses from the scientific community were completely positive. Lagarde received congratulatory letters from near and far, which showed the great value people placed on his edition. Adolf Erman was among the first well-wishers. Irrespective of his great admiration for Lagarde, the Egyptologist from Berlin had retained the ability to form his own opinions. He expressed his admiration at the speed at which Lagarde had completed the first volume of the Septuagint.[6]

Lagarde, however, who had just about reached the breaking point in the final months of work, reacted with great disappointment to the low sales figures. His wife's note from fall 1883 substantiates the grand illusions harbored in the Orientalist's home: "What expectations it had awakened! In England, 200 to 250 copies would be requested *immediately*. Oh, for heaven's sake. I would be surprised if there were more than five to begin with that crossed [the

Channel], except for the ones we gave away. After all that sacrifice!'"[7] As was so often the case, Lagarde's friend Georg Hoffmann tried to calm his irascible colleague. On October 19, he expressed his sympathy to Lagarde but said he did not consider the "slow sales" to be particularly surprising: "In England [. . .] people prefer not to purchase an incomplete work. And, in Germany, as you well know from your own experience, very few scholars are seriously interested in the LXX. Among those who are, there are some to whom a purchase would be most annoying." But this well-intended intervention missed its mark. With a typical mixture of resentment and self-pity, Lagarde decided to drastically apportion blame to the academic world.

On May 9, 1884, Lagarde published a leaflet about the reception of his edition that shows clear signs of bitterness. The leaflet included his report on a petition to the Prussian king that contained his reaction to the low sales of his Septuagint. Once again, Lagarde adopted a characteristically proud tone and pointed to the importance of the monarch in promoting the sciences. But the purpose of the petition was rather more secular in nature. Lagarde wanted his book to be purchased for the teachers' libraries at Prussian grammar schools. In early 1884, however, the Ministry of Education and Cultural Affairs had decided on purchasing just nine copies for the evangelical-theological departments of its universities. Even this modest figure could well have been a gesture of goodwill. But Lagarde had dreamed of selling more than two hundred books, and he was infuriated by the position of the Prussian state. He only exempted the institution of the monarchy from criticism and, for his part, counted on the beneficence of the Hohenzollerns. "The king is above political parties and, as ruler, above the ministries," he stated apodictically. He continued by projecting far into the future: "The king's son will see the disappearance of what they call theology today, and the king's grandson will see the development of a genuine theology. Theology will be indebted to me and to King Wilhelm, and it will be remembered that, in 1865, he took me under his wing as he did."[8] As always, Lagarde expected very little from the present, however.

People in professional circles knew about the erratic nature of Lagarde's decisions and tried to pacify the enraged scholar. On May 11, 1884, the eminent theologian and Orientalist Hermann Strack wrote these appreciative words from Berlin: "It was a great joy to me that the first volume of the LXX edition, the work which is the true mission of your scholarly life, has become available." But Lagarde was undeterred in his anger at the alleged indifference of his colleagues. On May 12, he grimly answered Strack by return messenger: "If people want to see additional volumes, then they should buy my books. I couldn't care less about praise." Lagarde hit rock bottom on New Year's Eve of that same year. He interpreted his own situation as an expression of political conditions in Germany, where "might" went "before right." In the most dire terms, he depicted the paltriness of his quarters during research trips and announced that he would never again work "for the good of theology."[9]

Officials at the Prussian Ministry of Education and Cultural Affairs were fairly used to dealing with Lagarde. But this time there was a real danger that he would stop working on the Septuagint altogether. Nevertheless, people in Berlin could count on the irascible Orientalist's two idiosyncrasies. On the one hand, scholarly work was a kind of elixir of life for Lagarde, and he could not go on without it. On the other hand, his drive to have an impact usually exceeded his anger over the injustice of the world. In other words, he repeatedly found his way back to his writing desk. In June 1885, Lagarde and the minister of education and cultural affairs, Gustav von Gossler, reached a characteristic settlement. They agreed that 250 copies would be sent at cost and that the Septuagint edition would be placed in Prussian teachers' libraries. This was a compromise for both parties, in which the ministry paid a rather large sum of 3,500 marks while Lagarde gave up the hoped-for, but no longer realistic, profit.[10] This was basically a rather good outcome for him. But, as he so often did, Lagarde took the ministerial concessions as a personal defeat. On September 22, 1885, he complained to the Reverend Bernhard Pick in Pennsylvania that only "196 copies" of his Lucian edition "[had] sold, and 1,000 would cover the cost." Feeling depressed, he told Georg Hoffmann that his "path had gone into the darkness."[11] A good six months later, on July 20, 1886, Lagarde was in a similarly bleak mood when he wrote up his will.

Lagarde had much to bequeath. Aside from a spacious home and property, he owned an extensive library valued at thirty thousand marks, as well as savings account books and securities.[12] In line with how responsible and orderly he was, Lagarde settled the financial particulars in detail and, above all, made provisions for his wife, whom he wanted to be free of any financial worries. He was at least as concerned with the future of the "de Lagarde" name. This may well have been an expression of reverence for his great-aunt Ernestine de Lagarde, who both adopted him and left him a large inheritance. He considered a foundation the most important means of preserving her name and his own along with it. In the event that no one in academia was interested in his legacy, he foresaw the founding of a small hospital. It would be called the "Lagardesches Krankenhaus," and the family crest, depicting a "greyhound leaping to the left" with a torn leash, would grace the entryway. But the Königliche Gesellschaft der Wissenschaften zu Göttingen (Royal Academy of Sciences at Göttingen) was the next heir in line. Lagarde had been a member since 1876 and, time and again, the academy had offered him a forum for his scholarly results.

The main purpose of the "Lagarde Foundation" was to be the conscientious editing of Oriental texts. Only the most capable philologists were considered worthy of support, and Lagarde generally barred "unbaptized Jews" from such support. This pronouncement spoke to his hatred of Jews, both in its relentlessness and its basis in religion. He imagined the hundredth anniversary of his birth in 1927 as a festive occasion. But he also saw it as a day of reckoning. On that occasion, a biography would be presented that would shed light on the dark episodes of his life. And the biography would be based on his own manuscripts that had been entrusted for safekeeping in Göttingen. In this case, Lagarde had in mind, among other things, clarifications of why he had not been offered appointments in Giessen or Halle and of the alleged obstruction of his research by the Foreign Office, where he suspected the presence of a "powerful enemy." All this not only revealed Lagarde's inability to work through failures; it also showed that he was losing his grip on reality. His unsystematic way of working, rather than external factors, was primarily responsible for the sluggish progress on the Septuagint project. His creation of an imaginary enemy in the Foreign Office showed how his mistrust of the Prussian state bordered on paranoia. But, in a way, this powerful, unknown enemy served more generally as a foil to explain his failures. Overall, Lagarde's will illustrates that his mistrust and need for validation were highly interwoven. For example, it contains precise arrangements for what to do in the event that the Göttinger Gesellschaft der Wissenschaften were to be disbanded. In this instance, the inheritance would go to the University of Giessen.

Various factors may have argued for the selection of this small university. Giessen was located outside Prussia and had served as a springboard for talented young scholars for quite some time. Lagarde planned to establish endowed chairs in philology and history at the university, located in Hesse-Darmstadt. They were to be awarded according to strict performance standards and, sometime between five and ten years later, the professors chosen would be reevaluated by their colleagues. Once more, Lagarde barred "unbaptized Jews" from filling these positions. The positions were also closed to anyone associated with the University of Giessen. Moreover, he could not resist attacking colleagues and, contrary to every academic code of conduct, he mentioned them by name. He expressly dubbed Giessen a place for the study of rarefied subjects that would span the gamut from Assyriology to Sinology to medical history. Lagarde embellished his idea with details that were entirely unrealistic, if merely for the reason that the legacy did not have sufficient funds at that time.

To ensure, however, that the funds ultimately went to the Göttinger Gesellschaft der Wissenschaften, Lagarde did not plan for a "change in the statutes" until 2027. By then, his legacy would have "placed talented, well-educated, hardworking, male researchers with a passion for truth in a position to serve scholarship without financial worries." This statement overtly expressed both Lagarde's identification with his legacy and the wish to live on through his foundation. May "God's blessing" rest upon this institution, he intoned, so as to "carry the man to posterity who will not survive through his children." He wrote the codicil on December 12, 1891, just a few days before his death. Once again, it illustrates the unusual strain in his relationship with the University of Göttingen. Lagarde had always preferred working from home to spending time in a public institution, yet he required the university library to make sure that his manuscripts were only allowed to be used within their rooms. His peculiar justification stated: "I want to ensure that visitors will come to reprobate Göttingen." In the final years of his life, Lagarde's intense rejection of the academic establishment was certainly not limited to Georgia Augusta. Hardly a single institution or researcher was spared from his critical glance. And disappointment with his own life emerged ever more clearly from behind his merciless standards.

In the 1880s, Lagarde got caught up in numerous personal feuds. He always reproached his colleagues for their limited knowledge of languages while, at the same time, increasingly offering his comments on areas in which he was not really at home. The scope of his scholarly output alone is evidence of a feverish if impetuous work tempo.[13] In the last decade of his life, he produced an impressive seven thousand pages. But the work increasingly lacked conscientious editing, and important plans came to a halt in the initial stages. After the huge disappointment with the Lucian edition, Lagarde's interest in the Septuagint project also diminished. He actually began the enormous task of the Greek Psalter, but he did not finish editing it. The academic world came to believe ever more strongly, and rightly in this case, that Lagarde had too many irons in the fire. More than a few of his publications addressed marginal subject matter and must have seemed eccentric to the scientific community. At the same time, he was partial to solemn scholarly rhetoric that, from a purely linguistic perspective, nipped any objections in the bud.

A classic example of Lagarde's late scholarly publications is his essay "Altes und Neues über das Weihnachtsfest" (Old and New Ideas of Christmas). He strongly emphasized the importance of the philological method to scientific progress, which he saw as central to a positivistic increase in knowledge. But he simultaneously developed an unequivocally negative image of German universities against the backdrop of his own experience: "I have intentionally been prevented from anything worthy of being called teaching, not because I could not or did not wish to teach it, and not because what I would have taught would not have been worth learning, but because the various cliques that came into power, one after another, hated me, and because the results of my work compelled me to face unpleasant truths that seemed easier to eliminate by getting rid of me than by trying to refute them."[14] This explanation was hardly convincing, because the senior professor could proclaim his ideas from the lectern and the Göttinger Gesellschaft der Wissenschaften placed almost unlimited print space at his disposal. But Lagarde gladly took advantage of the opportunity to style himself a persecuted scholar who could only place his hope in the younger generation of academics.

As far as the essay's content, Lagarde offered a peculiar perspective that was equally shaped by his study of sources from late antiquity and by his culturo-philosophical convictions. His interpretation boiled down to the statement that, in the fourth century, the Church in Rome had "saved Christianity by introducing the celebration of Christmas." This particular statement was aimed at Aryanism, which did not speak to the human heart and had caused the downfall of the Goths, Suebi, and Vandals. The real point of this extremely ideologized picture of history was that, over a long period of time, the people of southern Europe had missed out on the "blessing of German blood." As if this were not enough, Lagarde drew a daring comparison to his own time, a time in which "modern Aryanism" had to be combated. He declined to address his ideological opponents more closely and ended with a historico-philosophical generalization instead: "Who knows how close the darkness is that humanity cries into for light? I wish that it were here."[15]

Needless to say, this eschatological interpretation of the present did not lead Lagarde to forgo ambition or give up his tenacious effort in the service of science, not even in his final years. He continued to find that his undertakings were often not properly acknowledged. On May 22, 1886, he protested to Minister Gossler that his "business travels [. . .] were often seen as pleasure trips." With resentment, he said: "It is a great sacrifice for me to leave my wife for eight months and to be away from home without anyone to talk to, transcribing and collating for nine to twelve hours, day after day, in miserable lodgings with meager fare." This was, of course, an attempt to show his own self-sacrificial work in a favorable, meaningful light. But the personal choice of words reveals anger and genuine suffering. Poem "No. 11," written in London in 1887, illustrates just how fragile his sense of self-worth could be, particularly when he traveled on research. We previously quoted the sad lines of this poem about the unresolved death of his mother. A few verses later, it reads:

Since I became a man, but remained a child,
I am neither man nor child, just a burden
to myself and all who come close to me.
What am I, then?
An eagle without wings, a painter without hands, a deaf violinist.[16]

Lagarde was one of those damaged human beings who knew he was psychologically unstable and openly expressed it on occasion. Not only were loneliness and self-pity a result of his early experience of loss, but unbridled rage as well. Since Lagarde was horribly afraid of losing face in public, he repeatedly got into messy situations. And the self-certainty that he exhibited made him look like a know-it-all to many of his contemporaries. His suggestions for reforming the Göttinger Gesellschaft der Wissenschaften are a classic example of Lagarde's ineptness. What alienated his contemporaries even more was the way he intended to put his ideas into practice.

Since the time of its annexation by Prussia, the Göttingen Academy had played only a minor role. And, in comparison to the Berlin Academy, it was poorly endowed. As was often the case, Lagarde wanted fundamental changes in the Göttingen Academy. And he advised the Ministry of Education and Cultural Affairs of his ideas without first having reached agreement with his colleagues. Such tactics were anything but clever, because an issue of this magnitude could not be kept secret in the long run, and his approach would have invariably cast his ideas in a dim light. Moreover, Lagarde had spoken freely, and his suggestions were conceived in connection with terse value judgments. He boldly emphasized that, "Protestantism was living off the last ounce of its strength."[17] He did not understand that crafting academic policy also consisted of the ability to form coalitions with smaller parties. And so he belittled officials, people from Lower Saxony, journalists, and Jews without giving a single thought to the detrimental effects of his invectives. What probably hurt him most was his pejorative assessment of the seniority system that was in its heyday during the Kaiserreich. The budding academy should "consist of men who are in the process of becoming and not of decrepit celebrities, nor of old men who are has-beens or who appeared to have once been someone of note."[18] In light of these kinds of derogatory judgments, many members of the Göttingen Academy became angry with Lagarde and refused to seriously discuss his ideas for long-term support of the smaller fields within the arts and humanities.

Furthermore, Berlin had other priorities. And the influential head of the department, Friedrich Althoff, mainly had it in mind to build Georgia Augusta into a center for the natural sciences. Picking up on this idea, the famous mathematician Felix Klein commented on Lagarde's opinion and presented his own ideas on academic affairs. His core ideas were aimed at promoting the natural sciences that were based on the objective qualities of mathematics, even if other fields were also under consideration.[19] Unlike Lagarde, Klein refrained from justifying his academic plans on a national or religious basis. His ideas undoubtedly struck a contemporary note, whereas Lagarde's thoughts concerning the support of the arts and humanities were presented with his own brand of pathos and must have appeared antiquated. This was precisely the area that the Berlin Academy had emphasized for some time, and Theodor Mommsen had initiated important long-term tasks.

A peculiarity of Lagarde's character was a frequent tendency to not notice when he'd been marginalized. He continued to bombard the university trustee and the Ministry of Education and Cultural Affairs with his ideas for improvement without the appreciable support of academics in Göttingen. Lagarde was particularly afraid that Prussia's increasing centralization would undermine scholarly independence in the long term. Finally, Lagarde attacked Felix Klein personally: Klein didn't even understand the basic difference between the university and the academy, whose respective goals lay in educating students and promoting pure science. To cap it all, Lagarde closed his statement with comments on the careless handling of money by academic bodies. In absolute repudiation of the principle of majority rule, he stressed: "On principle, I do not give any scholarly association a blank check, but provide it for specific purposes only, because earmarking the money is the only way to ensure that it is not squandered."[20] Whatever one may think of this judgment, Lagarde's having stated it publicly must have increased his isolation. Lagarde adopted an even sharper tone in his second memorandum. He expressly opposed all reviews written as favors and demanded that all professors in Göttingen be obliged to refrain from promoting their own books. Moreover, in contravention of all common practice, he enthusiastically communicated numerous details of internal matters pertaining to his dealings with the Ministry of Education and Cultural Affairs.[21] On July 6, 1889, at the climax of the conflict, Lagarde announced to the university trustee Ernst von Meier that he would soon resign from the Göttinger Gesellschaft der Wissenschaften. With reference to the intended reforms of the Prussian Ministry of Education and Cultural Affairs, he made this curt statement about his colleagues' restraint: "Things simply cannot go on this way." In light of Lagarde's indiscretion and the avalanche of petitions, people in Berlin had reached the same conclusion about him.

On November 12, 1889, Minister Gossler penned a letter to the university trustee in Göttingen, stridently asking "whether [. . .] Lagarde was in such an overwrought state that he no longer appeared responsible for his actions."[22] He expected an immediate report on the matter. However, if Lagarde were not in such a condition, then the Orientalist must be informed that he had to submit any future petitions via the university trustee. Moreover, Lagarde was to be informed that a repeat of his "impudence and impertinence" would invariably lead to disciplinary proceedings. We cannot ascertain from the university records what von Gossler was specifically alluding to. But there is certainly no shortage of verbal insults that Lagarde directed at the Ministry of Education and Cultural Affairs. On August 31, 1889, he emphasized the medieval character of the Prussian university system and made this disrespectful remark: "Given the state of things, the monetary support of my Septuagint would be nothing more than a pittance, and I am already too old to accept pittances from the state coffers. But perhaps I am a horse of another color." At any rate, the crux of the conflict between Lagarde and the ministry was financial. The willful senior professor acted as if Gossler had agreed to the additional payment for the Syrian typeface that had already been purchased by the Göttinger Gesellschaft der Wissenschaften. But this was not the case, as the minister subsequently explained with the greatest clarity. So that no further unwarranted claims about the ministry would be circulated, he considered it necessary to inform the Göttingen Academy of Lagarde's unreliable statements.[23]

Ernst von Meier had a considerable talent for resolving conflict. He immediately informed the Ministry of Education and Cultural Affairs that Lagarde had seen the error of his ways. But if the matter of acquiring the Syrian typeface had been widely circulated, then it could not feasibly be stopped. On January 21, 1890, Gossler relented, although he left no room for doubt that the difficult scholar had really not earned such "consideration."[24] Just one day later, he was again involved in Lagarde-related matters. The minister, who seems to have been truly angry about the Orientalist's arrogant behavior, had to have an anthology of Lagarde's essays compiled for the Göttinger Gesellschaft der Wissenschaften. On account of certain quotations in the anthology, he criticized Lagarde's subjective remarks "about state institutions, officials and scholars" and proposed that the printing of such statements no longer be authorized.[25] In looking at the collection of quotes for the dossier, one would immediately agree with Gossler's critique. The mere content of Lagarde's writing was almost tantamount to the justification of censorship, and no one at Georgia Augusta was interested in expanding the influence of the state. As a senior professor, Lagarde also belonged to the innermost core of the faculty and could count on its collective support.

The secretary of the Göttinger Gesellschaft der Wissenschaften, Hermann

Sauppe, undertook Lagarde's defense. The elderly connoisseur of classical rhetoric showed a great deal of understanding for the Orientalist. "It is certainly very regrettable," Sauppe told the university trustee, "that a man who is intellectually outstanding and erudite, and has contributed important works, can hardly resist the unfortunate inclination to insert caustic remarks in all directions into whatever he writes."[26] Needless to say, one should not exaggerate the importance of Lagarde's remarks. People in Göttingen were "used to" Lagarde's highly barbed comments "and were more inclined to laugh at them, rather than to feel deeply offended." Moreover, the scholarly importance of the essays was in no way limited to the incriminating passages. "In consideration of the importance of the man and his work," Sauppe recommended that, "the matter be allowed to rest for now." At the same time, he promised to restrain Lagarde with respect to ministerial concerns. This was both prudent and clever reporting and, as it happened, the Ministry of Education and Cultural Affairs refrained from taking further steps. However much Lagarde attacked his colleagues in Göttingen, people showed the very esprit de corps that was the guarantor of a cohesive academic world. And something else: regardless of his difficult character, Lagarde's scholarly reputation was beyond question, and people were proud of his continued work on his critical edition of the Septuagint in Göttingen.

Lagarde's prize student, Alfred Rahlfs, was among the few auditors at Lagarde's lectures. Rahlfs worked intensively on Syriac and even took part in difficult private tutoring sessions with his mentor. Rahlfs also stayed in written contact with his revered professor and reported on the course of his studies, as well as on private matters. The senior professor reciprocated by supporting Rahlfs's career to the best of his ability. He urged Rahlfs to quickly complete his studies and ensured that he got an impeccable final grade. In addition, he attached great importance to the fact that Rahlfs not only earned a doctorate in philosophy but also passed the first theological exam. The shy Rahlfs took the early distinctions as an obligation to apply himself even more. He set to work on a systematic reading of the Old Testament and concentrated intensively on Hebrew grammar. As much as Lagarde welcomed the idea of Rahlfs following in his footsteps, he nevertheless warned against following his example too closely. In a letter of April 18, 1888, he encouraged the young scholar to attack him straightaway on intellectual grounds. In the end, he saw it as just about his foremost duty to "make" his students "independent." Regardless of the combative style that Lagarde cultivated in his other relationships, he knew exactly what was right and proper for a tenured professor in his dealings with young scholars. And it was abundantly clear to him that freedom was a necessary component of intellectual growth.

A letter to the university board of trustees, dated November 13, 1889, shows how highly Lagarde thought of Rahlfs. The letter endorsed Rahlfs's application for an adjunct professor's grant. The senior professor firmly emphasized that Rahlfs was his best student in Göttingen and "expressly trained for an academic teaching post." At the same time, Lagarde vouched for Rahlfs's belief in the strictly historical character of theology: Rahlfs "would not have worked with me for four years if he didn't want to see that, in the event that theology is a science, it may only make use of scientific methods and [. . .], in the event that there is a belief, its first article must be the conviction that, in the final analysis, honest and adequately practiced research always reaches a goal." This statement contains hidden praise for Lagarde himself and was objectively tricky considering that not every positivistically conducted piece of research led to fruitful results. On the other hand, these lines also unmistakably show that Lagarde wholeheartedly supported the grant, which was then approved without further ado.

Rahlfs naturally found out how gruffly disparaging and unjust Lagarde's judgments could be. In the guise of the unerring love of truth, the senior professor gave free reign to his resentment and disregarded the conventional rules of academic courtesy. He also had little sense of gratitude toward his former supporters. He accused his long-standing mentor at the Ministry of Education and Cultural Affairs, Justus Olshausen, of having an accountant's mentality and criticized his inability "to understand facts as an internally organized whole."[27] At the end of his life, he was even more harshly vocal about his predecessor, Heinrich Ewald, whose seat on the Göttinger Gesellschaft der Wissenschaften he took over in 1876. He thought "in downright horror" about "the long list" of Ewald's publications that showed psychologists only one thing, which was "that in all essential matters, this scholar did not go upward, but always set off on a downward path." In light of the many half-finished writings that he himself published, this was an imprudent and almost presumptuous statement. But Lagarde had less and less hope of ever reaching his main goal, the full critical edition of the Septuagint.

Instead of preparing the Psalter, he now worked on the edition of the Books of Ezra and Nehemiah, but did not finish this work either. Once again, he had prepared a huge number of explanatory notes that could not reasonably be incorporated into the final print version. Lastly, he concentrated on detailed studies that might be important for a future edition of the Septuagint, laboring with such characteristic energy that his main task was pushed into the background. Shortly before his death, he gloomily told his friend Alfred Schöne: "The Septuagint studies are devouring the Septuagint."[28] But self-awareness was an infrequent visitor to the Lagarde home and, particularly in the final years of his life, was outweighed by the critique of the world's ingratitude. The fire at Mommsen's house, the envy of colleagues, or the ignorance of state officials served, whenever necessary, as explanations for the failure of the Septuagint project. In her search for excuses, Anna de Lagarde even surpassed her husband. On November 9, 1890, she gave her friend Gustav Bösche a dramatic account of how the authorities had impeded Lagarde's work. At the same time, she asked the philologically educated grammar school teacher to continue her husband's work into the future: "He [Lagarde] has shown the way and the goal. Now it is your, the younger generation's, task to carry on the work: not to *take exception* to small or irrelevant matters, but *to follow* on the whole."

More and more often, thoughts in the Lagarde house revolved around posthumous fame. Lagarde wrote a poem that indicated how he wanted to be remembered. It was titled "Nachwort" (Epilogue), and in it Lagarde positioned himself as the pioneer of a better future. The last verse reads:

What ere he lacked, will you forget,
for leniency befits you.
Were he not who *he* was,
then we would not be standing here.[29]

Even if these awkwardly naive verses were highly romanticized, they still had something of a connection to reality. In 1908, when the Septuagint research was about to be institutionalized in Göttingen, Rahlfs would naturally be chosen as director. And, fittingly, the undertaking found permanent residence in Lagarde's home on Friedländer Weg. Today, people are still working on the Greek version of the Old Testament in the massive stone home that the Orientalist built to store valuable manuscripts. An important reason for this was that Lagarde had bequeathed his not inconsiderable fortune to the Göttinger Gesellschaft der Wissenschaften, and people thus felt obliged to appropriately preserve the memory of the important Orientalist. Of course, many inherently good reasons spoke for the continuation of the Septuagint project; its importance for the history of Judaism, late antiquity, and the biblical record is clearly indisputable. Yet Lagarde's tireless activity of behalf of the Septuagint remains puzzling to this day. How could it happen that a quintessential positivist wanted to found or at least decisively support a religious ideology by means of empirical results? Why didn't Lagarde notice the aporetic nature of his efforts or the material difficulties that stood in the way of the Septuagint project?

Finally, it is worth clarifying why the scientific community reacted so positively to Lagarde's apparently unrealistic idea of a soon-to-appear Septuagint edition. The answers should be sought along two lines. First, Lagarde was truly a brilliant philologist with extensive knowledge of languages. He had an immense capacity for work and an intuitive sense for research desiderata. He found his staunchest supporters in the Anglo-Saxon world and was long considered the one scholar who most energetically called attention to the value of the Septuagint.[30] In Prussia, the king's backing ensured that Lagarde's project never entirely lost its aura, not to mention its basis of financial support. Moreover, basic research in the arts and humanities was in keeping with the times and was attentively followed by the bourgeois public. Well-known researchers enjoyed considerable social prestige and could afford to be somewhat quirky. As difficult as it was to deal with an extremely sensitive and headstrong Orientalist like Lagarde, tenured professors at universities enjoyed extensive rights throughout the period of the German Empire. Regardless of any fundamental reservations or annoyances, it would not have occurred to any of his colleagues to instruct him in the selection of his fields of activity or the appropriate scholarly methods.

Second, Lagarde was one of a kind in terms of his ideas and the history of science. As if his combination of strictly philological questions with the founding of his German national religion were not striking enough, he also cultivated his own sort of cultural pessimism. In contrast to nearly every other critic of the educational system, he had a positive approach to specialization, and that approach was indispensable to sound scholarly understanding.[31] Even if it would only be proven in the distant future, he felt that the value of his research to the textual framework of the Bible was beyond question. In any case, Lagarde believed that a prerequisite for an authentic new beginning for the German people was the overcoming of contemporary materialistic culture. As unequivocal as he was in his judgment of the degenerate German Empire, he had long since draped himself in the mantle of a prophet.

13 Prophet of German Culture

Toward the end of Lagarde's life, an increasing number of people considered him the "prophet of a new religion." The professor from Göttingen greatly valued this lofty image and did his utmost to foster its dissemination. From today's perspective, it seems strange for a renowned scholar to become the herald of his own increasingly radicalized ideology. And, even in Lagarde's time, it was not the norm. At the end of the nineteenth century, the heralds of spiritual renewal who garnered the most attention were seldom members of the university establishment. Rather, they were mainly intellectuals who lacked influence and used daring blueprints for reform to compensate for their own marginalized position in society. Nevertheless, there is no doubt that Lagarde's eccentricity and religious message had an effect on his followers. Like so many pundits, Lagarde promised that social fragmentation would be conquered and a new "sheltering society" would be founded.[1] And he drew on existing traditions and personal convictions that were still rooted in the Nachmärz world.

Lagarde was steeped in his religious mission from early on. The letters he wrote from London to his bride explain how deeply at odds he was with his own time. He regarded his contemporaries as superficial materialists who would never open themselves to the Gospel unless their worldview was gravely shaken. Even after he married and was working as an ordinary Berlin schoolteacher, Lagarde did not lose his religious vision. A letter to his wife, dated August 16, 1860, may best express his unappeased, metaphysical longing: "Last night there were four storms all around the island," he wrote to her from the North Sea isle of Norderney. "I stood all by myself on the highest dune. It was as if barrels of light had been overturned in the heavens. Long, straight bolts shot into the sea itself. As fast as lightning moves, it still seemed to visibly run up the blades of the dune grass. I've never seen anything like it." He built on this dramatic description of nature with these bold but unquestionably serious words: "Elijah may have stood on his mountains and fed his soul in this way. The sounds of the sea and the wind in the dune grasses were uniquely gripping."[2] Like Fichte before him, Lagarde was convinced that a special, metaphysical mission to save humanity fell to the German people. When economic and domestic crises reached grave proportions following the founding of the German Empire, a growing number of people listened to prophets of doom.

People of many different stripes were greatly interested in Lagarde's idea of national-spiritual renewal. They ranged from prominent scholars like Adolf Erman and Friedrich Paulsen to spiritually battered figures like Alfred Schöne. And they included people of all ages, which made it easier for Lagarde to speak with fatherly authority. In scrutinizing his correspondence, one discovers that when it came to religious questions, Lagarde was quite generous with his time. Even if the correspondents were casual acquaintances or total strangers, Lagarde fully discussed religious concerns with them. He spoke down to them and left his counterparts in no doubt that he had long since found his own way. On March 22, 1874, he made the passing remark to the Hamburg poet Johannes Wedde that he had "walked the same mystical and Gnostic paths thirty years ago" but had "long since [. . .] abandoned" them. Lagarde also warned against using populist language so that Wedde's readers would not be affected by his religious creed. Most addressees felt morally uplifted by Lagarde's serious, fundamental admonitions but also kept their distance. Only a few people, such as Alfred Schöne, were on familiar enough terms with the unapproachable scholar that they dared adopt a personal tone. Schöne, of course, knew just how closely Lagarde's self-image was tied to his being hailed as a prophet, and he was very skillful at doing this himself. To Anna de Lagarde, he sang the praises of her husband's "true and genuine poet's soul" that enabled him to prophesy.[3] But, as a rule, the prophet from Göttingen was very careful to ensure that his relationships with his followers did not become too close or endanger the charismatic impact of his message.

A letter of May 6, 1883, to the Viennese poet Siegfried Lipiner concerning the training of a young scholar is a classic example of Lagarde's private style of communication. Lagarde's patronizing wish for the problem child was "a post [. . .] that would force him to recognize the seriousness of life." He continued in a solemn tone: "I was also ambitious as a young man, not out of a desire for honor, I believe, but in order to be of greater use. Even a throne would have been alright with me. I thank God every day that I didn't come out on top, but had to walk, sunburned, on stony paths in the lowlands, and that I must still walk these paths today, albeit in a different way than before." In the 1880s, Lagarde's humble yet considerably prideful rhetoric struck the right chord with many readers. A man had found his own way out of the spiritual emptiness and religious groundlessness that characterized the time, or so it seemed.

Reading circles formed in various locations to discuss Lagarde's writings at length, and they happily turned to the "master" for encouragement. The language of these exchanges was mainly nebulous, which, in the absence of any concrete purpose, could hardly have been otherwise. On February 8, 1883, Bruno Kerry wrote to the revered professor: "Here in Vienna," there is "a small group of men" who are pressing for Lagarde "to do [. . .] his bit for the common cause." Exactly one month later, the effusive Kerry was already speaking to the Orientalist about a "sacred Lagarde community."

Since these groups existed on a completely informal basis, no one knows how many there were and who belonged to them. They mainly centered on an enthusiastic follower who considered the *Deutsche Schriften* a prophetic guide. Be that as it may, Lagarde had high expectations of these elite circles and did a number of things to help them expand. He got carried away in affirming the development of these groups and made bold generalizations. On July 22, 1888, he told the French philologist Gaston Paris: "The patriots of all nations [. . .], the true, silent, suffering, laboring patriots, form a single community across the globe." But if one took these radical formulations to mean that Lagarde rejected all forms of authority, one would be going too far. No matter how deeply convinced he was of the superficiality of religious life or how massively he rejected Protestantism in particular, Lagarde remained a rather restrained revolutionary in matters of faith. He looked upon religion as a "concern of the many," in line with his irrefutable view that people needed "one church, or one community at the very least."[4] Without some type of organizational structure to hold it together, faith would always be a fleeting thing.

These were thoughts that occupied many people's minds in the late nineteenth century. People feared the consequences of the universal "dechurchification" process. Lagarde occupied a special place among them: he was a renowned professor of Orientalism, and his well-respected *Deutsche Schriften* had brought him success. But there was a lot of competition among authors who offered the Protestant educated class a comprehensive new interpretation of the world. In 1890, Bismarck was forced to resign, the multifaceted activities of Wilhelm II heralded a new age, and a book appeared that created an immediate furor: *Rembrandt als Erzieher* (*Rembrandt as Educator*). By 1893, the work had gone through forty-three editions, twenty-five of them within the first nine months. It fulfilled the longings of many and sold for the meager sum of two marks. People everywhere speculated as to who the author could be, because the front matter only told them that the book was written "by a German." It soon became habitual for people to speak of him as one of the *Rembrandtdeutschen* (Rembrandt Germans) and how indebted they were to him for their deep culturo-philosophical insights. At the same time, the unsolved authorship drove up sales. The majority of the more than sixty thousand purchasers agreed that *Rembrandt als Erzieher* made an exceptional read. And many of them even believed that the secrecy surrounding the author was entirely in keeping with the mystical content of the work.

The author, August Julius Langbehn, also had personal reasons for not placing himself in the foreground. After all, his life story hardly corresponded to bourgeois ideals.[5] Born in 1851 in the Northern Schleswig town of Hadersleben, Langbehn studied numerous subjects in Kiel and Munich. But, unlike Lagarde, he dawdled considerably. It wasn't until the age of twenty-nine that he was awarded a doctorate in classical archeology. The Gothic type of his doctoral dissertation, *Flügelgestalten der ältesten griechischen Kunst* (*Winged Figures in the Early Art of Ancient Greece*), underscored his flamboyant nature. When he had to wait for a travel grant, the impulsive Langbehn broke with the academic establishment, which he felt was divorced from reality. He later shamed his dissertation supervisor, Heinrich Brunn, and the entire University of Munich by sending back his doctoral diploma in shreds when his wish to return his doctoral title was not granted. Langbehn's high-flown dreams were not suited to regular employment. He traveled around restlessly for ten years, living on private subsidies and odd jobs until his lucky strike with *Rembrandt als Erzieher*. The work largely owed its success to its distinctive style.

Langbehn had mastered many forms of expression: he tended toward aphorisms and daring mental leaps, and used apodictic language to present etymologies whose scholarly worth was virtually nil. He was especially fond of old German stave rhymes that reinforced the desired solemnity of his prose. Daring associations were generally of greater importance to Langbehn than sound arguments. Here is a passage that illustrates his lofty idea of the German nation and allows us to sample his style: "The color of iron, which brings peace to all peoples and has set the German people free, is black. Black is also the color of the earth that the farmer tills and which patriotic artists have to thank for their best creative energy. If one joins this darkest of all elements with those other two, blood and gold, then one has the colors of the erstwhile ideal Germany: black, red, gold."[6] This type of vague wording allowed for numerous interpretations and didn't force people to accept any one in particular. So what was the secret of its success?

The magic word is synthesis. In an increasingly incalculable world, Langbehn argued in favor of the artist's perspective (*Wesensschau*) over the analytical approach of the scholar. Genuinely political problems would be handled peripherally, as needed. Like Lagarde, Langbehn believed in the need for a good king, in the ethical substance of the aristocracy and the worth of the national spirit. But, in lieu of resorting to harsh antagonism, he generally opted for conciliatory diction. His exalted speech also hid the extent to which he avoided committing himself to any sort of content. "The concepts of state and people, people and intellectuals, should not be ratcheted up into artificial opposites, but should be eased into natural harmony," he said sanguinely. And Langbehn continued in a virtually euphoric vein: "All private and public instruction culminate in such a natural harmony: not so as to divide, but to reconcile and to unite the lower and upper, the outer and inner aspects of human life! In the face of this goal, all professional and class distinctions disappear, people meet only as one person to another, high and low shake one another's hands!"[7] Like almost no other intellectual, the *Rembrandtdeutsche* recognized that all people longed for the reenchantment of the world in an achievement-oriented age dominated by a belief in science.

Langbehn's antisemitism emerged strikingly in the second edition (1891) of the "Rembrandt book" and was primarily a matter of calculation. The edition contained two new chapters that were intended to underscore the foreignness and "greedy exploitation" of the Jewish people.[8] Langbehn also tried to attract new buyers for his work by automatically identifying Jews with modernity and emphasizing their baneful influence on artistic life. The tone of his rabid antisemitism was similar to Lagarde's and contrasted strangely with the patriarchal, idyllic character of the book. The *Rembrandtdeutsche* left no doubt about his rejection of the 1848 revolution and all forms of belief in progress and democratic participation. Only art could save humanity and usher in the rebirth of the German people. And rebirth also meant a return to their rural ancestors.

Langbehn was a polarizing author. While some condemned his daring images and associations as charlatanism, others praised his flights of fancy and speculative richness. His opponents found fault, above all, with the freewheeling dilettantism of this self-taught man who didn't shrink from making any judgment, no matter how outlandish. Many were simply confused by the formal composition of his text, which didn't even try to give the appearance of a systematic arrangement. And Langbehn's erratic ideas stood in apparent opposition to any logical train of thought. Even his friend, the arts writer Cornelius Gurlitt, wrote that *Rembrandt als Erzieher* seemed as if it had been "welded together from a series of feature articles."[9] On the other hand, the loose form fit in with the work's abrupt dismissal by the academic establishment and its alleged overestimation of the human intellect. But the book created such a sensation that no one could ignore it, and even the critics contributed to its spread.

Langbehn's followers frequently expressed themselves as effusively as their venerable role model. The *Deutsche Wochenblatt* stressed emphatically: "An electric shock rips through the German nervous system as one is reading this book. And that's why everyone should read it. This is a book in and for the spirit of the times." The *Kieler Wochenschau* proved unreservedly in agreement with the goal of "making Germans German again by returning to who they really are." The *Deutsche Lehrerzeitung* compared the avant-garde writer to those "great men [. . .] who, from time to time, confronted their fellow human beings with the truth." The respected *Deutsche Literaturzeitung* promoted Langbehn's slogan, "Figurative, not literal" (*Bild nicht Buchstabe*), affirming the expressive power of the pictorial arts over the printed word. Lagarde no longer wished to stand on the sidelines in this matter. Although he was otherwise very sparing in his public recommendations, he now praised Langbehn's "intrepid love of truth" and his "original means of expression and representation."[10] And his acquaintance with the author of the "Rembrandt book" for more than two years may have made it easier for him to take this step.

In December 1887, Langbehn had requested a copy of the *Deutsche Schriften*, which he read with enthusiasm. He extolled Lagarde's prophetic soul and referred to his personal desire for groundbreaking societal reform in which art would come into its own. But when he tried to establish a more personal connection to the overworked professor, Anna de Lagarde kept him at bay. On April 4, 1889, she told him affably, but plainly, that she did not believe her husband could tear himself away from his troubles.[11] Langbehn's correspondence nevertheless seems to have made an impression. In any case, Lagarde decided to make a trip to Dresden, although he did not meet with Langbehn. And because the overworked scholar could hardly spare a minute, his trip back to Göttingen turned out to be quite irksome. It is, therefore, not at all surprising that his correspondence with Langbehn did not go beyond a friendly, reserved tone. In January 1890, Langbehn had already intimated to the Lagardes that he was the author of *Rembrandt als Erzieher*, so the fact remains that they shared a bond of trust. Langbehn's openness proved useful, because several journalists had immediately assumed that Lagarde was the author of the work. From a purely stylistic standpoint, very little spoke for this assumption, but people believed Lagarde was capable of this kind of genius. The young Maximilian Harden was thus convinced that the "outstanding, peculiar, original" author could be none other than Lagarde.[12] For his part, Lagarde denied the claim immediately and kept a low profile otherwise, which quite suited Langbehn.

But the relationship soon deteriorated. Lagarde had no use for Langbehn's genius-posturing and hostility toward scholarship. And he felt that the reading public had misjudged him. The impulsive Langbehn, on the other hand, enjoyed fame and became less and less tolerant of rebukes. On April 30, 1890, he told Anna de Lagarde that, with all due respect, he did not belong to her husband's "community [. . .], and I still know nothing about it or its members." As far as content was concerned, he strictly rejected any "uniform mass that rallied around a center," because it was not compatible with his aristocratic worldview.

At this point, the enraged professor's wife accused him of impudence and lack of self-control. At the same time, her husband came to the damning conclusion that Langbehn was anything but thorough and added a host of critical remarks to his own copy of *Rembrandt als Erzieher*.[13] But the two writers obviously kept up appearances.

Lagarde combined support for Langbehn's book with the robust promotion of his own cause. He firmly pointed out that, as early as 1881, he had called for the emergence of a "new public sentiment" that would improve the state of affairs in Germany. In early 1891, he approached Langbehn's Leipzig publisher, C. L. Hirschfeld, in order to partake of the exceptional success of *Rembrandt als Erzieher*. In proposing a popular edition of his *Deutsche Schriften*, Lagarde was preaching to the choir. On February 19, 1891, Hirschfeld wrote to him urgently that they "must take advantage [. . .] of the extremely favorable trend and mustn't wait for the uncertainty of 1892." As was so often the case when unexpected opportunities came up, Lagarde appeared rather fainthearted. On February 24, he asked for the popular edition to indicate differences in pagination from earlier editions so that it would be easier to check quotations. He justified this by saying that, in his writings, he "had long ago (as early as 1853) judged and appraised matters in a way that people were beginning to judge and assess them today." This was not entirely implausible. Moreover, it matched Lagarde's self-image as a thinker who had been misunderstood for decades. For an edition that was supposedly geared to a wider public, though, this request seemed rather contrived. Hirschfeld responded somewhat impatiently a day later, telling Lagarde they should "not hold up the popular edition for any longer. Even in the book trade, people say, 'Strike while the iron is hot!'" They were considering a print run of three thousand, and Hirschfeld had conceived a correspondingly large-scale advertising campaign. Eighty review copies would go to the press, and two hundred books would be presented to all those who had advertised on behalf of *Rembrandt als Erzieher*.[14] But, due to Lagarde's stubbornness, the negotiations ultimately failed. He wanted to compel the publishing house to pay a contractual penalty in the event that it deviated too greatly from the advance. Moreover, he was about to leave for Italy on a research trip and was not in a position to read the galley proofs. In 1891, the "popular edition" of his *Deutsche Schriften* was therefore published by Diederichs in Göttingen, which significantly diminished its chances of success. And the support of Ludwig Schemann in the *Bayreuther Blätter* did little to change that.[15]

Lagarde and Langbehn are often named in the same breath as radical critics of contemporary culture. The historian George Mosse went so far as to suggest that Langbehn, whom he saw as the true founder of the Völkisch movement, was Lagarde's prophet.[16] Mosse was basing this judgment on conventions that developed during the fin de siècle, conventions that had some merit in their own right, even if they scarcely matched the protagonists' ideas of themselves. But this view has taken on a life of its own, one that favors schematic judgments. According to Mosse's conception, the similarity of the two men thus explains Langbehn's unsuccessful visit to Göttingen, a similarity that prevented them from intensively exchanging ideas.[17] Upon closer examination, this view of the two men's failure to connect is hardly plausible. It marginalizes the differences of habit and intellect that existed between the eminent professor of Orientalism and the successful writer who was one generation younger than Lagarde. Furthermore, it ignores the more idealistic reasons behind Lagarde and Langbehn's interest in each other. Although later leading figures of the Völkisch movement liked to present themselves as highly altruistic, they were also calculating and single-minded people, and their appeal was not only due to the favorable climate of the times. What's decisive in terms of historical reception is that Langbehn's success supplied the senior professor from Göttingen with new readers. On the cover of his manifesto, the Rembrandtdeutsche (i.e., Langbehn) forcefully promoted the *Deutsche Schriften* as a "work of similar yet entirely independent inclinations." Like Langbehn's second great role model, Nietzsche, Lagarde stood to gain from changes in the cultural climate at the beginning of the Wilhelmine era (1890–1914). Of course, Lagarde only hazily perceived the growing receptivity.

Visibly exhausted and already showing signs of illness, Lagarde returned to Germany from a long research trip in October 1891.[18] The Göttingen specialist Julius Rosenbach diagnosed him with intestinal cancer and didn't hold out much hope. Lagarde spent the final weeks of his life in total seclusion, accompanied only by his wife. He received his favorite student, Alfred Rahlfs, for the sole purpose of discussing upcoming editorial tasks, but avoided all mention of the seriousness of his illness. At first, the operation on December 21 at the Mariahilf Hospital in Göttingen appeared to have been successful. Under the circumstances, Lagarde looked relatively good, and he even had his wife read him a recent review of the *Deutsche Schriften* at his bedside. But the recovery was only temporary. On the following day, his condition worsened dramatically. His body failed, and Lagarde was tormented by feverish ravings. His last words were, "So now I want to go to sleep."[19] He died several hours later on the evening of December 22, 1891. Lagarde's death came as a surprise to his contemporaries. People would soon go to great effort to preserve his memory.

The academic world, both German and foreign, devoted laudatory obituaries to Lagarde. A detailed bibliography was published immediately and made his widely scattered literature accessible to the public. The author praised Lagarde as "the most remarkable writer on Semitic studies that the learned world has ever seen."[20] On the first anniversary of his death, a call went out for the establishment of a Lagarde Foundation, and it was quite well received in the scientific community. Within a short time, 120 scholars had signed on to the effort, and quite a few subsequently decided to make generous donations. The purpose of the foundation was to support Lagarde's most desirable scholarly publications. But one may safely assume that a goodly portion of its members also thought highly of his critique of the academic establishment and his radical nationalism. At any rate, the draft charter pointed out that, in the *Deutsche Schriften*, Lagarde quite naturally succeeded in connecting the most learned individual research with the demands and problems of life, so that a uniform worldview emerged. People didn't have to accept Maximilian Harden's offer to start a publicity campaign for the Lagarde Foundation: the publisher of *Die Zukunft* (*The Future*) was certainly a successful journalist, but his attacks on Wilhelm II made it seem inadvisable to accept his support.[21]

The Göttinger Gesellschaft der Wissenschaften displayed the requisite composure in dealing with Lagarde's last will and testament. Although Anna de Lagarde was not prepared to forgo the right to publish purely personal documents, the Academy took over the administration of the considerable estate. There were essentially three reasons for this: First, a significant amount of money was involved that could be used in the service of scholarship but that also aroused covetousness. Second, Friedrich Althoff gave the green light from Berlin. The peculiarities of the will would not pose any legal problems for the Prussian state. The dynamic ministerial official had already informed Wilhelm II about the notable features of Lagarde's last will and testament. Althoff closed his remarkable letter with the following words: "If 'do not speak ill of the dead' may be rightly applied, then it is valid for Lagarde, who, through his service to scholarship and the vigor of his patriotic disposition, reconciled much, as the ire of his pen and his deep bitterness and excitability persuaded him to do." But Althoff did not forget to point out that Lagarde's estate amounted to "at least 60,000" gold marks.[22] Third, and not least, the Göttingen Orientalist was highly renowned for his extraordinary linguistic skills and wide-ranging oeuvre. And the Septuagint project was still a matter of prestige. Since no one in Germany was interested in his extensive library, however, his former student Paul Haupt arranged for it to be sold in the United States. As the "Lagarde Library," it found a new home at the City University of New York. The opening ceremony took place in April 1893, and the library was then available to students and researchers in the field of Orientalism.

The considerable notice taken of Lagarde's death by the journalistic world is evidence of the scholar's importance. Many feature pages reported on him, and most of them devoted more space to his authorship of the *Deutsche Schriften* than to the Orientalist himself. Cornelius Gurlitt extolled his penetrating critique of liberalism and professed to be part of the deceased man's "community." The *Illustrierte Zeitung* dramatically compared the Orientalist to Carlyle. Emphasis was placed on the equally suggestive and nonverifiable statement that Lagarde had "a large throng of silent followers."[23] In the left-wing liberal *Vossische Zeitung*, the eminent Germanist Gustav Roethe compared Lagarde to Langbehn and reached a trenchant conclusion: he could not "understand how a person could mistake the poetry of the Rembrandt book, which sprang coquettishly from one topic to another, with Lagarde's unified, hard-fought, austere, but unostentatious ideology, in which there was only room for convictions and not for opinions."[24] Ultimately, Langbehn's readers were more likely to be found among the younger generation, while Lagarde's fateful prose also spoke to established, successful citizens. Lagarde had become the favorite author of the mainly Protestant educated class, so his appeal was in no way limited to social "winners."

Lagarde was hailed in the *Akademische Blätter* as the apostle of a "new national religion."[25] This was no small matter in terms of how his ideas were received, because this newspaper was the mouthpiece of the Verband der Vereine Deutscher Studenten (VVDSt: Association of German Student Societies) and reached a wide readership. Unnerved by the situation in the academic job market, the association turned against the alleged preferential treatment of Jewish students. Since 1896, almost every branch of the association at German universities had even rejected the admission of baptized Jews. Those in the student milieu admired Lagarde as a radical national who had proclaimed civil order and, most especially, the fight against liberalism. At the same time, party supporters of political antisemitism expressed great interest in and provided subsidized copies of the *Deutsche Schriften*. In 1893, for example, the *Deutsch-Sozialen Blätter* (*German Socialist Newspaper*) put out an edition for the price of four, rather than ten, gold marks "in order to enable less well-to-do party members to purchase the work."[26]

Among the many antisemites who cited Lagarde, Theodor Fritsch proved the most energetic. In numerous articles, he styled himself Lagarde's rightful successor and stressed the late scholar's prophetic role in the antisemitic movement. Early on, Fritsch had established a good relationship with Anna de Lagarde, who wanted to spread her husband's ideas. In 1892, she did not hesitate to send Fritsch a photo of the scholar, something that Lagarde had strictly forbidden during his lifetime. Fritsch thanked her politely and subsequently portrayed himself as a faithful student of Lagarde. Needless to say, he experienced some difficulty in propagating messages that Lagarde would have endorsed. In a letter of December 8, 1897, to Lagarde's widow, he balanced the reading of two Lagarde essays with the statement that "one always feels that one's manhood has been strengthened and revitalized whenever one reads the candid words of the immortal one." Even if the celebration of manly virtues had not always been central to his thinking, the Göttingen professor had still cottoned to the theme at one time. On the other hand, Fritsch's agreement with the idea of "community building" showed truly limited comprehension. He considered it necessary "to proceed on less of a religious and more of an economic basis for the time being," a view that certainly did not jibe with Lagarde's idea of national rebirth.

Whereas Fritsch had a strong business sense, idealistic considerations were quite foreign to him. In 1902, he founded the antisemitic newspaper *Der Hammer* (*The Hammer*) and started reproducing Lagardian quotes the following year. The passages were carefully selected, mainly abridged, and manageably complex. But they were perfectly adequate for Fritsch's purposes. Calling upon Lagarde lent his obscure paper a certain respectability and allowed him to present himself as the champion of a higher cause. The Leipzig publisher desperately needed this, because he was embroiled for his entire life in disputes and lawsuits that earned him a number of fines and prison sentences. Anna de Lagarde, who now lived primarily for her husband's memory, seems to have known nothing of Fritsch's dubious reputation. On October 1, 1905, she told the subversive antisemite about her conviction that the nation had to be schooled in devout patriotism. Despite deep disappointment in the course of events, she remained undeterred in her belief that the *Deutsche Schriften* could point the way to a better future. Fritsch agreed with her from on high: "'Though the mills of God grind slowly,'" he solemnly declared, he would not give up hope "in a new day for our unhappy German people."[27] Meanwhile, the publisher of the infamous *Handbuch zur Judenfrage* (*Handbook on the Jewish Question*) had become accustomed to dealing with national-religious incantations.

In the 1890s, Lagarde's importance became most pronounced for the antisemitic movement. He, of course, remained an esteemed Orientalist who could lend historical and philological legitimacy to antisemitic value judgments. In addition, his multifarious enemy stereotypes still offered many starting points in the daily political struggle. And Lagarde's writings now began to be seen as providing outstanding access to the nationalistic discourse. His vehement criticism of the state found as much favor among antisemites as the lofty heights to which he raised the German people. Lagarde's firm conviction that Germanness lay in the soul, not in the blood, had long since lost its incontrovertible character. The cultural critic himself was largely to blame for this, because the imagery of his late writings displayed an increasingly close relationship to racial ideas. Toward the end of his life, an "ideological brew" began to emerge among his followers that combined the "biology of the blood-related community" with traditional, idealistic ideas.[28] Lagarde's pessimistic view of history could have created even greater problems for the nascent Völkisch movement. But the generation that raised a powerful voice around 1900 did not worry about such "trifles" and reinterpreted Lagarde in an optimistic light. The most successful disseminator of his ideas was the Jena cultural publisher Eugen Diederichs.

Diederichs, born near Naumburg in 1867, was among the most noteworthy figures of the fin de siècle. Following a severe nervous breakdown, this farmer's son decided to make a fresh start and began an apprenticeship in bookselling. He pursued his new career with great passion. Diederichs was innovative and eager to live life to the fullest. He went to Florence in 1897 and founded a publishing house in this meeting place of European modernity. In 1904, he moved to Jena because he wanted to build this former center of German idealism into a haven of national rebirth and the counterpart to Berlin. Diederichs strikingly combined business sense with ideological convictions. For the most part, he concentrated on producing valuable books whose print layout and Jugendstil aesthetic played a major role in sales. He had a good feeling for book market trends and a strongly developed sense of quality. Since Diederichs could not acquire the rights to Nietzsche's works, he published his favorite authors, such as Stendhal and the American poet-philosopher Ralph Waldo Emerson, whenever possible. Of the modern Russian writers, he included Maxim Gorky and Anton Chekhov alongside Leo Tolstoy on his publisher's list. Through his editions, Diederichs participated in the rediscovery of Hölderlin and Novalis. And he began a Kierkegaard edition in 1909 that was more than just a theologico-historical event. A large number of authors were involved in fundamental questions of culture and contemporary criticism. Many of them, including Arthur Bonus and Christoph Schrempf, wanted to immediately venture a spiritual fresh start. Despite Diederichs's strong commitment to the German reform movement, the international scope of his undertakings was surely never at issue.[29] At first glance and against this backdrop, it would seem astounding that he selected Lagarde, of all people, as his house author.

Diederichs was inspired by the conviction that modern culture could only find its curative power in the past and considered Lagarde a source through whom meaningful witnesses for this belief could be found. Moreover, Lagarde's mythologizing rhetoric directly invited imitation. In Lagardian style, the publisher expressed himself apodictically: "We must return to our cultural sources so as to create something new from there."[30] There were actually many prophets around the turn of the century who tried to generate interest in their message among those unnerved by the fast pace of social change. But no prophet other than Lagarde enjoyed comparable scholarly esteem. At the same time, the cultural critic from Göttingen had followers from the very same Protestant milieu that Diederichs courted. And, around 1900, many people considered national-religious renewal of paramount importance.

In addition, the simple fact could not be ignored that Lagarde's death made it markedly easier to turn him into a reform-movement author. During his lifetime, the combative scholar had scrupulously refused to accept imprecise citations. Yet he now became an object of market-driven revisions. The edition by Friedrich Daab, titled *Deutscher Glaube, Deutsches Vaterland, Deutsche Bildung* (*German Belief, German Fatherland, German Culture*), was therefore limited to highly condensed passages. Lagarde's statements were taken out of their original context and made more palatable for public consumption through targeted reductions in complexity. Significantly, the richly illustrated edition showed a preference for those powerful figures of speech employed by Lagarde to herald a later age.[31] On the other hand, his ideas on education particularly delighted those readers who saw the excessive, contemporary imparting of knowledge as a threat to the political order. Among those readers was a landowner in Pomerania who ordered one thousand copies of the *Deutsche Schriften* in order to distribute them to grammar schools.[32]

But it would be inadequate for one to place the Diederichs publishing house mainly or exclusively on the political right. Discontent with modernity had gripped large portions of the middle class, particularly among the younger generation. For example, Karl Fischer, the founder of the Steglitz *Wandervogel*, was a passionate follower of Lagarde. And he made certain that Lagarde's ideas, along with those of Langbehn, shaped the youth movement in an enduring way. The Zionist student organization in Prague, Bar Kochba, had many fine minds among its members, including Max Brod, Hans Kohn, and Robert Weltsch. And its members were also fond of studying products from the Diederichs publishing house. People in Prague showed great admiration for Martin Buber, and even he did not express any reservations. He published one of his most successful works, the *Ekstatische Konfessionen* (*Ecstatic Confessions*), in Jena, which was growing into a center of new religious and mythical endeavors.[33]

In 1912, Diederichs took over the paper *Die Tat* (*Deed*) and immediately placed it at the service of his ideological goals. He attached great importance to Lagarde's idea of an "openly secret alliance." The intentional ambiguity of the elite fraternity precisely matched his taste. And so this Lagardian formulation would adorn the letterhead of his publishing house from 1913 on: "May there at least be conspirators among us, an openly secret alliance which may plan and create that great tomorrow."[34]

The following year, Karl Lamprecht's involvement showed just how extensive the veneration of Lagarde had become. The controversial historian, whose publications rocked the academic world, established his own "Hall of Culture" at the Leipzig Book and Graphic Arts Fair. Lamprecht dedicated the hall to the history of the book trade and made a room available to Diederichs for contemporary history. Diederichs used the opportunity to present his favorite author. The publisher decided in favor of a chapel-like structure and hired the well-known architect Oscar Rohde to design it. Decorated with two statues from the Naumburg Cathedral and bathed in blue light, the structure showed Lagarde as guardian of the past and herald of a better future. These words could be seen from far away: "We want it to be born in order for all of you to live with it. If only the winds would blow our way." This statement supposedly represented an authentic quote of Lagarde's idea of an "openly secret alliance." After comparing it to the *Deutsche Schriften*, however, it becomes clear that we are really talking about Diederichs's skillful arrangement of quotes, which was meant to facilitate the connection between the pious cultural critic's ideas and the prevailing trends in new religion.[35] Its success not only substantiates the publisher's skill in creating a "mystical atmosphere" but also points out that, to a large extent, the original context of Lagarde's thinking had already been forgotten.

At the beginning of the twentieth century, Lagarde's ideas were disseminated in a number of ways. They made the rounds as partial quotes in paraphrased, often distorted forms and served entirely different interests. To a politician like Friedrich Naumann, Lagarde was simply a "great and honorable guy." Boldly revising the facts, he described Lagarde's nature as equally "German and liberal."[36] Of course, one should not classify this opinion as something that only served political purposes. Like Naumann's assessment of Nietzsche, it expressed genuine sympathy for a kind of idealism that he felt was missing in his own time. He accorded less importance to Lagarde's vehement antiliberalism. In his work *Demokratie und Kaisertum* (*Democracy and Imperial Rule*), published in 1900, Naumann conceptualized the legitimacy of the state on the basis of its power, in contrast to its foundation in law or justice, and sought ideological justification for his integrative nationalism. And Germany's need for a lofty ideological position and status in the world had certainly not lessened since that time.

Lagarde's antisemitism also played a subordinate role in how his ideas resonated with the public. He was commonly seen as an idealist whose writings' value lay mainly in their adherence to principles and their radical contemporary criticism. Hermann Bahr, a declared opponent of antisemitism, had absolutely no interest in Lagarde's anti-Jewish writings. In 1894, he published a series of spectacular interviews on the rampant hatred of Jews in which he characterized antisemitism as a shrunken form of political identity and "the little people's morphinism." Yet the Viennese writer greatly respected the author of the *Deutsche Schriften* as an incorruptible critic of the ruined educational system. In a journal entry of February 2, 1906, he noted how greatly Lagarde's critique of Prussian rote learning had impressed him. The highly touted grammar schools only contributed to memorization, while preventing any real personality development.[37] Friedrich Paulsen, the senior professor from Berlin, saw things similarly. In his famous *Geschichte des gelehrten Unterrichts* (*History of Scholarly Instruction*), he approvingly quoted Lagarde's shattering view: "Three things are the fruits of our education: bad eyes, vast revulsion at all that was, and no capacity for the future."[38] In a more moderate tone, but with an orientation akin to Lagarde's, Paulsen attributed undesirable trends in the Prussian educational system to Hegel's catastrophic influence.

At the beginning of the twentieth century, idealistic ways of understanding the world enjoyed increasing popularity. Astounding advances in the natural sciences and technology nurtured the hope in a Golden Age. At German universities, people also hoped to preserve the valuable legacy of the past. The unusual achievement of Rudolf Eucken, who saw the mission of philosophy in terms of successful universal integration, was indicative of the new discourse. Although he is only known among specialists today, the Jena professor was even awarded the 1908 Nobel Prize in literature. In his Stockholm acceptance speech, Eucken identified "a hopeful reawakening of idealism."[39] Political hotheads and literary enthusiasts also cited Lagarde on the eve of the First World War. In his aphorisms, a brooding writer like Christian Morgenstern also grappled intensively with the Göttingen cultural pessimist. Above all, he was captivated by Lagarde's gloomy language that revolved around issues of impermanence and death. Consciously following Lagarde's example, Morgenstern wrote: "Every one of us has something unhewn, unresolved in him, and working on it is his most secret mission in life." As Lagarde did before him, he considered "finding a good mother" the "best method of bringing up a child."[40]

Many others tried very hard to ignore Lagarde. Although Stefan George's concept of a "secret Germany" is admittedly very close to Lagarde's "openly secret alliance," one can hardly detect any direct references to Lagarde. Ulrich

Raulff has rightly emphasized how tenuous the philological body of evidence is for Ernst Kantorowicz's claim that George's idea constitutes a direct reference to Lagarde.[41] But the mere expression of this tie makes it an interesting find for the history of ideas. Needless to say, one should not overestimate Lagarde's intellectual influence on the middle class since, by the beginning of the twentieth century, other forces would displace him. Word got around that similar culturally skeptical ideas could be found that were expressed more shrewdly and often more brilliantly by Nietzsche. For example, Morgenstern got to know Nietzsche's late works after already reading Tolstoy and Lagarde. And Nietzsche would decisively influence Morgenstern's intellectual world from then on. But even in the last years of his life, the melancholy humorist kept faith with Lagarde. In 1907, he wrote a few verses of his poem "Niblum" in his notebook. The title is named after a small village on the North Sea island of Föhr. Its tone is equally melancholy and festive:

At Niblum shall I be buried,
on the edge twixt marsh and geest.
[. . .]
At Niblum shall I rest
from all that now is hard.
There write upon my stony house
My name and "Read Lagarde!"
Yea, only two things, large and small,
Just this request and my name, all:
My name and "Read Lagarde!"[42]

Such an enthusiastic response to Lagarde among Germany's writers may well have been the exception. On the eve of World War I, more than a few innovative minds switched from the veneration of Lagarde to that of Nietzsche. And this was because Nietzsche's radical critique of Christian morality and his call for self-determination were more in keeping with the times. In a new era, Nietzsche's Superman (Übermensch) and the Will to Power (Wille zur Macht) became code words that hardly went unnoticed by any intellectual. Richard Wagner's son-in-law, Houston Stewart Chamberlain, was possibly an even bigger star in the intellectual firmament than Nietzsche.

A German by choice who was the son of an English admiral, Chamberlain had a good relationship to the reform movement and admired Langbehn's ideas on art in particular. One year after Langbehn's death in 1907, Chamberlain married Eva Wagner and thus became a key figure in what historians would subsequently call the "Bayreuth Circle." At this point, the ambitious ideological writer was already in an influential position. He had an excellent understanding with Cosima Wagner, who was well aware of her power. In 1899, he published a book that everyone was soon talking about, an extensive monograph with the impressive title *Die Grundlagen des neunzehnten Jahrhunderts* (*The Foundations of the Nineteenth Century*). The work pleased Wilhelm II so greatly that, during the winter of 1900–1901, he recited portions of it every evening to his wife and the ladies of the court. The Prussian king attached great educational importance to Chamberlain's magnum opus, as can be seen by his immediately making it a permanent part of higher education for teachers. Wilhelm II also took a liking to the urbane cultural writer and invited Chamberlain to dine with him more and more frequently. Naturally, this aroused envy among Chamberlain's peers. But Chamberlain was able to negotiate all types of terrain. When he was once accused of "skimming the cream off the top" of court society, he replied elegantly, "This is not my doing: the cream was served to me in a little pot."[43]

Chamberlain, who was born in 1855, had passionately worshipped at the shrine of Richard Wagner from a young age. But he first became a fanatical antisemite in fin de siècle Vienna. He looked deeply into the racial ideas of the Comte de Gobineau and couldn't help feeling that the Danube metropolis was a place of "degenerate existence." Henceforth, Chamberlain saw Wagner's art as the crucial path to freedom from the baneful present. He founded the so-called Neuer Wagner Verein (New Wagner Society), which was mainly interested in the "racial content" of Wagnerian musical art forms. It was in this spirit that he wrote *The Foundations of the Nineteenth Century*, which was supposed to point out the driving forces behind human history. As with many profitable books, the work had a mundane reason to thank for its success. The Munich publisher Hugo Brackmann had commissioned "a comprehensive cultural history of nineteenth-century Europe," and Chamberlain immediately set to work on writing the entire work, which was conceived in three parts.[44] Although the first part brought him a great deal of success, he would never get beyond it. But since the work perfectly reflected the inner conflict of the Wilhelmine era, a continuation was also not necessary. While it invoked the supremacy of Nordic peoples, it also warned of contemporary moral decline. And it spoke equally to the hopes and fears of its readers. On the positive side, the Nordic foundation of German culture ultimately seemed to guarantee positive future prospects. By 1915, the work had gone through twelve editions and more than one hundred thousand copies had sold. This was also a result of its distinctive style. Chamberlain was a master of the kinds of solemn formulations that the educated middle class simply loved, particularly if the author spiced them up with pinches of brutality. In addition, the work could be read as a prelude to the dawn of a new century and offered the seductive illusion that, at the beginning of the twentieth century, a clear view of the entire cultural universe was still possible.

The main hypothesis of *The Foundations of the Nineteenth Century* is the simplest thing imaginable: racial conflicts had shaped the course of history since time immemorial, and the development of European civilization was actually to be understood as nothing more than the conflict between Semitic and Aryan peoples. Chamberlain's interpretation of Christianity was an especially important point. He emphatically stressed that Jesus was an Aryan and argued for this view in very general terms. In particular, only Aryans had the sort of idealism that characterized Jesus' behavior at every turn. This was a historical hodgepodge of the highest order that denied the Jewish roots of the New Testament and fundamentally delegitimized Judaism. At the same time, Chamberlain was convinced that the future of mankind would also be marked by racial conflicts and that appropriate marriages were indispensable to a society's prosperity. Chamberlain justified his eugenic statements by referring to Charles Darwin's theory of the survival of the fittest, which he applied to society by means of bold analogies.[45] He made the controversial claim that he was more a follower of Darwin than Wagner, which, in Bayreuth, only led to an even greater emphasis on the racial dimension of Wagner's works.

Chamberlain chose Lagarde as one of his most important sources, even though the Orientalist from Göttingen showed no inclination to support the theory of an Aryan Jesus. But this was of secondary importance to the self-confident autodidact. He was interested in those passages in which Lagarde emphasized the intrinsic differences between Judaism and Christianity. In essence, this came down to the abasement of Yahweh, whom Chamberlain presented as the "prototype of [. . .] the quarrelsome, vengeful Jew."[46] Concerning the significance of post-Christian Judaism, he stated both categorically and pejoratively: "Nothing remained of true, Jewish thought after Jesus' lifetime. As when construction of the Temple was completed, the scaffolding could be removed." In the same vein, he referred back to Lagarde's idea that the word *messiah* came from Mesopotamia and gave it an antisemitic edge. To Chamberlain, only the aura of the Orientalist's specialized knowledge mattered; the actual substance of that knowledge no longer did. What he had in common with the "truly Germanic man, Paul de Lagarde" was somewhat nebulous anyway. Lagarde was of the opinion that religion was "absolutely contemporary." Chamberlain saw this as a mystical worldview that could open the way to national rebirth.

As vague as these notions may seem to us, they would absolutely have resonated with Chamberlain's contemporaries. One may wish to dispute whether Chamberlain's philosophy of history "widely corresponded to the self-image of the nationalist, Protestant educated middle class." After all, by speculatively forging ahead, he had distanced himself from many certainties of the scholarly worldview, whose achievements were there for all to see. In terms of the ability to connect to the "redemption scenarios circulating" around 1900, Chamberlain didn't need to fear comparison with anyone.[47]

After Chamberlain's success, many people in decidedly *völkisch* circles thought Lagarde was not radical enough. For purposes of illustration, we shall refer to Gustaf Kossinna, a linguist and professor of German archeology at the University of Berlin. He expressly distanced himself from Lagarde by stating: "The blood must first create the soul. [. . .] Our long-deceased ancestors have not only bequeathed us their flesh and blood, but their ideas, spirits, and character as well." Needless to say, this does not appear to have been the majority opinion. That is presumably in part because, at the beginning of the twentieth century, Lagarde's voluntarism harmonized superbly with the rhetoric of self-mobilization. At any rate, in scrutinizing the *völkisch* literature, one finds no lack of Lagarde citations. For example, Wilhelm Schwaner cited him very matter-of-factly in his *Germanen-Bibel* (*Bible of Germanic Peoples*). The Völkisch movement accorded Schwaner considerable importance in terms of codification. The selected passages from Lagarde appeared in randomly simplified form and, although unproved, were supposed to prove compatible with the sectarian Germanic cult. Lagarde was listed alongside his archenemy, Bismarck, under "men of words and deeds," a pairing that would surely have incensed the Orientalist.[48]

Lagarde also acquired new readers in the wake of broad receptivity to Chamberlain. The chairman of the Pan-German League, Heinrich Class, expressly mentioned Lagarde alongside Chamberlain and Gobineau. In 1912, under the pseudonym Daniel Frymann, he wrote the polemical pamphlet *Wenn ich der Kaiser wär* (*If I Were Kaiser*), which called for a culturally and racially homogeneous nation. In the spirit of Lagarde, he yearned for a strong *Führer* behind whom the elite among the German *Volk* could line up. Lagarde himself was enlisted as both a "Romantic conservative" and an "ultramodern imperialist," and his solemn words provided a variety of German nationalists with an important basis for legitimacy.[49] Lagarde's radical nationalism could be understood as an answer to the problems of the Danube monarchy and an approach to mending the culturally riven fabric of Wilhelmine society. People mainly praised him as a champion of Alldeutschtum (Pan-Germanness). And they hoped to use this resounding code word to mobilize discontented voter groups.

Needless to say, Lagarde had more to offer than strong, nationalistic language. His critique of education paved the way for followers of the Völkisch movement to take part in the central, bourgeois discourse. It worked in his favor that, for the most part, he was not considered a guiding force in Germanic ideology. In fact, his oeuvre contains comparatively few references to the culturally sustaining importance of Germanic peoples. His ideas came mainly from the world of the Brothers Grimm and German Romanticism. We should generally think of the fin de siècle boundaries of cultural history as fluid. In particular, the usual "left-right distinctions" rarely get us any further in terms of ideological positioning. Although their ideological differences were legion, many religious socialists waved "Lagarde's flag."[50] The highly idealistic tone of the *Deutsche Schriften* was what principally impressed people. And that idealism increasingly came to be seen as an up-to-date reconstruction of Fichte's ideas. The polarity of young and old was of greater significance than political positioning. Significantly, very different ideological factions could agree on the rejection of the "self-satisfied Gründerzeit." And many people thought that the novelty of an idea also spoke for its future viability.

A second factor also bears consideration. The highly fractious Völkisch movement was much smaller than it appears in many historical works. The inner core consisted of barely more than ten thousand activists who often belonged to a host of different organizations. In terms of conceptual history, the findings are also rather unspectacular. The term *völkisch* seems so characteristic to us today, yet it was nothing more than a neologism for *national(istic)* and, as a rule, that is precisely how it was used.[51] The dream of a golden past was no more exclusive to the Völkisch movement than the great hopes that people placed on the reform of child raising—and on the future altogether. On the eve of the First World War, the discussion of utopian models also reached the universities. "Dechurchification" and de-Christianization had created unease, yet theology had to respond to the major issues of the time. Given this situation, it is hardly surprising that Lagarde found numerous readers among the topmost faculty. During his lifetime, he considered himself a theologian and presented himself as such.

Lagarde's theological position centered on the link between his philological critique of the Bible and a nationalistic understanding of religion. The Orientalist shared his contemporaries' scientific beliefs. He used the body of historical knowledge to bring Christianity into question and to postulate a new national(istic) religion. But its character remained unclear, because Lagarde confined his role to that of a "prophet" who could only hint at the shape of the future. This gave his idea of a national religion a curious lack of focus. Yet it also provided that ambiguous, widely resonant veneer which was so essential to gaining broad acceptance. But this did not answer the question of how to found a radically historicized world, nor did it offer a final judgment about the soundness of biblical sources. A loosely structured group of ambitious theologians, which can be considered the nucleus of the early-twentieth-century highly controversial Religionsgeschichtliche Schule (Religio-Historical School), picked up on these problems.

It is difficult to gauge the extent of Lagarde's influence on the young Göttingen theologians who would later create havoc in their field. His rejection of epistemological speculation may be worthy of discussion, and people may have largely endorsed his call for philologically precise analysis. Surely his prize student, Alfred Rahlfs, kept the memory of the difficult scholar alive. And, in the area of apocalyptism, Lagarde possessed a good feeling for research desiderata. Nevertheless, Lagarde's violent hatred of Jews was certainly not everyone's cup of tea, and his fierce rejection of Luther naturally met with theological opposition. Moreover, by the 1890s, his strongly associative approach to religio-historical comparative studies was already fairly antiquated. An innovative thinker like Julius Wellhausen also had personal reasons to be ill disposed toward Lagarde. In 1901, on the occasion of the 150th anniversary of the Göttinger Gesellschaft der Wissenschaften, Wellhausen wrote an article about Heinrich Ewald and went so far as to avoid any mention of Lagarde.[52] Within the academic culture of the Wilhelmine era, however, this kind of *damnatio memoriae* was the exception to the rule. People in the university city knew about Wellhausen's predecessor anyway and would have understood the article as a pointed statement about the history of his own chair.

Even in the case of inherently great differences, members of the academic world usually recognized others' achievements. Although he thought Lagarde had missed the mark with his idea that "Paul had corrupted the Christian religion with his rabbinical theology," Adolf von Harnack still called Lagarde an "outstanding Protestant theologian" in his extremely influential book *Das Wesen des Christentums* (*The Essence of Christianity*). In a casual voice, he praised the willful Orientalist for his "outstanding work in patristics."[53] On the other hand, contemporaries struggled to know how to handle Lagarde's dramatic intertwining of historicist and patriotic religious motifs. Even his emphasis on religious experience could not automatically be linked to his radically historical understanding of biblical sources. The story of Ernst Troeltsch, who came into contact with Lagarde's religio-historical methodology through Alfred Rahlfs, offers a classic example of the intellectual conflicts that cropped up.

The young Troeltsch had experienced a meteoric rise. In 1891, the University of Göttingen awarded him the *venia legendi* at the age of twenty-six. He was appointed to a professorship in Bonn in 1892 and, beginning in 1894, held a chair at the University of Heidelberg. Unlike most theologians of his generation, he was clear-minded and fond of debating. For these reasons, he had a lasting impact on the intellectual atmosphere in Göttingen. The group that vigorously called for a stronger orientation toward the facticity of religion, which is shaped by life experiences in the world (*lebensweltlichen Faktizität von Religion*), and of which Troeltsch was a part, consisted of very different minds, including the New Testament scholars Wilhelm Bousset and William Wrede and the Old Testament scholars Hermann Gunkel and Alfred Rahlfs.[54] They shared the belief that theology should not lay claim to any special rights and had to follow the rules of the historico-critical method. Against this backdrop, it practically went without saying that a detailed analysis of Lagarde was necessary. Not only had the Orientalist called for a clear analysis of religio-historical sources; he had also stressed the unavoidable singularity of religious experience.

Troeltsch's 1901 lecture "Die Absolutheit des Christentums und die Religionsgeschichte" (The Absoluteness of Christianity and the History of Religion) became increasingly important. Philosophical theology held that questions concerning the nature of absolute truth could not be answered by historical means. For this reason, there was no room in history for absolute personalities. With a view to Lagarde, Troeltsch emphasized that "the construction of an absolute religion never [tended] to adhere to a historical religion [. . .] and [would] lead to the construction of a future religion on its own."[55] Thought through logically, this meant the necessary relativization of those *Geltungsansprüche* (Jürgen Habermas: validity claims) that Lagarde had championed in support of his national religion. Other aspects of Lagardian ideology were hardly capable of satisfying Troeltsch. In 1908, he expressed vehement opposition to the widespread contempt for Luther that, not least of all, found its expression in the ideological influence of Lagarde and Nietzsche: "Modern Romantics and aesthetes who" would only see in Luther "the uncouth farmer's son and the ignorant, petty bourgeois German without higher culture, the zealot and fanatic, and the scholastic who believed in devils and demons" lacked all sense of his historical importance.[56] Nevertheless, Troeltsch felt so bound to his academic teacher that he dedicated the second volume of his *Gesammelte Schriften* (*Collected Writings*) to him in 1913. Yet a more careful examination of the foreword points to an ambivalent assessment of Lagarde.

Troeltsch opposed Lagarde's antisemitism, his portrayals of Paul and Luther, and "his misjudgment of the great, modern social upheaval." These were plain words, given that rhetorical conventions permitted hardly any criticism within the context of a dedication. At the same time, he duly remarked on Lagarde's philological virtues, his "objective view of truth," and his "strong, self-assured religiosity." But the desire to draw boundaries finally overtook him, and Troeltsch ended the dedication with the hope that one would "not" search it for "the key to my teachers."[57] The surviving letters concerning this matter support this particular view by illustrating how fundamentally the "cultural Protestant" differentiated himself from Lagarde and how highly he respected his former teacher in spite of it.

On June 16, 1913, Troeltsch shared the entire dedication with Anna de Lagarde, and her reaction was anything but unreservedly positive.[58] In the sketch for her response, dated June 24, the widow's reaction was distinctly personal and pointed: "The fact that you appear as L[agarde]'s opponent in terms of very essential points and, in fact, strongly accentuate your opposition perhaps makes the approval offered elsewhere all the more effective." She reminded Troeltsch how highly her husband had once thought of him and William Wrede, and announced the publication of her Lagarde biography. The tone of the second letter, dated July 2, 1913, was more reserved. Anna de Lagarde stressed how much it would mean to her if the famous theologian would kindly accept "the little book." She asked him to consider whether the "position on the Jewish question" that she cited in it could be equated with the "conventional term *antisemitism*." In his letter of July 8, Troeltsch again brought up his clearly defined words and explained them by "the desire for truthfulness with which I wished to recognize a spiritual man who influenced me early on." He also opted for restrained wording in the matter of antisemitism. He, of course, knew very well "that this" was "no personal hatred of Jews." But since he only wished to explain his political position on Lagarde, any further distinctions had been unnecessary. Despite his conciliatory, polite tone, Troeltsch had made it clear that his attitude toward Judaism differed substantially from Lagarde's. No matter how highly one may wish to rate Troeltsch's sympathy for the author of the *Deutsche Schriften* and the cryptic cultural criticism of these writings, Lagarde's fanatical hatred of Jews was unacceptable to the liberal theologian.[59]

Two additional factors should be considered in evaluating Lagarde's influence on the educated middle class. By around 1900, the scholar from Göttingen was widely considered a selfless idealist who, in the materialistic Bismarck era, had been deprived of the acceptance he deserved. This was the result of Lagarde's unceasing effort during his own lifetime to present himself as the victim of an environment that lacked understanding. Lagarde's antisemitism was certainly a main component of his ideology. Yet, as with Langbehn, many readers viewed his hatred of Jews as a relatively unimportant side issue. On the other hand, granting antisemitism the importance of a shibboleth was anything but essential in the late nineteenth century. And that's why many cultural Zionists toyed with the idea that racial accusations waged by German society could possibly aid in their own discovery of Judaism. A key figure in the Jewish Renaissance like Martin Buber thought more highly of national awakening than he did of the antisemitic divide that opened up in the process.[60]

Lagarde's great personal magnetism was the central factor in how history would view him. He found admirers among Jews, Catholics, and Protestants who thought highly of his vague rhetoric and critique of civilization. Anarchistic idealists could show as much enthusiasm for his ideas as surly civil servants. The educated middle class loved the way he charismatically electrified the German nation. In many respects, the list of his fin de siècle exponents reads like a Who's Who of the intellectual world: the philosopher Paul Natorp, for example, and the educator Friedrich Paulsen. The sociologist Ferdinand Tönnies paid Lagarde's ideas as much respect as did those of Ernst Troeltsch and Friedrich Naumann. And the highly gifted journalist Maximilian Harden valued Lagarde's decisiveness and religious pathos every bit as much as did the brooding Christian Morgenstern. It may not be all that helpful to distinguish between the influence of the "hard" and "soft" Lagarde, at least not too categorically.[61] The majority of his readers responded indecisively and inconclusively to the many messages contained in the *Deutsche Schriften*. Hardly anyone was interested in just one aspect of his thinking, especially since the interconnected references were apparent. Harsh enemy stereotypes determined the inner and outer borders of his integrative nationalism, which also lived from his promises of participation.

Lagarde was an ecstatic visionary and a shrewd critic of the deplorable state of contemporary affairs. And it was precisely this double-sided persona that explained his attractiveness for so many intellectual followers in Wilhelmine society. His texts thematized "doubt concerning the casualties of modernity,"[62] yet still gave people hope of a better and, indeed, entirely different kind of future. The reason for this conception lay in Lagarde's eschatological historical thinking itself. Only the downfall of the degenerate present offered the possibility of the coming of God's kingdom and was, therefore, seen positively from an inner perspective. This idea, which seems strange to us today, was pretty much taken for granted around 1900 and made Lagarde seem like an absolutely classic author of the neo-Romantic–Vitalistic Zeitgeist. Needless to say, radical critics of contemporary life rarely considered the extent to which they were or were not part of bourgeois culture. An irreconcilable intertwinement of feelings of security, hopes of salvation, and intellectual eagerness to experiment shaped the Central European bourgeois world that, in August 1914, became the *Welt von gestern* (*World of Yesterday*, Stefan Zweig's autobiography).

Throughout the First World War, the importance of the history of ideas and mentalities can hardly be overestimated. The nineteenth-century belief in progress was swallowed up by mechanized mass death on the Western Front and the dismal daily routine of the trenches. In view of the brutal acts of war and hunger on the home front, people's trust in social values declined palpably. And the *Krieg der Geister* ("War of the Minds") was fought with great energy, nearly turning the battlefield success of one's own nation into the ultimate value. All of this fit in well with interest in Lagarde, who had tied his call for a national religion to the glorification of Germanness.

In the propaganda war, Lagarde's ideas served to shore up the call to victory and won broad popularity, albeit in a highly oversimplified form. The sharp social critic became the heroic author of nationalistic aphorisms whose idea of German superiority would have appealed to the simplest hearts and minds. At the same time, his views made their way into frontline books and armed forces' mail service editions. Anna de Lagarde rejoiced whenever she thought about the broader impact of the *Deutsche Schriften*. "Right at the start and in the course of our Great War, Lagarde has come to life," she said emphatically. Continuing with satisfaction, she said: "It is the good fortune of my stage in life to see the recognition of this often unappreciated, yea mocked and reviled, man."[63] Doubts concerning the justice of the matter itself did not plague her. Paul de Lagarde had clearly shown her the exceptional nature of the German nation. In the spirit of Lagarde, she stated incontrovertibly: "We *were* conceived and brought to life as God's greatest people." She had no problem with Diederichs's editorial intervention in Lagarde's texts. Rather, she explicitly praised the smart publisher for championing her husband "out of genuine patriotic feeling."

In the first months of the war, many voices were heard concluding that God's blessing was the result of the purity of German patriotism. Moderate cultural Protestants like Martin Rade, the publisher of *Die Christliche Welt* (*The Christian World*), lastingly supported mobilization and called for "Everyone to the trenches!" His article appeared in the previously mentioned weekly paper, which had earned considerable respect as the flagship publication of liberal German Protestantism. So it was hardly coincidental that the paper had opened its columns to Lagarde's ideas and presented him as a prophet of the German people since 1914. Rade's friendship with Arthur Bonus may have contributed to the inclusion of Lagardian ideas. At the beginning of the twentieth century,

Bonus had already begun to champion the Germanization of Christianity in the Lagardian sense. But the number of articles concerning Lagarde that appeared in *Die Christliche Welt* during World War I may also point to increased public interest in Lagarde.[64]

By 1900, the nationalization of God was no longer a rarity. In the Netherlands, *Theologennationalismus* (clerical nationalism) took on rigid traits and emphasized the uniqueness of its own Calvinist tradition. In large nations like England, France, and Germany, the sacred history of one's own country gained momentum and enjoyed increasing popularity. During the First World War, harsh enemy stereotypes and the need to make sense of the chaos and destruction caused a powerful intensification of this trend. The methodical theologian Hermann Mulert had already portrayed Lagarde as a "Classicist of Religion" in 1913. He also emphasized how important independent thought was to Lagarde's religious ideology. Rade's friend Mulert now automatically exalted Lagarde as a prophet of German faith and firmly stated: "Religion will inevitably become nationalistic. God's plan for the world will be realized in the history of the [German] people."[65] In general, Lagarde's followers felt validated by the course of events and did all they could to assist the German nation. A typical example would be the Berlin Germanist Gustav Roethe, who, among other things, condemned the "lethargic pleasure-seeking" and "despicable acquisitive greed" of the prewar era in a talk he gave on September 3, 1914.[66] Numerous intellectuals solemnly swore to him that the German nation had regained its unity and overcome peacetime partisan politics and greed.

Thomas Mann was probably the most well-known admirer of Lagarde throughout the Great War. In 1919, following the war's close, Mann sang the praises of the Göttingen scholar as "Germany's preceptor" in his *Betrachtungen eines Unpolitischen* (*Observations of a Nonpolitical Man*). He also expressed certainty that Lagarde, like Nietzsche and Wagner, would have to be counted among Germany's "great men."[67] Behind such statements were the defiant convictions that German culture went substantially deeper than superficial Western civilization and that Germany had found its own way into the Modern Age. The culturally pessimistic tone of Mann's criticism of Western democracy, a political form that was allegedly alien to the German people, rightly came under attack, and he later withdrew his claims to the notion. But the ease with which ideological criticism proved useful in this case should not obscure the ideological heights to which many people took Germanness during the First World War.

Essential attributes such as these are not the sole province of the political right, nor do they represent purely German traits. The mere intensity of the propaganda war against the Entente, particularly against Germany's ideological archenemy, England, prompted the need to invoke the past in monumentally nationalistic ways. Even Jewish intellectuals would occasionally cite Lagarde or Fichte with affirmative intent. Nahum Goldmann viewed each thinker as the latest embodiment of the Hebrew prophets. Goldmann also hoped to win the kaiser over to the Zionist idea.[68] But, in wartime, those voices that emphatically insisted on the essential affinity between Germanness and Jewishness became less important. The most important reason for this was rampant antisemitism and, despite the boldly proclaimed "truce," it would soon set the political tone on the domestic front.

Having reached the height of his fame during the First World War, Chamberlain probably did more harm than anyone. He pompously referred to the words of Wilhelm II that he was "God's gift to the German people in their fight for survival."[69] His *Kriegsaufsätze* (*Wartime Essays*) were the most widely read German-language works in the War of the Minds. The first edition alone sold 75,000 copies. It first appeared as if Chamberlain's work took aim at the materialistically oriented English nation. But a closer inspection showed that it favored topoi that already had antisemitic connotations prior to 1914. Chamberlain, who received German citizenship in 1916, accused the English of greed, envy, and obstinate rejection of the Christian faith. People at the Verein zur Abwehr des Antisemitismus (Society for the Resistance of Antisemitism) consciously decided to take action against Chamberlain's wartime writings. But the success of their campaign was negligible, if only because the society printed up so few explanatory brochures.

The self-educated Chamberlain valued Lagarde for his sharp invectives against the "corrupt professorial world," invectives that reinforced Chamberlain's own self-image as a heroic prophet of a new age. He repeatedly pointed out how important the cultural critic from Göttingen had been in the development of his own worldview and backed it up by invoking the outward perception of Lagarde as an ultranationalistic ideologue. Neo-Fichtian ideological writers like the pedagogue Ernst Krieck did one more thing to cement Lagarde's image as a harbinger of national rebirth. Krieck praised Lagarde as the ideal synthesis of Treitschke's nationalistic and Nietzsche's cultural fixations, thereby moving him closer to two other thinkers whom the English considered exponents of the sinister German *Sonderweg* (special path toward tyranny).[70] In the War of the Minds, it must surely have come down to argumentative clashes that could not simply be dismissed on purely ideological grounds. And many a scholar was fully aware that the "war" could not last forever, that a new way of life would have to be found. Nevertheless, one should not take the destruction of the international republic of scholars for a mere footnote in the history of ideas. Renowned scholars gave back their awards, universities dissolved partnership agreements, while belief in the absolute or, at least, the higher rightness of their own cause fostered a crusader mood. All this left a permanent mark on society.

The reminiscences of the Oxford Assyriologist Archibald Henry Sayce proved just how thoroughly the cultural climate had been poisoned. The recognized scholar, who had once corresponded with Lagarde, reported on Lagarde's habit of having his Hebrew books bound in pigskin, "as he said, 'to keep the dirty fingers of the Jews off them.'"[71] As abysmal as Lagarde's anti-semitism was, Sayce's recollection did not correspond to the facts and certainly did not contribute anything to the understanding of his intellectual world. The ideological aftereffects were even more profound in Germany. The academic elites who had propagated boundless wartime goals and invested the bulk of their fortunes in war loans stood speechless in the face of defeat. They had been deceived by hopes of victory, and the profound shock left hardly a single conviction of bourgeois ideology untouched. The far-reaching existentialization of the discourse that had already shaped wartime thinking carried on at the beginning of the Weimar Republic and gave rise to lasting interest in Lagarde's dark cultural pessimism.

14 Guiding Intellectual Force of National Socialism

Wide sections of the bourgeoisie mourned the Kaiserreich and looked upon the Weimar Republic as alien. The Treaty of Versailles, in particular, was seen as an expression of despotic "justice" on the part of the victors and was vehemently rejected. Hardly anyone expressed faith in the future, given the millions of dead and crippled, Germany's political isolation, and the debt burden of the Reich. The unusual success of Oswald Spengler's *Untergang des Abendlandes* (*The Decline of the West*) was characteristic of the prevailing bleak mood. Spengler's work was completed in 1917, when Germans still anticipated a victorious end to the war. By the time of publication in 1918, this extensive cultural morphology was seen as a portent of European decline. An atmosphere of pessimism and disaffection with the state predominated, leaving parliamentarianism open to every sort of radical critique. Precious few of the leading elites visibly defended the new polity. The nationalistic right finally won the fight over who benefited symbolically from the First World War. "National rebirth" was the watchword, and fascination with cultural criticism escalated along similar lines.[1]

Since his deification of art had yielded precious little in the propagandistic conflict, August Julius Langbehn had only played a minor role in the War of the Minds. After the war, his book, *Rembrandt als Erzieher*, was greeted with new interest in his enigmatic, yet fundamental, social criticism. A new edition and an illustrated popular edition compiled by Hans Kellermann appeared within a short time. The response to Lagarde was presumably even more favorable. In the resentment-filled climate of the first postwar years, he offered brusque antiliberal and antisemitic enemy stereotypes that were embraced beyond just the political right. His attacks on the ruling elite and his disaffection with the state struck a chord with many people. Lagarde's praise for the little man, combined with his wish to return to the good old days, offered an opportunity for personal identification and maudlin self-pity. Lastly, his solemn diction impressed those who felt damaged by wartime defeat and wanted to preserve the integrity of German culture without fail. Armin Mohler's attitude was indicative of such responses. His work about the so-called conservative revolution is not only useful as a source of biographical information but also as a means to better understand a world that has become remote to us. It seemed certain to Mohler, who was Ernst Jünger's secretary for a time, that the true impact of Lagarde and

Langbehn was not felt until after the wartime defeat, at which point their use in the tricky process of "regaining German identity" met with greater understanding.[2] Surely this was an exaggeration, but it still illustrates how intently people tried to solve the problems of the future by idealizing their national heritage.

The copyright on Lagarde's works ran out in December 1921, thirty years after his death, and many renowned publishers expressed interest in his oeuvre. Lagarde anthologies were published by Bärenreiter in Augsburg, Langenscheidt in Berlin, Insel, Kröner, Reclam, and J. B. Teubner in Leipzig, J. F. Lehmann in Munich, as well as Schöningh in Paderborn.[3] Even in consideration of Lagarde's heightened popularity and his approaching centenary in 1927, the sheer number of editions that made it onto the market is astounding. All publishers banked on the basic intelligibility of their books. They copied Diederichs's successful Wilhelmine era strategy and presented the cultural pessimist from Göttingen as a "prophet of *Deutschtum*" (Germanness). Yet Diederichs did not give up without a fight and, although he lacked a monopoly position, he continued to publish and vigorously promote Lagarde. The Munich publisher Julius Friedrich Lehmann occupied a key position in the *völkisch* arena on account of his numerous political contacts. Lehmann had been an avid reader of Lagarde before the Great War and was utterly captivated by the importance of the *Deutsche Schriften*. Like so many supporters of the Völkisch movement, he believed that the real cause of the contemporary cultural crisis lay in the betrayal of *Deutschtum*. And he placed the blame for losing the war on the actions of the "inner enemy." In October 1918, Lehmann called for a coup d'état and, shortly thereafter, supported the extreme right-wing Deutsch-Völkischer Schutz und Trutzbund (DVSTB: German Nationalist Protection and Defiance Federation). The slogan of the federation, "Germany for Germans," sounded very familiar to antisemitic ears.[4]

Even in the Weimar Republic, Lagarde never entirely lost his educated middle-class aura, which is why there was still a special quality in the way people responded to him. And so the name of the theologian and Orientalist lived on in cultural Protestantism. Regardless of his inordinate critique of Luther and his unacceptable rejection of Pauline Christianity, people valued Lagarde for his sense of history and his upright religious convictions. When Ernst Troeltsch died on February 1, 1923, the obituaries showed that people took Lagarde's influence on the left-wing liberal theologian very much for granted.[5] A sizable number of publications were meant to show Lagarde's importance for the German educational tradition. Even Ludwig Schemann's substantial biography largely avoided an aggressive political tone. He presented Lagarde as a heroic outsider whose admission to the pantheon of outstanding scholars was assured. And so the Wagnerian, Schemann, broadcast the very image of Lagarde that Bayreuthers held in high regard, one in which middle-class respectability and ideological radicality seemed to effortlessly converge.

The most influential intellectual in the Bayreuth Circle was still Chamberlain. His antisemitism had gone through a profound metamorphosis in the Great War. In place of salvation through "Aryan Christianity," the metaphysical significance of *Deutschtum* now stood at the center of his reflections and, beginning in 1916, he espoused increasingly totalitarian views. The hypostatization of the German people would not only legitimize draconian measures taken against national enemies but would also guarantee a successful outcome to the war. After the surrender of the Central Powers, Chamberlain's strategy of rhetorical one-upmanship made an understandably antiquated impression. And interest in his glorification of Nordic peoples declined in the wake of traumatic defeat.[6] With sales topping sixty thousand, Spengler's *Untergang des Abendlandes* now shaped the public discourse. Its maudlin but dark tone was a good match for the gloomy future outlook. Even so, Chamberlain still possessed considerable symbolic capital on the nationalistic right, which did not want to resign itself to the war's outcome or Germany's loss of status as a great power.

When Adolf Hitler visited Bayreuth in September 1923, he paid his respects to the then-frail ideological writer. Chamberlain was impressed with the party leader's energy and expressed his thanks in an unusual letter of October 7. In lofty diction, he praised Hitler as a creative man who would change the world. After just a single encounter, Chamberlain was irrevocably convinced of Hitler's national mission. "The fact that Germany has borne a Hitler in the hour of its greatest need is a testament to how alive Germany really is," he wrote euphorically, giving hard-to-beat legitimacy to the key figure of a small, sectarian party.[7] He accorded almost messianic importance to the chairman of the National Socialist German Workers' Party (NSDAP), and Chamberlain's admiration for him did not change one iota when Hitler served a sentence in Landsberg Prison after the failed Munich putsch. Hitler, in turn, studied *The Foundations of the Nineteenth Century* while working on *Mein Kampf*. After his release from prison, he published Chamberlain's letter for propagandistic purposes. In January 1927, Hitler put in an appearance at Chamberlain's funeral, which sent the message that he saw himself as the legitimate heir to antisemitism in Bayreuth. A January 11, 1927, obituary in the *Völkische Beobachter* (*National Observer*) extolled Chamberlain as a spiritual forger in the "struggle for survival that peoples must often persist in for centuries."[8]

Ernst Nolte may have rightly advocated the thesis that one does not have to invoke the prophets of German nationalism in order to understand the atmosphere in which Hitler's worldview could take effect.[9] But this in no way proves that studies in historical reception are futile as a means of understanding the nationalistic right. For there were very few ideological maxims in the works of Arndt, Fichte, Treitschke, or Lagarde that were cited favorably, and these mainly served to support contemporary interests. The nationalist "German Bible," for example, preferred to place Lagarde in the political sphere. Chamberlain thought of him as a necessary counterweight to Bismarck's state-centric approach and an "auxiliary political genius."[10] The range of responses to Lagarde among the right wing was also immense. It stretched from *völkisch* circles, which cited Lagarde's rejection of Prussia and his hymn of praise for the Germanic past, to strictly statist Hindenburg supporters in the presidential elections of 1925. The image of the prophet of German national religion sparkled in many colors, and that even extended to his assessment of Judaism.

A surprising take on Lagarde's perception of Judaism came from the journalist Mario Krammer, who in 1925 published an anthology with the highbrow title *Die Wiedergeburt durch Lagarde* (*Rebirth through Lagarde*), which he provided with an in-depth introduction. In solemn language, he placed the Orientalist in close proximity to Friedrich Nietzsche, Stefan George, Theodor Fontane, and Gottfried Keller. Krammer made positive comments about Lagarde's organic world-picture and emphasized the geopolitical dimension of his thinking. Lagarde's religious ideas were of outstanding importance and were not limited to his fundamental rejection of Protestantism. Rather, he had a pronounced feeling for the religious character of nations and "had emphasized the beauty of the Jewish rite" like no one else.[11] Krammer's strange synthesis of philosemitic and *völkisch* trains of thought led him to conclude that Judaism had to free itself from "the 'stale air' of the Pentateuch and the Talmud." As a result, he looked upon Lagarde as the immediate forerunner of Theodor Herzl and Herzl's idea of the "new Jewish man."

After their experiences in the First World War, however, Zionist circles had become more cautious in borrowing ideas from supporters of radical German nationalism. Moreover, the Balfour Declaration of 1917 opened up political options that were not especially conducive to ideological high-flying. Martin Buber no longer wanted to give much thought to his glorification of war, for example. In the movement known as Brit Shalom (Covenant of Peace), he made a dedicated yet ultimately futile attempt to support the peaceful coexistence of Arabs and Jews in Palestine. This does not mean, of course, that the pathos of Lagarde's nationalistic understanding of religion had no effect on young Jewish intellectuals. In 1924, Leo Strauss explicitly highlighted Lagarde's contemporaneity in Buber's leading cultural periodical, *Der Jude* (*The Jew*). "However great his leanings toward the Germano-Christian Middle Ages," Strauss wrote, Lagarde still belonged to modernity if only for his affirmative ideas on labor.[12] Despite his fascination with Lagarde, Strauss did not give the Orientalist's ideas his unconditional approval. He could admittedly relate to Lagarde's criticism of fossilized postbiblical Judaism, but Lagarde's Fichte-influenced metaphysics of *Deutschtum* remained alien to Strauss. He was also convinced that Lagarde's influence on Zionism had to be regarded as a fleeting phenomenon in the history of ideas.

On the other hand, there was a very close connection between Lagarde and the cultural criticism of the Weimar Republic. Even a dyed-in-the-wool republican like the Catholic historian Franz Schnabel did not shy away from approvingly citing Lagarde. At the 1929 New Year's celebration in Baden, he hailed the cultural pessimist as a critic "of alienation in German life" and a prophet of the approaching "spiritual catastrophe."[13] Schnabel generally admired the powerful diction and intellectual integrity that allowed Lagarde to spurn all half-measures. With this in mind, Schnabel interpreted the *Deutsche Schriften* as written proof of an upright idealism that one seldom encountered in the political life of the Weimar Republic. He assessed Langbehn's contemporary criticism along similarly positive lines. Both thinkers were assigned the "role of living consciences" of the nation. And their "reawakening" was, therefore, anything but a mere coincidence.

Even in the case of a once-in-a-century work like Heidegger's *Sein und Zeit* (*Being and Time*), one should not forget that, in addition to his own philosophical profundity, the author largely owed his success to meaningful contact with culturo-critical figures of thought. However much he disapproved of German idealism, Heidegger masterfully employed Romantic topoi whenever he wanted to unmask the alienation of modern life. In this respect, at least, he was part of the tradition of Nietzschean social criticism, which used the "uglification and banalization of the world" as an opportunity for fundamental reflection.[14] As did Lagarde before him, Heidegger felt like an outsider and a radical critic of a university system that glossed over every serious, intellectual debate with empty rhetoric. Despite a certain amount of biographical and intellectual common ground, Heidegger is unlikely to have had a great deal to do with Lagarde, who responded with obvious disinterest to genuinely philosophical questions. At any rate, Lagarde's culturally pessimistic images were taken so much for granted in post–World War I Germany that they were no longer inevitably associated with their author. But the fact that *Sein und Zeit*'s publication coincided with the hundredth anniversary of Lagarde's birth remains evocative.

Lagarde's favorite student, Alfred Rahlfs, gave the ceremonial address at the centenary celebration, which took place at the Göttinger Gesellschaft der Wissenschaften on November 5, 1927. The first archivally based biography came out of the centenary in 1928, and it focused on Lagarde's Orientalist oeuvre. In accordance with his last will and testament, the study was also devoted to several contentious incidents in his scholarly life that Lagarde wanted reexamined after his death. But, in the end, the solemnly pious, personally grateful work touched on very few delicate matters and created no major waves.

The Göttingen adjunct professor Wilhelm Mommsen wrote a paper just in time for the anniversary. Inasmuch as he was a decidedly left-wing liberal humanities scholar, the modern historian continued the legacy of his famous grandfather. An enthusiastic follower of Friedrich Naumann, Mommsen helped found the Reichsbund Demokratischer Studenten (National Federation of Democratic Students) in 1919. Along with his academic mentor, Friedrich Meinecke, he also took part in the founding of the Weimar Circle, an informal organization of professors who were loyal to the constitution and supported the republic out of rational considerations. The circle comprised such different thinkers as Hans Delbrück, Gustav Radbruch, and Alfred Weber, all of whom agreed that, for domestic and power-political reasons, the integration of the working class into the state was indispensable. Yet most of them remained committed to Kaiserreich values.[15]

Wilhelm Mommsen, whose ambitious topic was "Paul de Lagarde als Politiker" (Paul de Lagarde as Politician), ardently wished for an appointment, as did so many other adjunct professors in the wake of the economic catastrophe of 1923. Irrespective of the celebratory occasion, Mommsen opted for a critically differentiated presentation of Lagarde rather than a monumentally affirmative one. He underscored Lagarde's contemporary isolation and the ivory-tower, intellectual heaviness of his political reform proposals. To interpret the essay as a pointed rebuke of Lagarde's racial misinterpretations, which had gained importance among the *völkisch* right, would presumably be going too far. But Mommsen's rigorous historicization still showed that Lagarde was very deeply rooted in the intellectual world of the Romantic era. Johann Gottlieb Fichte and Jacob Grimm were named as the most important sources of Lagarde's ideas. And Lagarde's objectives were "not pan-German, as people often believed, but Central European."[16] Mommsen thus placed the cultural pessimist in close proximity to Friedrich Naumann, who, with peaceful intentions, had once called for an expansionist national policy. In the end, Mommsen adopted a historical approach that situated Lagarde more as a product of his own time than in terms of his modern influence. The modern historian fully presented

Lagarde's critique of Bismarck, which he personally felt was unrealistic and anachronistic in many respects.

Mommsen had presented an offprint to certain colleagues, and their replies illustrate the reservations that future historians had about Lagarde. On a postcard dated November 24, 1927, the Heidelberg professor Willy Andreas admitted that he had never liked Lagarde, because "all of his findings and insights" tended toward exaggeration and pettiness.[17] In Munich, the mighty Hermann Oncken saw things similarly. He pointed out that, "as a rule," Lagarde's judgments "lagged behind whatever he was criticizing." Oncken also expressed skepticism along similar lines when entrusted with providing a second opinion about a Munich dissertation. The study in question by Richard Breitling placed Lagarde within the history of pan-German thinking, but had to deal with the problem that Lagarde had not explicitly mentioned the arguably most important theoretician, Constantin Frantz. The long-winded dissertation, in which the author was reticent to form opinions, did not meet with much of a response, although Breitling's renowned "dissertation supervisor," Karl Alexander von Müller, had provided it with a foreword that stressed the topicality of the erstwhile unrecognized "prophet" Lagarde.[18] This reticence may be attributed to the liberal orientation of "Lesser Germany" in the historical scholarship of the German university. Thus, a liberal writer such as Breitling would have had great reservations about discussing concepts drawn from another political current such as Lagarde's archconservatism.

On the other hand, Hans Rothfels, who had surrounded himself with a group of disciples at the University of Königsberg, displayed genuine enthusiasm for Lagarde. Many students belonged to the Deutsch-Akademische Gildenschaft, an academic fraternity that espoused pursuing a revision of the Treaty of Versailles, the concept of a Greater Germany, and aggressive expansionist aspirations. In his anniversary article for the *Königsberger Allgemeine Zeitung*, the historian Rothfels emphasized Lagarde's "Faustian effort" and how deeply he had suffered in his own lifetime. He described the cultural critic as one "of the most peculiar and most original thinkers" of the nineteenth century: he was "the progenitor of antisemitism and, at the same time, the author of the statement that *Deutschtum* lay in the spirit and not in the blood." His inner turmoil and profound ambivalence were the very things that ensured Lagarde's contemporary relevance. "So he drifted," as Rothfels saw it, "on a tide of generational feeling that strikes one as extremely familiar today."[19] Karl Berger struck a similar, youth-movement-oriented tone in the paper of the Bund völkischer Lehrer Deutschlands (German Teachers Association). He expressly emphasized the timely need for a fight against parliamentarianism, liberalism, and Judaism. He hailed Lagarde as a German national prophet who had recognized decades ago that a "people without space (*Raum*)" was an ominous state of affairs.[20] He was alluding here to Hans Grimm's famous novel that was the "talk of the town" in the Weimar Republic.

The University of Göttingen was thinking along similar lines when, on the occasion of Lagarde's one-hundredth birthday, it decided to confer an honorary doctorate on Grimm, who hailed from Lippoldsberg. The official doctoral certificate praised "the creator of the epic of a people without space who, with the same independent spirit and the same passionate heart for a Greater Germany, made his fate visible with the prophetic power of the poet," as Lagarde had once done. These were words befitting Grimm, who pointed out in his acceptance speech that, in the course of his career and despite considerable resistance, he had come closer to "the life of his own *Volk*."[21] Lagarde had voiced his opinion on a wealth of controversial political issues and special scholarly problems. And he had long since become the classic example of an upright, universally comprehensible nationalist attitude. This perception reached its zenith with Alfred Rosenberg, who used the name Lagarde as a code word for national renewal.

From early on, the National Socialist (NS) ideologue was enthusiastic about Lagarde. He was captivated by the extreme nationalism of the *Deutsche Schriften* and the unyielding way in which Lagarde stated his ideological convictions. The ethnically German emigrant from the Baltics shared Lagarde's concept of a Greater Germany and his hatred for the smugly well-to-do bourgeois world. One can even see personal similarities between the two outsiders. Like Lagarde, Rosenberg oscillated between megalomaniacal fantasies and fear of failure. And both men suffered from the feeling that a hostile world had denied them true recognition. After both of his parents died at a young age, Rosenberg was raised by two aunts. He styled himself a real man who faced every problem with resolute seriousness. Of course, one should not rely too heavily on individual psychology to understand Rosenberg, because hardly any details about his early childhood are known. In addition, his involvement with the most renowned advocates of German national religion obviously had numerous explanations. Given the severity of political disputes, he was particularly convinced that National Socialism could only triumph if people followed NS ideology like a religion. Just two months before the scholar's one-hundredth birthday, Rosenberg wrote a eulogistic article for the *Völkischer Beobachter* (*National Observer*). He began with these words: "Among the men who were once called prophets of a new ideology and architects of the *völkisch* state, one shines especially brightly: Paul de Lagarde."[22] As was his wont, Rosenberg offered a collage of quotations that were intended to simulate authenticity. But their actual purpose was to serve his own objectives. He emphasized the topicality of the "conservative revolutionary," whose intention allegedly consisted of "preserving the old, ancient essential being of the [German] nation and race." At the same time, he saw Lagarde's idea of national rebirth as a weapon to self-confidently resist a hostile environment.

The crux of all radically *völkisch* Lagarde interpretations was that the professor from Göttingen had not professed his racism as unequivocally as he might have. Conversely, there were plenty of statements in his oeuvre that contained reservations about "materialistic racial ideology." But since the vehemence of Lagarde's hatred toward the Jews was scarcely in doubt and the original contexts of his thought had long since been forgotten, people were happy to place him on the extreme right as a committed racist. By dedicating his third period-novel, *Die Sünde wider die Liebe* (*The Sins against Love*), to Lagarde, an antisemitic writer like Artur Dinter could strategically harmonize these elements for his audience. The work was not actually as successful as his first, *Die Sünde wider das Blut* (*The Sins against Blood*), which sold two hundred thousand copies.

Rosenberg primarily tended to view scholarly documents in terms of their value for the political fight. Significantly, he presented Lagarde as an intellectual guiding force in the development of the National Socialist blood concept (*Blutsidee*) in the first volume of the 1930 *Nationalsozialistische Monatshefte* (*National Socialist Monthly Magazine*).[23] That same year, he published his magnum opus, *Der Mythus des 20.Jahrhunderts. Eine Wertung der seelisch-geistigen Gestaltungskämpfe unserer Zeit* (*The Myth of the Twentieth Century: An Assessment of the Spiritual-Intellectual Battle to Shape Our Time*). The title announced Rosenberg's ambitious intention to bring Chamberlain's ideas into the present and make himself heir to the metahistorical prophets of the Völkisch movement. At the same time, Rosenberg used the aftermath of the world economic crisis to portray liberalism as finished, since it could not prevent mass unemployment and poverty. He replaced "reason" and "history" with the myth of a community based on race (*blutmässige Gemeinschaft*) that reserved a better future for German nationals.[24]

The two million fallen German soldiers of the First World War constituted the starting point for Rosenberg's reflections and the resulting obligation to undergo national rebirth. Herein lay a central motive for his rejection of the "Weimar system," which had no feeling for the heroic victims of the past. Despite his considerable programmatic ambition, Rosenberg stood firmly within the tradition of Chamberlain, and this ultimately concerned the glorification of the

Bayreuth world. Seen from this perspective, Lagarde, like the "Master" Wagner himself, became a brave fighter "against Alberich's entire bourgeois-capitalist world." Yet Lagarde had never been able to acquire a taste for Richard Wagner's music. Lagarde's specific function was as the scholarly authority on Old Testament traces in the New Testament, which Rosenberg considered substantially "un-Christian" and wanted to eliminate to the extent possible.[25] Lagarde, who had become a virtual icon of the upright, scholarly way of thinking, was presented, like Meister Eckhart, as the quintessence of the noble-minded German. Lagarde's rejection of Luther had run into opposition from Chamberlain at one time, but this stance played no further role in Rosenberg's plan. He considered Lagarde the creator of a national religion and a "prophet of goals specific to his own race." Two years earlier, he had incorporated Lagarde into the nationalistic arsenal of myths by comparing him with Frederick Barbarossa, who was "awaiting resurrection."[26] For the most part, Hitler had no interest in such expectant ideas. His eye was on the uppermost goal of gaining political power. He seems to have viewed the exponents of the Völkisch movement with contempt, and his speeches very rarely showed interest in them.

Only one speech survives in which Hitler directly referred to Lagarde. It dates from the period of his incarceration in Landsberg Prison and examines the triumph of his own ideology over that of his political opponents. Even the programmatic title, "Die soziale Sendung des Nationalsozialismus" (The Social Mission of National Socialism), was aimed mainly at contemporary problems. He was less concerned with an in-depth treatment of the *völkisch* tradition, and his examination of the subject was predictably cursory. Hitler complained that, in Germany, a sense of nationalism had emerged too late and nationalist prophets had possessed very little ability to have an impact on politics. He then pointed to the *völkisch* ideas of Friedrich Jahn ("the father of gymnastics"), Fichte, Wagner, and Lagarde, who, in spite of their numerous merits, had failed "to prevent the other side from carrying the day."[27] Hitler expressed these reservations even more strikingly in *Mein Kampf*, in which he accused "German-*völkisch* itinerant scholars" of unworldly naiveté and almost dangerous misapprehension of political realities. Given this situation, it seems highly unlikely that Lagardian ideas influenced Hitler. Many researchers also believe that, by the mid-1920s, Hitler's ideology had been finalized.[28]

Considering the avalanche of Hitler literature, it is certainly astounding that, up to now, hardly anyone has looked into the bibliographically ascertainable and philologically editable sources of his worldview. Thus far, his private library in the Berghof has played almost no role in the relevant research. Hitler was an ardent reader who insured his library in 1934 and furnished a number of his approximately 16,000 books with countless markings. Approximately 1,200 specimens that were kept in a salt mine near Berchtesgaden survived the collapse of the Third Reich. They are now available for scholarly research in the Rare Book and Special Collections Division of the Library of Congress. Hitler's library contains many recollections of the First World War, as well as strange writings on spiritual and occult issues and parapsychological matters. The deluxe Fichte edition in white leather is exceptional. In June 1933, Leni Riefenstahl tried to win the favor of the "dear Führer" with this gift. She apparently piqued his interest, as the volumes show clear signs of having been read. The Hitler Library also has a convincing treasure trove of Lagarde materials at the ready.[29]

In November 1934, Lehmann's publishing house came out with a new edition of the *Deutsche Schriften* that aimed to reach a wider audience. Two copies of this edition are found in Hitler's private library. While one volume looks nearly unread, the other shows proof of intensive study. It bears the lofty inscription "From the German people's prophet of old as dedicated to his successor. Cordially, J. F. Lehmann." The volume contains numerous markings in fine lead and thick blue pencil. Most of the markings are quite precise. Not only have entire sentences frequently been underlined, but individual clauses as well. Brisk strokes generally seem to indicate agreement, while very occasional question marks point to factual reservations. Hitler used a hierarchical system that ran from the simplest underlining, to between one and three oblique strokes, to exclamation marks and crosses in the margins. The majority of the markings appear in the first half of the *Deutsche Schriften*, perhaps lending special weight to Lagarde's early thinking.

One can ascertain biographical similarities between the two men without going to great effort. The follower of an abstinent lifestyle emphasized the baneful effects of nicotine and other narcotics; the nationalist who got involved in politics in Vienna valued Lagarde's statements on the intellectual poverty of the Magyars.[30] Hitler also found Lagarde's critique of education interesting. He underlined the polemical remark that German youth were in danger of dying "of boredom by the end of their school days" (p. 360). Hitler stressed the creative dimension of his autodidactic efforts and sharply criticized state educational institutions. A prime example would be Hitler's demand in *Mein Kampf* that the "youthful brain" must not be weighed down by unnecessary knowledge.[31] Hitler and Lagarde both thought that they were responsible for the failings of humanity. At the same time, Hitler shared the scholar's fondness for heroic gestures and assigned particular importance to his *Führertum* (leadership).

Hitler marked the belief that Germany lacked a Cromwell (p. 21) with two oblique strokes. He highlighted the following sentence in similar fashion: "Great men are uncomfortable, because they force little men to recognize them (and that recognition is justifiably expressed by hate and love in equal measure)" (p. 72). This marking corresponded to his affirmation of Lagarde's statement that historical progress was always dependent upon "individual human beings" (p. 138). Finally, Hitler was impressed by the formulation that "only a man of great, firm, pure will" (p. 286) could save Germany from ruin. The cult of important figures was embedded in a tragic understanding of history: "Great events," as Lagarde put it theatrically, "depend on good societies. Great events don't have anything to do with the little people living now. Throughout world history, electricity has come down solely from on high: molehills are safe from all kinds of lightning" (p. 24). Hitler showed considerable interest in Lagarde's predictive statements. In light of subsequent developments, one sentence that is marked with a heavy cross in the margin seems particularly remarkable: "We are currently drifting toward war with Russia, on the one hand, England and France on the other" (p. 38). But however seriously Hitler took Lagarde's political statements, he grappled all the more with the subject of "religion."

Since his reading of these Lagarde passages coincided with deteriorating relations with the Vatican, it is hardly astonishing that the passages tended to be anti-Catholic. He held on to the idea that the Pope had always marginalized the principle of "nationality" (p. 58) and proclaimed his own infallibility instead. In general, Hitler seemed to be attracted to arguments in which Lagarde criticized aggressive papal policies. In the Middle Ages, these policies led the Curia to consider the German king a "vassal" (p. 62). The sharp dichotomy between Germany and the Pope served to legitimize Lagarde's own national-religious understanding. Hitler was particularly interested in those figures of speech that underscored the hopelessness and harshness of the conflict between church and state. The following comment seemed especially noteworthy to him: "If one wants to render Romanism harmless, then one must conquer Rome. And in order to defeat Rome, one must wage war against it" (p. 113). In addition, Lagarde criticized the utilitarian political understanding of the Catholic Church, an understanding that was incompatible with the German people's sense of justice. For special emphasis, Hitler underlined the laconic statement "the Curia never loves a country so much as when it needs it" (p. 159) in a paragraph that he'd already marked. Hitler showed just as great an interest in the cultural pessimist's anti-Protestant invectives as he did in the anti-Catholic ones.

While Catholicism appeared as a powerful institution in the passages marked by Hitler, it was the "corrupt elements" that stood out in the case of

Protestantism. The "revocation of celibacy" had already had a sinister effect, because it had become impossible for the "sons of good families" to take up positions as clergymen (p. 16). As to whether this led to an overall rejection of service to the church among "finer souls" (p. 16), Hitler does not seem to have considered the matter settled, since he marked this spot in the text with one of his infrequent question marks. But Hitler's support for Lagarde's drastic attack on Protestant disingenuousness was beyond doubt. Its clergy was "nothing but [. . .] maggots that take on the color of whatever fruit they are eating" (p. 18). Given Lagarde's devastating judgment about theology, it is not surprising that theological faculties were to be shut down. Indeed, Hitler went along with Lagarde in considering an out-and-out fight against Catholicism and Protestantism inevitable. If one bears in mind that the Christian religion was "doomed" anyway (p. 267) because of its Jewish components, then this assessment was not without consequences.

Hitler's gaze repeatedly fell on those statements that emphasized the close relationship between Protestantism and Judaism. Lagarde vigorously contrasted the "trashy rags of today's Protestantism" (p. 30) with the "old-fashioned, yet sturdy and warm attire" of the Jews. Against such a backdrop, the idea of a Christian mission to the Jews appeared hubristic, such that Hitler firmly stressed Lagarde's observation: "For every religion, even fetishism, is better than the mishmash of stale, cowardly sentimentality and the stagnant, putrid remains of Christendom that we call Protestantism today" (p. 30). This is not to say that Hitler was uninterested in the few halfway-balanced passages in Lagarde on the topic of Judaism. Rather, his intensive reading of genuinely scholarly arguments shows the desire to arm himself against Judaism with proven expertise. For example, Hitler's interest in useful information can be seen in his underlining of a list of allegedly immoral passages in the Old Testament (p. 214). In marked contrast to these rather specialized arguments, statements about the "timeless character" of the Jews also caught his attention. Hitler commented on this momentous sentence with an exclamation mark: "Jews have not been corrupted by history; it's simply in their nature" (p. 28). This annotation bothered one present-day journalist so greatly that he described Lagarde's statement as simply "insane."[32] The statement actually has to do with an essential attribute of antisemitism that had already cropped up fairly often in the early nineteenth century. Hitler emphasized the culminating statement by Lagarde, who had his very own way of combining historico-philosophical and physiognomical considerations, that the Jews had not changed in appearance since the days of the Patriarchs (p. 28). This assessment agreed with Lagarde's typical metaphysics of popular customs and traditions (*Volkstum*), according to which Germans were much too soft by nature to live together with Jews. But the question mark that Hitler placed next to Lagarde's wish that religion could somehow "meld" the Jews into the German nation indicates an intensification of Hitler's perspective (p. 31).

Hitler particularly favored statements about the culturo-historical significance of the Jews. Thus, the "basis of all civilization, monogamy" (p. 28) was so unknown to them that it was not accepted until the time of the Saxon emperors. And the belief in one God should also not be registered as a Jewish achievement. Hitler marked and underlined Lagarde's polemical statement for emphasis: "Monotheism is not specifically Jewish: the Chinese, Indians, Greeks and, presumably, even the Egyptians had it. It is not a necessary result of thinking and has no intrinsic ethical value whatsoever. Monotheism means as little to religion as knowing the total population of Germany does to German patriotism" (p. 29). In general, there was no lack of emphasis on disrespectful statements about the Jewish religion. This was equally true for the defamation of Yahweh as "a papier-mâché idol" (p. 29) and the characterization of Judaism as a primitive religion in which fortune telling played a decisive role (p. 258). By his marking with thick pencil in two colors, Hitler directed attention to Lagarde's idea that Jews bore the blame for the crucifixion of Jesus (p. 64). In addition, he highlighted Lagarde's theory that the Gospels were systematically falsified by Paul, who, as someone "entirely without a calling," should never have been allowed to gain "influence in the church" (p. 67).

Statements about Jews that were applicable to the present almost always caught Hitler's attention. This was the case, for example, with the statement that "transplanting Polish and Austrian Jews to Palestine" would mean "a great deal of work" (p. 41). The same was true of Lagarde's demand for a national religion that did not contain elements of the Jewish tradition. And an appeal for a fundamental *damnatio memoriae* accompanied that demand: "If ye want no orthodox statutes and notions, ye German forefathers, then first get ye rid of Old Testament biblical history, and do it so thoroughly that their names may never be mentioned in the presence of your children" (p. 213). This connected up with his approval for Lagarde's view that the "Jewish question" could not be solved by the state authorities and that "only the German people" could supply the answer (p. 370).

Lagarde's political thinking was based on the conviction that the inner unification of the Reich had in no way ended with the 1871 coronation festivities at Versailles. The Germans' real mission of finding their way to a true religion still lay ahead of them. Lagarde's normative elevation of the concept of nationhood resulted in a call for an ideal in politics, and Hitler highlighted the applicable text with three colored-pencil strokes in both side margins: "May Germany never believe that it could enter a new period in life without a new ideal. May Germany consider that true life grows from the ground up, not downward from above, and that it is earned, not given" (p. 193). Lagarde's future utopian transfiguration was related to his contempt for everyday politics, which stood by "wretchedly idle" (p. 194) and watched mankind.

In language that tolerated no contradiction, Lagarde defined Germany as "the totality of all German-feeling, German-thinking, German-leaning Germans" (p. 193). In general, Hitler showed considerable sympathy for the anti-universalist thrust of Lagardian ideology. He marked the statement that "a single nation stands higher than humanity" (p. 164) with two colored-pencil strokes and an exclamation point. He gave the same degree of importance to Lagarde's claim that, in spite of all the public controversy, Catholicism and liberalism converged in their fondness for humanitarian-universalist ideals. In the final analysis, it was not only a question of the "envy of two competitors, both of whom needed to be asked to leave the house" (p. 164); Lagarde's argumentation also contained a strongly anti-bourgeois feeling, as reflected in the highlighted statement that "religion does not grow at reform banquets" (p. 165). The ultimate goal of "Germanic peoples" must be a multitude of "national religions" that could only come into existence through energetic resistance to "Jesuitism" (p. 270).

Lagarde's apocalyptic historical thinking was the main prerequisite for a vast number of severe value judgments. The downfall of the degenerate present was a necessary precondition for the dawning of a better day. The following anti-intellectualistic image of the enemy is characteristic of the aggressiveness of the Lagardian view: "Literati float on the surface of the new German Empire; namely, those who are literary figures openly and those who are secretly led by some party head or other. These invasive weeds must be purged from our rivers and seas, and the political system without which they could not exist must be destroyed" (p. 276). Hardly less significant is the diction used to illustrate the new birth of the German nation: "All flowers on the shore and all stars in the heavens will be reflected in the pure mirror. The old gods will disappear from the waters, and no one will bear a grudge against us" (p. 260). Hitler, who was given to rapid mood swings and had a characteristically sentimental relationship to his own brutality, decided in favor of uniformly highlighting the entire quote. He may ultimately have shared Lagarde's eschatological perspective and the hope that a powerful upheaval would bring an end to the unholy present.

The biographical similarities between Lagarde and Hitler invite speculation. They go from the unprocessed deaths of their mothers to the tension-laden relationships with their domineering fathers to their self-styled images as independent autodidacts and true revolutionaries. The two outsiders were united in their hatred of the bourgeois world and in their typical mixture of sentimentality and violent fantasies, accompanied by notoriously clear consciences. Lagarde, however, remained a "perpetrator in thought." The differences between the persnickety philologist and the high-handed agitator are so great that they should not be ignored. Hitler's markings in the *Deutsche Schriften* may not be sufficient grounds for far-reaching psychological conclusions. From the perspective of the historian of ideas, however, such marginalia are anything but irrelevant.

At the beginning of the 1920s, Hitler saw himself as the embodiment of the political messiah to come. Since writing *Mein Kampf*, he was increasingly convinced that the political genius who would save Germany was none other than himself.[33] This also meant that the National Socialist movement had to fill the role of prophet. Thinkers like Chamberlain and Lagarde were predestined for such a position. According to Hitler, they had been defrauded of their true influence in a "liberal era." Since 1933, a lack of legitimacy had entered the political system, and that system could not draw on established traditions. An excellent example would be Treitschke's high standing in this new order. It was no coincidence that his bust was placed in the foyer of the Reichsinstitut für die Geschichte des neuen Deutschlands (Institute of the German Reich for the History of the New Germany).[34] Lagarde's special importance rested on his brilliant melding, during his lifetime, of his scholarly nimbus and his aura as an outsider.

Hitler's meticulous study of the *Deutsche Schriften* reveals that his interest in them was not limited to a mere search for political weapons. Among the noteworthy points of agreement were the ultimate value of the nation, the unreserved affirmation of power, and ideological enemy stereotypes. Lagarde and Hitler vehemently negated the bourgeois world. They delegitimized its liberal values, which they simultaneously interpreted as a "Jewish supremacy strategy." Finally, the idea of a "national religion" may well have appealed to Hitler.[35] Whether or not he was a believer himself, he viewed the steadfast convictions of religious people as entirely positive. Accordingly, he highlighted a passage in which Lagarde distanced himself from religiously indifferent scholars: "Whoever calls an ideology his own," he stated apodictically, "has either acquired it as a gift of his childhood religion or has earned it through hard struggles that led him, as a man, to a new faith. Every ideology is religious" (p. 363). Rosenberg cultivated a similarly heroic self-image and did his utmost to shape the ideological face of the Third Reich.

Although the racial foundation of Lagarde's ideas was questionable from a

National Socialist perspective, Hitler gave Rosenberg a free hand in spreading them. Rosenberg's own *Myth of the Twentieth Century* was not particularly well received upon publication. The feature-article editors at the big papers ignored it, and Christian denominations adopted attitudes ranging from wait-and-see to negative. Only those in *völkisch* circles praised the voluminous, evidently ambitious work. Theodor Fritsch's paper, *Der Hammer*, called it a "tower block in the armed fight against God-defying egalitarianism."[36] Objective and political reservations had already hampered Rosenberg's publishing efforts. Even the Munich publisher Julius Lehmann could not be won over. However much he had in common with Rosenberg ideologically, Lehmann considered an "open break" with the Catholic Church inadvisable.

But the map was redrawn after the Seizure of Power. Even if many people had smiled condescendingly at the allegedly naive ideologue, Rosenberg, his magnum opus brought him great success among average folk. By 1933, 73,000 copies had already been sold; sales reached a half million in 1938 and culminated at one million by 1942.[37] It is, of course, not easy to determine how many of these books were actually read. *Myth* was a stylistically unwieldy, long-winded work. After being flipped through cursorily, many copies must simply have ended up on people's bookshelves. But the mere fact that it directly attacked Christendom led the Pope to put it on the Index, assuring Rosenberg considerable attention. Numerous ecclesiastical statements impressively substantiate how greatly challenged people felt by the party's claims to power. Further, the approximately one thousand pages of personal letters received by Rosenberg's chancellery alone are a reflection of enormous public interest. Rosenberg must, therefore, have also succeeded in disseminating his heroic image of Lagarde. As a public speaker, he went to considerable effort to make the "prophet of the National Socialist movement" accessible to a wider audience.

Throughout his multifaceted activities, Rosenberg was convinced that the "National Socialist revolution" would have to conclude with a complete change of heart. Beginning in early 1934, his official title was the "Führer's representative in charge of all NSDAP mental and ideological training and education." Against this backdrop, one can better understand why Rosenberg attached great importance to the idea of a German religion. On account of his brilliantly controlled, national-religious semantics, Lagarde, it stands to reason, was designated the herald of this belief. At the fourth Nuremberg Rally in September 1934, Rosenberg called Lagarde, along with Goethe, Hölderlin, Wagner, Nietzsche, and Chamberlain, a champion "of the new birth of the German soul." At the same time, he benevolently confirmed that Lagarde had dreamed "of a powerful religious awakening,"[38] while emphasizing Lagarde's opposition to the authoritarian Bismarck state. Before an audience of Wehrmacht (armed forces) officers on March 7, 1935, Rosenberg declared that Lagarde saw blood as "the missing glue of the Second Empire" and that he had underscored the catastrophic effect of liberalism on German unity.[39] This rhetoric tied in superbly with the assessment that the academic establishment had fought Lagarde tooth and nail. On November 14, 1935, Rosenberg even dared to state in the presence of foreign diplomats that Lagarde, like Chamberlain and Nietzsche, had been unable to find a position at any German university. The party ideologue had a quick explanation on hand, as confidently stated as it was incorrect: "People did not allow for any philosophy of history that opposed the old historical view."[40] Yet it presumably did not escape some listeners that, in making such statements, the Weltanschauung's expert on National Socialism was primarily speaking for himself.

Rosenberg stressed the close relationship between Lagarde and Langbehn in his *Geschichte des deutschen Volkes* (*History of the German People*), which he published under the pseudonym Widukind. He sharply contrasted their concept of a "racially related national bond" (*Blutsmässige Volksverbundenheit*) with "Nietzsche's ultimately pathological individualism." He linked the glorification of the Duke of Saxony to the deliberate effort toward a Germanic historical view, a view that always remained in dispute on account of its remoteness.[41] But Rosenberg held on to the premises of his national ideology with an iron will. In 1936, a publication put out by the main educational office of the NSDAP and the Deutsche Arbeitsfront (DAP: German Labor Front) ensured that Lagarde's thought was widely disseminated among NS functionaries. The publication contained an essay by Josef Becker that went by the lofty title "Paul de Lagarde. Ein Seher der deutschen Nation" (Paul de Lagarde: A Seer of the German Nation). The text offered a condensed version of Lagarde's *völkisch* ideas from a National Socialist perspective and emphatically presented him as a forward-looking figure. He was the "solitary Great," the allegedly "unrecognized and silenced" scholar about whom people spoke solemnly during his lifetime. At any rate, the promotion of Lagarde within Rosenberg's sphere was not without semantic consequences. A rather overattentive article appeared in the *Göttinger Tageblatt* (*Göttingen Daily News*) under a similarly pompous heading.[42]

Rosenberg also went to great lengths to spread Lagarde's ideas during the Second World War. When suitable literature was shipped to members of the Wehrmacht in 1940, Rosenberg arranged for Lagarde to be represented alongside his own *Myth* and Alfred Bauemler's work on Nietzsche. The Lagarde text was called *Deutsche Politik und Religion* (*German Politics and Religion*) and was put out by the Insel publishing house in Leipzig, which presented its readers with a barely eighty-page selection of forceful key passages from the Göttingen scholar. Under the headword *Führer*, it principally offered quotes that made Bismarck appear as an accomplice of the prevailing liberalism. In general, Lagarde was styled a "model of the German man," whose blueprint for a "national religion" was the badly needed answer to Luther's failure.[43] On December 22, 1941, Rosenberg insisted on speaking at the Kroll Opera House in Berlin for the fiftieth anniversary of Lagarde's death. A total of no fewer than 180 Lagarde celebrations supposedly took place in the German Reich.[44] If one considers that, by this time, the war against the Soviet Union had already been under way for many months, and the party and population had many other concerns, then the number of celebrations held for Lagarde feels astounding.

But the Romantic, idealistic coloring of Lagarde's ideas made them difficult to disseminate and only marginally compatible with "scholarly racist" thought. In the prestigious *Zeitschrift für Theologie und Kirche* (*Journal of Theology and the Church*), the Leipzig adjunct professor Heinz Erich Eisenhuth had already stated categorically in 1934 that it would be "a misapprehension of racial diversity [. . .] for L[agarde] to consider the Germanization of the Jews possible."[45] There were some German Christians who considered Lagarde's attitude toward the "Jewish question" antiquated. As a consequence of the eternal conflict among Hitler's paladins, pressure intensified to profess loyalty to National Socialist beliefs, an obligation that applied all the more strongly throughout the Second World War. In 1943, a passionate Lagarde reader like the historian Erich Botzenhart almost prophylactically disputed the accusation that he was not racist enough. The Festschrift for Karl Alexander von Müller stated: "Lagarde saw the Jewish question predominantly as a spiritual and not a biological problem. For this reason, the racial antisemitism of his younger contemporary, Schönerer, did not get through to him." In the Orientalist's defense, the Festschrift pointed mainly to his "unequivocal and uncompromising attitude" toward the Jews.[46]

For all Rosenberg's hustling and bustling, one should still not overestimate his influence. In the battle for power, the tactically inflexible desk worker was no match for the dynamic, single-minded Goebbels. The "Führer's ideological representative" was late in setting up his own, independent power apparatus. From time to time, he seems to have been taken less than seriously by the grandees of the Third Reich. And so his ideological initiatives repeatedly ran into obstacles. The wartime emphasis shifted to whatever was immediately useful anyway. On December 29, 1941, Rosenberg informed the head of the party chancellery, Martin Bormann, that an "Hour of Remembrance for Paul de Lagarde would take place" and a celebration of "Frederick the Great" in the following month. Given the reservations expressed by "several gauleiters and their staffs," Rosenberg apparently softened his tone, saying that he "would only go ahead with" the Lagarde celebration "if the requirements for a worthy event were in place."[47] The strategic nature of this statement is apparent, while its veracity is equally difficult to ascertain. Yet what may hardly be debatable is that the longer and more severe the war became, the more unrealistic the visions of a new National Socialist individual like Rosenberg must have seemed. Like most functionaries, Hitler's chief ideologue had not shaped the thinking of the population to the degree that he believed and, to a large extent, this also applied to the acceptance of national-religious ideas.

Alongside efforts to establish Lagarde as a prophet of National Socialism, members of the middle class also gave him a friendly reception during the era of the Third Reich. The middle-class response was able to build on Franz Schnabel's and others' interpretations of Lagarde. A typical example would be Theodor Heuss, who wrote an article to commemorate the fiftieth anniversary of Lagarde's death for the *Frankfurter Zeitung*. The paper was forbidden by "order of the Führer" to publish anything under Heuss's name, so the parties involved decided on the abbreviation D, which is how insiders hid his nickname, Dorle. The outright liberal highlighted the extent to which Lagarde had been out of step with his own time. Heuss was not silent about Lagarde's difficult personality traits but expressed great respect "for the deep seriousness of the man" who had suffered so greatly over the spiritual superficiality of the Kaiserreich.[48] He particularly praised Lagarde's language. Its "lyrical tenderness, along with alternately brooding and sincere pathos[,]" was as impressive as the "effortless richness of [his] imagery and examples." Those with ears to hear it could also pick out subtle notes of contemporary criticism in Heuss's empathy for Lagarde's culturally pessimistic views. A hidden barb appeared in the closing sentence of the article, which stated that Lagarde's energetic protest had maintained "awareness of timeless powers that were responsible for free nations."

At the time when Heuss's newspaper article appeared, National Socialist power extended from the Pyrenees to the gates of Moscow, and a robust propaganda apparatus announced the triumph of its "blood and soil" ideology (*Blut-und-Boden-Ideologie*). Hitler had, in fact, already passed the zenith of his power. From today's point of view, his declaration of war on the United States on December 11, 1941, was already the beginning of the end.[49] Given the defeat that loomed on the horizon, the National Socialist worldview turned out to be an extremely fleeting phenomenon. No matter how greatly Rosenberg put forward its importance, the ensuing fall from power made such efforts hardly necessary. So the ideological initiatives that he developed as head of the Eastern Ministry fell on rocky soil. In the remaining years of the war, he focused mainly on art theft of the highest order. The Reich director's "Special Task Force on Fine Arts" alone confiscated 21,788 art objects.[50] In a certain sense, Rosenberg's actions showed the real extent to which he felt bound to his own ideals. In 1945, only remnants of the NS historical view remained, and no more cocks crowed for the supposed prophets of the "thousand-year Reich." Lagarde changed from the "prophet of national rebirth" into a nonperson. And that has not changed to this very day.

Epilogue

Ten years after writing his memorial article for the *Frankfurter Zeitung*, Theodor Heuss visited the University of Göttingen. In the meantime, he was no longer a threatened journalist but president of the German federation and a central figure in public life. The occasion was the two-hundredth anniversary of the Göttingen Academy of Sciences, which had asked Heuss to give the commemorative speech. For the well-read, highly educated Heuss, this trip was among his more pleasant duties. At the ceremony on November 10, 1951, the politician reviewed the history of the academy, recalling the achievements of outstanding scholars and taking a stand against its Nazi past. Heuss sharply criticized the development of "German mathematics" as the "ultimate perversion" of disastrous, abortive nationalism.[1] He also stressed the human suffering of the emigrants, whose loss the former mecca of scientific research would never recover from entirely. Heuss approached the topic of Lagarde at some length, but expressed his opposition to the "strange man" in very moderate tones. Like that of Lichtenberg, the Orientalist's journalistic impact had been considerable, which was not at all typical for Göttingen. Heuss showed remarkable understanding for the fact that, "due to all sorts of dark human inscrutability," no historian dared approach Lagarde's works.

When I first encountered Lagarde's papers during work on my dissertation, I came under their spell. There was a heavy suitcase filled with reviews. After studying them, I no longer saw the notion of a "despised outsider," an idea that originated with Lagarde, as very credible in spite of its historically accepted importance. Impressed by the wealth of evidence, I gave initial consideration to writing a biography. But the realization of historical projects is mainly tied to favorable circumstances, above all to the availability of research time and source materials. In this case, nearly a decade passed before I could devote all my energy to this peculiar cultural pessimist and outstanding scholar. Like most biographers, I had to grapple with transference problems while trying to help Lagarde come into his own. However, it became increasingly clear that his impressive narratives did not stand up to scrutiny. Over time, source work confirmed the contemporary image of a misanthropic scholar whose specific character traits were not at all suitable for heroizing or mythmaking.

Lagarde was an unusually difficult man. Having grown up in a cold, loveless atmosphere, this highly talented scholar became lonely early on and felt misjudged by his contemporaries. Neither his wife's love nor the recognition that went with being a renowned professor could make up for his joyless childhood. On the contrary, his outward successes were accompanied by a kind of mental petrification that caused him to increasingly view his life as a burden. Some aspects of Franz Overbeck's verdict on Nietzsche also apply to the tireless, speedy, precise, and hardworking Orientalist: he was a "product of the violence with which he was treated."[2] Lagarde, of course, lacked the philosopher's delight in intellectual experimentation, and his most prominent character traits, like envy, greed, and bitterness, showed signs of inner hardening. He often harbored resentment toward particular colleagues for years before exploding in public. Time and again, he inwardly relived long-forgotten slights.

While the energetic cultural pessimist so gladly presented himself as a leader of men, he was helpless in the face of his own contradictory existence. Equipped only with fragile self-esteem, he vacillated between judgmental extremes and, in fact, his entire worldview entailed contradictions that he himself was unable to resolve. Lagarde remained convinced of his own idealistic persuasion, yet he also preached the purifying power of hate. His idealistic vision of a national community produced the very de-Christianization that he was fighting against. He tended to make extravagant scholarly plans that contained the seeds of their own failure. Lagarde compensated for his dissatisfaction with the slow progress of his Septuagint edition with verbal gaffes, and people at the University of Göttingen often turned a blind eye to his conflicts. Through the years, his hatred of the outside world took on an almost pathological dimension. Lagarde expressed his antisemitism in misanthropic language that outraged many of his contemporaries, language that has an even more distressing impact today. Nevertheless, it would be wrong to merely emphasize his aggressive character traits. Lagarde was someone who needed a great deal of love, and he repeatedly expressed that need in an oppressive yet touching manner. With elegant detachment and absolute clarity, the writer Golo Mann described Lagarde as a "person with the most fatal, long-term political beliefs and dreams," and called his antisemitism "abominable." Yet he approvingly quoted the following lines by Lagarde:

> You know that only in a richer you,
> Thirsting away, may I to peace win through.
> The world just gives us things in lieu of you,
> Forever human, we, without a you.

Golo Mann certainly seemed to feel that, "in spite of everything, a pure light must have shone within Lagarde's black soul," or else the Göttingen scholar would not have managed to write verses like these.[3] Whatever one may think of this opinion, Lagarde's sensitive side should not be ignored by historians. For, without it, his overbearing nationalism would have met with a significantly lesser response. Countless readers sympathized with his equally lachrymose and energetic critique of modernity. Yet only a few of them understood that his extreme judgments were not rooted merely in his character but in his chiliastic worldview as well.

Lagarde certainly had a huge impact on the *völkisch* right. All the same, it would be extremely tricky to call him the primary or even the exclusive forerunner of National Socialism. In doing so, one would be in danger of adopting Rosenberg's view. Without respect for the resistance expressed in the sources, Rosenberg claimed the Orientalist from Göttingen, as well as German nationalism in general, for the tradition of the Third Reich. Among the traditional and noble tasks of historiography is the assignment of historical meaning. But historiography is also connected to entrenched teleologies. As a result, a great danger lies in the potential sacrificing of the scholarliness of historical understanding to the prevailing modern perspective. George Bataille's prima facie critique of Lagarde as "one of the fathers of the National Socialist church" expresses a platitude whose origins have largely been forgotten.[4] But neither should Lagarde's Romantic roots be overemphasized. As strong as the youthful impressions of Rückert's keen students may have been, Rückert's greatest influence came in the heyday of the European nation-state. Marc Bloch's belief that men are generally more similar to their contemporaries than to their fathers applies even to this solitary Orientalist, and historiography "falls into disrepute" by ignoring this fact.[5]

Lagarde's sectarian criticism of Bismarck cannot hide the fact that the development of a "national religion" was a sign of the times. The scholar from Göttingen shared in the prevailing scholarly beliefs, used his philological tools to call Christianity fundamentally into question, and postulated a new national religion. Yet this religion's exact nature remained unclear, because Lagarde confined his role to that of a "prophet" who could only hint at the specific shape of things to come. This made his idea of a national religion strangely blurry, but also provided that dazzling ambiguity which was indispensable to its broad acceptance in the fin de siècle world. Lagarde's presentist understanding of religion admittedly did not help answer the question of how true faith would be possible in a historicized world. It is no coincidence, likewise, that his seemingly coherent worldview contained numerous heterogeneous elements. These elements were superficially joined together with a teleological view of history that assigned the German people a decisive role in the emergence of God's kingdom. In addition, stereotypical enemy images had an important unifying function in Lagarde's worldview. His temperament led him to engage in vehement attacks on political opponents, but his ideas did not offer any realistic solutions to the many interwoven problems of the era. Yet this is precisely what furthered the impact of his national-religious semantics, which glorified the future of the German people in daring metaphors and extolled the power of Providence at the same time.

Historical fairness demands that we place Lagarde within the intellectual world of the outgoing nineteenth century and also opens up the possibility of new discoveries. The theory of "German exceptionalism" has seen its best days and was probably never terribly fruitful for the history of ideas. When the theory was mapped onto centuries of German experience, its path became much too convoluted. A narrative that leads directly from the German idiosyncrasies of Fichte, Lagarde, Chamberlain, and Rosenberg to the "Third Reich" is too neglectful of the diversity of modern cultural criticism, which also has some convincing arguments in its favor. What may be even more important is that this historical perspective marginalizes the great variety of meaning contained in demanding texts. Through his command of delicate language, and because he had something to say, Lagarde impressed many thinkers, from Christian Morgenstern to Franz Schnabel. The depth of his misanthropic ideas could not be covered up, not at all. The dangerous nature of his national-religious understanding is illustrated by the significant impact exerted by his harsh enemy stereotypes during very different periods of time. Even Hitler did not see Lagarde as a prophet of the Völkisch movement in the stereotypical way that many did. In 1934, he picked up the *Deutsche Schriften*, and it seems that he found an astounding number of points in common with the Orientalist.

Lagarde was essentially moved by the problem of alienation from life. He had come to doubt his faith, and he created powerful images that held the promise of spiritual rebirth and personal religious experience. In the battle against his own inner emptiness, which expressed itself in massive fatigue and world-weariness, Lagarde tried to encourage himself in a loud voice. Even his contemporaries confused Lagarde's heroic self-promotion with an insecure personality, thereby creating decisive room for the acceptance of his "prophet of *Deutschtum*" myth. And this view was in full bloom for more than one hundred years. Even when the critical repercussions of the Second World War prevailed, people stressed the uniformity of his personality and the erratic character of his ideology. Without wanting to, people remained under the spell of Lagarde's own self-image, the dissemination of which had been so important to the Göttingen fisher-of-men. Even at a time of fierce ideological conflict, new light was being shed on the false prophets of nationalism. Lagarde's fate shows just how closely connected mental disability, deliberate self-stylization, and a charismatic impact can be.

Notes

1. A MAN OF CONTRADICTIONS

1. Details of Lagarde's funeral on December 25, 1891, are recorded in the Universitätsarchiv Göttingen, Kur 5903, fol. 107ff.; see also Paul Fischer, *Überblick über Paul de Lagardes Lebensgang*, in: Paul de Lagarde, *Ausgewählte Schriften* (Munich, 1924), XIII–XVIII, especially XVIII, and Alfred Rahlfs, *Paul de Lagardes wissenschaftliches Lebenswerk im Rahmen einer Geschichte seines Lebens dargestellt* (Göttingen, 1928), p. 94. A directory of obituaries is offered by: Anna de Lagarde, *Paul de Lagarde. Erinnerungen aus seinem Leben zusammengestellt* (Berlin, 1894), p. 5.

2. See the description of the funeral in Ulrich von Wilamowitz-Moellendorf, *Erinnerungen* 1848–1914, 2nd expanded edition (Leipzig, 1929), pp. 330–335; see same pages for the quotations that follow.

3. Whether these private passages also include an instance of self-identification can be difficult to decide in retrospect. William M. Calder III, in his essay "Wilamowitz' Call to Göttingen," asserts that the fervent nationalist Wilamowitz viewed Lagarde's prophetic self-stylization with some sympathy. "Paul de Lagarde to Friedrich Althoff on Wilamowitz-Moellendorf," in: *Studi italiani di filologia classica 3* (1985), pp. 136–160, especially pp. 139ff.

4. Robert Hanhart, "Paul Anton de Lagarde und seine Kritik an der Bibel," in: Bernd Moeller (ed.), Theologie in Gottingen. Eine Vorlesungsreihe (Göttingen, 1987), pp. 271–305, especially p. 274. Fritz Stern, *Kulturpessimismus als politische Gefahr. Eine Analyse nationaler Ideologie in Deutschland* (*The Politics of Cultural Despair: A Study in the Rise of Germanic Ideology*) (Stuttgart, 2005) [first published 1961], p. 54, mistakenly claims that Lagarde had left the church and therefore "no priest was allowed to bury him." Actually the "list of those buried at St. Albani parish in Göttingen" only indicates the absence of the superintendent and the collaborator. Lagarde's leaving the church is as little documented here as it is by his resident registration card. The Göttingen certificate of residence, issued on June 9, 1870, lists him as "of the Protestant faith." These findings are in line with Lagarde's general attitude, which, for all his reservations regarding the official church and its representatives, involved avoiding an open break with tradition.

5. Julius Wellhausen, "Gedächtnisrede auf Paul de Lagarde," in: *Aus den Nachrichten der K. Gesellschaft der Wissenschaften zu Göttingen. Geschäftliche Mittheilungen* (1894), p. 1.

6. It is thus unmistakably described in the article "Lagarde": "Mit seiner ausserordentlichen wissenschaftlichen Begabung gingen [. . .] krankhafte Rechthaberei und Misstrauen gegenüber den Bestrebungen anderer Hand in Hand": Meyers Konversations-Lexikon, 5th newly revised ed. (Leipzig and Vienna, 1897), pp. 947ff.

7. Niedersächsische Staats und Universitätsbibliothek Göttingen, Cod. Ms. Lagarde, letter to Adalbert Bezzenberger of October 21, 1881, estate of Paul de Lagarde. During the writing of this biography, Lagarde's papers have been newly listed as part of the database Hans on the Internet; see www.sub.uni-goettingen.de/hans. This renders the old call numbers obsolete and, since 2004, has enabled searches concentrating on authors' names. The

huge estate reflects Lagarde's energy for work. It includes more than 250 catalog numbers, with no. 150 alone containing his collected general correspondence to more than a thousand addresses. The letters contained in the Göttingen estate will henceforth be quoted with the sender, recipient, and date, and without any special certification. In general, the spelling of the contemporaneous documents has been carefully modernized.

8. Anonymous [Theodor Fritsch], "Paul de Lagarde," in: *Deutsch-Soziale Blätter*, no. 195, May 8, 1892, p. 222.

9. One can read the following in Fritsch's self-righteous display: "Lagarde, however, had a certain aversion to being photographed. Years ago, when asked for his picture for the antisemitic *Volks-Kalender*, he replied: 'I do not like to be photographed, I have a *hard, unsympathetic look* on my face'!—
In whose sad self-deception a sublime, but humble spirit can yet be found."—
The emphases can be found here and in the following from the original.

10. Ludwig Schemann, "Paul de Lagarde. Ein Nachruf," in: *Bayreuther Blätter 6* (1892), pp. 1–26.

11. See Anna de Lagarde, p. 1, and the emphatic statement: "I have not myself to think about, but of Him whom I would like to serve with all of my strength to the end of my life."

12. Ludwig Schemann, *Paul de Lagarde. Ein Lebens und Erinnerungsbild* (Leipzig and Hartenstein, 1919), p. x. The educated, wished-for, middle-class tone in this biography is illustrated by: Johannes Heinssen, *Historismus und Kulturkritik. Studien zur deutschen Geschichtskultur im späten 19. Jahrhundert* (Göttingen, 2003), pp. 485ff.

13. Rahlfs, p. 84; see p. 87, for the next quote.

14. Regarding the historical impact, see Ina Ulrike Paul, "Paul Anton de Lagarde," in: Uwe Puschner, Walter Schmitz, and Justus H. Ulbricht (eds.), *Handbuch zur "Völkischen Bewegung"* (Munich et al., 1996), pp. 45–93, especially pp. 74–90; Ulrich Sieg, "Ein Prophet nationaler Religion. Paul de Lagarde und die völkische Bewegung," in: Friedrich Wilhelm Graf (ed.), *Intellektuellengötter. Das religiöse Laboratorium der klassischen Moderne* (Munich, 2007), and below, the chapter "Prophet of German Culture."

15. Helmut Walser Smith, "Deutsche Geschichte als imperiale Geschichte. Polen, slawophone Minderheiten und das Kaiserreich als kontinentales Empire," in: Sebastian Conrad and Jürgen Osterhammel (eds.), *Das Kaiserreich transnational. Deutschland in der Welt, 1871–1914* (Göttingen, 2004), pp. 149–169, especially p. 152.

16. For a constellation of historical ideas, see J[ohn] W. Burrow, *The Crisis of Reason: European Thought, 1848–1914* (New Haven and London, 2000).

17. This is also true of the extensive, highly descriptive study by Jean Favrat, *La Pensée de Paul de Lagarde (1827–1891). Contribution à la étude des rapports de la religion et de la politique dans le nationalisme et le conservatisme au XIXeme siècle* (Lille and Paris, 1979), as well as the important handbook article by Ina Ulrike Paul.

18. Instructive as well: Friedrich Wilhelm Graf, *Die Wiederkehr der Götter. Religion in der modernen Kultur* (Munich, 2004). Stimulating, as always, regarding the complexity of religious conflict in the German Empire: Thomas Nipperdey, *Religion im Umbruch. Deutschland, 1870–1918* (Munich, 1988).

19. Peter G. J. Pulzer, *Die Entstehung des politischen Antisemitismus in Deutschland und Österreich 1867 bis 1914*. With the author's research report (Göttingen, 2004) [first published 1964]; regarding the lack of interest in historical biographical research on antisemitism, see

Moshe Zimmermann and Wilhelm Marr, *The Patriarch of Antisemitism* (New York and Oxford, 1986), p. vii.

20. Gangolf Hübinger, "Der Verlag Eugen Diederichs in Jena. Wissenschaftskritik, Lebensreform und völkische Bewegung," in: *Geschichte und Gesellschaft* 22 (1996), pp. 31–45, especially p. 40. For general information regarding publication policies inside the Diederichs publishing house: Meike G. Werner, *Moderne in der Provinz. Kulturelle Experimente im Fin de Siècle Jena* (Göttingen, 2003), pp. 183–186.

2. DISMAL CHILDHOOD

1. For a condensed introduction, see Hartwig Brandt, *Europa 1815–1850. Reaktion—Konstitution—Revolution* (Stuttgart, 2002), and Dieter Langewiesche, *Europe zwischen Restauration und Revolution, 1815–1849*, 4th ed. (Munich, 2004).

2. Paul de Lagarde, *Erinnerungen an Friedrich Rückert. Ueber einige Berliner Theologen, und was von ihnen zu lernen ist. Zwei Aufsätze.* Reprinted and presented by Anna de Lagarde (Göttingen, 1897), p. 5. The potential for urban conflict before March is made clear by: Rüdiger Hachtmann, *Berlin 1848. Eine Politik- und Gesellschaftsgeschichte der Revolution* (Berlin, 1997).

3. See Volker Gerhardt, Reinhard Mehring, and Jana Rindert, *Berliner Geist. Eine Geschichte der Berliner Universitätsphilosophie bis 1946* (Berlin, 1999), pp. 63–108.

4. A good impression of William Bötticher's character is conveyed by: Rahlfs, pp. 7–16.

5. Anna de Lagarde, p. 7; see p. 13 for the next quote.

6. Paul de Lagarde, *Erinnerungen an Friedrich Rückert*, p. 13; on Kant's strict upbringing, which also took aim at religious seriousness: Manfred Kühn, *Kant: A Biography* (Cambridge, 2002), pp. 21–60.

7. "Gedichte von Paul Bötticher als Handschrift für Freunde" (Halle, 1850). The unpaginated booklet contains twelve poems; the reproduced verses are concerned with "No. 5."

8. Regarding contact with Schleiermacher, see *Lagarde, Berliner Theologen*, p. 50; from the secondary literature, see the important study by Robert W. Lougee, *Paul de Lagarde: A Study of Radical Conservatism in Germany* (Cambridge, Mass., 1962), p. 38.

9. Thus, emphatically: Otto Pflanze, *Bismarck der Reichsgründer* (Munich, 1997), p. 53; also, pp. 44–55 offer an utterly opinionated description of Bismarck's school years.

10. Lagarde, *Berliner Theologen*, p. 97. Romanticizing the Orientalist's contact with Friedrich Wilhelm IV: Richard Breitling, *Paul de Lagarde und der grossdeutsche Gedanke.* With a foreword by Karl Alexander von Müller (Vienna and Leipzig, 1927), pp. 101ff. General information regarding the dazzling figure of Frederick William IV: Peter Krüger and Julius H. Schoeps (eds.), *Der verkannte Monarch. Friedrich Wilhelm IV in seiner Zeit* (Potsdam, 1997).

11. The following is based on the "certificate of maturity for the pupil of the Berlin Royal Friedrich Wilhelm Gymnasium, *Paul Bötticher*, a native of Berlin," from March 19, 1844, Universitätsarchiv Halle, Rep. 21 II, no. 74, fol. 553r–557r.

12. On Lagarde's studies: Hanhart, pp. 271ff; Rahlfs, pp. 19–25; and Stern, *Kulturpessimismus*, pp. 33ff.

13. See Lagarde, *Erinnerungen an Friedrich Rückert*, pp. 10–24. Regarding the atmosphere in Rückert's seminars: Hartmut Bobzin, *Friedrich Rückert in Berlin (1844–45).* From the memoirs of Max Müller, in: *Oriens 29/30* (1986), pp. 102–109; their importance to

scholarly history is outlined by: Sabine Mangold, *Eine "weltbürgerliche Wissenschaft"—Die deutsche Orientalistik im 19. Jahrhundert* (Stuttgart, 2004), p. 135.

14. Rahlfs, p. 24; see p. 27 for the next quotation.

15. The initial work of the Orientalists is found with separate pagination: Paul de Lagarde, *Frühe Schriften. Neudruck der Ausgaben, 1847–1854* (Osnabrück and Wiesbaden, 1967).

16. Its Latin title was *Initia chromatologiae arabicae*. The documents covering Lagarde's doctoral process are found in: Archiv der Humboldt Universität zu Berlin, *Acta der Königl. Friedrich-Wilhelms-Universität zu Berlin betreffend die Promotionen 1849, 1850*, fol. 189r, v u. fol. 222r–241r.

17. See Anna de Lagarde, p. 11; on Lagarde's attitude to the Revolution of 1848–1849: Favrat, pp. 44ff., and Stern, *Kulturpessimismus*, p. 30f.

18. Anna de Lagarde, p. 17.

19. Ibid., p. 18. Regarding Bötticher's assessment of Catholicism, see Hans Walter Schütte, *Lagarde und Fichte. Die verborgenen spekulativen Voraussetzungen des Christentumsverständnisses Paul de Lagardes* (Gütersloh, 1965), pp. 20ff.

20. Rahlfs, p. 34; see p. 32 for the following quotes.

21. The description of the procedure follows the "Habilitationsakte Paul Anton Bötticher," recorded in the Universitätsarchiv Halle, Rep. 21 II, no. 74, fol. 548r–567r. Important bits of information are offered by Hanhardt, p. 271, and Rahlfs, p. 33.

22. The text can be found at: Niedersächsische Staats und Universitätsbibliothek Göttingen, Cod. Ms. Lagarde 60, fol. 29–36; the quote appears in fol. 31.

23. Ibid., fol. 46–60, "Manuskript für meine Probevorlesung in gremio facultatis behufs meiner Habilitierung, Halle 1851"; the quote appears in fol. 59.

24. Pertinent monograph: Micha Brumlik, *Deutscher Geist und Judenhass. Das Verhältnis des philosophischen Idealismus zum Judentum* (Munich, 2000).

25. However much respect Rückert offered his master's student can be found in his letter of recommendation dated January 13, 1847. It states: "I must acknowledge his [Paul Bötticher's] considerable abilities and determined work for this subject, and I only wish that he receive all necessary encouragement and support to pursue his diversely difficult studies."

26. Lagarde, *Erinnerungen an Friedrich Rückert*, p. 23; see p. 24 for the next quote.

27. Regarding Jacob Grimm's political views, see Hans-Christof Kraus, "Jacob Grimm—Wissenschaft und Politik," in: Bernd Heidenreich and Ewald Grothe (eds.), *Kultur und Politik—Die Grimms* (Frankfurt am Main, 2003), pp. 149–178; Grimm's importance to the elevation of the National Idea in Germany is stressed by: Burrow, p. 87.

28. They can be found today in the Krakauer Jagellionen-Bibliothek as part of the wartime relocation of the Berliner Staatsbibliothek; I am grateful to Ewald Grothe for this information.

29. This is stressed by Julius Wellhausen and Heinrich Ewald, in: *Festschrift zur Feier des hundertfünfzigjährigen Bestehens der Königlichen Gesellschaft der Wissenschaften zu Göttingen. Beiträge zur Gelehrtengeschichte Göttingens* (Berlin, 1901), pp. 61–88, especially p. 70. A good insight into Ewald's dark side is offered by: Lothar Perlitt, "Heinrich Ewald. Der Gelehrte in der Politik," in: Bernd Möller (ed.), Theologie in Göttingen. Eine Vorlesungsreihe (Göttingen, 1987), p. 157–212.

30. R[ichard] Fick and G[ötz] Sölle (eds.), letter to Ewald. From his estate (Göttingen, 1932), p. 117.

31. Paul Bötticher's letter to the Prussian minister of education and cultural affairs of January 1, 1851; Staatsbibliothek Berlin, Darmstadt collection, Paul de Lagarde; the following quotations are also found there.

32. Edited by: Favrat, pp. 599–602. For readability, the reproduction smoothens out many linguistic peculiarities in the text; the emphases are thus found in the original.

33. Only a few scholars in the humanities have seen this clearly. All too often, they ascribe the Orientalist with romantic beliefs, to which he used all his power to overcome. Perhaps the best characterization of his scholarly worldview is offered by: Stefan Breuer, *Ordnungen der Ungleichheit—die deutsche Rechte im Widerstreit ihrer Ideen, 1871–1945* (Darmstadt, 2001), pp. 312ff.

34. On the following, see Helmuth M. Pölcher, "Symphilologein. Briefe von Paul de Lagarde an Adolf Hilgenfeld aus den Jahren 1862–1887," in: Hellmut Diwald (ed.), *Lebendiger Geist. Hans-Joachim Schoeps zum 50. Geburtstag von Schülern dargebracht* (Leiden and Cologne, 1959), pp. 19–47, especially pp. 24ff., and Rahlfs, pp. 38ff.

35. Staatsbibliothek Berlin, Nachlass Hengstenberg.

36. Rahlfs, p. 30, where the next quote also appears.

37. He is well documented: Paul de Lagarde, *Aus dem deutschen Gelehrtenleben. Aktenstücke und Glossen* (Göttingen, 1880), pp. 8–25. The quotes are found in Rahlfs, pp. 16ff.

38. See Rahlfs, pp. 40ff. The life of cosmopolitan diplomats and ambitious promoters of scholarship is described by: Frank Foerster, *Christian Carl Josias Bunsen. Diplomat, Mäzen und Vordenker in Wissenschaft, Kirche und Politik* (Bad Arolsen, 2001).

3. WITH SCHOLARSHIP INTO THE WORLD

1. Anna de Lagarde, p. 23.

2. Ibid., pp. 22ff. For Bötticher's irritability within academic company, see Stern, *Kulturpessimismus*, pp. 34ff.

3. Quoted in: Francis Wheen, *Karl Marx* (Munich, 2002), p. 182. Just how many people came under its spell in nineteenth-century London is illustrated by: Peter Ackroyd, *London: The Biography* (London, 2001), pp. 573–581.

4. Lagarde, *Notizen und Auszüge*, Niedersächsische Staats- und Universitätsbibliothek Göttingen, Cod. Ms., vol. 1, p. 76.

5. Anna de Lagarde, p. 32.

6. Ibid., p. 40.

7. Regarding these plans, see Rahlfs, p. 44, note 3; Anna de Lagarde, p. 13, for the next quote.

8. Rahlfs, p. 45.

9. See Manfred Botzenhart, *1848/49. Europa im Umbruch* (Paderborn, 1998), pp. 21ff.

10. Rahlfs, pp. 46ff.; regarding Bunsen's effectiveness in London, see Wilhelm Höcker, *Der Gesandte Bunsen als Vermittler zwischen Deutschland und England* (Göttingen, 1951).

11. The fact that the Orientalist and his glorification of English life was not a rare exception is illustrated by: Ian Buruma, *Anglomania. Europas englischer Traum* (Munich and Vienna, 2002).

12. Rahlfs, p. 87.

13. Anna de Lagarde, p. 37.

14. David Blackbourn, "Das Kaiserreich transnational. Eine Skizze," in: Sebastian Con-

rad and Jürgen Osterhammel (eds.), *Das Kaiserreich transnational. Deutschland in der Welt 1871–1914* (Göttingen, 2004), pp. 302–324, especially p. 313. The previous quote appears in: Rahlfs, p. 34, note 2.

15. A concise characterization of Renan, which does not spare the downsides of the major scholar, is offered by: Peter Gay, *Die Macht des Herzens. Das 19. Jahrhundert und die Erforschung des Ich* (Munich, 1999), pp. 160ff. Regarding the friendship between the two Orientalists, see also Lougee, pp. 80ff.

16. Quoted in: Rahlfs, p. 44.

17. See *Paul de Lagarde and Syrian Church History* with a foreword by Prof. D. Hermann Doerrie, ed. by the Göttinger Arbeitskreis für syrische Kirchengeschichte (Göttingen, 1968), p. 3. A reprint of the *Didascali apostolorum syriace* appeared in Osnabrück and Wiesbaden, 1967.

18. Staatsbibliothek Berlin, Darmstadt collection, Paul de Lagarde: Paul Bötticher's letter to the minister of education of October 7, 1853, where the following quotations also appear.

19. The following quotations are all based on: Geheimes Staatsarchiv Berlin, Nachlass Althoff B107, fol. 123r–126r; however palliative and largely untestable, see: *Lagarde: Aus dem deutschen Gelehrtenleben*, pp. 74ff., and Anna de Lagarde, p. 46.

20. See Heike Behlmer, "Ein neo-koptischer Brief Adolf Ermans an Paul de Lagarde. Zeugnis für eine wissenschaftsgeschichtliche Wende in der Erforschung des Koptischen," in: *Lingua Aegyptia 11* (2003), pp. 1–12, especially p. 6. Brugsch's scathing critique hurt Lagarde so much that, twenty-seven years later, he still meticulously rejected the accusation of lack of conscientiousness; see Lagarde, *Aus dem deutschen Gelehrtenleben*, pp. 25–65.

21. Both quotes are found in: Rahlfs, p. 16.

22. Paul de Lagarde, "Information about a Few Families with the Name Bötticher. Printed [. . .] as Manuscript" (Berlin, 1867), p. 27.

23. Ibid., p. 50. In any case, with "de Lagarde" it's not about "aristocratic fantasy names," as Stephan Malinowski: *Vom König zum Führer. Sozialer Niedergang und politische Radikalisierung im deutschen Adel zwischen Kaiserreich und NS-Staat* (Berlin, 2003), p. 191, erroneously asserted.

24. Fick and Sölle, p. 118.

25. The essay "Conservative?" is quoted according to the print version in *Paul de Lagarde, Deutsche Schriften. Gesamtausgabe letzter Hand. Mit einem Bild des Verfassers*, 5th ed. (Göttingen, 1920), pp. 5–12. The pagination can be found in the body text.

26. Regarding syntagma peculiar to "radical conservatism," see Vincent Viaene, "Paul de Lagarde: A Nineteenth-Century 'Radical' Conservative—and Precursor of National Socialism?" in: *European History Quarterly 26* (1996), pp. 527–555, especially pp. 528ff.; also see Lougee, pp. 2ff. and passim.

27. Generalities regarding England as a role model in the debates among German conservatives: Robert von Friedeburg, "England as a Model in the Debate about Aristocratic Reform between the Late Enlightenment and the Empire," in: Heinz Reif (ed.), *Adel und Bürgertum in Deutschland*, vol. 1 (Berlin, 2000), pp. 29–51.

28. Additionally as a monograph: Malinowski, *Vom König zum Führer.*

29. The text of the current tasks of the German policy is cited by: Paul de Lagarde, *Deutsche Schriften*, 5th ed. (Göttingen, 1920), pp. 18–39. For its historical influence during the Reichsgründungsjahrzehnt, see chapter 8, "Future Conspirators."

30. Thus emphasized by: Rüdiger Safranski, *Nietzsche: Biographie seines Denkens* (Munich and Vienna, 2000), p. 105. For general information regarding the mental characteristics of the Nachmärz period, when 750,000 Germans left their homeland and a surveillance mentality took hold—and not just in the universities: Wolfram Siemann, *Der Polizeiverein deutscher Staaten: Eine Dokumentation zur Überwachung der Öffentlichkeit nach der Revolution von 1848/49* (Tübingen, 1983), and Christian Jansen, *Einheit, Macht und Freiheit: Die Paulskirchenlinke und die deutsche Politik in der nachrevolutionären Epoche (1849–1866)*, (Düsseldorf, 2000).

31. Ludwig August von Rochau, *Grundsätze der Realpolitik—angewandt auf die staatlichen Zustände Deutschlands*. Reprint edited by Hans-Ulrich Wehler (Frankfurt, Berlin, and Vienna, 1972), p. 25. A bold but eminently worth reading interpretation of Rochau's ideas is offered by: Wolfgang Kraushaar, "Realpolitik als Ideologie: Von Ludwig August von Rochau zu Joschka Fischer," in: Wolfgang Kraushaar, *Fischer in Frankfurt: Karriere eines Aussenseiters* (Hamburg, 2001), pp. 120–188.

32. So said Kierkegaard from on high regarding the revolutionary course of events on March 23, 1848: "They stormed the palace in Paris, an indeterminate amount of people who did not themselves know what they wanted, without any clear thoughts. Then the king fled—and voila, the republic. Nonsense." Quoted in: Joakim Garff, *Kierkegaard: Biographie* (Munich and Vienna, 2004), p. 571.

33. Søren Kierkegaard, *Geheime Papiere. Aus dem Dänischen übersetzt, kommentiert und herausgegeben von Tim Hagemann* (Frankfurt am Main, 2004), p. 22.

34. Lagarde's letter of December 12, 1852: Niedersächsische Staats und Universitätsbibliothek Göttingen, Cod. Ms. Lagarde, *Notizen und Auszüge*, vol. 1, p. 82.

35. See the comments in the previous chapter regarding Lagarde's trial lecture in Halle; instructive as a case study: Michael Brenner, "Gott schütze uns vor unseren Freunden: Zur Ambivalenz des Philosemitismus im Kaiserreich," in: *Jahrbuch für Antisemitismusforschung* 2 (1993), pp. 174–199.

36. Niedersächsische Staats und Universitätsbibliothek Göttingen, Cod. Ms. Lagarde, *Notizen und Auszüge*, vol. 1, 24.

4. A DOUBLE LIFE

1. See Lagarde, *Aus dem deutschen Gelehrtenleben*, p. 67; *allgemein zu seiner Lehrerzeit*: Anna de Lagarde, pp. 50–84, as well as Rahlfs, pp. 50–53 and pp. 88–94.

2. See G. Nathanael Bonwetsch, "Aus vierzig Jahren deutscher Kirchengeschichte. Briefe an E.W. Hengstenberg," in: *Beiträge zur Förderung der christlichen Theologie*, 2nd series, XXIV/2 (Gütersloh, 1919), pp. 5ff.

3. Niedersächsische Staats und Universitätsbibliothek Göttingen, Cod. Ms. Ewald, No. 837, "Brief Lagardes an Ewald vom 22.Dezember 1856."

4. Lagarde, *Aus dem deutschen Gelehrtenleben*, p. 65.

5. Anna de Lagarde, pp. 55ff.

6. Rahlfs, p. 89; the next quotation is found in: Anna de Lagarde, p. 58.

7. Niedersächsische Staats und Universitätsbibliothek Göttingen, Cod. Ms. Lagarde, *Notizen und Auszüge*, vol. 1, p. 140; for the next quotation, see p. 143.

8. See Stern, *Kulturpessimismus*, pp. 52ff. Lagarde's Göttingen estate contains numerous letters from his former students. Among them is a letter from Georg Ruge of June 1, 1869, that captures Lagarde's encouragement of free thinking.

9. For the teacher's salary and status, see Heinz-Elmar Tenorth, "Lehrerberuf und Lehrerbildung," in: *Handbuch der deutschen Bildungsgeschichte*, vol. 3: *1800–1870*, ed. by Karl-Ernst Jeismann and Peter Lundgreen (Munich, 1987), pp. 250–270, especially p. 264.

10. Rahlfs, p. 71; regarding the private atmosphere that struck Lagarde's former students, see the birthday letters from Hans Wegschneider of October 31, 1866 and 1867.

11. Uffa Jensen, *Gebildete Doppelgänger. Bürgerliche Juden und Protestanten im 19. Jahrhundert* (Göttingen, 2005), p. 119.

12. Affirming Lagarde's editorial practices: Paul Richard Berger, "Zur Herstellung einer kritischen Textedition nach den gegenwärtigen Möglichkeiten der Lexikographie," in: *Paul de Lagarde und die syrische Kirchengeschichte mit einem Geleitwort von Prof. D. Hermann Dörries*, ed. by Göttinger Arbeitskreis für syrische Kirchengeschichte (Göttingen, 1968), pp. 27–31; rather critical: Rahlfs, p. 54. Also worth mentioning regarding relevant editions: Paul de Lagarde, *Analecta Syriaca*, 1858 (Neudruck Osnabrück, 1967); Lagarde, *Titi Bostreni. Contra manichaeos libri quatuor syriace* (Berlin, 1859); Lagarde, *Clementis Romani. Recognitiones Syriace* (Leipzig and London, 1861); Lagarde, *Constitutiones Apostolorum*, 1862, as well as Lagarde (ed.), *Die vier Evangelien. Arabisch aus der Wiener Handschrift*, reprint of the 1864 edition (Osnabrück, 1972).

13. Hermann-Peter Eberlein, *Flamme bin ich sicherlich! Friedrich Nietzsche, Franz Overbeck und ihre Freunde* (Köln, 1999), p. 53. Kierkegaard's justification for his excessive consumption: "My extravagances have [. . .] a substantial relationship to my productivity, which I saw as my only option and, on the other hand, an indescribable blessing from God, to attach such meaning to my life. Therefore, every extravagance was allowed, to let me be productive." (Garff, p. 598); regarding Schopenhauer's more moderate behavior patterns, see Garff, pp. 803–810.

14. Paul de Lagarde, "d'à côté du chemin," printed as manuscript (Berlin, 1859). Lagarde later placed the poem in his *Deutsche Schriften*, where, without a separate title, it now heads up the round of Lagarde's poetry. The closing lines are even more dramatic: "You will forget for time and eternity."

15. Kierkegaard, *Geheime Papiere*, p. 254.

16. Paul de Lagarde, *Symmicta*, vol. 2 (Berlin, 1880), p. 140.

17. See Rahlfs, p. 55; Lagarde's letter to Ewald on January 27, 1855, is found at: Fick and Sölle, pp. 119ff.

18. Rahlfs, pp. 120ff.; the next quote: Rahlfs, p. 123.

19. Niedersächsische Staats und Universitätsbibliothek Göttingen, Cod. Ms. Ewald, No. 853.

20. Staatsbibliothek Berlin, Mommsen's estate. General information regarding Mommsen's key position in Classical studies: Stefan Rebenich, *Theodor Mommsen. Eine Biographie* (Darmstadt, 2002).

21. Quoted in: Gangolf Hübinger, *Theodor Mommsen und das Kaiserreich* (Friedrichsruh, 2003), p. 15. The next statement from Lagarde is found in his letter to Mommsen of November 22, 1864: Staatsbibliothek Berlin, Mommsen's estate.

22. The text of the petition and a brief sketch of the historical context is to be found in: Lagarde, *Symmicta*, vol. 2, pp. 80–86; see p. 82 for the next two quotes.

23. Lagarde's letter to Adolf Hilgenfeld of June 2, 1862, quoted from: Pölcher, p. 28. The allusion was to the *Neue Preussische Zeitung*, appearing twice daily and the mouthpiece of

the archconservatives. Echoing the Iron Cross on its front page, the Berlin paper was called the *Kreuzzeitung* by supporters and opponents alike.

24. Lagarde's letter to Hase of February 2, 1864; the previous quotation is found in: Lagarde, *Symmicta*, vol. 2, p. 29.

25. Niedersächsische Staats und Universitätsbibliothek Göttingen, Cod. Ms. Lagarde, *Notizen und Auszüge*, vol. 1, pp. 95ff.; in her reproduction of the December 15 letter, Anna de Lagarde omitted her husband's criticism of German classics (Anna de Lagarde, pp. 56ff.).

26. The text, "Ueber das Verhältnis des deutschen Staates zu Theologie, Kirche und Religion. Ein Versuch Nicht-Theologen zu orientieren," is cited by: Lagarde, *Deutsche Schriften*, 5th ed. (Göttingen, 1920) pp. 40–83; for its genesis, see p. 40.

27. The nineteenth-century introduction of the heliocentric view of the world was a particularly popular example of the irreversibility of the cognitive process. How complex the state of discussions actually was is illustrated by Paul K. Feyerabend, *Wider den Methodenzwang. Skizze einer anarchistischen Erkenntnistheorie* (Frankfurt am Main, 1976), thereby provoking heavy epistemological discussions in a very different time.

28. See the documents in the Universitätsarchiv Halle, Philosophische Fakultät I, no. 93; the following quotations appear in the same source. The family perspective about the events in Halle is offered by: Anna de Lagarde, pp. 62–68. This prime example of Protestant aggression in the nineteenth century is still worth reading: Johannes Gildemeister and Heinrich von Sybel, *Der heilige Rock zu Trier und die zwanzig andern heiligen ungenähten Röcke. Eine historische Untersuchung* (Düsseldorf, 1844).

29. Niedersächsische Staats- und Universitätsbibliothek Göttingen, Cod. Ms. Ewald, No. 848; the quoted passage from Lagarde's letter of July 20, 1862, is found in: Anna de Lagarde, p. 67.

30. The description of the Giessen incident follows the relevant documents in Lagarde's Göttingen estate; Anna de Lagarde, pp. 68–74, who was used for support, justified the behavior of her husband unconditionally.

31. A prime example of the worldview of a German mandarin would be that of Wilamowitz, who did not have long to wait for his first professorship. The full professor, who knew his subject like no other, states from on high "that the misjudged and benighted lecturer belongs in the realm of academic mythology. Anyone who felt so had themselves to thank": Wilamowitz-Moellendorf, memoirs, p. 174.

32. *Neue Evangelische Zeitung*, vol. 1863, no. 47, col. 751ff.

33. This underestimates Schutte, p. 37, who occasionally falls under the spell of his own rhetoric when discussing Lagarde's scholarly objectives; for the consequences, see Rahlfs, pp. 58–62.

34. A copy of the lost letter is found in: Niedersächsische Staats- und Universitätsbibliothek Göttingen, Cod. Ms. Lagarde, *Notizen und Auszüge*, vol. 1, p. 134. Lagarde's letter of May 3, 1863, is found in the partial estate of Jacob Grimm of the Jagiellonian Library in Krakow.

35. Lagarde, *Die vier Evangelien*, p. xxxi; the previous quotation is found in: Pölcher, p. 29.

36. Staatsbibliothek Berlin, Mommsen's estate. Legend has it that seventy-two scholars on the island of Pharos created the Greek translation of the Old Testament. Among scholars, it was quite common to use the Latin numerals LXX instead of the word Septuagint.

37. Anna de Lagarde, p. 77; see also Rahlfs, p. 53.

5. FINALLY A PROFESSOR

1. For the consequences, see Anna de Lagarde, pp. 78ff. General information regarding the normatively charged understanding of scholarship in Prussia: Bernhard vom Brocke, "Preussische Bildungspolitik (und Wissenschaftspolitik) . . . ," in: Wolfgang Böhme (ed.), *Preussen—eine Herausforderung* (Bad Herrenalb, 1981), pp. 54–99. For a different view regarding dealing with the nonentity "Humboldt": Rüdiger vom Bruch, "Abschied von Humboldt? Etappen deutscher Universitätsgeschichte, 1810–1945," in: Mitchell Ash (ed.), *Mythos Humboldt. Vergangenheit und Zukunft der deutschen Universitäten* (Vienna, Cologne, and Weimar, 1999), pp. 29–57.

2. Anna de Lagarde, p. 80. The previous quotation can be found in: Hans Georg Kippenberg, *Die Entdeckung der Religionsgeschichte. Religionswissenschaft und Moderne* (Munich, 1997), p. 62.

3. Pölcher, p. 32.

4. Paul de Lagarde, *Gesammelte Abhandlungen. Neudruck der Ausgabe 1866* (Osnabrück, 1966), p. xi.

5. Deutsches Literaturarchiv Marbach, Cotta estate; the former, quite typical quote comes from a letter from Lagarde to Wilhelm Hertz of January 14, 1867.

6. Pölcher, p. 38, on which page the next quote in Lagarde's letter of July 17, 1867, to Hilgenfeld also appears.

7. Niedersächsische Staats und Universitätsbibliothek Göttingen, Cod. Ms. Lagarde, *Notizen und Auszüge*, vol. 1, p. 156; the following quotes are found on p. 162 of the same source and in Anna de Lagarde, p. 167.

8. Quoted in: Rebenich, p. 167. General information regarding the degree to which war was accepted: Kolaus Buschmann, *Einkreisung und Waffenbruderschaft. Die öffentliche Deutung von Krieg und Nation in Deutschland, 1850–1871* (Göttingen, 2003).

9. Niedersächsische Staats und Universitätsbibliothek Göttingen, Cod. Ms. Lagarde, *Notizen und Auszüge*, vol. 1, p. 164.

10. Anna de Lagarde, p. 86.

11. Within the extensive body of literature regarding the importance of universalism in scholarship, there is only mention of the classic treatise by Robert Merton, "The Normative Structure of Scholarship," in: Norman W. Stroyer (ed.), *The Sociology of Scholarship: Theoretical and Empirical Investigations* (Chicago, 1973), pp. 267–278.

12. Lagarde, *Nachrichten*, pp. 14ff.

13. Lagarde, *Beiträge zur baktrischen Lexikographie. Neudruck der Ausgabe*, 1867 (Osnabrück and Wiesbaden, 1967).

14. Lagarde, *Materialien zur Kritik und Geschichte des Pentateuchs. Neudruck der Ausgabe*, 1867 (Osnabrück and Wiesbaden, 1967), p. xi. For the consequences, see Otto Eissfeldt, *Entstehungsgeschichte des Alten Testaments*, 3rd newly revised ed. (Tübingen, 1964), pp. 928ff.

15. Pölcher, pp. 32ff.

16. Paul de Lagarde, *Genesis graece, e fide editionis Sixtinae addita scripturae discrepantia e libris manu scriptis a se ipso conlatis et editionibus Complutensi et Aldina adcuratissime enotata edita* (Leipzig, 1868). Regarding the objective of Lagarde's Genesis edition, see Rahlfs, p. 67.

17. In the original, Lagarde declined mentioning Paul's quotation, giving only "Corinthians 4:2."

18. Regarding the smooth process preceding the awarding of the doctorate, see the documentation in the Universitätsarchiv Halle, rep. 27, no. 889.

19. General information concerning this: Ute Frevert, *Ehrenmänner. Das Duell in der bürgerlichen Gesellschaft* (Munich, 1991), which, not by accident, tells many stories about the academic world.

20. Letter from Prussian culture minister Heinrich von Mühler to University of Gottingen curator Adolf Warnstedt on March 5, 1869; Universitätsarchiv Göttingen, Kur 5903, fol. 1r.

21. Fick and Sölle, p. 111.

22. Universitätsbibliothek Tübingen Md 782–131.

23. See Perlitt, p. 192.

24. Lagarde, *Symmicta*, vol. 2, p. 95.

25. Lagarde, *Erinnerungen an Friedrich Rückert*, p. 20; see p. 14 for the previous quote.

26. Lagarde, *Übersicht über die im Aramäischen, Arabischen und Hebräischen übliche Bildung der Nomina nebst Register und Nachträgen.* Reprinted from the 1889 and 1891 editions (Osnabrück, 1972), p. 2.

27. Niedersächsische Staats und Universitätsbibliothek Göttingen, Cod. Ms. Lagarde, *Notizen und Auszüge*, vol. 1, pp. 174ff.

28. Quoted from: Favrat, p. 77, note 1.

29. Thus, Lagarde in his letter of August 28, 1870, to the editor of the *Magdeburger Zeitung*; for the consequences, see Rebenich, p. 168.

30. Ernest Renan, *Was ist eine Nation? Und andere politische Schriften* (Vienna and Bozen, 1995), p. 99. For the discursive context, see Dieter Langewiesche, "Was heisst Erfindung der Nation? Nationalgeschichte als Artefakt—oder Geschichtsdeutung als Machtkampf," in: *Historische Zeitschrift* 277 (2003), pp. 593–617, especially pp. 599ff.

31. Quoted in: Rebenich, p. 168, where the next passage can also be found.

32. A brief interpretation of this key document is found in Stern, *Kulturpessimismus*, p. 47, which assumes, albeit erroneously, that Lagarde directed his letter to Prussian King Wilhelm I; see also Lougee, p. 111.

33. See Lagarde's letter from January 28, 1871, to the provost of the Münchener Hofkirche, Ignaz von Döllinger, which was designed to lobby Ludwig II for the annexation of Luxembourg. It culminates with these words: "What Germany wins is won for the kingdom of God, so that for us there can be no less than a present, no less than a ruling power, which really *can* come to pass for us, whereas in France, unfortunately, there is by all human reckoning little chance of breaking fresh ground."

34. Pölcher, pp. 43ff., See Stern, *Kulturpessimismus*, p. 47.

35. Henri Bordier (ed.), *L'Allemagne aux Tuileries de 1850 à 1870* (Paris, 1872).

36. Anonymous, "German Letters to Napoleon III," in: *Deutsche Allgemeine Zeitung No.* 75 of March 31, 1872; the following quote appears in the same source.

37. Niedersächsische Staats und Universitätsbibliothek Göttingen, Cod. Ms. Lagarde, *Notizen und Auszüge*, vol. 2, p. 2; the next quotation appears on p. 3.

38. Staatsbliothek Berlin, Darmstadt collection, Paul de Lagarde: source of the following quotations.

39. The following: according to documents in the Geheimes Staatsarchiv Berlin I, rep. 76 V, in sect. 6, title IV, vol. 4.

40. Universitätsarchiv Göttingen, Kur 5903, fol. 13r; see also Hanhardt, pp. 280ff., who

first drew attention to the side notes (marginalia) and offers a slightly different interpretation of Lagarde's behavior.

41. Regarding Jaffé's suicide, which greatly occupied his contemporaries, see Horst Fuhrmann, "Sind eben alles Menschen gewesen," in: *Gelehrtenleben im 19. und 20. Jahrhundert. Dargestellt am Beispiel der Monumenta Germaniae Historica und ihrer Mitarbeiter* (Munich, 1996), pp. 108–115.

42. Niedersächsische Staats und Universitätsbibliothek Göttingen, Cod. Ms. Lagarde, *Notizen und Auszüge*, vol. 1, p. 177.

6. A HOUSE LIKE A FORTRESS

1. Heike Behlmer, "Heinrich Friedrich Karl Brugsch (1827–1894) Ägyptologe. Rede anlässlich der Enthüllung einer Gedenktafel am 26.09.2003, Untere Masch 16," in: *Göttinger Jahrbuch 51* (2003), pp. 165–169, especially p. 168; the previous quotation is found in: Wilamowitz, *Erinnerungen*, p. 198.

2. Paul de Lagarde, "Zum Unterrichtsgesetze," in: Paul de Lagarde, *Deutsche Schriften*, 5th ed. (Göttingen, 1920), pp. 183–235, especially p. 224.

3. Schemann, *Lagarde. Lebens und Erinnerungsbild*, p. 381; The next quote: Anna de Lagarde, pp. 25ff.

4. Niedersächsische Staats und Universitätsbibliothek Göttingen, Cod. Ms. Lagarde, *Notizen und Auszüge*, vol. 2, p. 29.

5. Concerning Lagarde's anger about the practices in Basel and Smend's failure: Niklaus Peter and Andreas Urs Sommer (eds.), "Franz Overbecks Briefwechsel mit Paul de Lagarde," in: *Zeitschrift für Neuere Theologiegeschichte 4* (1997), pp. 127–171, especially pp. 164–168.

6. See Heike Behlmer, " 'As Safe as in the British Museum': Paul de Lagarde and His Borrowing of Manuscripts from the Collection of Robert Curzon," in: *The Journal of Egyptian Archeology 89* (2003), pp. 231–238, especially p. 236, and Rebenich, pp. 204ff.

7. Lagarde's letter to the Göttingen Police of May 6, 1877; the preceding quotations are found in Lagarde's letter to the same recipient of June 4, 1876. General information about the heated political climate in the decade of the founding of the Empire: Thomas Nipperdey, *Deutsche Geschichte, 1866–1918*, vol. 2: *Machtstaat vor der Demokratie* (Munich, 1992), pp. 359–381, and Hans-Ulrich Wehler, *Deutsche Gesellschaftsgeschichte, Bd.3: Von der "Deutschen Doppelrevolution" bis zum Beginn des Ersten Weltkrieges, 1848–1914* (Munich, 1995), pp. 889–934.

8. *Göttinger Zeitung*, no. 4727, from June 19, 1879.

9. See Adelheid von Saldern, "Göttingen im Kaiserreich," in: Rudolf von Thadden and Günther J. Trittel (eds.), *Göttingen. Geschichte einer Universitätsstadt, Bd.3: Von der preussischen Mittelstadt zur südniedersächsischen Grosstadt, 1866–1989* (Göttingen, 1989), pp. 5–62, especially pp. 47ff.; Lagarde's article appeared in the *Göttinger Zeitung*, no. 4032, of March 7, 1877.

10. See Lagarde's letters to the Royal Library in Berlin of September 22 and October 2, 1882.

11. See Lagarde's letter to Sauppe of July 25, 1871.

12. Heinrich August Winkler, *Der lange Weg nach Westen*, vol. 1: *Deutsche Geschichte vom Ende des Alten Reiches bis zum Untergang der Weimarer Republik* (Munich, 2000), p. 235.

13. Regarding the trouble-free postdoctoral lecturing qualification procedure, see the

documentation at the Universitätsarchiv Göttingen, Philosophische Fakultät Dekanatsband, no. 155ff. 253r–259r.

14. Lagarde's letter to Overbeck of December 5, 1874; quoted from: Peter and Sommer, 149.

15. See her letter to Ludwig Stern of March 4, 1885, which states in a conciliatory tone: "What is left for an Egyptologist save universities and museums? In the latter case you can well retain enough time for scholarly work, which can sometimes lead to a professorship. It does not really require an illness for a loyal officer to be denied an upcoming directorship, only to have it awarded to someone younger. Look at the whole situation from this viewpoint firmly and calmly before you decide."

16. Niedersächsische Staats und Universitätsbibliothek Göttingen, Cod. Ms. Lagarde, *Notizen und Auszüge*, vol. 2, p. 54; the following quotation appears on p. 56 of the same source.

17. See ibid., p. 58, for Anna de Lagarde's subsequent side notes on one of her husband's letters from Turin of March 13, 1883: "Smooth roads were always my fear: he was not careful."

18. Ibid., pp. 13ff.

19. Ibid., p. 60, for Lagarde's letter to his wife of March 16, 1883. Monograph on the idea that Jews were unable to speak standard German, and therefore were "mumbling": Sander L. Gilman, *Jüdischer Selbsthass. Antisemitismus und die verborgene Sprache der Juden* (Frankfurt am Main, 1993).

20. Lagarde's letter to his wife of April 14, 1881; Niedersächsische Staats und Universitätsbibliothek Göttingen, Cod. Ms. Lagarde, *Notizen und Auszüge*, vol. 2, p. 48.

21. Ibid., Lagarde, vol. 1, pp. 108ff.

22. This applies, in my opinion, despite the different account by Peter Gay, *Die zarte Leidenschaft. Liebe im bürgerlichen Zeitalter* (Munich, 1987), because it only shows a few cosmopolitan university towns like Heidelberg as having a tangible display of interaction.

23. Fundamental information regarding Althoff, who long deserved a modern biography: Bernhard vom Brocke, *Hochschul und Wissenschaftspolitik in Preussen im Deutschen Kaiserreich, 1882–1907*. The "Althoff system," in: Peter Baumgart (ed.), *Bildungspolitik in Preussen zur Zeit des Kaiserreichs* (Stuttgart, 1980), pp. 9–118.

24. Anna de Lagarde's letter to Gustav Bösche of November 9, 1890.

25. Presumably it is about the essay "Die Religion der Zukunft," which concluded Lagarde's *Deutsche Schriften*. For his interpretation, see chapter 8.

26. This is demonstrated by Lagarde's note in the margin of his birthday letter to his wife.

27. Niedersächsische Staats und Universitätsbibliothek Göttingen, Cod. Ms. Lagarde, *Notizen und Auszüge*, vol. 2, p. 76; copy of Lagarde's London letter is missing a proper date.

28. Ibid., p. 88, where the next quote can also be found.

29. Paul de Lagarde, *Gedichte. Gesamtausgabe besorgt von Anna de Lagarde, 2. verm. Aufl.* (Göttingen, 1911), p. 21.

30. Anna de Lagarde's memo of April 30, 1912: Niedersächsische Staats und Universitätsbibliothek Göttingen, Cod. Ms. Lagarde, *Notizen und Auszüge*, foreword.

31. Lagarde, *Gedichte*, p. 39; the next quote appears on the same page.

32. Ibid., p. 80; For an explanation, see Anna de Lagarde, p. 10; Hanhart, p. 278, and Stern, *Kulturpessimismus*, pp. 56ff.

33. Lagarde, *Gedichte*, p. 81.

34. Lagarde's letter to Theodor Nöldeke of July 7, 1878.

35. Instructive as well: Klaus Christian Köhnke, *Entstehung und Aufstieg des Neukantianismus. Die deutsche Universitätsphilosophie zwischen Idealismus und Positivismus* (Frankfurt am Main, 1986), pp. 302–319.

36. Draft of Anna de Lagarde's letter to Georg Hoffmann of November 19, 1879, with the handwritten note in the margin "copy to be verbatim." Hoffmann was no more than twenty-six years old at his appointment at Kiel in 1870.

37. Lagarde's letter to Eugen Wolff of September 1, 1890.

38. Niedersächsische Staats und Universitätsbibliothek Göttingen, Cod. Ms. Lagarde, *Notizen und Auszüge*, vol. 2, pp. 81–87.

39. Joachim Fest, *Hitler. Eine Biographie* (Frankfurt am Main and Berlin, 1973), p. 521.

40. Willy Real, "Paul Lagarde, der Politiker," in: Ernst Heinen and Hans Julius Schoeps (eds.), *Geschichte in der Gegenwart. Festschrift für Kurt Kluxen zu seinem 60. Geburtstag* (Paderborn, 1972), pp. 161–178, especially p. 163.

41. Stated emphatically: Safranski, p. 107.

7. AN ESTABLISHED OUTSIDER

1. The discussions are found in the unordered part of Lagarde's estate, which is rarely consulted for research.

2. The holiday requests are contained in Lagarde's personal file, Universitätsarchiv Göttingen, Kur 5903.

3. Rahlfs, p. 92.

4. On Lagarde's lecturing style, see Schemann, *Lagarde. Lebens und Erinnerungsbild*, pp. 401ff. Lagarde described his identity as grammar school teacher in a submission to Minister of Education and Cultural Affairs Gustav von Gossler of September 21, 1886, with these proud words: "My teaching is of the sort in which the subjects assigned to me are pursuant to exclusively private teaching, and therefore [. . .] considerably more laborious, more accountable and less predictable than my classroom lectures or my colleague's dictations."

5. This judgment is handed down by Ernst Troeltsch in his essay "Meine Bücher" from the year 1921, as quoted from: Friedemann Voigt (ed.), *Ernst Troeltsch Lesebuch. Ausgewählte Texte* (Tübingen, 2003), pp. 372–385, especially p. 384.

6. Geheimes Staatsarchiv Berlin, Nachlass Althoff, B107, fol. 151r.

7. See vom Brocke, *Hochschul und Wissenschaftspolitik*.

8. Lagarde's letter to Richard Schöne of November 4, 1879.

9. See Lagarde, *Symmicta*, vol. 2, p. 146; regarding the "Ära Puttkamer," in which political motives regarding the placing of officials played an important role: Norbert Kampe, *Studenten und "Judenfrage" im Deutschen Kaiserreich. Die Entstehung einer akademischen Trägerschicht des Antisemitismus* (Göttingen, 1988), pp. 60–70.

10. To the widow of the recently deceased Classical philologist Friedrich Wilhelm Schneidewin, who openly criticized the expulsion of the "Göttingen Seven," Lagarde wrote officially on September 13, 1882: her husband had "fought against the idea that violence in Germany should ever be allowed to be tried in court." The university, Lagarde continued, will honor his reputation.

11. Thus the derisive contemporary term for the forgeries. A brief description of the events is offered by: Adolf Erman, *Mein Werden und mein Wirken. Erinnerungen eines alten Berliner Gelehrten* (Berlin, 1929), pp. 237ff.

12. See the text with the heading "War in der Probe nicht unterzubringen," which contains a report about Mommsen's alleged mistakes and failures; Niedersächsische Staats und Universitätsbibliothek Göttingen, Cod. Ms. Lagarde, *Notizen und Auszüge*, no. 154, p. 7.

13. Paul de Lagarde, "Der angebliche Petrus-Papyrus," in: *Protestantische Kirchenzeitung für das evangelische Deutschland*, April 28, 1880, pp. 29ff.

14. Niedersächsische Staats und Universitätsbibliothek Göttingen, Cod. Ms. Lagarde: "'Einige aus der Vorrede der Symmicta vor der Drucklegung gestrichene Sätze' vom 10.März 1877," p. xiv.

15. Lagarde, *Symmicta*, p. 153.

16. Lagarde, *Symmicta*, vol. 2, p. vii; the next quotation appears on p. 98 of the same source.

17. Ibid., p. 109; the next quote is found on p. 114 of the same source.

18. Lagarde, *Gelehrtenleben*, p. 5. Regarding confusion about these prospects, see Georg Hoffmann's letter to Anna de Lagarde of November 22, 1880: "But of what use is it to draw the position of a party into the debate, be it political or religious? Does such a thing depend on Lagarde's perfect right, or anyone else's? Should indecency be limited to parties?"

19. Also instructive as a case study: Gangolf Hübinger, *Kulturprotestantismus und Politik. Zum Verhältnis von Liberalismus und Protestantismus im wilhelminischen Deutschland* (Tübingen, 1994).

20. Lagarde's letter to Wilhelm Nowack of January 1, 1888.

21. See Niels Pettersson, "Das Kaiserreich in Prozessen ökonomischer Globalisierung," in: Sebastian Conrad and Jürgen Osterhammel (eds.), *Das Kaiserreich transnational. Deutschland in der Welt, 1871–1914* (Göttingen, 2004), pp. 49–67, especially p. 60.

22. Lagarde's letter to Otto Benndorf of October 27, 1889.

23. Paul Haupt's letter to Lagarde of July 23, 1879. For general information regarding Haupt's career: Rykle Borger, "Ein Jahrhundert Assyriologie an der Universität Göttingen," in: *Universität Göttingen Informationen*, no. 9, December 6–8, 1980, pp. 3–9.

24. Lagarde's letter to Minister of Education and Cultural Affairs Gossler of December 2, 1881.

25. Lagarde's letter to Althoff of May 18, 1888: Geheimes Staatsarchiv Berlin, Nachlass Althoff, B18. May, fol. 151v.

26. Borger, p. 6; see also Erman, pp. 233ff., for Haupt's disrespectful characterization, which, however, does not refer to Lagarde.

27. Otto Baumgarten, *Zum Gedächtnis an Alfred Schöne, geb. 16.oktober 1836—gest. 8.Januar 1918, Kiel 1928*, no pagination.

28. *Nürnberger Anzeiger*, no. 249, of December 16, 1874. The following description accords with Schöne's mere ten-page personnel file in the Archives of the University of Erlangen, A 2/1, No. S 37.

29. See Schöne's letter to Lagarde of February 9, 1877, in which he effusively assures him that he is "the quantum of knowledge, will, ability, learning and intellectual activity, hidden in so many of your books, nevermore to be compared with the graceful, pleasant chatter and occasional thoughtlessness of the late Livius."

30. In a letter to Erlangen lawyer Heinrich Marquardsen of June 2, 1878; regarding Mommsen's influence in matters of appointment, see Rebenich, p. 123.

31. Quoted from: Hanhart, p. 279.

32. See Calder, "Wilamowitz' Call to Göttingen," pp. 145ff.

33. In his letter to Althoff of January 29, 1887, Lagarde stressed that he saw "the university as Schöne's own field of operations." He continued: "[S]ince he comes to my home once a week in the evening, I now know him well enough to be able to credit him with lots of teaching ability, a strong sense of duty, orientation capabilities, and lofty points of view." Geheimes Staatsarchiv Berlin, Nachlass Althoff, B107, fol. 135v; see fol. 137v of the same source for the next quotation.

34. Also knowledgeable and amusing: Behlmer, "Ein neo-koptischer Brief Adolf Ermans an Paul de Lagarde."

35. On Lagarde's promotion in England: Rahlfs, pp. 94ff.; the previous quote is found in Olshausen's letter to Lagarde of January 10, 1880.

36. See Marc Schalenberg, "Die Rezeption des deutschen Universitätsmodells in Oxford 1850–1914," in: Rudolf Muhs, Johannes Paulmann, and Willibald Steinmetz (eds.), *Aneignung und Abwehr. Interkultureller Transfer zwischen Deutschland und Grossbritanien im 19. Jahrhundert* (Munich and Vienna, 1998), pp. 198–226. As a characteristic detail, Schalenberg, p. 216, stresses that the term *scholarship* was often left untranslated in English texts [. . .].

37. Barend Sijmons's letter to Lagarde of May 14, 1885.

38. Quoted from: Kippenberg, p. 65.

39. See Heike Behlmer, "Schenute, Besa und Lagarde—Eine unbekannte Episode der Forschungsgeschichte," in: *Journal of Coptic Studies* 5 (2003), pp. 55–66, especially p. 58.

40. See Lagarde's letter to Falk of March 15, 1877.

41. So wrote Spitta in his letter to Lagarde of August 5, 1882.

42. See Lagarde's "Bericht über meine Reise nach Czernowitz," October 13, 1874: Niedersächsische Staats und Universitätsbibliothek Göttingen, Cod. Ms. Lagarde, *ungeordneter Teil*; the next quote appears in the same source.

43. See Lagarde's letter to the senate of the University of Czernowitz of December 13, 1875.

44. To differentiate: Schutte, p. 23.

45. Quoted from: Stern, *Kulturpessimismus*, p. 46.

46. Rudolf Smend, "1887—die Universität in Preussen," in: Bernd Moeller (ed.), *Stationen der Göttinger Universitätsgeschichte. 1737–1787–1837–1887–1937. Eine Vortragsreihe* (Göttingen, 1988), pp. 68–90, especially pp. 76ff.

47. See the relevant message in the Universitätsarchiv Göttingen, Kur 5903, fol. 58r; see also Lagarde, fol. 68r of the same source, for the next quotation.

48. See Lagarde's "Bericht für die Gesellschaft der Wissenschaften über seine Bologna-Reise vom 6. bis 15. Juni 1888": Niedersächsische Staats und Universitätsbibliothek Göttingen, Cod. Ms. Lagarde, *ungeordneter Teil.*

49. Lagarde, *Symmicta*, vol. 2, p. 81; see also Lagarde's letter to Richard Schöne of December 16, 1879, where a similar confessional appears: "You know, my happiness and unhappiness is that I take everything seriously, very seriously."

50. The document is reproduced in full in Lagarde's article "Noch einmal meine Ausgabe der Septuaginta," in: *Mittheilungen*, vol. 3 (Göttingen, 1889), pp. 229–256, especially pp. 236–239. The following quotations appear in the same source, pp. 238ff.

8. FUTURE CONSPIRATORS

1. Quoted from: Winkler, *Der lange Weg nach Westen*, vol. 1, p. 212.

2. See the classical depiction by Hans Rosenberg, *Grosse Depression und Bismarckzeit. Wirtschaftsablauf, Gesellschaft und Politik in Mittel-europa* (Berlin, 1967). Data regarding feverish speculation during the Gründerjahre and the great stock market crash is described by: Fritz Stern, *Gold und Eisen. Bismarck und sein Bankier Bleichröder*, (Berlin, 1999), pp. 264ff., and Massimo Ferrari Zumbini, *Die Wurzeln des Bösen. Gründerjahre des Anti-semitismus: Von der Bismarckzeit zu Hitler* (Frankfurt am Main, 2003), pp. 112–128.

3. See Barbara Besslich, *Wege in den Kulturkrieg. Zivilisationskritik in Deutschland, 1890–1914* (Darmstadt, 2000), p. 57.

4. Also, at the start of pp. 81–84: this reprint of quotes adheres to the fifth edition of the *Deutsche Schriften*.

5. Ernest Renan, *Paulus. Autorisierte deutsche Ausgabe* (Leipzig and Paris, 1869); the historical scholarly background is sketched by: Daniel Havemann, "Evangelische Polemik. Nietzsches Paulusdeutung," in: *Nietzsche-Studien 30* (2001), pp. 175–186, especially p. 179.

6. Niedersächsische Staats und Universitätsbibliothek Göttingen, Cod. Ms. Lagarde, *Notizen und Auszüge*, vol. 2, p. 38.

7. See Jensen, pp. 52ff.

8. Niedersächsische Staats und Universitätsbibliothek Göttingen, Cod. Ms. Lagarde, *Notizen und Auszüge*, vol. 2, p. 12.

9. Personal documents substantiating the up-to-now untroubled relationship between Lagarde and Ritschl. Later, Lagarde did his best to ensure that this fact would be forgotten. On December 11, 1886, he wrote to Karl Johannes Neumann: "Ritschl has called them scrawlings and scribblings, ever since my first essay appeared in 1873, which he approved, but then declared he had to fight, in full opposition to me, and never declared his reasons: he is thus Göttingen's worst polluter, has laid waste to its theologians, has become a burden to my life, whose objective powers I recognize and subjectively regard as immoral, even devilish."

10. Johannes Wedde, "Das Verhältnis des deutschen Staates zu Theologie, Kirche und Religion," in: *Die Literatur. Wochenschrift für das nationale Geistesleben der Gegenwart*, no. 7, February 13, 1874, pp. 97ff. For discursive context, see Friedrich Wilhelm Graf, "Protestantische Theologie in der Gesellschaft des Kaiserreichs," in: Graf, *Profile des neuzeitlichen Protestantismus*, vol. 2, part 1 (Gütersloh, 1992), pp. 12–117, especially pp. 23ff.

11. See Lagarde's letters to Peter Reichensperger of January 4, 1873, and February 14, 1874.

12. Overbeck's letter of February 1, 1871, is found in the scholarly edition by Peter and Sommer, pp. 140–144, with the quote appearing on p. 140; for what follows, see Eberlein, pp. 97–101.

13. Peter and Sommer, p. 142, where the next quote also appears.

14. Franz Overbeck, "Ueber die Christlichkeit unserer heutigen Theologie. Streit und Friedensschrift," in: Overbeck, *Werke und Nachlass*, vol. 1 (Stuttgart and Weimar, 1994), pp. 167–256, especially pp. 244ff.

15. Andreas Urs Sommer, "Zwischen Agitation, Religionsstiftung und 'Hoher Politik': Friedrich Nietzsche und Paul de Lagarde," in: *Nietzscheforschung. Ein Jahrbuch 4* (1998), pp. 169–194, especially p. 170, note 5. For historical context: Karlfried Gründer (ed.), *Der*

Streit um Nietzsches "Geburt der Tragödie." Die Schriften von E. Rohde, R. Wagner, U. von Wilamowitz-Moellendorf (Hildesheim, 1969).

16. Friedrich Nietzsche, *Briefwechsel. Kritische Gesamtausgabe*, part 2, vol. 3 (Berlin and New York, 1978), p. 121.

17. See Ernst Schulin, "Zeitgemässe Historie um 1870. Zu Nietzsche, Burckhardt und zum "Historismus," in: *Historische Zeitschrift 281* (2005), pp. 33–58, especially pp. 45–48.

18. A reconstruction of the Aphorismus, which was originally planned for the second volume of *Menschliches, Allzumenschliches*, is offered by: Sommer, p. 185.

19. See Friedrich Nietzsche, "Der Antichrist. Fluch auf das Christenthum," *Werke. Kritische Gesamtausgabe*, part VI, vol. 3 (Berlin, 1969), pp. 161–252, especially pp. 211–221; the next citation appears in the same source, p. 209.

20. Paul de Lagarde, "Diagnose," *Deutsche Schriften*, 5th ed., pp. 95–105, especially p. 95; the next two quotes appear on p. 101 of the same source.

21. Moltke's letter to Lagarde of December 17, 1874.

22. Reproduced in: Richard Fick, "Lagarde und Carlyle," in: *Mitteilungen des Universitätsbundes Göttingen 21* (1941), no. 2, pp. 19–22, especially pp. 20ff. Their pathos-filled speeches prove the two cultural pessimists to be forerunners of Nazism. For general information regarding Carlyle's prophetic rhetoric, which led to his derisive labeling by Johan Huizinga: Jens Nordalm, "Der gegängelte Held. 'Heroenkult' im 19.Jahrhundert am Beispiel Thomas Carlyles und Heinrich von Treitschkes," in: *Historische Zeitschrift 276* (2003), pp. 647–675, especially pp. 655ff.

23. Niedersächsische Staats und Universitätsbibliothek Göttingen, Cod. Ms. Lagarde, *Notizen und Auszüge*, vol. 1, p. 43; the next quotation appears on p. 60 of the same source.

24. Lagarde's letter to Overbeck of December 12, 1875, Peter and Sommer, p. 154.

25. Lagarde was thereby taking passages from the "Diagnose" essay; the citation in the text follows, as usual, the fifth edition of the *Deutsche Schriften*.

26. To this end, and pointedly: Wolfgang Schivelbusch, *Die Kultur der Niederlage. Der amerikanische Süden 1865, Frankreich 1871, Deutschland 1918* (Darmstadt, 2001), p. 434, note 139.

27. On the importance of Central European thinking to Lagarde's worldview, see Stern, *Kulturpessimismus*, pp. 95ff.; general information regarding Central Europe's significance as a German equivalent to the British and French colonies: Blackbourn, p. 322.

28. The crisis of Hegelianism in the Nachmärz is illustrated by: Hermann Lübbe, *Politische Philosophie in Deutschland. Studien zu ihrer Geschichte* (Munich, 1974), pp. 27–82; monograph on the rise of neo-Kantianism: Köhnke.

29. On the peculiarities of everyday *Selbstsein* (being oneself), Heidegger states: "In using public transportation, or in using news sources (newspapers), each is the same as the other. This triggers its own existence with one another completely in the mode of being of the 'others,' so much so that the others disappear into their diversity and explicitness more. Within this inconspicuousness and unascertainability, man unfolds his true dictatorship." Martin Heidegger, *Sein und Zeit*, 16th ed. (Tübingen, 1986), p. 126.

30. *Neue Evangelische Kirchenzeitung*, no. 6, February 5, 1876, col. 86ff.; *Merkur. Zeitschrift für nationale Handelspolitik und Volkswirtschaft*, no. 18, April 29, 1876, pp. 139ff., especially p. 140; *Protestantische Kirchenzeitung für das evangelische Deutschland*, no. 5, January 29, 1876, cols. 86–97, especially col. 91.

31. Peter and Sommer, p. 155.

32. Richard Wagner, "Was ist deutsch?" in: Wagner, *Dichtungen und Schriften. Jubiläumsausgabe*, edited by Dieter Borchmeyer, vol. 10 (Frankfurt am Main, 1983), pp. 84–103, especially p. 103.

33. Niedersächsische Staats und Universitätsbibliothek Göttingen, Cod. Ms. Lagarde, *Notizen und Auszüge*, vol. 2, p. 21, where the next quote can also be found. General information on Lagarde's reservations about Richard Wagner: Stern, *Kulturpessimismus*, pp. 133ff.

34. See Graf, *Theologie*, pp. 38ff., and Heinssen, *Historismus und Kulturkritik*, p. 476.

35. Regarding Schmeitzner, see Curt Paul Janz, *Friedrich Nietzsche. Biographie*, vol. 1: *Kindheit und Jugend. Die zehn Basler Jahre* (Munich, 1981), pp. 834ff., passim.

36. Paul de Lagarde, *Deutsche Schriften* (Göttingen, 1878), p. 3; in the following, in order to avoid Lagarde's Grimms-like use of small capital letters and other linguistic peculiarities, the fifth edition is cited as usual.

37. Lagarde's letter to the Office of Statistics of October 2, 1877.

38. Thus, I follow Viaene, pp. 544ff.; Stern, *Kulturpessimismus*, p. 120, is erroneous, viewing the Lagardian "state schools" as forerunners of Nazi "Ordensburgen."

39. On the significance of this phenomenon: Otto Gerhard Oexle, *Geschichtswissenschaft im Zeitalter des Historismus. Studien zu Problemgeschichten der Moderne* (Göttingen, 1996).

40. As stated in: Lougee, p. 315; the complexity of religio-semantic interpretation in the late nineteenth century is stressed by: Graf, *Wiederkehr der Götter*, pp. 122ff.

41. Lagarde's spelling of the supreme Germanic God, which is usually encountered as "Wotan." The "pithecoids" referred to in the next sentence illustrate the transitional stage between apes and humans, whose existence troubled science in the late nineteenth century.

42. Bismarck's systematic manipulation of the press was already a subject of contemporary conjecture. Unfortunately, the "Iron Chancellor" obliterated his tracks so well that many questions remain open to this day about the "Bismarck system." Insufficient: Nöll Nahmer, *Bismarcks Reptilienfonds. Aus den Geheimakten Preussens und des deutschen Reichs* (Mainz, 1968).

43. For what follows with appropriate documentation: Ulrich Sieg, *Aufstieg und Niedergang des Marburger Neukantianismus. Die Geschichte einer philosophischen Schulgemeinschaft* (Würzburg, 1994), pp. 159ff. and pp. 495ff.

44. Lagarde's letter to Erman of July 2, 1880.

45. Lagarde, *Symmicta*, vol. 2, p. 106.

46. See, for example, Tönnies's letter to Lagarde of January 8, 1884, which is about the approval of a "community of professionals."

47. Heinrich von Treitschke, "Einige Bemerkungen über das Gymnasialwesen," in: *Preussische Jahrbücher* 51 (1883), pp. 158–190, especially p. 177.

48. Lagarde's letter to Max Koch of July 4, 1884; Bayerische Staatsbibliothek Munich, Ana 328, I.

49. Safranski, p. 187.

50. *De Portefeuille. Nieuw Kunst en Letterbode*, no. 10, June 4, 1881, pp. 102ff. The review ends with these words of agreement: "Over den hedendagschen toestand zijns vaderlands spreekt de schriver menig bitter woord; maar wie duft hem tegenspreken?" (Concerning the present-day conditions, the writer speaks many bitter words; but who can argue against them?)

51. See Georg Hoffmann's letter to Lagarde of October 2, 1878.

52. Paul de Lagarde, "Essays and Semitic Essays," in: *The Academy* of September 28, 1878.

53. Ernest Renan, "Was ist eine Nation?" Lecture at the Sorbonne, held on March 11, 1882, in: Renan, *"'Was ist eine Nation?' und andere politische Schriften" [. . .]* (Vienna and Bolzano, 1995), pp. 41–58, especially p. 56.

54. Niedersächsische Staats und Universitätsbibliothek Göttingen, Cod. Ms. Lagarde, *Notizen und Auszüge*, vol. 1, p. 121.

55. Paul de Lagarde, "Zum letzten Male Albrecht Ritschl," *Ausgewählte Schriften. Als Ergänzung zu Lagardes Deutschen Schriften*, compiled by Paul Fischer (Munich, 1924), pp. 255–279, especially p. 279.

9. LIBERALISM: IMAGE OF THE ENEMY

1. Thus distinctly: Heinrich August Winkler, "Vom linken zum rechten Nationalismus: Der deutsche Liberalismus in der Krise von 1878/79," in: Winkler, *Liberalismus und Antiliberalismus. Studien zur politischen Sozial Geschichte des 19. und 20. Jahrhunderts* (Göttingen, 1979), pp. 36–51 and pp. 294–300. For the main conceptual questions, see Dieter Langewiesche, *Nation, Nationalismus, Nationalstaat in Deutschland und Europa* (Munich, 2000).

2. Regarding the necessary political conditions for the success of new demagogues: Helmut Berding, *Moderner Antisemitismus in Deutschland* (Frankfurt am Main, 1988), pp. 85–110.

3. The text, which has no separate title, is found in the fifth edition of the *Deutsche Schriften*, pp. 88–94.

4. See Anna de Lagarde's letter to Luise Kapp of February 14, 1873.

5. Lagarde, *Symmicta*, vol. 2, p. 106.

6. The citation that follows comes from the fifth edition of *Deutsche Schriften*. On Lagarde's anti-liberalism see Corona Hepp, *Avantgarde. Moderne Kunst, Kulturkritik und Reformbewegungen nach der Jahrhundertwende* (Munich, 1987), p. 60; Lougee, p. 197, and Stern, *Kulturpessimismus*, pp. 104ff.

7. Carl Wilmanns, *Die "goldene" Internationale und die Nothwendigkeit einer socialen Reformpartei* (Berlin, 1876); for the historical background, see Stern, *Gold und Eisen*, pp. 690ff., and Winkler, *Der lange Weg nach Westen*, vol. 1, pp. 228ff.

8. See Thomas Nipperdey and Reinhard Rürup, "Antisemitismus," in: Otto Brunner, Werner Conze, and Reinhart Koselleck (eds.), *Geschichtliche Grundbegriffe. Historisches Lexikon zur politisch-sozialen Sprache in Deutschland*, vol. 1 (Stuttgart, 1972), pp. 129–153, especially pp. 138ff.

9. Heinrich von Treitschke, "Unsere Aussichten," in: *Preussische Jahrbücher 44* (1879), pp. 559–576.

10. For a source book on the conflict, which should perhaps be labeled a nationwide event, see Karsten Krieger (ed.), *Der Berliner Antisemitismusstreit, 1879–1881. Eine Kontroverse um die Zugehörigkeit der Juden zur deutschen Nation*, 2 vols. (Munich, 2004); the most comprehensive presentation of the debate is now offered by Jensen.

11. For nuanced historical context: Jörn Leonhard, "Semantische Deplazierung und Entwertung. Deutsche Deutungen von liberal und Liberalismus im europäischen Vergleich," in: *Geschichte und Gesellschaft 29* (2003), pp. 5–39, especially p. 30.

12. Paul de Lagarde's reformation writings, in: *Deutsches Tageblatt*, no. 164, June 19, 1882.

13. Lagarde's approach to answering Pernersdorfer on July 22, 1883.

14. Paul de Lagarde, "Die graue Internationale," in: *Deutsche Worte. Politische Zeitschrift für das deutsche Volk in Oesterreich*, no. 18, September 16, 1883, pp. 1–6, especially p. 1, asterisk footnote at the bottom of the page.

15. Niedersächsische Staats und Universitätsbibliothek Göttingen, Cod. Ms. Lagarde, *Notizen und Auszüge*, vol. 2, pp. 36ff.

16. The text is easy to grasp: Lagarde, *Deutsche Schriften*, 5th ed., pp. 307–314; the following quote can also be found there.

17. First published separately in Göttingen, 1884; here quoted from the *Deutsche Schriften*, 5th ed.

18. See Paul de Lagarde, "Die Finanzpolitik Deutschlands," *Deutsche Schriften*, 5th ed., pp. 316–336, especially p. 324 and pp. 334ff.

19. The historical background is outlined by: Blackbourn, p. 310; Wehler, *Deutsche Gesellschafts Geschichte*, vol. 3, p. 544, and Ferrari Zumbini, p. 30.

20. For the anti-egalitarian and antiliberal thrust of Lagarde's argument, see Breuer, *Ordnungen der Ungleichheit*, p. 12.

21. Here quoted from: Lagarde, *Deutsche Schriften*, 5th ed., p. 4.

22. This, in oppostion to Stern, *Kulturpessimismus*, p. 110; the following quote according to the copy of the essays "Die nächsten Pflichten deutscher Politik" in the fifth edition of the *Deutsche Schriften*.

23. Sober and knowledgeable on this topic: Magnus Brechtken, "Madagascar für die Juden," *Antisemitische Idee und politische Praxis, 1885–1945* (Munich, 1997)

24. Quoted from: Eberhard Kolb, "Gezähmte Halbgötter? Bismarck und die militärische Führung, 1871–1890," in: Lothar Gall (ed.), *Otto von Bismarck und Wilhelm II. Repräsentanten eines Epochenwechsels?* (Paderborn et al., 2000), pp. 41–60, especially p. 52.

25. On Lagarde's anti-Slavic prejudices, which are often treated *en passant*: Wolfgang Wippermann, "Antislawismus," in: Uwe Puschner, Walter Schmitz, and Justus H. Ulbricht (eds.), *Handbuch zur "Völkischen Bewegung"* (Munich et al., 1996), pp. 512–524, especially pp. 521ff.

26. Thus Lagarde in the cover letter dated April 6, 1886, to the "General Administration of His Grand Ducal Highness, Prince Alexander of Hesse," Geheimrat Menges. The preceding quotes are from Lagarde's letter of November 22, 1885, which was sent to the prince directly.

27. Masaryk's letter to Lagarde of March 30, 1881.

28. See Viaene, pp. 541 and 549.

29. Anna de Lagarde, p. 107; see also Stern, *Kulturpessimismus*, p. 106.

30. The document can be found in: Anna de Lagarde, pp. 104ff.

31. Eugene Wolff on Lagarde's letter of October 3, 1885, where the following quotations appear. General information about the "rightward shift" in the student body in the 1880s, fed to new readers by Lagarde: Norbert Kampe, *Studenten und "Judenfrage" im Deutschen Kaiserreich. Die Entstehung einer akademischen Trägerschicht des Antisemitismus* (Göttingen, 1988).

32. Paul de Lagarde, *Le opere di Giordano Bruno ristampata da Paolo de Lagarde, 2 Bde.*

(Göttingen, 1888 and 1889), in: *Göttingische gelehrte Anzeigen*, February 1, 1889, pp. 113–145; quoted from: Lagarde, *Mittheilungen*, vol. 3 (Göttingen, 1889), pp. 131–163, especially p. 145.

33. Ibid., p. 153.

34. Ibid., p. 161 and p. 163; on p. 161, see the emotional statement: "Dante loved ardently, thus earning the right to criticize harshly. The consequences of loving and hating are his to bear."

35. Ibid., p. 163.

36. Niedersächsische Staats und Universitätsbibliothek Göttingen, Cod. Ms. Lagarde, *Notizen und Auszüge*, vol. 2, pp. 91ff.

37. Ibid., pp. 93ff.

10. THE CAMEL SPARROW

1. Quoted from: David Kaufmann, *Paul de Lagarde's jüdische Gelehrsamkeit. Eine Erwiederung* (Leipzig, 1887), p. 42.

2. See Max Buber's letter to Lagarde of April 10, 1882.

3. Matthias Manthey, "Juden in Göttingen," in: *Göttingen. Geschichte einer Universitätsstadt*, vol. 3, pp. 675–683, especially p. 678. The previous quotation is found in: Staatsbibliothek Berlin, Darmstäder collection, Paul de Lagarde.

4. See Lagarde's letter to Minister of Education Robert von Puttkamer, of December 17, 1880, where the heavy judgmental bias and inaccuracy of the citation can also be found.

5. Quoted from: Fuhrmann, "Sind eben alles Menschen gewesen," p. 106.

6. See Ulrich Sieg, "Der Preis des Bildungsstrebens. Jüdische Geisteswissenschaftler im Kaiserreich," in: Andreas Gotzmann, Rainer Liedtke, and Till van Rahden (eds.), *Juden, Bürger, Deutsche. Zur Geschichte von Vielfalt und Differenz, 1800–1933* (Tübingen 2001), pp. 67–95.

7. All citations in Lagarde's letter to Steindorff are of December 26, 1884.

8. See Helmut Walser Smith, *Die Geschichte des Schlachters. Mord und Antisemitismus in einer deutschen Kleinstadt* (Göttingen, 2002), pp. 136ff., as well as for general information: I. Michael Aronson, *Troubled Waters: The Origins of the 1881 Anti-Jewish Pogroms in Russia* (Pittsburgh, 1990).

9. As an instructive case study: Christhard Hoffmann, "Politische Kultur und Gewalt gegen Minderheiten. Die antisemitischen Ausschreitungen in Pommern und Westpreussen, 1881," in: *Jahrbuch für Antisemitismusforschung 3* (1994), pp. 93–120.

10. See, for a general account, Andrew Handler, *Blood Libel in Tiszaeslar* (New York, 1980).

11. Lagarde's letter to August Rohling on January 25, 1885.

12. Regarding this strange episode in the history of theology: Ulrich Sieg, *Jüdische Intellektuelle im Ersten Weltkrieg. Kriegserfahrungen, weltanschauliche Debatten und kulturelle Neuentwürfe* (Berlin, 2001), pp. 218ff.

13. Christian testimony against the blood libel of Jews, Berlin, 1882; Lagarde's opinion is found in ibid.

14. August Rohling, *Die Polemik und das Menschenopfer des Rabbinismus. Eine wissenschaftliche Antwort ohne Polemik für die Rabbiner und ihre Genossen* (Paderborn, 1883); for what follows, see Favrat, p. 98, and Ferrari Zumbini, pp. 135ff.

15. Rohling, *Die Polemik und das Menschenopfer des Rabbinismus* [. . .], 2nd ed. (Prague 1884), p. 88. Two sets of conclusions in p. 106 of the same text may help characterize the

hate-filled arguments: "Die Stellen, welche wir durchgenommen haben, zeigen uns den Rabbinismus in seiner wahren Gestalt. Nicht blos die Erde, sondern auch den Himmel will er nur für Israel."

16. Apropos hereto: Elisabeth Albanis, *German-Jewish Cultural Identity from 1900 to the Aftermath of the First World War* (Tübingen, 2002), p. 27.

17. Niedersächsische Staats und Universitätsbibliothek Göttingen, Cod. Ms. Lagarde, *Notizen und Auszüge*, vol. 2, p. 22.

18. Paul de Lagarde, *Gesammelte Abhandlungen. Neudruck der Ausgabe 1866* (Osnabrück, 1966), pp. 282ff.

19. Lagarde's letter to his wife of August 3, 1879; Niedersächsische Staats und Universitätsbibliothek Göttingen, Cod. Ms. Lagarde, *Notizen und Auszüge*, p. 44.

20. The citation in the body text follows the fifth edition of Lagarde's *Hauptwerk*, pp. 270–286.

21. Niedersächsische Staats und Universitätsbibliothek Göttingen, Cod. Ms. Lagarde, *Notizen und Auszüge*, vol. 2, p. 99.

22. Apropos: Stefan Breuer, *Ordnungen der Ungleichheit*, p. 86.

23. Regarding references to the history of systematically relevant ideas, see Peter Berghoff, "Der 'Jude' als Todesmetapher des politischen Körpers und der Kampf gegen die Zersetzung des nationalen 'Über-Lebens,'" in: Peter Alter, Claus Ekkehard Bärsch, and Peter Berghoff (eds.), *Die Konstruktion der Nation gegen die Juden* (Munich, 1999), pp. 159–172.

24. Lagarde, *Programm*, pp. 396–400.

25. Rather than including the now fairly extensive body of literature regarding Mommsen's understanding of the nation, I will only mention the study by Christian Hoffmann, *Juden und Judentum im Werk deutscher Althistoriker des 19. und 20. Jahrhunderts* (Leiden, 1988) to illuminate the history of scientific context.

26. Regarding the elections, in: *Neue Evangelische Kirchenzeitung*, no. 42, October 18, 1884, see pp. 659ff.

27. From Lagarde's school, in: *Jüdisches Litteratur-Blatt*, no. 24, June 11, 1885, pp. 93ff., especially p. 94. General information regarding what follows: Elisabeth Hollender, "Verachtung kann Unwissenheit nicht entschuldigen. Die Verteidigung der Wissenschaft des Judentums gegen die Angriffe Paul de Lagarde's 1884–1887," in: *Frankfurter Judaistische Beiträge 30* (2003), pp. 169–205.

28. The essay was published in Göttingen in 1886; it is quoted from this easily understandable edition: Paul de Lagarde, *Mittheilungen*, vol. 2 (Göttingen, 1887), pp. 108–162.

29. Including this monograph: Michaela Haibl, *Zerrbild als Stereotyp. Visuelle Darstellungen von Juden zwischen 1850 und 1900* (Berlin, 2000).

30. Kaufmann, *Paul de Lagarde's jüdische Gelehrsamkeit*, p. 45.

31. A[braham] Berliner, *Professor Paul de Lagarde, nach seiner Natur gezeichnet* (Berlin, 1887), p. 24; see p. 2 of the same source for the next citation.

32. Moritz Güdemann, "Der 'deutsche Nationalheilige' Paul de Lagarde," in: *Die Presse*, no. 42, February 12, 1887, pp. 1ff.

33. Paul de Lagarde, *Juden und Indogermanen. Eine Studie nach dem Leben*, in: Lagarde, *Mittheilungen*, vol. 2 (Göttingen, 1887), pp. 262–351, especially p. 321. The other citations are shown in the main text. General information regarding the extent to which Lagarde responded to the accusations of Jewish scholars: Hollender, pp. 198–202.

34. How Viaene, p. 546, in the face of such statements, came to the conclusion that Lagarde had always rejected violence against Jews is not obvious to me.

35. Clear-sighted, to this end: Ernst Piper, "Der Orient als Dystopie. Paul de Lagarde und der Mythos der deutschen Nation," in: Irene A. Dieckmann, Thomas Gerber, and Julius H. Schoeps (eds.), *Der Orient im Okzident. Sichtweisen und Beeinflussungen* (Potsdam, 2003), pp. 161–176.

36. Regarding Schönerer, the most comprehensive source remains: Andrew G. Whiteside, *Georg von Schönerer. Alldeutschland und sein Prophet*, 2 vols. (Graz, Vienna, and Cologne, 1981); for what follows, see Lagarde, *Juden und Indogermanen*, pp. 268ff., and the relevant documents in Lagarde's Göttingen papers.

37. See Ruhler's letter to Lagarde of June 23, 1887.

38. Quoted from: Peters, p. 80. For what follows, see pp. 147–152 of the same source and scattered throughout; Curt Paul Janz, *Friedrich Nietzsche. Biographie*, vol. 2: *Die zehn Jahre des freien Philosophen* (Munich, 1981), pp. 416–421.

39. Bernhard Förster, *Deutsche Colonien in dem oberen Laplata-Gebiete* (Naumburg, 1886), p. 418.

40. Theodor Fritsch's letter to Lagarde of May 13, 1886. Now essential for Fritsch: Ferrari Zumbini, pp. 321–422, who also analyzed his contact with Lagarde in pp. 355–359 of the same text.

41. Thomas Frey (i.e., Theodor Fritsch), *Antisemiten-Katechismus. Eine Zusammenstellung des wichtigsten Materials zum Verständnis der Judenfrage, 25. verm. Edition* (Leipzig, 1893); see also Paul, p. 79.

42. Lagarde's letter to Salomon Buber of February 5, 1887.

43. Peter Pulzer, "Die Wiederkehr des alten Hasses," in: *Deutsch-jüdische Geschichte in der Neuzeit*, vol. 3: *Umstrittene Integration, 1871–1918*, Steven M. Lowenstein et al. (eds.) (Munich, 1997), pp. 193–248, especially p. 217.

44. Apropos: Smith, *Deutsche Geschichte als imperiale Geschichte*, p. 163.

11. THE TALMUD ON TRIAL

1. The quote is found in the instructive essay by Andrea Hopp, "Auf Stimmenfang mit dem Vorurteil: Antisemitismus im Wahlkampf," in: Lothar Gall (ed.), *Regierung, Parlament und Öffentlichkeit im Zeitalter Bismarcks. Politikstile im Wandel* (Paderborn, 2003), pp. 263–280, especially p. 271; for the instrumentalization of antisemitism analyzed by the conservatives, see Nipperdey, *Deutsche Geschichte, 1866–1918*, vol. 2, pp. 306ff.

2. Regarding the north Hessian agricultural crisis and its political implications, see David Peal, "Antisemitism by Other Means? The Rural Cooperative Movement in Late Nineteenth-Century Germany," in: *Leo Baeck Institute Yearbook 32* (1987), pp. 135–153, and Ferrari Zumbini, pp. 264–275.

3. Otto Böckel-Capistrano, *Germania. Eine Frühlingselegie* (Kassel, 1887), p. 16; the historical context is not without problems but is unsurpassed in detail and conviction: Rüdiger Mack, "Otto Böckel und die antisemitische Bauernbewegung in Hessen, 1887–1894," in: *Neunhundert Jahre Geschichte der Juden in Hessen. Beiträge zum politischen, wirtschaftlichen und kulturel-len Leben*, Christine Heinemann (ed.) (Wiesbaden, 1983), pp. 377–410.

4. Otto Böckel, *Die Juden, die Könige unserer Zeit. Rede des Herrn Dr. Otto Böckel aus Marburg gehalten in der öffentlichen Versammlung des Deutschen Antisemiten-Bundes auf*

der Bockbrauerei zu Berlin am 4.oktober 1886; quoted here according to the 108th edition in Marburg, 1887, p. 4.

5. For more detail: Arne Sudhoff, "Agitation und Mobilisierung ländlicher Bevölkerung im ausgehenden 19.Jahrhundert. Die kurhessische Zeitung Reichsherold im Schnittpunkt von Antisemitismus und Agrargesellschaft," in: *Aschkenas 11* (2001), pp. 87–120.

6. See Winkler, *Der lange Weg nach Westen*, vol. 1, p. 319, which, however, Class's predecessor does not mention.

7. Emphasized by: Bernhard vom Brocke, "Marburg im Kaiserreich, 1866–1918. Geschichte und Gesellschaft, Parteien und Wahlen einer Universitätsstadt im wirtschaftlichen Wandel der industriellen Revolution," in: Erhart Dettmering and Rudolf Grenz (eds.), *Marburger Geschichte. Rückblick auf die Stadtgeschichte in Einzelbeiträgen*, 2nd ed. (Marburg, 1982), pp. 367–540, especially p. 486, and Ferrari Zumbini, pp. 276–280.

8. More details regarding the following are contained in my essays "'Der Wissenschaft und dem Leben tut dasselbe not: Ehrfurcht vor der Wahrheit' Hermann Cohens Gutachten im Marburger Antisemitismusprozess 1888," in: Reinhard Brandt and Franz Orlik (eds.), *Philosophisches Denken—Politisches Wirken. Hermann-Cohen-Kolloquium 1992* (Hildesheim, Zurich, and New York, 1993), pp. 222–249, and "Der Talmud vor Gericht. Die ideengeschichtliche Bedeutung des Marburger Antisemitismusprozesses," in: Hans-Martin Barth and Christoph Elsas (eds.), *Religiöse Minderheiten. Potentiale für Konflikt und Frieden* (Schenefeld, 2004), pp. 129–144, offered for general information.

9. Hessisches Staatsarchiv Marburg, 330 C, Marburg no. 3176.

10. Same as the former, fol. 43.

11. Regarding the success of Rohling's "Der Talmudjude. Zur Beherzigung für Juden und Christen aller Stände dargestellt" (Münster, 1871), these six editions were heavily debated in the press: Olaf Blaschke, *Katholizismus und Antisemitismus im Deutschen Kaiserreich* (Göttingen, 1997), pp. 74ff.

12. The Fenner trial, in: *Antisemitische Correspondenz. Central-Organ der Antisemiten*, no. 27, May 15, 1888, pp. 2–5. Regarding the spread of this journal: Ferrari Zumbini, pp. 332–340.

13. See the reproduction of their article of May 6, 1888: "Paul de Lagarde, Ein preussischer Staatsanwalt," in: Lagarde, *Mittheilungen*, vol. 3 (Göttingen, 1889), pp. 85–99, especially pp. 85ff. The charged atmosphere, which was reflected also in the vehemence of the reporting, is neglected by: Gesine Palmer, "The Case of Paul de Lagarde," in: Hubert Cancik and Uwe Puschner (eds.), *Antisemitismus, Paganismus, Völkische Religion* (Munich, 2004), pp. 37–53, especially p. 38, which characterized the Marburg antisemitism trial as a "strange little lawsuit."

14. Lagarde, *Juden und Indogermanen*, p. 338.

15. Paul de Lagarde, "Ein Gutachten," in: Lagarde, *Mittheilungen*, vol. 3 (Göttingen, 1889), pp. 3–23, especially p. 5. In the following, Lagarde's note regarding this version is reproduced from the body text. In the micro edition, five pieces of the printed original version could not be found; the reprint in antisemitic publications proved to be considerably shortened and with arbitrary commentary.

16. Bezzenberger's letter to Lagarde of February 27, 1888.

17. Hermann Cohen, "Die Nächstenliebe im Talmud. Ein Gutachten dem Königlichen Landgericht zu Marburg erstattet," in: Cohen, *Jüdische Schriften*, Bruno Strauss (ed.), vol. 1

(Berlin, 1924), pp. 145–174, especially p. 150. Regarding Cohen's attitude toward Treitschke in the "Berlin antisemitism dispute," see Ulrich Sieg, "Bekenntnis zu nationalen und universalen Werten. Jüdische Philosophen im Deutschen Kaiserreich," in *Historische Zeitschrift 263* (1996), pp. 609–639, especially pp. 617ff., and Jensen, pp. 229ff.

18. Cohen, *Nächstenliebe im Talmud*, p. 148; see p. 151 of the same source for the next citation.

19. Ibid., p. 174.

20. Anonymous [Otto Böckel], *Der Prozess Fenner nach den Akten dargestellt und beleuchtet* (Marburg, 1888), p. 43.

21. See Cohen's letter to the Zurich philosopher August Stadler of May 16, 1888; quoted from: Cohen, *Jüdische Schriften*, vol. 1, p. 338.

22. *Theologisches Literaturblatt 9* (1888), col. 297ff.; the previous quotation is found in: *Sächsisches Kirchen und Schulblatt*, no. 1, January 3, 1889, col. 12.

23. Niedersächsische Staats und Universitätsbibliothek Göttingen, Cod. Ms. Lagarde, no. 154, p. 57.

24. Ibid., no. 154, p. 59.

25. Lagarde, *Ein preussischer Staatsanwalt*, pp. 97ff.; regarding Lagarde's furious protest, see also Schemann, *Lagarde. Lebens und Erinnerungsbild*, p. 233.

26. See Anna de Lagarde's letter to Fenner of December 21, 1888.

27. This shows in Lagarde's letter to Frederich Stehlich of August 28, 1889. On the historical background of the consequences: Barbara Suchy, "The Association for the Defense of Anti-Semitism I: From Its Beginnings to the First World War," in: *Leo Baeck Institute Yearbook 28* (1993), pp. 205–239.

28. This is strongly emphasized by: Stefan Breuer, "Gescheiterte Milieubildung. Die Völkischen im deutschen Kaiserreich," in: *Zeitschrift für Geschichtswissenschaft 52* (2004), pp. 995–1016, especially p. 1003. And especially regarding the decline of the Böckel movement: Mack, pp. 398ff., and Peal.

29. Lagarde, *Ein preussischer Staatsanwalt*, p. 85.

30. Lagarde, *Gutachten*, p. 20.

12. SCHOLARLY FAILURE

1. See Rahlfs, pp. 70ff., and Stern, *Kulturpessimismus*, pp. 50ff.

2. But between the autumns of 1881 and 1884, the Orientalist, with slow sales of his scientific (academic) works, lost more than nine thousand gold marks. (Lagarde, once again in my edition of the Septuagint, pp. 253ff.) The sum, which can be estimated to just under seven times that amount in euros, also allows for some conclusions regarding his overall wealth.

3. Paul de Lagarde, preliminary remarks to my edition of the Septuagint, in: Lagarde, *Symmicta*, vol. 2 (Göttingen, 1880), pp. 137–148, especially p. 146.

4. Lagarde's letter to William Aldis Wright of September 5, 1880. Thereafter, on October 9, 1880, Lagarde sent a detailed timetable for further steps.

5. Thus, I follow Rahlfs, pp. 78ff., who believes the Lucian edition to be the "biggest failure" of Lagarde's scholarship.

6. Erman's letter to Lagarde of August 4, 1884. Five days later came the printing of the *Librororum Veteris Testamenti pars prior graece*, which was completed by Diederichs, Lagarde's responsible publishing house.

7. Quoted from: Rahlfs, p. 16, note 1.

8. The text of the petition is reproduced: Lagarde, once again from my edition of the Septuagint, pp. 239ff., asterisk footnote at the bottom of the page.

9. Lagarde, pp. 249 and 254.

10. See Lagarde's letter to Gossler of June 4, 1885, and his letter to Althoff on June 30, 1885, wherein he presented a detailed distribution plan for the Lucian edition. The description of the facts is misleading in Stern, *Kulturpessimismus*, p. 51, which does not mention purchase of the Septuagint edition by the Prussian Ministry of Education and Cultural Affairs.

11. The passage is found in a lost letter by Lagarde, dated autumn 1885, which is quoted by Hoffmann in his reply of November 1, 1885.

12. Lagarde's last will is recorded: Universitätsarchiv Göttingen, Kur 7013, fol. 6r–28r, where the following quote can also be found. A concise interpretation of his last testament is offered by: Hanhart, p. 284.

13. See Rahlfs, p. 13, note 4.

14. Paul de Lagarde, *Altes und Neues über das Weihnachtsfest*, in: Lagarde, *Mittheilungen*, vol. 4 (Göttingen, 1891), pp. 241–323, especially p. 241.

15. All quotations: ibid., pp. 322ff. Regarding spreading the interests of Ludwig Schemann, Lagarde's bold mentor among the Wagnerians, see Schemann's collective discussion "Ueber die neuesten Publikationen Paul de Lagarde's," *Bayreuther Blätter 5* (1891), pp. 409–412, especially p. 411.

16. Lagarde, *Gedichte*, p. 81.

17. Lagarde, *Die königliche Gesellschaft der Wissenschaften in Göttingen betreffend. Ein Gutachten*, in: Anna de Lagarde, pp. 164–179, especially p. 165. Details of the historical context: Martin Gierl, *Geschichte und Organisation. Institutionalisierung als Kommunikationsprozess am Beispiel der Wissenschaftsakademien um 1900* (Göttingen, 2004), pp. 30–43 and passim.

18. Lagarde, *Die königliche Gesellschaft der Wissenschaften in Göttingen*, p. 169.

19. See Gierl, pp. 44–50, as well as Renate Tobies, *Wissenschaftliche Schwerpunktbildung: der Ausbau Göttingens zum Zentrum der Mathematik und Naturwissenschaften*, in: Bernhard vom Brocke (ed.), *Wissenschaftsgeschichte und Wissenschaftspolitik im Industriezeitalter. Das "System Althoff" in historischer Perspektive* (Hildesheim, 1991), pp. 87–108.

20. Paul de Lagarde, *Bemerkungen zu einem von Herrn Professor Felix Klein über die Reorganisation der königlichen Gesellschaft der Wissenschaften zu Göttingen abgegebenen Gutachten. Als Handschrift gedruckt* (Göttingen, 1889), p. 16.

21. Paul de Lagarde, *Die königliche Gesellschaft der Wissenschaften in Göttingen betreffend. Ein zweites und letztes Gutachten. Als Handschrift gedruckt* (Göttingen, 1889).

22. Universitätsarchiv Göttingen, Kur 5903, fol. 76r–77r, where the following quote can also be found.

23. See the letter from the Göttingen Academy of Science to the Prussian Ministry of Culture on May 6, 1889, and the second letter from Gossler to Meier of November 12, 1889; Universitätsarchiv Göttingen, Kur 5903, fols. 74r–v and 81r–v.

24. Gossler's letter to Meier of January 21, 1890; Universitätsarchiv Göttingen, Kur 5903, fol. 89r–v.

25. Gossler, fol. 93r; the list of "Bemerkenswerthe Stellen aus Paul de Lagardes Schriften" can be found: Universitätsarchiv Göttingen, Kur 5903, fol. 94r–97r.

26. Sauppe's letter to Meier on July 12, 1890; Universitätsarchiv Göttingen, Kur 5903, fol. 99r–v, where the following quotes can also be found.

27. Lagarde, *Übersicht über die im Aramäischen, Arabischen, und Hebräischen übliche Bildung der Nomina*, p. 3; also see the double-asterisk footnote on p. 2 for the following quotes.

28. Lagarde's letter to Alfred Schöne of December 6, 1891, as quoted from: Schemann, *Lagarde. Lebens und Erinnerungsbild*, p. 395; regarding his last works, see also Rahlfs, pp. 82ff.

29. Lagarde, *Gedichte*, pp. 117ff., especially p. 118.

30. See, for example, D. Winton Thomas, "The Textual Criticism of the Old Testament," in: Harold H. Rowley (ed.), *The Old Testament and Modern Study: A Generation of Discovery and Research* (Oxford, 1961), pp. 243ff. and pp. 250–255, or Sydney Jellicoe, *The Septuagint and Modern Study* (Oxford, 1968), pp. 5–9.

31. Apropos hereto: Heinssen, *Historismus und Kulturkritik*, p. 483.

13. PROPHET OF GERMAN CULTURE

1. Graf, *Wiederkehr der Götter*, p. 231.

2. Niedersächsische Staats und Universitätsbibliothek Göttingen, Cod. Ms. Lagarde, *Notizen und Auszüge*, vol. 1, pp. 112ff.

3. Alfred Schöne's letter to Anna de Lagarde of August 22, 1878.

4. Lagarde's letter to Elise von Seidlitz of April 25, 1890.

5. Essential source material, but only to be used with caution: Benedict Momme Nissen, *Der Rembrandtdeutsche Julius Langbehn. Von seinem Freunde* (Freiburg im Breisgau, 1937). As a biographical introduction, see also: Bernd Behrendt, "August Julius Langbehn, der 'Rembrandtdeutsche,'" in: Uwe Puschner, Walter Schmitz, and Justus H. Ulbricht (eds.), *Handbuch zur "Völkischen Bewegung"* (Munich et al., 1996), pp. 94–113, and Stern, *Kulturpessimismus*, pp. 143–166.

6. [August Julius Langbehn], *Rembrandt als Erzieher. Von einem Deutschen*, 7th edition (Leipzig, 1890), p. 283. An ideological interpretation of Langbehn's main work is offered by: Stern, *Kulturpessimismus*, pp. 167–212; the tense interplay of backward values and avant-garde linguistic resources is discussed by: Heinssen, *Historismus und Kulturkritik*, pp. 436–463.

7. [Langbehn], *Rembrandt als Erzieher*, 7th edition, p. 101.

8. [August Julius Langbehn], *Rembrandt als Erzieher. Von einem Deutschen*, 29th ed. (Leipzig, 1891), p. 42. Regarding the radicalization of Langbehn's antisemitism, which soon led him to adopt the racist ideology: Behrendt, *Langbehn*, pp. 102ff.; Breuer, *Ordnungen der Ungleichheit*, p. 342; Pulzer, *Entstehung des politischen Antisemitismus*, pp. 257ff., and Ferrari Zumbini, pp. 362ff.

9. Quoted from: Johannes Heinssen, "Ein Indikator für die Probleme der Problemgeschichte: Kulturkritische Entdifferenzierung am Ende des 19. Jahrhunderts," in: Otto Gerhard Oexle (ed.), *Das Problem der Problemgeschichte, 1800–1932* (Göttingen, 2001), pp. 41–84, especially p. 42, which presents an impressive anthology of derogatory judgments.

10. All quotes from the book prospectus of *Rembrandt als Erzieher* are in Lagarde's papers; general information regarding the many positive votes: Stern, *Kulturpessimismus*, pp. 213–230.

11. The document is missing in the too-edifying and thus unreliable edition by Joseph Becker, "Paul de Lagarde und Julius Langbehn, die Begegnung zweier Seher der deutschen Zukunft. Unveröffentlichte Briefe," in: *Deutsche Rundschau 239* (April/May/June 1934), pp. 96–104.

12. Quoted from: Stern, *Kulturpessimismus*, p. 221.

13. Stern, p. 159, asterisk footnote at the bottom of the page; the previous quotations are found in: Becker, p. 103.

14. Hirschfeld's letter to Lagarde of March 6, 1891; for the consequences, see Lagarde's letters to the Leipzig publisher of March 12 and 22, 1891.

15. See Schemann, "Ueber die neuesten Publikationen Paul de Lagarde's," in: *Bayreuther Blätter 5* (1891), pp. 409–412, especially p. 409, which speaks of the *Deutsche Schriften* as having become "a house of ghosts" for the Wagners' followers.

16. George Mosse, *Ein Volk—Ein Reich—Ein Führer. Die völkischen Ursprünge des Nationalsozialismus* (Königsstein im Taunus, 1979) [first published 1964], p. 40.

17. Bernd Behrendt, *Zwischen Paradox und Paralogismus. Weltanschauliche Grundzüge einer Kulturkritik in den neunziger Jahren des 19.Jahrhunderts am Beispiel August Julius Langbehn* (Frankfurt am Main et al., 1984), pp. 211ff.

18. The following according to: Anna de Lagarde, pp. 116–121, and Rahlfs, pp. 93ff.

19. Anna de Lagarde, p. 121.

20. Richard J. H. Gottheil, "Bibliography of the Works of Paul de Lagarde," in: *Proceedings of the American Oriental Society 15* (1892), pp. ccxi–ccxxix, especially p. ccxi.

21. Calder, "Wilamowitz' Call to Göttingen," pp. 142ff., note 45; the call for the Foundation of Friends of Paul de Lagarde of December 22, 1892, is found in: Staatsbibliothek Berlin, Nachlass Twesten.

22. Althoff's letter to Wilhelm II of June 1, 1892: Universitätsarchiv Göttingen, Kur 7013, fol. 92r–97r.

23. Friedrich Kirchner, "Paul de Lagarde," in: *Illustrierte Zeitung*, no. 2543, March 26, 1892, p. 329; the previous quotation is found in: Cornelius Gurlitt, "Paul de Lagardes Deutsche Schriften," in: *Die Gegenwart 39* (1891), pp. 386–389, especially p. 386.

24. Gustav Roethe, "Zur Erinnerung an Paul Anton de Lagarde," in: *Sonntagsbeilage zur Vossischen Zeitung*, no. 51, January 31, 1892, pp. 1–4, especially p. 1.

25. Paul Heinze, "Paul de Lagarde," in: *Akademische Blätter*, no. 6, January 16, 1892, pp. 252ff.; for the consequences, see Berding, pp. 118ff.

26. Niedersächsische Staats und Universitätsbibliothek Göttingen, Cod. Ms. Lagarde, no. 205.

27. Theodor Fritsch's letter to Anna de Lagarde of October 4, 1905.

28. See Nipperdey, *Deutsche Geschichte, 1866–1918*, vol. II, p. 305.

29. Richly faceted detail about the Diederichs house and its various enterprises: Gangolf Hübinger, *Versammlungsort moderner Geister. Der Eugen Diederichs Verlag—Aufbruch ins Jahrhundert der Extreme* (Munich, 1996); regarding culture in Jena, equally covering its ultramodern scientific enterprises, civil saturation, and bold attempts at reform, see Werner, *Moderne in der Provinz*.

30. Hans-Jörg Uther, "Märchen und Sagen im Eugen Diederichs Verlag," in: Gangolf Hübinger (ed.), *Versammlungsort moderner Geister. Der Eugen Diederichs Verlag—Aufbruch ins Jahrhundert der Extreme* (Munich, 1996), pp. 376–410, especially p. 382.

31. Paul de Lagarde, *Deutscher Glaube. Deutsches Vaterland, Deutsche Bildung. Das Wesentliche aus seinen Schriften ausgewählt und eingeleitet von Friedrich Daab* (Jena, 1913).

32. This is evidenced by the letter from publishing editor Buchwald to the philosopher Paul Natorp of April 9, 1914: Natorp partial estate, Seijo University Library, Tokyo.

33. See Ulrich Sieg, *Jüdische Intellektuelle*, pp. 42ff. Nuanced for the Jewish renaissance in Prague: Philipp Blom, "Martin Buber and the Spiritual Revolution of the Prague Bar Kochba: Nationalist Rhetorics and the Politics of Beauty," phil. diss. (Oxford, 1997).

34. See Andreas Meyer, "Der Verlagsgründer und seine Rolle als Kulturverleger," in: Gangolf Hübinger (ed.), *Versammlungsort moderner Geister. Der Eugen Diederichs Verlag—Aufbruch ins Jahrhundert der Extreme* (Munich, 1996), pp. 26–89, especially p. 49.

35. Quoted from: Edith Hanke and Gangolf Hübinger, "Von der 'Tat'-Gemeinde zum 'Tat'-Kreis. Die Entwicklung einer Kulturzeitschrift," in: Gangolf Hübinger (ed.), *Versammlungsort moderner Geister. Der Eugen Diederichs Verlag—Aufbruch ins Jahrhundert der Extreme* (Munich, 1996), pp. 299–334, especially p. 306. The original version of the quote is found in the first edition of the *Deutsche Schriften*, pp. 101ff.; Lagarde made no changes in later editions.

36. Friedrich Naumann, "Ein Radikalkonservativer," in: *Die Hilfe 18* (1912), pp. 779ff., especially p. 781. General information regarding the text that follows: Peter Theiner, *Liberalismus und Weltpolitik. Friedrich Naumann im Wilhelminischen Deutschland (1860–1919)* (Baden-Baden, 1983).

37. Hermann Bahr, *Tagebuch* (Berlin, 1909), pp. 114ff. Related information on the politically alert defender of literary modernism in the German-speaking world: Besslich, pp. 192–260; see p. 235 of the same source for the previous quotation.

38. Friedrich Paulsen, *Geschichte des gelehrten Unterrichts auf den deutschen Schulen und Universitäten vom Ausgang des Mittelalters bis zur Gegenwart*, 3rd expanded ed., vol. 2 (Berlin and Leipzig, 1921) [first published 1904], p. 388.

39. Quoted from: Besslich, p. 81; regarding the reasons behind Eucken's wide-ranging influence, see Friedrich Wilhelm Graf, "Die Positivität des Geistigen. Rudolf Euckens Programm neoidealistischer Universalintegration," in: Rüdiger vom Bruch, Friedrich Wilhelm Graf, and Gangolf Hübinger (eds.), *Kultur und Kulturwissenschaften um 1900*, vol. 2 (Stuttgart, 1997), pp. 53–85.

40. Christian Morgenstern, *Aphorismen und Sprüche. Auswahl aus dem Gesamtwerk und Nachwort von Margareta Morgenstern* (Munich, 1960) [first published 1913], pp. 126ff.; regarding Morgenstern's Lagarde lectures, see Stern, *Kulturpessimismus*, pp. 129ff.

41. Ulrich Raulff, "'In unterirdischer Verborgenheit.' Das geheime Deutschland—Mythogenese und Myzel," in: Barbara Schlieben, Olaf Schneider, and Kerstin Schulmeyer (eds.), *Geschichtsbilder im George-Kreis. Wege zur Wissenschaft* (Göttingen, 2004), pp. 93–115, especially p. 98.

42. Quoted from: Christian Morgenstern, "Autobiographische Notiz," in: Morgenstern, *Aphorismen und Sprüche. Auswahl [. . .] von Margareta Morgenstern* (Munich, 1960) [first published 1913], pp. 7–13, especially p. 9. At the time of writing this little résumé, Morgenstern had already turned to his last great role model, Rudolf Steiner, with whom he joined, last but not least, in admiration of Lagarde.

43. Wolfram Kinzig (ed.), "Der Kaiser und der 'Evangelist des Rassismus.' Houston Stewart Chamberlains Brief an Anne Guthrie über seine erste Begegnung mit Wilhelm II. Mit einer

Einleitung," in: *Zeitschrift für Neuere Theologiegeschichte 11* (2004), pp. 79–125, especially p. 103. General information regarding Chamberlain's breathtaking rise: Geoffrey G. Field, *Evangelist of Race: The German Vision of Houston Stewart Chamberlain* (New York, 1981).

44. David Clay Large, "Ein Spiegelbild des Meisters? Die Rassenlehre von Houston Stewart Chamberlain," in: Dieter Borchmeyer, Ami Maayani, and Susanne Vill (eds.), *Richard Wagner und die Juden* (Stuttgart and Weimar, 2000), pp. 144–158, especially p. 150.

45. See Houston Stewart Chamberlain, *Die Grundlagen des neunzehnten Jahrhunderts*; quoted here according to the thirteenth edition (Munich, 1919), pp. 56ff. and pp. 631ff.

46. Chamberlain, p. 122; the next quotes are found on pp. 279 and 573 of the same text.

47. Thus, the pithy assessments in Breuer, *Ordnungen der Ungleichheit*, p. 315.

48. See Wilhelm Schwaner (ed.), *Germanen-Bibel. Aus heiligen Schriften germanischer Völker, 2. vollst. umgearb. Edition, Schlachtensee—Berlin 1910*, pp. 298–302. The previous quotation comes from the thorough work of Rainer Kipper, *Der Germanenmythos im Deutschen Kaiserreich. Formen und Funktionen historischer Selbstthematisierung* (Göttingen, 2002), p. 271.

49. Thus, the concise characterization by Pulzer, *Entstehung des politischen Antisemitismus*, p. 133. General information regarding the importance of the Pan-German League before World War I: Roger Chickering, *We Men Who Feel Most German: A Cultural Study of the Pan-German League, 1866–1914* (London and Sydney, 1984). The full title of Class's widely read polemic, *Wenn ich der Kaiser wär* (Leipzig, 1912), already illustrates the brash self-assurance associated with the *Deutsche Schriften*.

50. Friedrich Wilhelm Graf, "Das Laboratorium der religiösen Moderne. Zur 'Verlagsreligion' des Eugen Diederichs Verlags," in: Gangolf Hübinger (ed.), *Versammlungsort moderner Geister. Der Eugen Diederichs Verlag—Aufbruch ins Jahrhundert der Extreme* (Munich, 1996), pp. 243–298, especially p. 256.

51. Uwe Puschner, *Die völkische Bewegung im wilhelminischen Kaiserreich. Sprache—Rasse—Religion* (Darmstadt, 2001), p. 14.

52. Wellhausen, *Heinrich Ewald.*

53. Quoted from: Kurt Nowak, *Theologie, Philologie und Geschichte. Adolf von Harnack als Kirchenhistoriker*, in: Nowak and Otto Gerhard Oexle (eds.), *Adolf von Harnack, Theologe, Historiker, Wissenschaftspolitiker* (Göttingen, 2001), pp. 189–237, especially p. 201; the previous quotations are found in: Adolf von Harnack, *Das Wesen des Christentums*, edited and commented on by Trutz Rendtorff (Gütersloh, 1999), p. 177.

54. Friedrich Wilhelm Graf, "Der 'Systematiker' der 'Kleinen Göttinger Fakultät.' Ernst Troeltschs Promotionsthesen und ihr Göttinger Kontext," in: Graf and Horst Renz (eds.), *Troeltsch-Studien. Untersuchungen zur Biographie und Werkgeschichte. Mit den unveröffentlichten Promotionsthesen der "Kleinen Göttinger Fakultät"* (Gütersloh, 1982), pp. 235–290, especially p. 289. General information regarding Troeltsch's early days: Hans-Georg Drescher, *Ernst Troeltsch. Leben und Werk* (Göttingen, 1991), pp. 21–85.

55. Ernst Troeltsch, *Die Absolutheit des Christentums und die Religionsgeschichte (1902/1912) mit den Thesen von 1901 und den handschriftlichen Zusätzen*, edited by Trutz Rendttorff in collaboration with Stefan Pautler (Berlin and New York, 1998), p. 143.

56. Ernst Troeltsch, "Luther und die moderne Welt," in: Troeltsch, *Schriften zur Bedeutung des Protestantismus für die moderne Welt (1906–1913)*, edited by Trutz Rendttorff in collaboration with Stefan Pautler (Berlin and New York, 1998), pp. 53–97, especially p. 67.

57. Ernst Troeltsch, *Gesammelte Schriften*, vol. 2: *Zur religiösen Lage. Religionsphilosophie und Ethik* (Tübingen, 1913), p. viii.

58. The following is based on: Ulrich Sieg, "Ernst Troeltsch und Paul de Lagarde. Einige Unbekannte Dokumente," in: *Mitteilungen der Ernst-Troeltsch-Gesellschaft 19* (2006), pp. 31–54.

59. Another view is presented by David N. Myers, *Resisting History: Historicism and Its Discontents in German-Jewish Thought* (Princeton and Oxford, 2003), pp. 64ff., but this text does not account for the dedication of Troeltsch's letters to Anna de Lagarde.

60. A monograph hereto: Manfred Voigts, *"Wir sollen alle kleine Fichtes werden!" Johann Gottlieb Fichte als Prophet der Kultur-Zionisten* (Berlin and Vienna, 2003).

61. This distinction, which was long decisive to the research, is offered by Stern, *Kulturpessimismus*, p. 127. It served not least the separation of bourgeois cultural critics from their inglorious adepts on the political right and created an ideological clarity foreign to the sense of crisis around 1900.

62. Apropos: Nipperdey, *Deutsche Geschichte, 1866–1918*, vol. 1, p. 826.

63. Niedersächsische Staats und Universitätsbibliothek Göttingen, Cod. Ms. Lagarde, *Notizen und Auszüge*, vol. 2, p. 101; the next citation appears on p. 103 of the same source.

64. A list of relevant titles is found in: Niedersächsische Staats und Universitätsbibliothek Göttingen, Cod. Ms. Lagarde, *Notizen und Auszüge*, vol. 2, pp. 106ff.; general information regarding Rade's behavior in World War I: Anne Chr. Nagel, *Martin Rade—Theologe und Politiker des Sozialen Liberalismus. Eine politische Biographie* (Gütersloh, 1996), pp. 134–156.

65. Hermann Mulert, "Lagarde als Prophet deutscher Religion," in: *Monatshefte der Comenius-Gesellschaft für Kultur und Geistesleben NF 8* (1916), pp. 14–27, especially p. 20. His book, *Paul de Lagarde*, had come out in 1913 in Berlin-Schöneberg as volume 7 of the series Die Klassiker der Religion.

66. Quoted from: Besslich, p. 4.

67. Thomas Mann, *Betrachtungen eines Unpolitischen* (Berlin, 1918), in: Thomas Mann, *Gesammelte Werke*, vol. 12 (Frankfurt am Main, 1960), pp. 7–589, especially pp. 275ff. For the intellectual historical context, see Paul, pp. 85ff., and Stern, *Kulturpessimismus*, p. 129.

68. Nachum Goldmann, *Von der weltkulturellen Bedeutung und Aufgabe des Judentums* (Munich, 1916), p. 36.

69. Quoted from: Large, p. 151. The extent of Chamberlain's activities is shown by: Erik Lindner, *Houston Stewart Chamberlain: The Abwehrverein and the "Praeceptor Germaniae," 1914–1918*, in: *Leo Baeck Institute Yearbook* 37 (1992), pp. 213–236.

70. See Peter Hoeres, *Krieg der Philosophen. Die deutsche und die britische Philosophie im Ersten Weltkrieg* (Paderborn et al., 2004), pp. 396ff.

71. Archibald H. Sayce, *Reminiscences* (London, 1923), p. 53.

14. GUIDING INTELLECTUAL FORCE OF NATIONAL SOCIALISM

1. Distinctly pertinent: Hans-Ulrich Wehler, *Deutsche Gesellschaftsgeschichte*, vol. 4: *Vom Beginn des Ersten Weltkriegs bis zur Gründung der beiden deutschen Staaten, 1914–1949* (Munich, 2003), p. 547. As a captivating analysis of the antirepublican climate at the time: Sebastian Haffner, *Geschichte eines Deutschen. Die Erinnerungen, 1914–1933*, 6th ed. (Stuttgart and Munich, 2000).

2. Armin Mohler, *Die Konservative Revolution in Deutschland. Ein Handbuch*, 2nd ed. (Darmstadt, 1972), p. 29. With special resonance for "Rembrandtdeutschen": Behrendt, *Langbehn*, p. 112.

3. See Paul, p. 75, note 110.

4. On Lehmann's attitude: Brigitte Lohff, "'Das Buch als Tat in Deutschlands Namen.' Die Medienpolitik des Verlegers Julius Friedrich Lehmann," in: Sigrid Stöckel (ed.), *Die "rechte Nation" und ihre Verleger. Politik und Popularisierung im J.F.Lehmanns Verlag 1890–1979* (Berlin, 2002), pp. 241–258; general information regarding nationalist publishers: Justus H. Ulbricht, "'Ein heimlich offener Bund für das grosse Morgen . . .' Methoden systematischer Weltanschauungsproduktion während der Weimarer Republik," in: Hubert Cancik and Uwe Puschner (eds.), *Antisemitismus, Paganismus, Völkische Religion* (Munich, 2004), pp. 65–81.

5. See the rich material in the book *Ernst Troeltsch in Nachrufen*, edited by Friedrich Wilhelm Graf in collaboration with Christian Nees (Gütersloh, 2002).

6. For Chamberlain's "Erlösungsantisemitismus": Saul Friedländer, *Das Dritte Reich und die Juden*, vol. 1: *Die Jahre der Verfolgung, 1933–1939* (Munich, 1998), pp. 102–105; especially regarding the ideological shift in emphasis in World War I: Sieg, *Jüdische Intellektuelle*, pp. 186ff.

7. See Joachim Fest, *Hitler. Eine Biographie* (Berlin, 1973), p. 259.

8. Quoted from: Large, p. 157.

9. Ernst Nolte, *Der Faschismus in seiner Epoche. Action française. Italienischer Faschismus. Nationalsozialismus. Mit einem Vorwort zur Taschenbuchausgabe*, 6th ed. (Munich, 1984), p. 345.

10. Houston Stewart Chamberlain, *Politische Ideale*, 3rd ed. (Munich, 1926), p. 114.

11. Mario Krammer, *Die Wiedergeburt durch Lagarde. Eine Auswahl und Würdigung* (Gotha and Stuttgart, 1925), p. 68; see p. 71 of the same source for the quotations that follow.

12. Here quoted from: Leo Strauss, "Paul de Lagarde," in: Strauss, *Philosophie und Gesetz—Frühe Schriften. Unter Mitw. von Wiebke Meier hg. von Heinrich Meier* (Stuttgart and Weimar, 1997), pp. 323–331, especially p. 324.

13. Franz Schnabel, "Zehn Jahre nach dem Kriege." Speech delivered at the New Year's celebration of the Baden state government in the State Theater in Karlsruhe on January 1, 1929 (Karlsruhe, 1929), p. 19; the next quote is from Schnabel's discussion of Fritz Krog's work, published in Munich in 1930, "Lagarde und der deutsche Staat" (literary supplement to the *Karlsruhe Tageblatt*, no. 91, April 1, 1930). A historical analysis of Schnabel's attitude is offered by: Thomas Hertfelder, *Franz Schnabel und die deutsche Geschichtswissenschaft. Geschichtsschreibung zwischen Historismus und Kulturkritik (1910–1945)* (Göttingen, 1998), pp. 171ff.

14. See Heinz Dieter Kittsteiner, *Mit Marx für Heidegger. Mit Heidegger für Marx* (Munich, 2004), p. 139, as well as Richard Wolin, *Heidegger's Children: Hannah Arendt, Karl Löwith, Hans Jonas, and Herbert Marcuse* (Princeton and Oxford, 2001), pp. 48ff. and passim.

15. See Herbert Döring's classic study, *Der Weimarer Kreis. Studien zum politischen Bewusstsein verfassungstreuer Hochschullehrer in der Weimarer Republik* (Meisenheim am Glan, 1975).

16. Wilhelm Mommsen, *Paul de Lagarde als Politiker. Zu seinem 100. Geburtstag am*

2. *November 1927* (Göttingen, 1927), p. 22. For an interpretation, see Paul, p. 80; general information regarding Mommsen's left-liberal involvement in the Weimar Republic: Helga Grebing, "Zwischen Kaiserreich und Diktatur. Göttinger Historiker und ihr Beitrag zur Interpretation von Geschichte und Gesellschaft (M.Lehmann, A.O.Meyer, W.Mommsen, S.A.Kaehler)," in: Hartmut Boockmann and Hermann Wellenreuter (eds.), *Geschichtswissenschaft in Göttingen. Eine Vorlesungsreihe* (Göttingen, 1987), pp. 204–238, especially pp. 235ff., and Anne Chr. Nagel, "'Der Prototyp der Leute, die man entfernen soll, ist Mommsen.' Entnazifizierung in der Provinz oder die Ambiguität moralischer Gewissheit," in: *Jahrbuch zur Liberalismus-Forschung 10* (1998), pp. 55–91, pp. 55ff. and passim.

17. This and the following cited documents can be found in the Bundesarchiv Koblenz, N 1178 (Nachlass Wilhelm Mommsen), no. 85. For pointing out the unusually meaningful testimony, I warmly thank Anne Chr. Nagel.

18. Richard Breitling, *Paul de Lagarde und der grossdeutsche Gedanke. Mit einem Geleitwort von Karl Alexander von Müller* (Vienna and Leipzig, 1927), p. iii.

19. All quotes: entertainment supplement of the *Königsberg Allgemeine Zeitung* on November 2, 1927. For Rothfels's earlier effectiveness at the East Prussian university, see Ingo Haar, *Historiker im Nationalsozialismus. Deutsche Geschichtswissenschaft und der "Volkstumskampf" im Osten* (Göttingen, 2000), pp. 70–76, and Jan Eckel, *Hans Rothfels. Eine intellektuelle Biographie im 20.Jahrhundert* (Gottingen, 2005), pp. 99–182, which crafts a very different picture of the charismatic scholar.

20. Karl Berger, "Paul de Lagarde, ein deutscher Prophet," in: *Die völkische Schule 5* (1927), pp. 153–156, especially p. 155; the article is interpreted in detail: Paul, pp. 86ff.

21. Hans Grimm, address to the Philosophy Faculty of the University of Göttingen, in: Grimm, *Über mich selbst und meine Arbeit* (Lippoldsberg, 1975), pp. 46ff.; see pp. 46 and 48 of the same source for the quotations. For historical context, see Annette Gümbel, *"Volk ohne Raum." Der Schriftsteller Hans Grimm zwischen nationalkonservativem Denken und völkischer Ideologie* (Darmstadt and Marburg, 2003).

22. Alfred Rosenberg, "Paul de Lagarde," in: Rosenberg, *Blut und Ehre. Ein Kampf für deutsche Wiedergeburt. Reden und Aufsätze von 1919–1933*, edited by Thilo von Trotta (Munich, 1935), pp. 228ff. [first published in the *Völkischer Beobachter* September 10, 1927], especially p. 228. Regarding Rosenberg, whose historical significance has long been underestimated, now significantly: Ernst Piper, *Alfred Rosenberg, Hitlers Chefideologe* (Munich, 2005).

23. Alfred Rosenberg, "Um die Erfüllung," in: *Nationalsozialistische Monatshefte* (1930), pp. 1–5; regarding Dinter's political classification and the enthusiastic response to his low-brow literary works, see Wehler, *Deutsche Gesellschaftsgeschichte*, vol. 4, pp. 502ff.

24. For historical context, which should not be ignored even in such prima facie timeless works as *Der Mythus des 20.Jahrhunderts*: Heinrich August Winkler, *Weimar 1918–1933. Die Geschichte der ersten deutschen Demokratie* (Munich, 1993), pp. 334–407; regarding the contemporary view that liberalism has survived: Wolfgang Schivelbusch, *Entfernte Verwandtschaft. Faschismus, Nationalsozialismus, New Deal 1933–1939* (Munich and Vienna, 2005), pp. 10ff.

25. Alfred Rosenberg, *Der Mythus des 20.Jahrhundert. Eine Wertung der seelisch-geistigen Gestaltungskämpfe unserer Zeit* (Munich, 1930); reproduced here after the twenty-first and twenty-second editions (Munich, 1934); the quotation appears on p. 443 of the same

source. Regarding Rosenberg's principled rejection of the Old Testament, see Frank-Lothar Kroll, *Utopie als Ideologie. Geschichtsdenken und politisches Handeln im Dritten Reich* (Paderborn et al., 1998), pp. 139ff., and Piper, *Alfred Rosenberg*, pp. 195ff.

26. Alfred Rosenberg, *Dietrich Eckhart. Ein Vermächtnis* (Munich, 1928); quoted here from the 5th ed. (Munich, 1938), pp. 157ff.; the previous quotation is found in: Rosenberg, *Mythus des 20. Jahrhunderts*, p. 457.

27. Adolf Hitler, *Die soziale Sendung des Nationalsozialismus. Rede auf der NSDAP-Versammlung in Stuttgart am 16. Dezember 1925*, in: Hitler, *Reden, Schriften, Anordnungen*, vol. 1: *Die Wiedergründung der NSDAP. Februar 1925–Juni 1926*, edited and with commentary by Clemens Vollnhals (Munich et al., 1994), pp. 239–262, especially p. 257.

28. Thus also Fest, *Hitler*, p. 295; the previous passage is found in: Adolf Hitler, *Mein Kampf*, quoted here from the 444–448th ed. (Munich, 1939), p. 395.

29. Regarding the contents of Hitler's library, see Philipp Gassert and Daniel S. Mattern, *The Hitler Library: A Bibliography* (Westport, Conn., and London, 2001); regarding his taste in reading: Timothy W. Ryback, "Hitler's Forgotten Library: The Man, His Books, and His Search for God," *Atlantic Monthly 291* (May 2003), pp. 76–90.

30. Paul de Lagarde, *Deutsche Schriften*, edited by Karl August Fischer, 2nd ed. (Munich, 1934), pp. 21 and 245. Hitler's emphases, in this volume, are reproduced in the main text that follows with the relevant page numbers.

31. Hitler, *Mein Kampf*, p. 464.

32. Jordan Mejias, "Hitlers Bücher. Was hat er gelesen? Wer hat ihm Bücher geschenkt? Besuch in einer vergessenen Bibliothek," in: *Frankfurter Allgemeine Sonntagszeitung*, no. 15, April 13, 2003, pp. 23 and 25.

33. Stefan Breuer, *Ordnungen der Ungleichheit*, p. 143. Regarding the historical implications of these ideas, see Klaus Schreiner, "'Wann kommt der Retter Deutschlands?' Formen und Funktionen von politischem Messianismus in der Weimarer Republik," in: *Saeculum 49* (1998), pp. 107–160.

34. Hagen Schulze, "Walter Frank," in: Hans-Ulrich Wehler (ed.), *Deutsche Historiker*, vol. 7 (Göttingen, 1980), pp. 69–81, especially p. 74.

35. Regarding Hitler's interest in religion and especially in the theological ideas of Fichte: Ryback, "Hitler's Forgotten Library."

36. Quoted from: Piper, *Rosenberg*, p. 181; also on pp. 179–188 and pp. 212–226, rich material regarding the impact of the myth, which I myself support in the passages that follow.

37. Statements according to: ibid., p. 184; the previous quotation is found in: ibid., p. 183.

38. Alfred Rosenberg, "Die Welt des Auges. Eröffnungsrede zur Kulturtagung auf dem Reichsparteitag am 5. 9. 1934," in: Alfred Rosenberg, *Gestaltung der Idee. Reden und Aufsätze von 1933–1935*, edited by Thilo von Trotta (Munich, 1936), pp. 140–147, especially p. 142. For this passage, see Paul, p. 87, and Piper, *Rosenberg*, p. 190.

39. Alfred Rosenberg, "An die deutsche Wehrmacht," in: Rosenberg, *Gestaltung der Idee. Reden und Aufsätze von 1933–1935*, edited by Thilo von Trotta (Munich, 1936), pp. 285–304, especially p. 288.

40. Alfred Rosenberg, "Nationalsozialismus und Ausland," in: Rosenberg, *Gestaltung der Idee. Reden und Aufsätze von 1933–1935*, edited by Thilo von Trotta (Munich, 1936), pp. 379–394, especially p. 384.

41. Quoted from: Paul, p. 87. Regarding academic reservations against the glorification of

Widukind, which are usually directed against Charlemagne and his "un-Germanic" policy for Saxony, see: Karl-Ferdinand Werner, *Das NS-Geschichtsbild und die Geschichtswissenschaft* (Stuttgart, 1967), pp. 74–79, and Anne Christine Nagel, *Im Schatten des Dritten Reichs. Mittelalterforschung in der Bundesrepublik Deutschland, 1945–1970* (Göttingen, 2005), pp. 53–60.

42. "M., Paul de Lagarde, der Seher. Zu seinem 45. Todestage am 22.Dezember," in: *Göttinger Tageblatt* of December 22, 1936. The article by Josef Becker, "Paul de Lagarde. Ein Seher der deutschen Nation," was published in: *Der Schulungsbrief*, 3. Jg., 5. Folge, May 1936, pp. 162–165; the quotations appear on p. 163 of the same source.

43. Paul de Lagarde, *Deutsche Politik und Religion. Eine Auswahl aus den Schriften* (Leipzig, no date), p. 77.

44. W. G., "Imperiale Träume eines schrulligen Altphilologen. Vor 75 Jahren starb der Orientalist und Verfasser der *Deutsche Schriften* Paul de Lagarde," in: *Die Welt*, no. 294, December 17, 1966, suppl. p. I. Regarding celebrations in the Kroll Opera House, see Bundesarchiv Berlin Lichterfelde NS 8 [Amt Rosenberg], no. 36; for the list of books for members of the Wehrmacht, see the same source, no. 183, fol. 12ff.

45. Heinz Erich Eisenhuth, "Die Idee der nationalen Kirche bei Paul de Lagarde," in: *Zeitschrift für Theologie und Kirche NF 15* (1934), pp. 145–166, especially p. 149.

46. Erich Botzenhart, "Paul de Lagarde," in: Kurt von Raumer and Theodor Schieder (eds.), *Stufen und Wandlungen der deutschen Einheit. In Verb. mit Ludwig Bittner* (Stuttgart and Berlin, 1943), pp. 420–431, especially pp. 427ff.

47. Bundesarchiv Berlin Lichterfelde NS 8, no. 186.

48. "D., Paul de Lagarde. Zum fünfzigsten Todestage am 22. Dezember," in: *Frankfurter Zeitung*. Reichsausgabe of December 21, 1941, pp. 3ff., where the following quotations also appear. For pointing out this article and for his important support, I warmly thank the managing director of the President Theodor-Heuss-Haus Foundation, Thomas Hertfelder.

49. Still exciting regarding this: Sebastian Haffner, *Anmerkungen zu Hitler*, 25th ed. (Frankfurt am Main, 2003) [first published 1978], pp. 135–141.

50. Piper, *Rosenberg*, p. 494. Instructive regarding looting in the German-occupied territories: Anja Heuss, *Kunst und Kulturgutraub. Eine vergleichende Studie zur Besatzungspolitik der Nationalsozialisten in Frankreich und der Sowjetunion* (Heidelberg, 2000).

EPILOGUE

1. Speech by Federal President Prof. Dr. Theodor Heuss on the bicentennial of the Academy of Sciences in Göttingen, in: *Jahrbuch der Akademie der Wissenschaften in Göttingen, 1944–1960*, pp. 39–44, especially p. 40; see p. 42 of the same source for the following quotations.

2. Quoted from: Eberlein, p. 207.

3. Golo Mann, *Erinnerungen und Gedanken. Eine Jugend in Deutschland*, 3rd ed. (Frankfurt am Main, 1986), p. 158. The verses quoted are from the poem "No. 7" from the Am Strande collection; Lagarde, *Gedichte*, p. 79.

4. George Bataille, "Nietzsche," in: Jörg Salaquarda (ed.), *Nietzsche*, 2nd ed. (Darmstadt, 1996), pp. 45–49, especially p. 47.

5. Marc Bloch, *Apologie der Geschichte oder Der Beruf des Historikers*, edited by Lucien Febvre, 3rd ed. (Stuttgart, 1992), p. 49.

Index